Human-Computer Interaction

Human-Computer Interaction
An Empirical Research Perspective

I. Scott MacKenzie

AMSTERDAM • BOSTON • HEIDELBERG • LONDON
NEW YORK • OXFORD • PARIS • SAN DIEGO
SAN FRANCISCO • SINGAPORE • SYDNEY • TOKYO

Morgan Kaufmann is an imprint of Elsevier

Acquiring Editor: Meg Dunkerley
Development Editor: Heather Scherer
Project Manager: Mohanambal Natarajan
Designer: Greg Harris

Morgan Kaufmann is an imprint of Elsevier
225 Wyman Street, Waltham, MA 02451, USA

Library of Congress Cataloging-in-Publication Data
Application submitted

British Library Cataloguing-in-Publication Data
A catalogue record for this book is available from the British Library

ISBN: 978-0-12-405865-1

For information on all Morgan Kaufmann publications
visit our website at www.mkp.com

Printed and bound by CPI Group (UK) Ltd, Croydon, CR0 4YY
Transferred to Digital Printing, 2013

Working together to grow
libraries in developing countries

www.elsevier.com | www.bookaid.org | www.sabre.org

ELSEVIER   BOOK AID International   Sabre Foundation

Contents

Preface xi
Acknowledgments xv
Author Biography xvii

CHAPTER 1   Historical Context 1
    1.1 Introduction 2
    1.2 Vannevar Bush's "as we may think" (1945) 3
    1.3 Ivan Sutherland's Sketchpad (1962) 5
    1.4 Invention of the mouse (1963) 6
    1.5 Xerox star (1981) 11
    1.6 Birth of HCI (1983) 15
          1.6.1 First ACM SIGCHI conference (1983) 15
          1.6.2 The psychology of human-computer interaction (1983) 17
          1.6.3 Launch of the Apple Macintosh (1984) 22
    1.7 Growth of HCI and graphical user interfaces (GUIs) 23
    1.8 Growth of HCI research 24
    1.9 Other readings 26
    1.10 Resources 26
    Student Exercises 26

CHAPTER 2   The Human Factor 27
    2.1 Time scale of human action 28
    2.2 Human factors 29
    2.3 Sensors 30
          2.3.1 Vision (Sight) 30
          2.3.2 Hearing (Audition) 34
          2.3.3 Touch (Tactition) 36
          2.3.4 Smell and taste 36
          2.3.5 Other senses 38
    2.4 Responders 38
          2.4.1 Limbs 38
          2.4.2 Voice 42
          2.4.3 Eyes 42
    2.5 The brain 44
          2.5.1 Perception 44
          2.5.2 Cognition 47
          2.5.3 Memory 48

2.6 Language...50

    2.6.1 Redundancy in language..52

    2.6.2 Entropy in language...53

2.7 Human performance 54

    2.7.1 Reaction time 56

    2.7.2 Visual search 59

    2.7.3 Skilled behavior 62

    2.7.4 Attention 63

    2.7.5 Human error..65

Student Exercises 67

CHAPTER 3 Interaction Elements...**71**

3.1 Hard controls and soft controls...72

3.2 Control-display relationships...74

    3.2.1 Spatial relationships..75

    3.2.2 CD gain and transfer function.................................80

    3.2.3 Latency...81

    3.2.4 Property sensed and order of control 84

3.3 Natural versus learned relationships.............................86

3.4 Mental models and metaphor...88

3.5 Modes 93

3.6 More about degrees of freedom 101

3.7 Mobile context 106

3.8 Interaction errors..111

Student Exercises 117

CHAPTER 4 Scientific Foundations...**121**

4.1 What is research?..121

    4.1.1 Research must be published..123

    4.1.2 Citations, references, impact.....................................124

    4.1.3 Research must be reproducible.........................126

    4.1.4 Research versus engineering versus design 126

4.2 What is empirical research?..129

4.3 Research methods 130

    4.3.1 Observational method 130

    4.3.2 Experimental method...130

    4.3.3 Correlational method 132

4.4 Observe and measure 132

    4.4.1 Observation..132

    4.4.2 Measurement scales 133

    4.4.3 Nominal 134

    4.4.4 Ordinal data 136

4.4.5 Interval data 136
4.4.6 Ratio data..137
4.5 Research questions 139
4.6 Internal validity and external validity.....................................140
4.7 Comparative evaluations 143
4.8 Relationships: circumstantial and causal................................145
4.9 Research topics...147
4.9.1 Ideas..148
4.9.2 Finding a topic..150
4.9.3 Tip #1: Think small! 150
4.9.4 Tip #2: Replicate! 151
4.9.5 Tip #3: Know the literature! 151
4.9.6 Tip #4: Think inside the box! 152
Student Exercises 155

Chapter 5   **Designing HCI Experiments**...**157**
5.1 What methodology? 157
5.2 Ethics approval 159
5.3 Experiment design..160
5.4 Independent variables...161
5.5 Dependent variables 163
5.6 Other variables...165
5.6.1 Control variables...166
5.6.2 Random variables 166
5.6.3 Confounding variables 166
5.7 Task and procedure...169
5.8 Participants 171
5.9 Questionnaire design 173
5.10 Within-subjects and between-subjects 175
5.11 Order effects, counterbalancing, and latin squares..................177
5.12 Group effects and asymmetric skill transfer............................181
5.13 Longitudinal studies 184
5.14 Running the experiment 187
Student Exercises 188

CHAPTER 6   **Hypothesis Testing**..**191**
6.1 Analysis of variance 192
6.1.1 Why analyze the variance?..193
6.1.2 More than two test conditions 199
6.1.3 Post hoc comparisons 201
6.1.4 Between-subjects designs...202
6.1.5 Two-way analysis of variance 203

    6.1.6 ANOVA tool..206
    6.1.7 Counterbalancing and testing for a group effect..............207
  6.2 Chi-square test 209
  6.3 Non-parametric tests for ordinal data 214
    6.3.1 Example 1 215
    6.3.2 Example 2 216
    6.3.3 Example 3 218
    6.3.4 Example 4 220
    6.3.5 Discussion..221
  6.4 Parametric versus non-parametric tests 223
  Student Exercises 227

CHAPTER 7 Modeling Interaction..................................**233**
  7.1 Descriptive models..233
    7.1.1 Delineating a problem space...............................234
    7.1.2 Quadrant model of groupware 235
    7.1.3 Key-action model (KAM).................................236
    7.1.4 Model of bimanual control 238
    7.1.5 Three-state model for graphical input......................242
  7.2 Predictive models...244
    7.2.1 Linear regression model...................................245
    7.2.2 Fitts' law 249
    7.2.3 Choice reaction time 255
    7.2.4 The keystroke-level model.................................258
    7.2.5 Skill acquisition 274
    7.2.6 More than one predictor...................................279
  7.3 A model continuum model 283
  Student Exercises 283

CHAPTER 8 Writing and Publishing a Research Paper..................**293**
  8.1 Conference papers, journal papers............................293
  8.2 Parts of a research paper 295
    8.2.1 Title 296
    8.2.2 Abstract..296
    8.2.3 Keywords 297
    8.2.4 Introduction..298
    8.2.5 Method 299
    8.2.6 Results and Discussion 301
    8.2.7 Conclusion 303
    8.2.8 References..303

8.3 Preparing the manuscript 303

    8.3.1 Formatting 304

    8.3.2 Citations and references 305

    8.3.3 Visual Aids 308

    8.3.4 Writing for clarity 311

    Student Exercises 313

References 319

Appendix 343

Index 345

Preface

A few months ago, my son approached me with a problem. It was November, daylight saving time had arrived, and his watch was an hour fast. He was having trouble adjusting the time. Could I help? "Sure," I said. He gave me the watch. By most standards, I am an expert in user interfaces. Modern watches have many features and just a few buttons. They have modes. I understand modes. Repeatedly press one button to cycle through the modes. Press and hold another button and the device is ready for change. That sort of thing. It might take some trial and error, but the task seemed simple enough. I was wrong. Try as I may, the watch resisted. I couldn't change the time! I borrowed the watch and brought it to work. At the time I was teaching a course called Advanced Human-Computer Interaction. The students, all MSc or PhD candidates, are more tech-savvy than their instructor. After all, these students were born in the digital age. Technology to them is like food or air. They consume it! I explained the situation and then gave the watch to the closest student. A few minutes later the watch was passed to the next student, then the next. About 30 minutes later, the watch was returned to me. The time was unchanged. Not a single student was able to change the time.

I am thankful for stories like this. They give you and me something to do—something to think about and work on. Human-computer interaction (HCI) as a field of research and practice extends back 30 years. Despite the accomplishments, we still confront technology that utterly perplexes and frustrates us. Yes, there is work to do.

This book is not about designing a better watch. Of course, the end game is better designs and products, but the focus here is on the ideas—ideas for new and improved user interfaces or interaction techniques. The journey from idea to product is long, however. Before embedding in a product, an idea must be implemented, refined, tested, refined again, tested again, and so on. Testing is key: Is the idea any good? How good? Does it improve on current practice? According to what criteria and by how much? Will users like it? Is it intuitive, efficient, even fun, or will users find it awkward or frustrating? This book is about answering questions like these.

The questions above are expressions of curiosity. They capture the true and unstructured spirit of innovative thought. But answering these questions is a challenge. Terms like "any good" and "improve on" are highly subjective. To answer with clarity and assurance, the questions must be recast and narrowed—to make them answerable, so to speak. Well-formed questions about new ideas for user interfaces invite observation and measurement of human interaction with the technology of interest. In the narrowed form, the questions are "research questions." Furthermore, questions that are pursued through observation and measurement are empirical. With this, we arrive at this book's theme: human-computer interaction, with an empirical research perspective.

This book's study of empirical research in HCI is admittedly narrow. The reader is implored not to view this as dismissive of research methods in HCI that are also empirical but with a qualitative or non-experimental emphasis. HCI is a tremendously broad field with a considerable amount of empirical research, particularly in the social sciences, that uses observational methods as opposed to experimental methods. The emphasis on experimental methods in the pages ahead is a by-product of the book's single-author design. To expand the treatment of observational methods here, giving them equal page space with experimental methods, would be a disservice to the substantial community of researchers skilled in these methods. This book reflects one researcher's perspective and that perspective has more to do with the author's personal experience and expertise than with any suggestion that certain methods are superior to others. For this reason, the "empirical research" label is delegated to the book's subtitle, or secondary title. Bracketing empirical research with "perspective" and the indefinite article "an" is deliberate. The book presents one perspective on empirical research in HCI. Often, the focus is broad (*What is empirical? What is research?*); but when laying down the details, there is an emphasis on research that is empirical and experimental. If there is one deliverable in this book, it is the knowledge and skills required to design and conduct a "user study"—a factorial experiment with human participants where two or more facets of a user interface are empirically and quantitatively compared.

This book is organized into eight chapters. It begins with a historical context of the field in Chapter 1, chronicling significant work leading to the emergence in the 1980s of HCI as a field of research and practice. This is followed with an overview of the human factor in Chapter 2, where the sensory, motor, and cognitive characteristics of the human are introduced and summarized. Chapter 3 presents the core elements of human interaction with computers. The examination focuses on human actions and the responses they invoke in the computer. Of course, the goal is to distinguish action-response pairings that work well from those that are awkward or confusing. The scientific foundations of research and, in particular, experimental research are elaborated in Chapter 4. Here I reveal how to craft narrow and testable research questions. The underlying principles of science and research are studied, as well. Following this, Chapter 5 provides a step-by-step guide on how to design and conduct an HCI experiment, or user study. The focus is on controlled experiments, with independent variables, dependent variables, within- and between-subjects assignment of conditions, counterbalancing, etc. Chapter 6 is on hypothesis testing; that is, answering research questions in a statistical sense. The review is introductory, cookbook-like, and is limited to the analysis of variance (causal relationships), the chi-square test (circumstantial relationships), and non-parametric tests on ordinal data. One important theme in HCI research is building and testing models of interaction. This is the subject of Chapter 7, where two approaches to modeling are presented. Descriptive models partition a problem space, usually with visual aids, to help understand an aspect of human interaction with technology. Predictive models are equations that predict human performance from task characteristics. The final and essential step in research is publishing the results, so the book concludes in Chapter 8 with tips and discussions on writing and publishing a research paper.

In style, the book has several approaches. It is not a research monograph, although some original and unpublished research is included. An example is the experiment on visual search, leading to a predictive model. The model gives the time to scan n items on a display while searching for a particular item. The task is common in HCI. For example, soft keyboards on touchscreen devices often include word completion. As entry progresses, the system offers candidates completing the current key sequence. If there are n candidates in the list, how much time is needed for a user to determine if the desired word is present? The cost of viewing the list can be traded against the cost of not viewing it. Design choices follow. Herein is the essence of predictive modeling, a subject well-traveled in HCI (and in this book).

The book is not a work of fiction, but stories and anecdotes help frame many of the discussions (with an HCI motivation). In the pages ahead, you will read about the sitcom character Dobie Gillis' pensive moments by *The Thinker* (how to find a research topic), the unusual definition of a false start in the 100 meter dash in the Olympics (human reaction time to an auditory stimulus), the danger in feeding a Tamagotchi digital pet while driving (visual attention; secondary tasks), the use of duct tape to fix a bad user interface (importance of tactile feedback; form versus function), and the framing of important achievements in science, such as microbiologist Louis Pasteur's development of a standardized research methodology (research must be reproducible; the importance of a consistent methodology for user studies). And the writing style occasionally slips into the first person, where a personal experience seems relevant. An example is my experience in 1981 at the National Computer Conference (NCC). The event of note was the introduction of the Xerox *Star* – the first commercially available computer system to use a graphical user interface (GUI) and a mouse.

Mostly this book is a textbook, though it also serves as a handbook. The intended audience is students of HCI, but anyone undertaking empirical or experimental research in HCI will likely find it of interest. Many topics are presented with a pedagogical intent, such as designing and conducting experiments (user studies), building a regression model from experimental data, or performing and explaining an analysis of variance. As well, there are student exercises to hone one's skill on the topics within.

A website supplements the book. The primary purpose is to host downloadable files supporting topics in the book. There is Java-based software, including full source code and detailed APIs. An analysis of variance application (Anova2) and other statistics utilities are included as are several complete packages for HCI experiments. Here's the URL: www.yorku.ca/mack/HCIbook.

The website will evolve as more resources become available. Most of the software is intended for desktop computing environments. There is, at present, one application for tablets running the Android operating system. More will be added later.

Acknowledgments

Many people helped in various and significant ways along this book's path from conception to draft to realization. Let me begin by thanking the three anonymous reviewers who provided critical and helpful suggestions on an early draft of the manuscript. Those I have the pleasure to name include Steven Castellucci, Alison Chong, John Paulin Hansen, Howell Istance, Kari-Juoko Räihä, Janet Read and William Soukoreff. This book has arrived (whew!) and is better in no small measure because of your support and direction. Thank you.

Author Biography

I. Scott MacKenzie is Associate Professor of Computer Science and Engineering at York University, Canada. For the past 25 years, MacKenzie has been an active member of the human-computer interaction (HCI) research community, with over 130 peer-reviewed publications, including more than 30 papers in the Association for Computing Machinery Conference on Human Factors in Computing Systems (ACM SIGCHI) conference proceedings. MacKenzie's interests include human performance measurement and modeling, interaction devices and techniques, text entry, mobile computing, accessible computing, touch-based interaction, eye tracking, and experimental methodology.

Historical Context

Human-computer interaction. In the beginning, there were humans. In the 1940s came computers. Then in the 1980s came interaction. Wait! What happened between 1940 and 1980? Were humans not *interacting* with computers then? Well, yes, but not just any human. Computers in those days were too precious, too complicated, to allow the average human to mess with them. Computers were carefully guarded. They lived a secluded life in large air-conditioned rooms with raised floors and locked doors in corporate or university research labs or government facilities. The rooms often had glass walls to show off the unique status of the behemoths within.

If you were of that breed of human who was permitted access, you were probably an engineer or a scientist—specifically, a computer scientist. And you knew what to do. Whether it was connecting relays with patch cords on an ENIAC (1940s), changing a magnetic memory drum on a UNIVAC (1950s), adjusting the JCL stack on a System/360 (1960s), or *grep*ing and *awk*ing around the *unix* command set on a PDP-11 (1970s), you were on home turf. *Unix* commands like *grep*, for *global regular expression print*, were obvious enough. Why consult the manual? You probably wrote it! As for *unix*'s *vi* editor, if some poor soul was stupid enough to start typing text while in command mode, well, he got what he deserved.[1] Who gave him a login account, anyway? And what's all this talk about *make the state of the system visible to the user*? What user? Sounds a bit like ... well ... socialism!

Interaction was not on the minds of the engineers and scientists who designed, built, configured, and programmed the early computers. But by the 1980s interaction was an issue. The new computers were not only powerful, they were useable—by anyone! With usability added, computers moved from their earlier secure confines onto people's desks in workplaces and, more important, into people's homes. One reason human–computer interaction (HCI) is so exciting is that the field's emergence and progress are aligned with, and in good measure responsible for, this dramatic shift in computing practices.

---

[1] One of the classic UI foibles—told and re-told by HCI educators around the world—is the *vi* editor's lack of feedback when switching between modes. Many a user made the mistake of providing input while in *command mode* or entering a command while in *input mode*.

This book is about research in human-computer interaction. As in all fields, research in HCI is the force underlying advances that migrate into products and processes that people use, whether for work or pleasure. While HCI itself is broad and includes a substantial applied component—most notably in design—the focus in this book is narrow. The focus is on research—the what, the why, and the how— with a few stories to tell along the way.

Many people associate research in HCI with developing a new or improved interaction or interface and testing it in a user study. The term "user study" some-times refers to an informal evaluation of a user interface. But this book takes a more formal approach, where a user study is "an experiment with human participants." HCI experiment are discussed throughout the book. The word *empirical* is added to this book's title to give weight to the value of experimental research. The research espoused here is empirical because it is based on observation and experience and is carried out and reported on in a manner that allows results to be verified or refuted through the efforts of other researchers. In this way, each item of HCI research joins a large body of work that, taken as a whole, defines the field and sets the context for applying HCI knowledge in real products or processes.

1.1 Introduction

Although HCI emerged in the 1980s, it owes a lot to older disciplines. The most central of these is the field of *human factors*, or *ergonomics*. Indeed, the name of the preeminent annual conference in HCI—the Association for Computing Machinery Conference on Human Factors in Computing Systems (ACM SIGCHI)—uses that term. SIGCHI is the special interest group on computer-human interaction sponsored by the ACM.[2]

Human factors is both a science and a field of engineering. It is concerned with human capabilities, limitations, and performance, and with the design of systems that are efficient, safe, comfortable, and even enjoyable for the humans who use them. It is also an art in the sense of respecting and promoting creative ways for practitioners to apply their skills in designing systems. One need only change *systems* in that statement to *computer systems* to make the leap from human factors to HCI. HCI, then, is human factors, but narrowly focused on human interaction with computing technology of some sort.

That said, HCI itself does not feel "narrowly focused." On the contrary, HCI is tremendously broad in scope. It draws upon interests and expertise in disciplines such as psychology (particularly cognitive psychology and experimental psychology), sociology, anthropology, cognitive science, computer science, and linguistics.

---

[2]The Association of Computing Machinery (ACM), founded in 1947, is the world's leading educational and scientific computing society, with over 95,000 members. The ACM is organized into over 150 special interest groups, or "SIGs." Among the services offered is the ACM Digital Library, a repository of online publications which includes 45+ ACM journals, 85+ ACM conference proceedings, and numerous other publications from affiliated organizations. See www.acm.org.

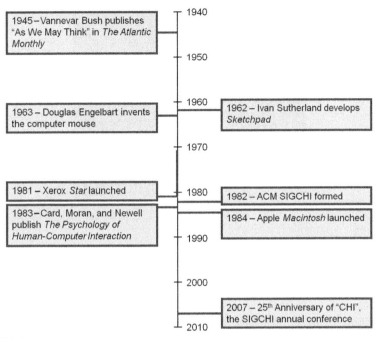

FIGURE 1.1

Timeline of notable events in the history of human–computer interaction HCI.

Figure 1.1 presents a timeline of a few notable events leading to the birth and emergence of HCI as a field of study, beginning in the 1940s.

1.2 Vannevar Bush's "as we may think" (1945)

Vannevar Bush's prophetic essay "As We May Think," published in the *Atlantic Monthly* in July, 1945 (Bush, 1945), is required reading in many HCI courses even today. The article has garnered 4,000+ citations in scholarly publications.[3] Attesting to the importance of Bush's vision to HCI is the 1996 reprint of the entire essay in the ACM's *interactions* magazine, complete with annotations, sketches, and biographical notes.

Bush (see Figure 1.2) was the U.S. government's Director of the Office of Scientific Research and a scientific advisor to President Franklin D. Roosevelt. During World War II, he was charged with leading some 6,000 American scientists in the application of science to warfare. But Bush was keenly aware of the possibilities that lay ahead in peacetime in applying science to more lofty and humane

---

[3] Google Scholar search using *author: "v bush."*

FIGURE 1.2

Vannevar Bush at work (circa 1940–1944).

pursuits. His essay concerned the dissemination, storage, and access to scholarly knowledge. Bush wrote:

> *the summation of human experience is being expanded at a prodigious rate, and the means we use for threading through the consequent maze to the momentarily important item is the same as was used in the days of square-rigged ships (p. 37).*[4]

Aside from the reference to antiquated square-rigged ships, what Bush says we can fully relate to today, especially his mention of the *expanding human experience* in relation to HCI. For most people, nothing short of Olympian talent is needed to keep abreast of the latest advances in the information age. Bush's *consequent maze* is today's *information overload* or *lost in hyperspace*. Bush's *momentarily important item* sounds a bit like a blog posting or a tweet. Although blogs and tweets didn't exist in 1945, Bush clearly anticipated them.

Bush proposed navigating the knowledge maze with a device he called *memex*. Among the features of memex is *associative indexing*, whereby points of interest can be connected and joined so that selecting one item immediately and automatically selects another: "When the user is building a trail, he names it, inserts the name in his code book, and taps it out on his keyboard" (Bush, 1945, p. 44). This sounds like a description of hyperlinks and bookmarks. Although today it is easy to equate memex with hypertext and the World Wide Web, Bush's inspiration for this idea came from the contemporary telephone exchange, which he described as a "spider web of metal, sealed in a thin glass container" (viz. vacuum tubes) (p. 38). The maze of connections in a telephone exchange gave rise to Bush's more general theme of a spider web of connections for the information in one's mind, linking one's experiences.

It is not surprising that some of Bush's ideas, for instance, *dry photography*, today seem naïve. Yet the ideas are naïve only when juxtaposed with Bush's

---

[4]For convenience, page references are to the March 1996 reprint in the ACM's *interactions*.

(a)   (b)

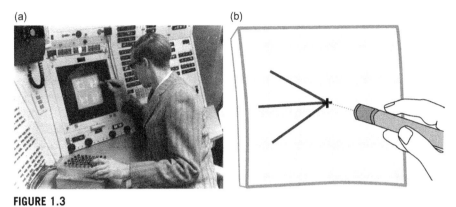

FIGURE 1.3

(a) Demo of Ivan Sutherland's Sketchpad. (b) A light pen dragging ("rubber banding") lines, subject to constraints.

brilliant foretelling of a world we are still struggling with and are still fine-tuning and perfecting.

1.3 Ivan Sutherland's Sketchpad (1962)

Ivan Sutherland developed Sketchpad in the early 1960s as part of his PhD research in electrical engineering at the Massachusetts Institute of Technology (M.I.T.). Sketchpad was a graphics system that supported the manipulation of geometric shapes and lines (*objects*) on a display using a light pen. To appreciate the inferior usability in the computers available to Sutherland at the time of his studies, consider these introductory comments in a paper he published in 1963:

> *Heretofore, most interaction between man and computers has been slowed by the need to reduce all communication to written statements that can be typed. In the past we have been writing letters to, rather than conferring with, our computers (Sutherland, 1963, p. 329).*

With Sketchpad, commands were not typed. Users did not "write letters to" the computer. Instead, objects were drawn, resized, grabbed and moved, extended, deleted—directly, using the light pen (see Figure 1.3). Object manipulations worked with constraints to maintain the geometric relationships and properties of objects.

The use of a pointing device for input makes Sketchpad the first *direct manipulation* interface—a sign of things to come. The term "direct manipulation" was coined many years later by Ben Shneiderman at the University of Maryland to provide a psychological context for a suite of related features that naturally came together in this new genre of human–computer interface (Shneiderman, 1983). These features included visibility of objects, incremental action, rapid feedback, reversibility, exploration, syntactic correctness of all actions, and replacing language with action. While Sutherland's Sketchpad was one of the earliest examples of a direct manipulation system, others soon followed, most notably the *Dynabook* concept system by Alan Kay of the Xerox Palo Alto Research Center (PARC) (Kay and Goldberg, 1977). I will say more about Xerox PARC throughout this chapter.

Sutherland's work was presented at the Institute of Electrical and Electronics Engineers (IEEE) conference in Detroit in 1963 and subsequently published in its proceedings (Sutherland, 1963). The article is available in the ACM Digital Library (http://portal.acm.org). Demo videos of Sketchpad are available on YouTube (www.youtube.com). Not surprisingly, a user study of Sketchpad was not conducted, since Sutherland was a student of electrical engineering. Had his work taken place in the field of industrial engineering (where human factors is studied), user testing would have been more likely.

1.4 Invention of the mouse (1963)

If there is one device that symbolizes the emergence of HCI, it is the computer mouse. Invented by Douglas Engelbart in 1963, the mouse was destined to fundamentally change the way humans interact with computers.[5] Instead of typing commands, a user could manipulate a mouse to control an on-screen tracking symbol, or cursor. With the cursor positioned over a graphic image representing the command, the command is issued with a select operation—pressing and releasing a button on the mouse.

Engelbart was among a group of researchers at the Stanford Research Institute (SRI) in Menlo Park, California. An early hypertext system called NLS, for oN-Line System, was the project for which an improved pointing device was needed. Specifically, the light pen needed to be replaced. The light pen was an established technology, but it was awkward. The user held the pen in the air in front of the display. After a few minutes of interaction, fatigue would set in. A more natural and comfortable device might be something on the desktop, something in close proximity to the keyboard. The keyboard is where the user's hands are normally situated, so a device beside the keyboard made the most sense. Engelbart's invention met this requirement.

The first prototype mouse is seen in Figure 1.4a. The device included two potentiometers positioned at right angles to each other. Large metal wheels were attached to the shafts of the potentiometers and protruded slightly from the base of the housing. The wheels rotated as the device was moved across a surface. Side-to-side motion rotated one wheel; to-and-fro motion rotated the other. With diagonal movement, both wheels rotated, in accordance with the amount of movement in each direction. The amount of rotation of each wheel altered the voltage at the wiper terminal of the potentiometer. The voltages were passed on to the host system for processing. The x and y positions of an on-screen object or cursor were indirectly

---

[5]Engelbart's patent for the mouse was filed on June 21, 1967 and issued on November 17, 1970 (Engelbart, 1970). U.S. patent laws allow one year between public disclosure and filing; thus, it can be assumed that prior to June 21, 1966, Engelbart's invention was not disclosed to the public.

(a)   (b)

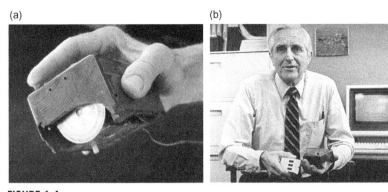

FIGURE 1.4

(a) The first mouse. (b) Inventor Douglas Engelbart holding his invention in his left hand and an early three-button variation in his right hand.

controlled by the two voltage signals. In Figure 1.4a, a selection button can be seen under the user's index finger. In Figure 1.4b, Engelbart is shown with his invention in his left hand and a three-button version of a mouse, which was developed much later, in his right.

Initial testing of the mouse focused on selecting and manipulating text, rather than drawing and manipulating graphic objects. Engelbart was second author of the first published evaluation of the mouse. This was, arguably, HCI's first user study, so a few words are in order here. Engelbart, along with English and Berman conducted a controlled experiment comparing several input devices capable of both selection and *x-y* position control of an on-screen cursor (English, Engelbart, and Berman, 1967). Besides the mouse, the comparison included a *light pen*, a *joystick*, a *knee-controlled lever*, and a *Grafacon*. The joystick (Figure 1.5a) had a moving stick and was operated in two control modes. In absolute or position-control mode, the cursor's position on the display had an absolute correspondence to the position of the stick. In rate-control mode, the cursor's velocity was determined by the amount of stick deflection, while the direction of the cursor's motion was determined by the direction of the stick. An embedded switch was included for selection and was activated by pressing down on the stick.

The light pen (Figure 1.5b) was operated much like the pen used by Sutherland (see Figure 1.3). The device was picked up and moved to the display surface with the pen pointing at the desired object. A projected circle of orange light indicated the target to the lens system. Selection involved pressing a switch on the barrel of the pen.

The knee-controlled lever (Figure 1.5c) was connected to two potentiometers. Side-to-side knee motion controlled side-to-side (*x*-axis) cursor movement; up-and-down knee motion controlled up-and-down (*y*-axis) cursor movement. Up-and-down knee motion was achieved by a "rocking motion on the ball of the foot" (p. 7). The device did not include an integrated method for selection. Instead, a key on the system's keyboard was used.

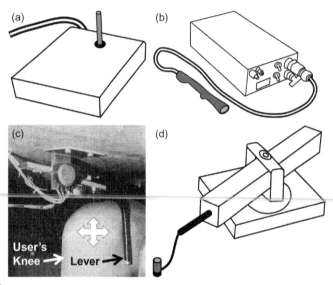

FIGURE 1.5

Additional devices used in the first comparative evaluation of a mouse: (a) Joystick.
(b) Lightpen. (c) Knee-controlled lever. (d) *Grafacon*.

(Source: a, b, d, adapted from English et al., 1967; c, 1967 IEEE. Reprinted with permission)

The Grafacon (Figure 1.5d) was a commercial device used for tracing curves. As noted, the device consisted "of an extensible arm connected to a linear potentiometer, with the housing for the linear potentiometer pivoted on an angular potentiometer" (1967, 6). Originally, there was a pen at the end of the arm; however, this was replaced with a knob-and-switch assembly (see Figure 1.5). The user gripped the knob and moved it about to control the on-screen cursor. Pressing the knob caused a selection.

The knee-controlled lever and Grafacon are interesting alternatives to the mouse. They illustrate and suggest the processes involved in empirical research. It is not likely that Engelbart simply woke up one morning and invented the mouse. While it may be true that novel ideas sometimes arise through "eureka" moments, typically there is more to the process of invention. Refining ideas—deciding what works and what doesn't—is an iterative process that involves a good deal of trial and error. No doubt, Engelbart and colleagues knew from the outset that they needed a device that would involve some form of human action as input and would produce two channels (*x-y*) of analog positioning data as output. A select operation was also needed to produce a command or generate closure at the end of a positioning operation. Of course, we know this today as a *point-select*, or *point-and-click*, operation. Operating the device away from the display meant some form of on-screen tracker (a *cursor*) was needed to establish correspondence between the *device space* and the *display space*. While this seems obvious today, it was a newly emerging form of human-to-computer interaction in the 1960s.

In the comparative evaluation, English et al. (1967) measured users' *access time* (the time to move the hand from the keyboard to the device) and *motion time* (the time from the onset of cursor movement to the final selection). The evaluation included 13 participants (eight experienced in working with the devices and three inexperienced). For each trial, a character target (with surrounding distracter targets) appeared on the display. The trial began with the participant pressing and releasing the spacebar on the system's keyboard, whereupon a cursor appeared on the display. The participant moved his or her hand to the input device and then manipulated the device to move the cursor to the target. With the cursor over the target, a selection was made using the method associated with the device. Examples of the test results from the inexperienced participants are shown in Figure 1.6. Each bar represents the mean for ten sequences. Every sequence consists of eight target-patterns. Results are shown for the mean task completion time (Figure 1.6a) and error rate (Figure 1.6b), where the error rate is the ratio of missed target selections to all selections.

While it might appear that the knee-controlled lever is the best device in terms of time, each bar in Figure 1.6a includes both the access time and the motion time. The access time for the knee-controlled lever is, of course, zero. The authors noted that considering motion time only, the knee-controlled lever "no longer shows up so favorably" (p. 12). At 2.43 seconds per trial, the light pen had a slight advantage over the mouse at 2.62 seconds per trial; however, this must be viewed with consideration for the inevitable discomfort in continued use of a light pen, which is operated in the air at the surface of the display. Besides, the mouse was the clear winner in terms of accuracy. The mouse error rate was less than half that of any other device condition in the evaluation (see Figure 1.6b).

The mouse evaluation by English et al. (1967) marks an important milestone in empirical research in HCI. The methodology was empirical and the write-up included most of what is expected today in a user study destined for presentation at a conference and publication in a conference proceedings. For example, the write-up contained a detailed description of the participants, the apparatus, and the procedure. The study could be reproduced if other researchers wished to verify or refute the findings. Of course, reproducing the evaluation today would be difficult, as the devices are no longer available. The evaluation included an independent variable, input method, with six levels: mouse, light pen, joystick (position-control), joystick (rate-control), and knee-controlled lever. There were two dependent variables, task completion time and error rate. The order of administering the device conditions was different for each participant, a practice known today as counterbalancing. While testing for statistically significant differences using an analysis of variance (ANOVA) was not done, it is important to remember that the authors did not have at their disposal the many tools taken for granted today, such as spreadsheets and statistics applications.

The next published comparative evaluation involving a mouse was by Card, English, and Burr (1978), about 10 years later. Card et al.'s work was carried out at Xerox PARC and was part of a larger effort that eventually produced the first windows-based graphical user interface, or GUI (see next section). The mouse

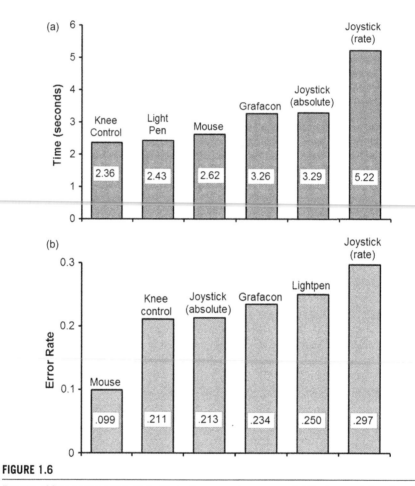

FIGURE 1.6

Results of first comparative evaluation of a computer mouse: (a) Task completion time in seconds. (b) Error rate as the ratio of missed selections to all selections.

(Adapted from English et al., 1967)

underwent considerable refining and reengineering at PARC. Most notably, the potentiometer wheels were replaced with a rolling ball assembly, developed by Rider (1974). The advantage of the refined mouse over competing devices was reconfirmed by Card et al. (1978) and has been demonstrated in countless comparative evaluations since and throughout the history of HCI. It was becoming clear that Engelbart's invention was changing the face of human-computer interaction.

Years later, Engelbart would receive the ACM Turing Award (1997) and the ACM SIGCHI Lifetime Achievement Award (1998; 1st recipient). It is interesting that Engelbart's seminal invention dates to the early 1960s, yet commercialization of the mouse did not occur until 1981, when the Xerox Star was launched.

1.5 **Xerox star (1981)**

There was a buzz around the floor of the National Computer Conference (NCC) in May 1981. In those days, the NCC was *the* yearly conference for computing. It was both a gathering of researchers (sponsored by the American Federation of Information Processing Societies, or AFIPS) and a trade show. The trade show was huge.[6] All the players were there. There were big players, like IBM, and little players, like Qupro Data Systems of Kitchener, Ontario, Canada. I was there, "working the booth" for Qupro. Our main product was a small desktop computer system based on a single-board computer known as the *Pascal MicroEngine*.

The buzz at the NCC wasn't about Qupro. It wasn't about IBM, either. The buzz was about Xerox. "Have you been to the Xerox booth?" I would hear. "You gotta check it out. It's really cool." And indeed it was. The Xerox booth had a substantial crowd gathered around it throughout the duration of the conference. There were scripted demonstrations every hour or so, and the crowd was clearly excited by what they were seeing. The demos were of the Star, or the *Xerox 8100 Star Information System*, as it was formally named. The excitement was well deserved, as the 1981 launch of the Xerox Star at the NCC marks a watershed moment in the history of computing. The Star was the first commercially released computer system with a GUI. It had windows, icons, menus, and a pointing device (WIMP). It supported direct manipulation and what-you-see-is-what-you-get (WYSIWYG) interaction. The Star had what was needed to bring computing to the people.

The story of the Star began around 1970, when Xerox established its research center, PARC, in Palo Alto, California. The following year, Xerox signed an agreement with SRI licensing Xerox to use Engelbart's invention, the mouse (Johnson et al., 1989, p. 22). Over the next 10 years, development proceeded along a number of fronts. The most relevant development for this discussion is that of the *Alto*, the Star's predecessor, which began in 1973. The Alto also included a GUI and mouse. It was used widely at Xerox and at a few external test sites. However, the Alto was never released commercially—a missed opportunity on a grand scale, according to some (D. K. Smith and Alexander, 1988).

Figure 1.7 shows the Star workstation, which is unremarkable by today's standards. The graphical nature of the information on the system's display can be seen in the image. This was novel at the time. The display was bit-mapped, meaning images were formed by mapping bits in memory to pixels on the display. Most systems at the time used character-mapped displays, meaning the screen image was composed of sequences of characters, each limited to a fixed pattern (e.g., 7×10 pixels) retrieved from read-only memory. Character-mapped displays required considerably less memory, but limited the richness of the display image. The mouse—a two-button variety—is featured by the system's keyboard.

---

[6] Attendance figures for 1981 are unavailable, but the NCC was truly huge. In 1983, NCC attendance exceeded 100,000 (Abrahams, 1987).

FIGURE 1.7

Xerox Star workstation.

As the designers noted, the Star was intended as an *office automation system* (Johnson et al., 1989). Business professionals would have Star workstations on their desks and would use them to create, modify, and manage documents, graphics tables, presentations, etc. The workstations were connected via high-speed Ethernet cables and shared centralized resources, such as printers and file servers. A key tenet in the Star philosophy was that workers wanted to get their work done, not fiddle with computers. Obviously, the computers had to be easy to use, or *invisible*, so to speak.

One novel feature of the Star was use of the *desktop metaphor*. Metaphors are important in HCI. When a metaphor is present, the user has a jump-start on knowing what to do. The user exploits existing knowledge from another domain. The desktop metaphor brings concepts from the office desktop to the system's display. On the display the user finds pictorial representations (*icons*) for things like documents, folders, trays, and accessories such as a calculator, printer, or notepad. A few examples of the Star's icons are seen in Figure 1.8. By using existing knowledge of a desktop, the user has an immediate sense of what to do and how things work. The Star designers, and others since, pushed the limits of the metaphor to the point where it is now more like an office metaphor than a desktop metaphor. There are windows, printers, and a trashcan on the display, but of course these artifacts are not found on an office desktop. However, the metaphor seemed to work, as we hear even today that the GUI is an example of the desktop metaphor. I will say more about metaphors again in Chapter 3.

In making the system usable (invisible), the Star developers created interactions that deal with files, not programs. So users "open a document," rather than "invoke an editor." This means that files are associated with applications, but these details are hidden from the user. Opening a spreadsheet document launches the spreadsheet application, while opening a text document opens a text editor.

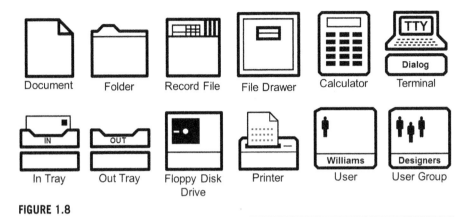

FIGURE 1.8

Examples of icons appearing on the Xerox Star desktop.

(Adapted from Smith, Irby, Kimball, and Harslem, 1982)

With a GUI and point-select interaction, the Star interface was the archetype of direct manipulation. The enabling work on graphical interaction (e.g., Sutherland) and pointing devices (e.g., Engelbart) was complete. By comparison, previous command-line interfaces had a single channel of input. For every action, a command was needed to invoke it. The user had to learn and remember the syntax of the system's commands and type them in to get things done. Direct manipulation systems, like the Star, have numerous input channels, and each channel has a direct correspondence to a task. Furthermore, interaction with the channel is tailored to the properties of the task. A continuous property, such as display brightness or sound volume, has a continuous control, such as a slider. A discrete property, such as font size or family, has a discrete control, such as a multi-position switch or a menu item. Each control also has a dedicated location on the display and is engaged using a direct point-select operation. Johnson et al. (1989, 14) compares direct manipulation to driving a car. A gas pedal controls the speed, a lever controls the wiper blades, a knob controls the radio volume. Each control is a dedicated channel, each has a dedicated location, and each is operated according to the property it controls.

When operating a car, the driver can adjust the radio volume and then turn on the windshield wipers. Or the driver can first turn on the windshield wipers and then adjust the radio volume. The car is capable of responding to the driver's inputs in any order, according to the driver's wishes. In computing, direct manipulation brings the same flexibility. This is no small feat. Command-line interfaces, by comparison, are simple. They follow a software paradigm known as *sequential programming*. Every action occurs in a sequence under the system's control. When the system needs a specific input, the user is prompted to enter it. Direct manipulation interfaces require a different approach because they must accept the user's actions according to the user's wishes. While manipulating *hello* in a text editor, for example, the user might change the font to Courier (hello) and then change the style to bold (**hello**). Or the user might first set the style to bold (**hello**) and then change the font to Courier (**hello**). The result is the same, but the order of actions differs. The point here is that the user is in control, not the system. To support this, direct manipulation systems are designed using a software paradigm known as *event-driven programming*, which is substantially more complicated than sequential programming. Although event-driven programming was not new (it was, and still is, used in process-control to respond to *sensor events*), designing systems that responded asynchronously to *user events* was new in the early 1970s when work began on the Star. Of course, from the user's perspective, this detail is irrelevant (remember the invisible computer). We mention it here only to give credit to the Herculean effort that was invested in designing the Star and bringing it to market.

Designing the Star was not simply a matter of building an interface using windows, icons, menus, and a pointing device (WIMP), it was about designing a system on which these components could exist and work. A team at PARC led by Alan Kay developed such a system beginning around 1970. The central ingredients were a new object-oriented programming language known as Smalltalk and a software architecture known as Model-View-Controller. This was a complex programming environment that evolved in parallel with the design of the Star. It is not surprising, then, that the development of the Star spanned about 10 years, since the designers were not only inventing a new style of human-computer interaction, they were inventing the architecture on which this new style was built.

In the end, the Star was not a commercial success. While many have speculated on why (e.g., D. K. Smith and Alexander, 1988), probably the most significant reason is that the Star was not a personal computer. In the article by the Star interface designers Johnson et al. (1989), there are numerous references to the Star as a *personal computer*. But it seems they had a different view of "personal." They viewed the Star as a beefed-up version of a terminal connected to a central server, "a collection of personal computers" (p. 12). In another article, designers Smith and Irby call the Star "a personal computer designed for office professionals" (1998, 17). "Personal"? Maybe, but without a doubt the Star was, first and foremost, a networked workstation connected to a server and intended for an office environment. And it was expensive: $16,000 for the workstation alone. That's a distant world from personal computing as we know it today. It was also a distant world from personal computing as it existed in the late 1970s and early 1980s. Yes, even then personal computing was flourishing. The *Apple II*, introduced in 1977 by Apple Computer, was hugely successful. It was the platform on which *VisiCalc*, the first spreadsheet application, was developed. VisiCalc eventually sold over 700,000 copies and became known as the first "killer app." Notably, the Star did not have a spreadsheet application, nor could it run any spreadsheet or other application available in the market place. The Star architecture was "closed"—it could only run applications developed by Xerox.

Other popular personal computer systems available around the same time were the *PET*, *VIC-20*, and *Commodore 64*, all by Commodore Business Machines, and the *TRS-80* by Tandy Corp. These systems were truly personal. Most of them were located in people's homes. But the *user interface* was terrible. These systems worked with a traditional command-line interface. The operating system—if you could call it that—usually consisted of a BASIC-language interpreter and a console prompt. LOAD, SAVE, RUN, EDIT, and a few other commands were about the extent of it. Although these systems were indeed personal, a typical user was a hobbyist, computer enthusiast, or anyone with enough technical skill to connect components together and negotiate the inevitable software and hardware hiccups. But users loved them, and they were cheap. However, they were tricky to use. So while the direct manipulation user interface of the Star may have been intuitive and had the potential to be used by people with no technical skill (or interest in having it!), the system just didn't reach the right audience.

1.6 **Birth of HCI (1983)**

Nineteen eighty-three is a good year to peg as the birth of HCI. There are at least three key events as markers: the first ACM SIGCHI conference, the publication of Card, Moran, and Newell's *The Psychology of Human-Computer Interaction* (1983), and the arrival of the Apple Macintosh, pre-announced with flyers in December 1983. The *Mac* launch was in January 1984, but I'll include it here anyway.

1.6.1 **First ACM SIGCHI conference (1983)**

Human-computer interaction's roots reach as early as 1969, when ACM's Special Interest Group on Social and Behavioral Computing (SIGSOC) was formed. (Borman, 1996). Initially, SIGSOC focused on computers in the social sciences. However, emphasis soon shifted to the needs and behavioral characteristics of the users, with talk about the user interface or the human factors of computing. Beginning in 1978, SIGSOC lobbied the ACM for a name change. This happened at the 1982 *Conference on Human Factors in Computing Systems* in Gaithersburg, Maryland, where the formation of the ACM Special Interest Group on Computer-Human Interaction (SIGCHI) was first publicly announced. Today, the ACM provides the following articulate statement of SIGCHI and its mission:

> The ACM Special Interest Group on Computer-Human Interaction is the world's largest association of professionals who work in the research and practice of computer-human interaction. This interdisciplinary group is composed of computer scientists, software engineers, psychologists, interaction designers, graphic designers, sociologists, and anthropologists, just to name some of the domains whose special expertise come to bear in this area. They are brought together by a shared understanding that designing useful and usable technology is an interdisciplinary process, and believe that when done properly it has the power to transform persons' lives.[7]

The interdisciplinary nature of the field is clearly evident in the list of disciplines that contribute to, and have a stake in, HCI.

---

[7] Retrieved from http://www.acm.org/sigs#026 on September 10, 2012.

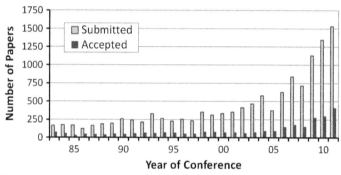

FIGURE 1.9

Number of papers submitted and accepted by year for the ACM SIGCHI Conference on Human Factors in Computing Systems ("CHI"). Statistics from the ACM Digital Library.

In the following year, 1983, the first SIGCHI conference was held in Boston. Fifty-nine technical papers were presented. The conference adopted a slightly modified name to reflect its new stature: *ACM SIGCHI Conference on Human Factors in Computing Systems*. "CHI," as it is known (pronounced with a hard "k" sound), has been held yearly ever since and in recent years has had an attendance of about 2,500 people.

The CHI conference brings together both researchers and practitioners. The researchers are there for the technical program (presentation of papers), while the practitioners are there to learn about the latest themes of research in academia and industry. Actually, both groups are also there to network (meet and socialize) with like-minded HCI enthusiasts from around the world. Simply put, CHI is *the* event in HCI, and the yearly pilgrimage to attend is often the most important entry in the calendar for those who consider HCI their field.

The technical program is competitive. Research papers are peer reviewed, and acceptance requires rising above a relatively high bar for quality. Statistics compiled from 1982 to 2011 indicate a total of 12,671 paper submissions with 3,018 acceptances, for an overall acceptance rate of 24 percent. Figure 1.9 shows the breakdown by year, as provided on the ACM Digital Library website.[8] The technical program is growing rapidly. For example, the number of accepted contributions in 2011 (410) exceeded the number of submissions in 2005 (372).

Once accepted, researchers present their work at the conference, usually in a 15–20 minute talk augmented with visual slides and perhaps a video demonstration of the research. Acceptance also means the final submitted paper is published in the conference proceedings and archived in the ACM Digital Library. Some tips on writing and publishing a research paper are presented in Chapter 8.

---

[8] Data retrieved from http://portal.acm.org. (Click on "Proceedings," scroll down to any CHI conference proceedings, click on it, then click on the "Publication" tab.)

CHI papers have high visibility, meaning they reach a large community of researchers and practitioners in the field. One indication of the quality of the work is *impact*, the number of citations credited to a paper. Since the standards for acceptance are high, one might expect CHI papers to have high impact on the field of HCI. And indeed this is the case (MacKenzie, 2009a). I will say more about research impact in Chapter 4.

Although the annual CHI conference is SIGCHI's flagship event, other conferences are sponsored or co-sponsored by SIGCHI. These include the annual *ACM Symposium on User Interface Software and Technology* (*UIST*), specialized conferences such as the *ACM Symposium on Eye Tracking Research and Applications* (*ETRA*) and the *ACM Conference on Computers and Accessibility* (*ASSETS*), and regional conferences such as the *Nordic Conference on Computer-Human Interaction* (*NordiCHI*).

1.6.2 The psychology of human-computer interaction (1983)

If two HCI researchers speaking of "Card, Moran, and Newell" are overheard, there is a good chance they are talking about *The Psychology of Human-Computer Interaction*—the book published in 1983 and co-authored by Stuart Card, Tom Moran, and Allen Newell. (See Figure 1.10.) The book emerged from work done at Xerox PARC. Card and Moran arrived at PARC in 1974 and soon after joined PARC's *Applied Information-Processing Psychology Project* (AIP). Newell, a professor of computer science and cognitive psychology at Carnegie Mellon University in Pittsburgh, Pennsylvania, was a consultant to the project. The AIP mission was "to create an applied psychology of human-computer interaction by conducting requisite basic research within a context of application" (Card et al., 1983, p. ix).

The book contains 13 chapters organized roughly as follows: scientific foundation (100 pages), text editing examples (150 pages), modeling (80 pages), and extensions and generalizations (100 pages). So what is an "applied psychology of human-computer interaction"? Applied psychology is built upon basic research in psychology. The first 100 or so pages in the book provide a comprehensive overview of core knowledge in basic psychology as it pertains to the human sensory, cognitive, and motor systems. In the 1980s, many computer science students (and professionals) were challenged with building simple and intuitive interfaces for computer systems, particularly in view of emerging interaction styles based on a GUI. For many students, Card, Moran, and Newell's book was their first formalized exposure to human perceptual input (e.g., the time to visually perceive a stimulus), cognition (e.g., the time to decide on the appropriate reaction), and motor output (e.g., the time to react and move the hand or cursor to a target). Of course, research in human sensory, cognitive, and motor behavior was well developed at the time. What Card, Moran, and Newell did was connect low-level human processes with the seemingly innocuous interactions humans have with computers (e.g., typing or using a mouse). The framework for this was the *model human processor* (MHP). (See Figure 1.11.) The MHP had an eye and an ear (for sensory input to a perceptual processor), a

FIGURE 1.10

Card, Moran, and Newell's *The Psychology of Human-Computer Interaction.*

(Published by Erlbaum in 1983)

brain (with a cognitive processor, short-term memory, and long-term memory), and an arm, hand, and finger (for motor responses).

The application selected to frame the analyses in the book was text editing. This might seem odd today, but it is important to remember that 1983 predates the World Wide Web and most of today's computing environments such as mobile computing, touch-based input, virtual reality, texting, tweeting, and so on. Text editing seemed like the right framework in which to develop an applied psychology of human-computer interaction.[9] Fortunately, all the issues pertinent to text editing are applicable across a broad spectrum of human-computer interaction.

An interesting synergy between psychology and computer science—and it is well represented in the book—is the notion that human behavior can be understood, even modeled, as an information processing activity. In the 1940s and 1950s the work of Shannon (1949), Huffman (1952), and others, on the transmission of information through electronic channels, was quickly picked up by psychologists like Miller (1956), Fitts (1954), and Welford (1968) as a way to characterize human perceptual, cognitive, and motor behavior. Card, Moran, and Newell

---

[9]At a panel session at *CHI 2008*, Moran noted that the choice was between text editing and programming.

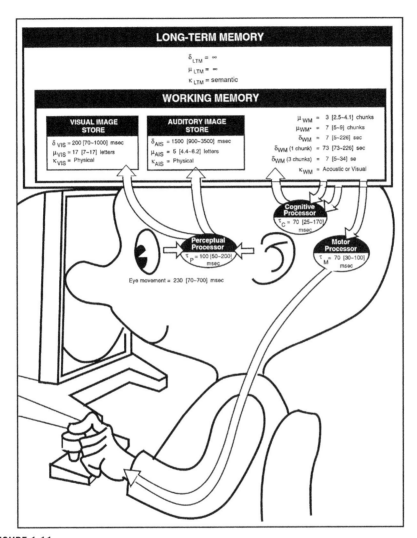

FIGURE 1.11

The model human processor (MHP) (Card et al., 1983, p. 26).

adapted information processing models of human behavior to interactive systems. The two most prominent examples in the book are Hick's law for choice reaction time (Hick, 1952) and Fitts' law for rapid aimed movement (Fitts, 1954). I will say more about these in Chapter 7, Modeling Interaction.

Newell later reflected on the objectives of *The Psychology of Human-Computer Interaction*:

> *We had in mind the need for a theory for designers of interfaces. The design of the interface is the leverage point in human-computer interaction. The classical emphasis of human factors and man-machine psychology on experimental*

analysis requires that the system or a suitable mock-up be available for experimentation, but by the time such a concrete system exists, most of the important degrees of freedom in the interface have been bound. What is needed are tools for thought for the designer—so at design time the properties and constraints of the user can be brought to bear in making the important choices. Our objective was to develop an engineering-style theory of the user that permitted approximate, back-of-the-envelope calculations of how the user would interact with the computer when operating at a terminal. (Newell, 1990, pp. 29–30)

There are some interesting points here. For one, Newell astutely identifies a dilemma in the field: experimentation cannot be done until it is too late. As he put it, the system is built and the degrees of freedom are bound. This is an overstatement, perhaps, but it is true that novel interactions in new products always seem to be *followed* by a flurry of research papers identifying weaknesses and suggesting and evaluating improvements. There is more to the story, however. Consider the Apple *iPhone*'s two-finger gestures, the Nintendo *Wii*'s acceleration sensing flicks, the Microsoft *IntelliMouse*'s scrolling wheel, or the Palm *Pilot*'s text-input gestures (aka *Graffiti*). These "innovations" were not fresh ideas born out of engineering or design brilliance. These breakthroughs, and many more, have context, and that context is the milieu of basic research in human-computer interaction and related fields.[10] For the examples just cited, the research preceded commercialization. Research by its very nature *requires* dissemination through publication. It is not surprising, then, that conferences like CHI and books like *The Psychology of Human-Computer Interaction* are fertile ground for discovering and spawning new and exciting interaction techniques.

Newell also notes that an objective in the book was to generate "tools for thought." This is a casual reference to models—models of interaction. The models may be quantitative and predictive or qualitative and descriptive. Either way, they are tools, the carver's knife, the cobbler's needle. Whether generating quantitative predictions across alternative design choices or delimiting a problem space to reveal new relationships, a model's purpose is to tease out strengths and weaknesses in a hypothetical design and to elicit opportunities to improve the design. The book includes exemplars, such as the keystroke-level model (KLM) and the goals, operators, methods, and selection rules model (GOMS). Both of these models were presented in earlier work (Card, Moran, and Newell, 1980), but were presented again in the book, with additional discussion and analysis. The book's main contribution on modeling, however, was to convincingly demonstrate why and how models are important and to teach us how to build them. For this, HCI's debt to

---

[10]Of the four examples cited, research papers anticipating each are found in the HCI literature. On multi-touch finger gestures, there is Rekimoto's "pick-and-drop" (1997), Dietz and Leigh's DiamondTouch (Dietz and Leigh, 2001), or, much earlier, Herot and Weinzapfel's two-finger rotation gesture on a touchscreen (Herot and Weinzapfel, 1978). On acceleration sensing, there is Harrison et al.'s "tilt me!" (1998). On the wheel mouse, there is Venolia's "roller mouse" (Venolia, 1993). On single-stroke handwriting, there is Goldberg and Richardson's "Unistrokes" (1993).

Card, Moran, and Newell is considerable. I will discuss descriptive and predictive models further in Chapter 7, Modeling Interaction.

Newell suggests using approximate "back of the envelope" calculations as a convenient way to describe or predict user interaction. In *The Psychology of Human-Computer Interaction*, these appear, among other ways, through a series of 19 interaction examples in Chapter 2 (pp. 23–97). The examples are presented as questions about a user interaction. The solutions use rough calculations but are based on data and concepts gleaned from basic research in experimental psychology. Example 10 is typical:

> *A user is presented with two symbols, one at a time. If the second symbol is identical to the first, he is to push the key labeled YES. Otherwise he is to push NO. What is the time between signal and response for the YES case? (Card et al., 1983, p. 66)*

Before giving the solution, let us consider a modern context for the example. Suppose a user is texting a friend and is entering the word *hello* on a mobile phone using predictive text entry *(T9)*. Since the mobile phone keypad is ambiguous for text entry, the correct word does not always appear. After entering 4(GHI), 3(DEF), 5(JKL), 5(JKL), 6(MNO), a word appears on the display. This is the *signal* in the example (see above). There are two possible responses. If the word is *hello*, it matches the word in the user's mind and the user presses 0(SPACE) to accept the word and append a space. This is the YES response in the example. If the display shows some other word, a collision has occurred, meaning there are multiple candidates for the key sequence. The user presses *(NEXT) to display the next word in the ambiguous set. This is the NO response in the example. As elaborated by Card, Moran, and Newell, the interaction just described is a type of *simple decision* known as *physical matching*. The reader is walked through the solution using the model human processor to illustrate each step, from stimulus to cognitive processing to motor response. The solution is approximate. There is a nominal prediction accompanied by a *fastman* prediction and a *slowman* prediction. Here's the solution:

$$\text{Reaction time} = t_p + 2 \times t_c + t_M$$
$$= 100[30 \sim 200] + 2 \times (70[25 \sim 170]) + 70[30 \sim 100] \quad (1)$$
$$= 310[130 \sim 640]\,\text{ms}$$

(Card et al., 1983, p. 69). There are four low-level processing cycles: a perceptual processor cycle (t_P), two cognitive processor cycles (t_C), and a motor processor cycle (t_M). For each, the nominal value is bracketed by an expected minimum and maximum. The values in Equation 1 are obtained from basic research in experimental psychology, as cited in the book. The fastman–slowman range is large and demonstrates the difficulty in accurately predicting human behavior. The book has many other examples like this. There are also modern contexts for the examples, just waiting to be found and applied.

It might not be apparent that predicting the time for a task that takes only one-third of a second is relevant to the bigger picture of designing interactive systems.

But don't be fooled. If a complex task can be deconstructed into primitive actions, there is a good chance the time to do the task can be predicted by dividing the task into a series of motor actions interlaced with perceptual and cognitive processing cycles. This idea is presented in Card, Moran, and Newell's book as a *keystroke-level model* (KLM), which I will address again in Chapter 7.

The Psychology of Human-Computer Interaction is still available (see http://www.amazon.com) and is regularly and highly cited in research papers (5,000+ citations according to Google Scholar). At the ACM SIGCHI conference in Florence, Italy in 2008, there was a panel session celebrating the book's 25th anniversary. Both Card and Moran spoke on the book's history and on the challenges they faced in bringing a psychological science to the design of interactive computing systems. Others spoke on how the book affected and influenced their own research in human-computer interaction.

1.6.3 Launch of the Apple Macintosh (1984)

January 22, 1984 was a big day in sports. It was the day of Super Bowl XVIII, the championship game of the National Football League in the United States. It was also a big day in advertising. With a television audience of millions, companies were jockeying (and paying!) to deliver brief jolts of hype to viewers who were hungry for entertainment and primed to purchase the latest must-have products. One ad—played during the third quarter—was a 60-second stint for the Apple Macintosh (the Mac) personal computer. The ad, which is viewable on YouTube, used Orwell's *Nineteen Eighty-Four* as a theme, portraying the Mac as a computer that would shatter the conventional image of the home computer.[11] The ad climaxed with a female athlete running toward, and tossing a sledgehammer through, the face of Big Brother. The disintegration of Big Brother signaled the triumph of the human spirit over the tyranny and oppression of the corporation. Directed by Ridley Scott,[12] the ad was a hit and was even named the 1980s Commercial of the Decade by *Advertising Age* magazine.[13] It never aired again.

The ad worked. Soon afterward, computer enthusiasts scooped up the Mac. It was sleek and sported the latest input device, a computer mouse. (See Figure 1.12.) The operating system and applications software heralded the new age of the GUI with direct manipulation and point-select interaction. The Mac was not only cool, the interface was simple and intuitive. Anyone could use it. Part of the simplicity was its one-button mouse. With one button, there was no confusion on which button to press.

There are plenty of sources chronicling the history of Apple and the events leading to the release of the Mac (Levy, 1995; Linzmayer, 2004; Moritz, 1984). Unfortunately, along with the larger-than-life stature of Apple and its flamboyant

---

[11] Search using "1984 Apple Macintosh commercial."

[12] Known for his striking visual style, Scott directed many off-beat feature-length films such as *Alien* (1979), *Blade Runner* (1982), *Thelma and Louise* (1991), and *Gladiator* (2000).

[13] http://en.wikipedia.org/wiki/1984 (advertisement).

FIGURE 1.12 The Apple Macintosh.

leaders comes plenty of folklore to untangle. A few notable events are listed in Figure 1.13. Names of the key players are deliberately omitted.

1.7 Growth of HCI and graphical user interfaces (GUIs)

With the formation of ACM SIGCHI in 1983 and the release and success of the Apple Macintosh in 1984, human-computer interaction was off and running. GUIs entered the mainstream and, consequently, a much broader community of users and researchers were exposed to this new genre of interaction. Microsoft was a latecomer in GUIs. Early versions of Microsoft *Windows* appeared in 1985, but it was not until the release of *Windows 3.0* (1990) and in particular *Windows 3.1* (1992) that Microsoft Windows was considered a serious alternative to the Macintosh operating system. Microsoft increased its market share with improved versions of Windows, most notably *Windows 95* (1995), *Windows 98* (1998), *Windows XP* (2001), and *Windows 7* (2009). Today, Microsoft operating systems for desktop computers have a market share of about 84 percent, compared to 15 percent for Apple.[14]

With advancing interest in human-computer interaction, all major universities introduced courses in HCI or user interface (UI) design, with graduate students often choosing a topic in HCI for their thesis research. Many such programs of study were in computer science departments; however, HCI also emerged as a legitimate and popular focus in other areas such as psychology, cognitive science, industrial engineering, information systems, and sociology. And it wasn't just universities that recognized the importance of the emerging field. Companies soon

---

[14]www.statowl.com.

1976	April – Apple Computer Inc. founded in Cupertino, California.
1977	Launch of Apple II. Sells for $1300 U.S. with 4KB RAM. Hugely successful (more than one million units sold). Works with a text-based command-line interface.
1978	*Lisa* project started . Goal of producing a powerful (and expensive!) personal computer.
1979	September – *Macintosh* project started. Goal of producing a low-cost easy-to-use computer for the average consumer. December – Apple and Xerox sign an agreement that allows Xerox to invest in Apple. In return Apple's engineers visit Xerox PARC and see the Xerox *Alto*. The GUI ideas in the *Alto* influence *Lisa* and *Macintosh* development.
1980	December – Apple goes public through initial public offering (IPO) of its stock.
1981	May – Xerox *Star* launched at the National Computer Conference (NCC) in Chicago. Members of the *Lisa* design team are present and see the *Star* demo. They decide to re-vamp the *Lisa* interface to be icon-based. August – IBM PC announced. Highly successful, but embodies traditional text-based command-line interface.
1982	*Lisa* and *Macintosh* development continue. Within Apple, there is an atmosphere of competition between the two projects.
1983	January – *Lisa* released. *Lisa* incorporates a GUI and mouse input. Sells for $10,000 U.S. In the end, *Lisa* is a commercial failure. December – brochures distributed in magazines (e.g., *Time*) pre-announcing the *Macintosh*.
1984	January 22 – *Macintosh* ad plays during Super Bowl XVIII. January 24 – *Macintosh* released. Sells for $2500 U.S.

FIGURE 1.13

Some notable events leading to the release of the Apple Macintosh.[15]

realized that designing good user interfaces was good business. But it wasn't easy. Stories of bad UIs are legion in HCI (e.g., Cooper, 1999; Johnson, 2007; Norman, 1988). So there was work to be done. Practitioners—that is, specialists applying HCI principles in industry—are important members of the HCI community, and they form a significant contingent at many HCI conferences today.

1.8 Growth of HCI research

Research interest in human-computer interaction, at least initially, was in the quality, effectiveness, and efficiency of the interface. How quickly and accurately can people do common tasks using a GUI versus a text-based command-line interface? Or, given two or more variations in a GUI implementation, which one is quicker or more accurate? These or similar questions formed the basis of much empirical research in the early days of HCI. The same is still true today.

A classic example of a research topic in HCI is the design of menus. With a GUI, the user issues a command to the computer by selecting the command from a menu rather than typing it on the keyboard. Menus require *recognition*; typing

---

[15] www.theapplemuseum.com, http://en.wikipedia.org/wiki/History_of_Apple, and www.guidebook-gallery.org/articles/lisainterview, with various other sources to confirm dates and events.

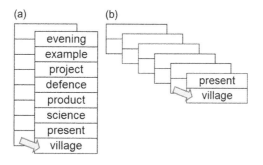

FIGURE 1.14

Breadth versus depth in menu design: (a) 8×8 choices in a broad hierarchy.
(b) 2×2×2×2×2×2 choices in a deep hierarchy.

requires *recall*. It is known that recognition is preferred over recall in user interfaces (Bailey, 1996, p. 144; Hodgson and Ruth, 1985; Howes and Payne, 1990),
at least for novices, but a new problem then surfaces. If there are numerous commands in a menu, how should they be organized? One approach is to organize menu
commands in a hierarchy that includes depth and breadth. The question arises: what
is the best structure for the hierarchy? Consider the case of 64 commands organized
in a menu. The menu could be organized with depth $=8$ and breadth $=2$, or with
depth $=2$ and breadth $=6$. Both structures provide access to 64 menu items. The
breadth-emphasis case gives $8^2=64$ choices (Figure 1.14a). The depth-emphasis
case gives $2^6=64$ choices (Figure 1.14b). Which organization is better? Is another
organization better still (e.g., $4^3=64$)? Given these questions, it is not surprising
that menu design issues were actively pursued as research topics in the early days
of HCI (e.g., Card, 1982; Kiger, 1984; Landauer and Nachbar, 1985; D. P. Miller,
1981; Snowberry, Parkinson, and Sisson, 1983; Tullis, 1985).

Depth versus breadth is not the only research issue in menu design; there are
many others. Should items be ordered alphabetically or by function (Card, 1982;
Mehlenbacher, Duffy, and Palmer, 1989)? Does the presence of a title on a sub-
menu improve menu access (J. Gray, 1986)? Is access improved if an icon is added
to the label (Hemenway, 1982)? Do people in different age groups respond differently to broad versus deep menu hierarchies (Zaphiris, Kurniawan, and Ellis,
2003)? Is there a depth versus breadth advantage for menus on mobile devices
(Geven, Sefelin, and Tschelig, 2006)? Does auditory feedback improve menu
access (Zhao, Dragicevic, Chignell, Balakrishnan, and Baudisch, 2007)? Can the
tilt of a mobile phone be used for menu navigation (Rekimoto, 1996)? Can menu
lists be pie shaped, rather than linear (Callahan, Hopkins, Weiser, and Shneiderman,
1988)? Can pie menus be used for text entry (D. Venolia and Neiberg, 1994)?

The answers to these research questions can be found in the papers cited. They
are examples of the kinds of research questions that create opportunities for empirical research in HCI. There are countless such topics of research in HCI. While
we've seen many in this chapter, we will find many more in the chapters to come.

1.9 **Other readings**

Two other papers considered important in the history of HCI are:

- "Personal Dynamic Media" by A. Kay and A. Goldberg (1977). This article describes *Dynabook*. Although never built, Dynabook provided the conceptual basis for laptop computers, tablet PCs, and e-books.
- "The Computer for the 21st Century" by M. Weiser (1991). This is the essay that presaged ubiquitous computing. Weiser begins, "The most profound technologies are those that disappear. They weave themselves into the fabric of everyday life until they are indistinguishable from it" (p. 94).

Other sources taking a historical view of human-computer interaction include: Baecker, Grudin, Buxton, and Greenberg, 1995; Erickson and McDonald, 2007; Grudin, 2012; Myers, 1998.

1.10 **Resources**

The following online resources are useful for conducting research in human-computer interaction:

- Google Scholar: http://scholar.google.ca
- ACM Digital Library: http://portal.acm.org
- HCI Bibliography: http://hcibib.org

This website is available as a resource accompanying this book:

- www.yorku.ca/mack/HCIbook
  Many downloads are available to accompany the examples presented herein.

STUDENT EXERCISES

1-1. The characteristics of direct manipulation include visibility of objects, incremental action, rapid feedback, reversibility, exploration, syntactic correctness of all actions, and replacing language with action. For each characteristic consider and discuss an example task performed with modern GUIs. Contrast the task with the same task as performed in a command-line environment such as unix, linux, or DOS.

The Human Factor

The deepest challenges in human-computer interaction (HCI) lie in the human factor. Humans are complicated. Computers, by comparison, are simple. Computers are designed and built and they function in rather strict terms according to their programmed capabilities. There is no parallel with humans. Human scientists (including those in HCI) confront something computer scientists rarely think about: variability. Humans differ. We're young, old, female, male, experts, novices, left-handed, right-handed, English-speaking, Chinese-speaking, from the north, from the south, tall, short, strong, weak, fast, slow, able-bodied, disabled, sighted, blind, motivated, lazy, creative, bland, tired, alert, and on and on. The variability humans bring to the table means our work is never precise. It is always approximate. Designing systems that work well, period, is a lofty goal, but unfortunately, it is not possible to the degree we would like to achieve. A system might work well for a subset of people, but venture to the edges along any dimension (see list above), and the system might work poorly, or not at all. It is for this reason that HCI designers have precepts like "know thy user" (Shneiderman and Plaisant, 2005, p. 66).

Researchers in HCI have questions—lots of them. We are good at the small ones, but the big ones are difficult to answer: Why do humans make mistakes? Why do humans forget how to do things? Why do humans get confused while installing apps on their computers? Why do humans have trouble driving while talking on a mobile phone? Why do humans enjoy *Facebook* so much? Obviously, the human part is hugely important and intriguing. The more we understand humans, the better are our chances of designing interactive systems—interactions—that work as intended. So in this chapter I examine the human, but the computer and the interaction are never far away.

The questions in the preceding paragraph begin with *why*. They are big questions. Unfortunately, they do not lend themselves to empirical enquiry, which is the focus of this book. Take the first question: *Why do humans make mistakes?* From an empirical research perspective, the question is too broad. It cannot be answered with any precision. Our best bet is to narrow in on a defined group of humans (a *population*) and ask them to do a particular task on a particular system in a particular environment. We observe the interaction and measure the behavior. Along the way, we log the mistakes, classify them, count them, and take note of where and how the mistakes occurred. If our methodology is sound, we might assimilate enough information to put forth an answer to the *why* question—in a narrow sense.

If we do enough research like this, we might develop an answer in a broad sense. But a grounded and rigorous approach to empirical research requires small and narrowly focused questions.

Descriptive models, which will be discussed in Chapter 7, seek to delineate and categorize a problem space. They are tools for thinking, rather than tools for predicting. A descriptive model for "the human" would be useful indeed. It would help us get started in understanding the human, to delineate and categorize aspects of the human that are relevant to HCI. In fact there are many such models, and I will introduce several in this chapter.

2.1 Time scale of human action

Newell's *Time Scale of Human Action* is a descriptive model of the human (Newell, 1990, p. 122). It delineates the problem space by positioning different types of human actions in timeframes within which the actions occur. (See Figure 2.1.) The model has four bands, a *biological band*, a *cognitive band*, a *rational band*, and a *social band*. Each band is divided into three levels. Time is ordered by seconds and appears on a logarithmic scale, with each level a factor of ten longer than the level below it. The units are microseconds at the bottom and months at the top. For nine levels, Newell ascribes a label for the human system at work (e.g., *operations* or *task*). Within these labels we see a connection with HCI. The labels for the bands suggest a worldview or theory of human action.

The most common dependent variable in experimental research in HCI is time—the time for a user to do a task. In this sense, Newell's time-scale model is relevant to HCI. The model is also appropriate because it reflects the multidisciplinary nature of the field. HCI research is both *high level* and *low level*, and we see this in the model. If desired, we could select a paper at random from an HCI conference proceedings or journal, study it, then position the work somewhere in Figure 2.1. For example, research on selection techniques, menu design, force or auditory feedback, text entry, gestural input, and so on, is within the cognitive band. The tasks for these interactions typically last on the order of a few hundred milliseconds (ms) to a few dozen seconds. Newell characterizes these as deliberate acts, operations, and unit tasks.

Up in the rational band, users are engaged in tasks that span minutes, tens of minutes, or hours. Research topics here include web navigation, user search strategies, user-centered design, collaborative computing, ubiquitous computing, social navigation, and situated awareness. Tasks related to these research areas occupy users for minutes or hours.

Tasks lasting days, weeks, or months are in the social band. HCI topics here might include workplace habits, groupware usage patterns, social networking, online dating, privacy, media spaces, user styles and preferences, design theory, and so on.

Another insight Newell's model provides pertains to research methodology. Research at the bottom of the scale is highly quantitative in nature. Work in the biological band, for example, is likely experimental and empirical—at the level of neural

Scale (sec)	Time Units	System	World (theory)
10^7	Months		**SOCIAL BAND**
10^6	Weeks		
10^5	Days		
10^4	Hours	Task	**RATIONAL BAND**
10^3	10 min	Task	
10^2	Minutes	Task	
10^1	10 sec	Unit task	**COGNITIVE BAND**
10^0	1 sec	Operations	
10^{-1}	100 ms	Deliberate act	
10^{-2}	10 ms	Neural circuit	**BIOLOGICAL BAND**
10^{-3}	1 ms	Neuron	
10^{-4}	100 μs	Organelle	

FIGURE 2.1

Newell's time scale of human action.

(From Newell, 1990, p. 122)

impulses. At the top of the scale, the reverse is true. In the social band, research methods tend to be qualitative and non-experimental. Techniques researchers employ here include interviews, observation, case studies, scenarios, and so on. Furthermore, the transition between qualitative and quantitative methods moving from top to bottom in the figure is gradual. As one methodology becomes more prominent, the other becomes less prominent. Researchers in the social band primarily use qualitative methods, but often include some quantitative methods. For example, research on workplace habits, while primarily qualitative, might include some quantitative methods (e.g., counting the number of personal e-mails sent each day while at work). Thus, qualitative research in the social band also includes some quantitative assessment. Conversely, researchers in the cognitive band primarily use quantitative methods but typically include some qualitative methods. For example, an experiment on human performance with pointing devices, while primarily quantitative, might include an interview at the end to gather comments and suggestions on the interactions. Thus, quantitative, experimental work in the cognitive band includes some qualitative assessment as well.

Newell speculates further on bands above the social band: a *historical band* operating at the level of years to thousands of years, and an *evolutionary band* operating at the level of tens of thousands to millions of years (Newell, 1990, p. 152). We will forgo interpreting these in terms of human-computer interaction.

2.2 **Human factors**

There are many ways to characterize the human in interactive systems. One is the model human processor of Card et al. (1983), which was introduced in Chapter 1.

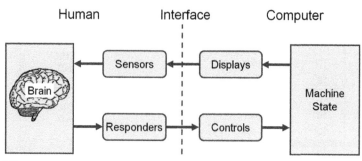

FIGURE 2.2

Human factors view of the human operator in a work environment.

(After Kantowitz and Sorkin, 1983, p. 4)

Other characterizations exist as well. Human factors researchers often use a model showing a human operator confronting a machine, like the image in Figure 2.2. The human monitors the state of the computer through sensors and displays and controls the state of the computer through responders and controls. The dashed vertical line is important since it is at the interface where interaction takes place. This is the location where researchers observe and measure the behavioral events that form the interaction.

Figure 2.2 is a convenient way to organize this section, since it simplifies the human to three components: sensors, responders, and a brain.

2.3 Sensors

Rosa: You deny everything except what you want to believe. That's the sort of man you are.
Bjartur: I have my five senses, and don't see what need there is for more.
(Halldór Laxness, *Independent People*)

The five classical human senses are vision, hearing, taste, smell, and touch. Each brings distinctly different physical properties of the environment to the human. One feature the senses share is the reception and conversion into electrical nerve signals of physical phenomena such as sound waves, light rays, flavors, odors, and physical contact. The signals are transmitted to the brain for processing. Sensory stimuli and sense organs are purely physiological. Perception, discussed later, includes both the sensing of stimuli and use of the brain to develop identification, awareness, and understanding of what is being sensed. We begin with the first of the five senses just noted: vision.

2.3.1 Vision (Sight)

Vision, or sight, is the human ability to receive information from the environment in the form of visible light perceived by the eye. The visual sensory channel

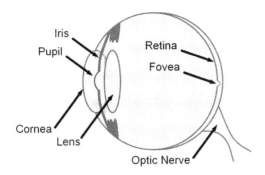

FIGURE 2.3

The eye.

FIGURE 2.4

The fovea image spans a region a little more than one degree of visual angle.

is hugely important, as most people obtain about 80 percent of their information though the sense of light (Asakawa and Takagi, 2007). The act of seeing begins with the reception of light through the eye's lens. The lens focuses the light into an image projected on to the retina at the back of the eye. (See Figure 2.3.) The retina is a transducer, converting visible light into neurological signals sent to the brain via the optic nerve.

Near the center of the retina is the fovea, which is responsible for sharp central vision, such as reading or watching television. The fovea image in the environment encompasses a little more than one degree of visual angle, approximately equivalent to the width of one's thumb at arm's length (see Figure 2.4). Although the fovea is only about 1 percent of the retina in size, the neural processing associated with the fovea image engages about 50 percent of the visual cortex in the brain.

As with other sensory stimuli, light has properties such as intensity and frequency.

Frequency. Frequency is the property of light leading to the perception of color. Visible light is a small band in the electromagnetic spectrum, which ranges from

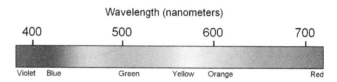

FIGURE 2.5

The visible spectrum of electromagnetic waves.

radio waves to x-rays and gamma rays. Different colors are positioned within the visible spectrum of electromagnetic waves, with violet at one end (390 nanometers) and red at the other (750 nm). (See Figure 2.5; colors not apparent in grayscale print).

Intensity. Although the frequency of light is a relatively simple concept, the same cannot be said for the intensity of light. Quantifying light intensity, from the human perspective, is complicated because the eye's light sensitivity varies by the wavelength of the light and also by the complexity of the source (e.g., a single frequency versus a mixture of frequencies). Related to intensity is *luminance*, which refers to the amount of light passing through a given area. With luminance comes *brightness*, a subjective property of the eye that includes perception by the brain. The unit for luminance is candela per square meter (cd/m^2).

Fixations and saccades. Vision is more than the human reception of electromagnetic waves having frequency and intensity. Through the eyes, humans look at and perceive the environment. In doing so, the eyes engage in two primitive actions: *fixations* and *saccades*. During a fixation, the eyes are stationary, taking in visual detail from the environment. Fixations can be long or short, but typically last at least 200 ms. Changing the point of fixation to a new location requires a saccade—a rapid repositioning of the eyes to a new position. Saccades are inherently quick, taking only 30–120 ms. Early and influential research on fixations and saccades was presented in a 1965 publication in Russian by Yarbus, translated as *Eye Movements and Vision* (reviewed in Tatler, Wade, Kwan, Findlay, and Velichkovsky, 2010). Yarbus demonstrated a variety of inspection patterns for people viewing scenes. One example used *The Unexpected Visitor* by painter Ilya Repin (1844–1930). Participants were given instructions and asked to view the scene, shown in Figure 2.6a. Eye movements (fixations and saccades) were recorded and plotted for a variety of tasks. The results for one participant are shown in Figure 2.6b for the task "remember the position of people and objects in the room" and in Figure 2.6c for the task "estimate the ages of the people." Yarbus provided many diagrams like this, with analyses demonstrating differences within and between participants, as well as changes in viewing patterns over time and for subsequent viewings. He noted, for example, that the similarity of inspection patterns for a single viewer was greater than the patterns between viewers.

HCI research in eye movements has several themes. One is analyzing how people read and view content on web pages. Figure 2.7 shows an example of a

(a)

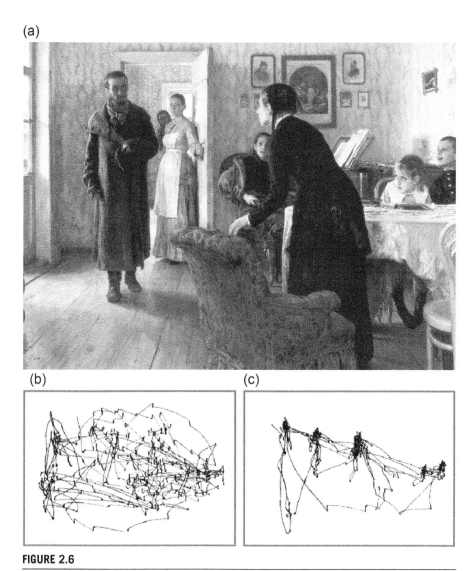

(b)   (c)

FIGURE 2.6

Yarbus' research on eye movements and vision (Tatler et al., 2010). (a) Scene. (b) Task: *Remember the position of the people and objects in the room.* (c) Task: *Estimate the ages of the people.*

scanpath (a sequence of fixations and saccades) for a user viewing content at different places on a page. (See also J. H. Goldberg and Helfman, 2010, Figure 2.) The results of the analyses offer implications for page design. For example, advertisers might want to know about viewing patterns and, for example, how males and females differ in viewing content. There are gender differences in eye movements

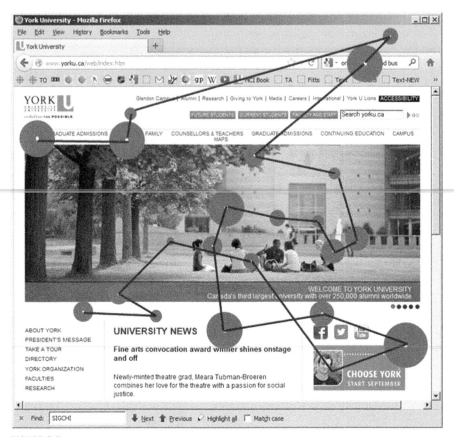

FIGURE 2.7

Scanpath for a user locating content on a web page.

(Pan et al., 2004), but it remains to be demonstrated how low-level experimental results can inform and guide design.

2.3.2 Hearing (Audition)

Hearing, or audition, is the detection of sound by humans. Sound is transmitted through the environment as sound waves—cyclic fluctuations of pressure in a medium such as air. Sound waves are created when physical objects are moved or vibrated, thus creating fluctuations in air pressure. Examples include plucking a string on a guitar, slamming a door, shuffling cards, or a human speaking. In the latter case, the physical object creating the sound is the larynx, or vocal cords, in the throat.

Hearing occurs when sound waves reach a human's ear and stimulate the ear drum to create nerve impulses that are sent to the brain. A single sound from a single source has at least four physical properties: intensity (loudness), frequency (pitch), timbre, and envelope. As a simple example, consider a musical note played from an instrument such as a trumpet. The note may be loud or soft (intensity); high or low (frequency). We hear and recognize the note as coming from a trumpet, as opposed to a flute, because of the note's timbre and envelope. Let's examine each of these properties.

Loudness. Loudness is the subjective analog to the physical property of intensity. It is quantified by *sound pressure level*, which expresses the pressure in a sound wave relative to the average pressure in the medium. The unit of sound pressure level is the decibel (dB). Human hearing begins with sounds of 0–10 dB. Conversational speech is about 50–70 dB in volume. Pain sets in when humans are exposed to sounds of approximately 120–140 dB.

Pitch. Pitch is the subjective analog of frequency, which is the reciprocal of the time between peaks in a sound wave's pressure pattern. The units of pitch are cycles per second, or Hertz (Hz). Humans can perceive sounds in the frequency range of about 20 Hz–20,000 Hz (20 kHz), although the upper limit tends to decrease with age.

Timbre. Timbre (aka richness or brightness) results from the harmonic structure of sounds. Returning to the example of a musical note, harmonics are integer multiples of a note's base frequency. For example, a musical note with base frequency of 400 Hz includes harmonics at 800 Hz, 1200 Hz, 1600 Hz, and so on. The relative amplitudes of the harmonics create the subjective sense of timbre, or richness, in the sound. While the human hears the note as 400 Hz, it is the timbre that distinguishes the tone as being from a particular musical instrument. For example, if notes of the same frequency and loudness are played from a trumpet and an oboe, the two notes sound different, in part, because of the unique pattern of harmonics created by each instrument. The purest form of a note is a sine wave, which includes the base frequency but no harmonics above the base frequency. The musical notes created by a flute are close to sine waves.

Envelope. Envelope is the way a note and its harmonics build up and transition in time—from silent to audible to silent. There is considerable information in the onset envelope, or attack, of musical notes. In the example above of the trumpet and oboe playing notes of the same frequency and same loudness, the attack also assists in distinguishing the source. If the trumpet note and oboe note were recorded and played back with the attack removed, it would be surprisingly difficult to distinguish the instruments. The attack results partly from inherent properties of instruments (e.g., brass versus woodwind), but also from the way notes are articulated (e.g., staccato versus legato).

Besides physical properties, sound has other properties. These have to do with human hearing and perception. Sounds, complex sounds, can be described as being harmonious (pleasant) or discordant (unpleasant). This property has to do with how different frequencies mix together in a complex sound, such as a musical chord. Sounds may also convey a sense of urgency or speed.

Humans have two ears, but each sound has a single source. The slight difference in the physical properties of the sound as it arrives at each ear helps humans in identifying a sound's location (direction and distance). When multiple sounds from multiple sources are heard through two ears, perceptual effects such as stereo emerge.

Sounds provide a surprisingly rich array of cues to humans, whether walking about while shopping or sitting in front of a computer typing an e-mail message. Not surprisingly, sound is crucial for blind users, for example, in conveying information about the location and distance of environmental phenomena (Talbot and Cowan, 2009).

2.3.3 Touch (Tactition)

Although touch, or tactition, is considered one of the five traditional human senses, touch is just one component of the somatosensory system. This system includes sensory receptors in the skin, muscles, bones, joints, and organs that provide information on a variety of physical or environmental phenomena, including touch, temperature, pain, and body and limb position. Tactile feedback, in HCI, refers to information provided through the somatosensory system from a body part, such as a finger, when it is in contact with (touching) a physical object. Additional information, such as the temperature, shape, texture, or position of the object, or the amount of resistance, is also conveyed.

All user interfaces that involve physical contact with the user's hands (or other body parts) include tactile feedback. Simply grasping a mouse and moving it brings considerable information to the human operator: the smooth or rubbery feel of the mouse chassis, slippery or sticky movement on the desktop. Interaction with a desktop keyboard is also guided by tactile feedback. The user senses the edges and shapes of keys and experiences resistance as a key is pressed. Tactile identifiers on key tops facilitate eyes-free touch typing. Identifiers are found on the 5 key for numeric keypads and on the F and J keys for alphanumeric keyboards. Sensing the identifier informs the user that the home position is acquired. (See Figure 2.8a.)

Augmenting the user experience through active tactile feedback is a common research topic. Figure 2.8b shows a mouse instrumented with a solenoid-driven pin below the index finger (Akamatsu et al., 1995). The pin is actuated (pulsed) when the mouse cursor crosses a boundary, such as the edge of a soft button or window. The added tactile feedback helps inform and guide the interaction and potentially reduces the demand on the visual channel. A common use of tactile feedback in mobile phones is vibration, signaling an incoming call or message. (See Figure 2.8c.)

2.3.4 Smell and taste

Smell (olfaction) is the ability to perceive odors. For humans, this occurs through sensory cells in the nasal cavity. Taste (gustation) is a direct chemical reception of sweet, salty, bitter, and sour sensations through taste buds in the tongue and oral cavity. Flavor is a perceptual process in the brain that occurs through a partnering of the

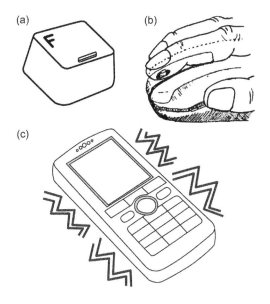

FIGURE 2.8

Tactile feedback: (a) Identifier on key top. (b) Solenoid-driven pin under the index finger.
(c) Vibration signals an in-coming call.

(Adapted from Akamatsu, MacKenzie, and Hasbrouq, 1995)

smell and taste senses. Although smell and taste are known intuitively by virtually all humans—and with expert-like finesse—they are less understood than the visual and auditory senses. Complex smells and tastes can be built up from simpler elements, but the perceptual processes for this remain a topic of research. For example, classification schemes have been developed for specific industries (e.g., perfume, wine) but these do not generalize to human experiences with other smells and tastes.

While humans use smell and taste all the time without effort, these senses are not generally "designed in" to systems. There are a few examples in HCI. Brewster et al. (2006) studied smell as an aid in searching digital photo albums. Users employed two tagging methods, text and smell, and then later used the tags to answer questions about the photos. Since smell has links to memory, it was conjectured that smell cues might aid in recall. In the end, recall with smell tags was poorer than with word tags. Related work is reported by Bodnar et al. (2004) who compared smell, auditory, and visual modalities for notifying users of an interruption by an incoming message. They also found poorer performance with smell. Notable in both examples, though, is the use of an empirical research methodology to explore the potential of smell in a user interface. Both studies included all the hallmarks of experimental research, including an independent variable, dependent variables, statistical significance testing, and counterbalancing of the independent variable.

2.3.5 **Other senses**

The word *sense* appears in many contexts apart from the five senses discussed above. We often hear of a sense of urgency, a sense of direction, musical sense, intuitive sense, moral sense, or even common sense. The value of these and related senses to HCI cannot be overstated. Although clearly operating at a higher level than the five primary senses, these additional senses encapsulate how humans feel about their interactions with computers. Satisfaction, confidence, frustration, and so on, are clearly steeped in how users feel about computing experiences. Are there receptors that pick up these senses, like cells in the naval cavity? Perhaps. It has been argued and supported with experimental evidence that humans may have a moral sense that is like our sense of taste (Greene and Haidt, 2002). We have natural receptors that help us pick up sweetness and saltiness. In the same way, we may have natural receptors that help us recognize fairness and cruelty. Just as a few universal tastes can grow into many different cuisines, a few moral senses can grow into different moral cultures.

2.4 **Responders**

Through movement, or motor control, humans are empowered to affect the environment around them. Control occurs through *responders*. Whether using a finger to text[1] or point, the feet to walk or run, the eyebrows to frown, the vocal chords to speak, or the torso to lean, movement provides humans with the power to engage and affect the world around them. Penfield's *motor homunculus* is a classic illustration of human responders (Penfield and Rasmussen, 1990). (See Figure 2.9.) The illustration maps areas in the cerebral motor cortex to human responders. The lengths of the underlying solid bars show the relative amount of cortical area devoted to each muscle group. As the bars reveal, the muscles controlling the hand and fingers are highly represented compared to the muscles responsible for the wrist, elbow, and shoulders. Based partially on this information, Card et al. (1991) hypothesized that "those groups of muscles having a large area devoted to them are heuristically promising places to connect with input device transducers if we desire high performance," although they rightly caution that "the determinants of muscle performance are more complex than just simple cortical area" (Card et al., 1991, p. 111). (See also Balakrishnan and MacKenzie, 1997).

See also student exercise 2-1 at the end of this chapter.

2.4.1 **Limbs**

Human control over machines is usually associated with the limbs, particularly the upper body limbs. The same is true in HCI. With fingers, hands, and arms we

---

[1] "Text" is now an accepted verb in English. "I'll text you after work," although strange in the 1980s, is understood today as sending a text message (SMS) on a mobile phone.

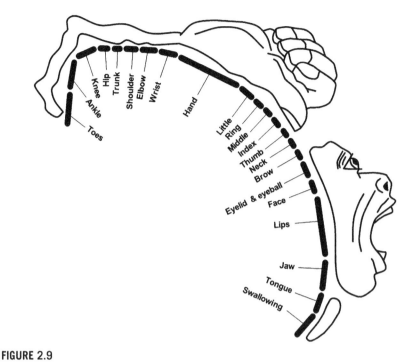

FIGURE 2.9

Motor homunculus showing human responders and the corresponding cortical area.

(Adapted from Penfield and Rasmussen, 1990)

type on keyboards, maneuver mice and press buttons, hold mobile phones and press keys, touch and swipe the surfaces of touchscreen phones and tablets, and wave game controllers in front of displays. Of course, legs and feet can also act as responders and provide input to a computer. For users with limited or no use of their arms, movement of the head can control an on-screen cursor. Some example scenarios are seen in Figure 2.10.

Movement of the limbs is tightly coupled to the somatosensory system, particularly proprioception (Proprioception is the coordination of limb movement and position through the perception of stimuli within muscles and tendons.), to achieve accuracy and finesse as body parts move relative to the body as a whole. Grasping a mouse without looking at it and typing without looking at the keyboard are examples.

In Figure 2.10a, the user's left hand grips the mouse. Presumably this user is left-handed. In Figure 2.10b, the user's right index finger engages the surface of the touchpad. Presumably, this user is right-handed. Interestingly enough, handedness, or hand dominance, is not an either-or condition. Although 8 to 15 percent of people are deemed left-handed, handedness exists along a continuum, with people considered, by degree, left-handed or right-handed. Ambidextrous people are substantially indifferent in hand preference.

(a)   (b)   (c)

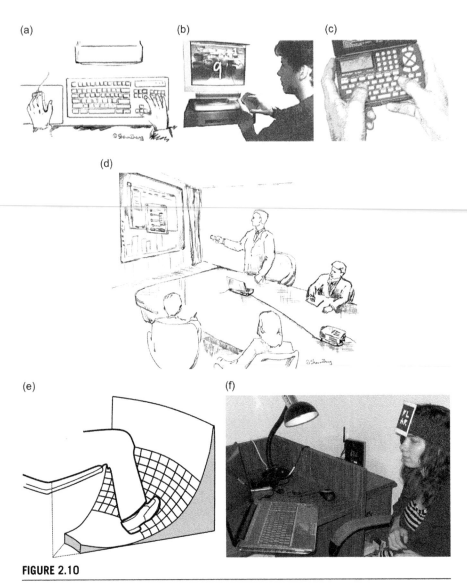

(d)

(e)   (f)

FIGURE 2.10

Use of the limbs in HCI: (a) Hands. (b) Fingers. (c) Thumbs. (d) Arms. (e) Feet. (f) Head.

(sketches a and d courtesy of Shawn Zhang; e, adapted from Pearson and Weiser, 1986)

A widely used tool to assess handedness is the Edinburgh Handedness Inventory, dating to 1971 (Oldfield, 1971). The inventory is a series of self-assessments of the degree of preference one feels toward the left or right hand in doing common tasks, such as throwing a ball. The inventory is shown in Figure 2.11

	Left	Right
1. Writing	☐☐	☐☐
2. Drawing	☐☐	☐☐
3. Throwing	☐☐	☐☐
4. Scissors	☐☐	☐☐
5. Toothbrush	☐☐	☐☐
6. Knife (without fork)	☐☐	☐☐
7. Spoon	☐☐	☐☐
8. Broom (upper hand)	☐☐	☐☐
9. Striking a match	☐☐	☐☐
10. Opening box (lid)	☐☐	☐☐
Total (count checks)	☐	☐

Difference	Cumulative Total	RESULT
☐	☐	☐

Instructions
Mark boxes as follows:
x   preference
xx   strong preference
blank   no preference

Scoring
Add up the number of checks in the "Left" and "Right" columns and enter in the "Total" row for each column. Add the left total and the right total and enter in the "Cumulative Total" cell. Subtract the left total from the right total and enter in the "Difference" cell. Divide the "Difference" cell by the "Cumulative Total" cell (round to 2 digits if necessary) and multiply by 100. Enter the result in the "RESULT" cell.

Interpretation of RESULT
−100 to −40 left-handed
−40 to +40 ambidextrous
+40 to 100 right-handed

FIGURE 2.11

Edinburgh Handedness Inventory for hand dominance assessment (Oldfield, 1971).

along with the instructions, scoring, and interpretation of results.[2] People scoring −100 to −40 are considered left-handed, whereas those scoring +40 to +100 are considered right-handed. People scoring −40 to +40 are considered ambidextrous.

There are several examples in HCI where the Edinburgh Handedness Inventory was administered to participants in experiments (Hancock and Booth, 2004; Hegel, Krach, Kircher, Wrede, and Sagerer, 2008; Kabbash, MacKenzie, and Buxton, 1993; Mappus, Venkatesh, Shastry, Israeli, and Jackson, 2009; Masliah and Milgram, 2000; Matias, MacKenzie, and Buxton, 1996). In some cases, the degree of handedness is reported. For example, Hinckley et al. (1997) reported that all participants in their study were "strongly right-handed," with a mean score of 71.7 on the inventory.

Handedness is often relevant in situations involving touch- or pressure-sensing displays. If interaction requires a stylus or finger on a display, then the user's hand may occlude a portion of the display. Occlusion may lead to poorer performance (Forlines and Balakrishnan, 2008) or to a "hook posture" where users contort the arm position to facilitate interaction (Vogel and Balakrishnan, 2010). This can be avoided by positioning UI elements in a different region on the display (Hancock and Booth, 2004; Vogel and Baudisch, 2007). Of course, this requires sensing or determining the handedness of the user, since the occlusion is different for a left-handed user than for a right-handed user.

---

[2]Dragovic (2004) presents an updated version of the Edinburgh Inventory, using more contemporary and widely-understood tasks.

2.4.2 **Voice**

The human vocal cords are responders. Through the combination of movement in the larynx, or voice box, and pulmonary pressure in the lungs, humans can create a great variety of sounds. The most obvious form of vocalized sound—speech—is the primary channel for human communication. As an input modality, the speech must be *recognized* by algorithms implemented in software running on the host computer. With this modality, the computer interprets spoken words as though the same words were typed on the system's keyboard. Vertanen and Kristensson (2009) describe a system for mobile text entry using automatic speech recognition. They report entry rates of 18 words per minute while seated and 13 words per minute while walking.

Computer input is also possible using non-speech vocalized sounds, a modality known as *non-verbal voice interaction* (NVVI). In this case, various acoustic parameters of the sound signal, such as pitch, volume, or timbre, are measured over time and the data stream is interpreted as an input channel. The technique is particularly useful to specify analog parameters. For example, a user could produce an utterance, such as "volume up, aaah." In response, the system increases the volume of the television set for as long as the user sustains "aaah" (Igarashi and Hughes, 2001). Harada et al. (2006) describe the *vocal joystick*—a system using NVVI to simulate a joystick and control an on-screen cursor (e.g., "eee" = move cursor left). Applications are useful primarily for creating accessible computing for users without a manual alternative.

2.4.3 **Eyes**

In the normal course of events, the human eye receives sensory stimuli in the form of light from the environment. In viewing a scene, the eyes combine fixations, to view particular locations, and saccades, to move to different locations. This was noted earlier in considering the eye as a sensory organ. However, the eye is also capable of acting as a responder—controlling a computer through fixations and saccades. In this capacity, the eye is called upon to do double duty since it acts both as a sensor and as a responder. The idea is illustrated in Figure 2.12, which shows a modified view of the human-computer interface (see Figure 2.2 for comparison). The normal path from the human to the computer is altered. Instead of the hand providing motor responses to control the computer through physical devices (set in grey), the eye provides motor responses that control the computer through *soft controls*—virtual or graphical controls that appear on the system's display.

For computer input control using the eyes, an eye tracking apparatus is required to sense and digitize the gaze location and the movement of the eyes. The eye tracker is usually configured to emulate a computer mouse. Much like point-select operations with a mouse, the eye can *look-select*, and thereby activate soft controls such as buttons, icons, links, or text (e.g., Zhang and MacKenzie, 2007). The most common method for selecting with the eye is by fixating, or dwelling, on a selectable target for a predetermined period of time, such as 750 ms.

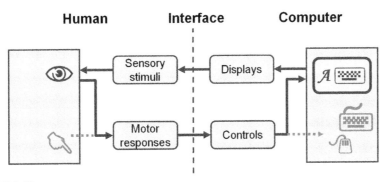

FIGURE 2.12

The human-computer interface with an eye tracker. The eye serves double duty, processing sensory stimuli from computer displays and providing motor responses to control the system.

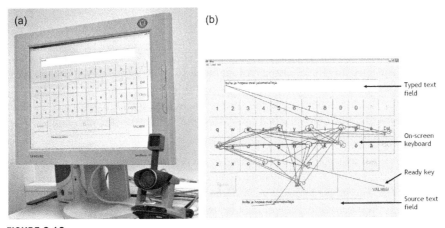

FIGURE 2.13

Eye typing: (a) Apparatus. (b) Example sequence of fixations and saccades (Majaranta et al., 2006).

Text entry is one application of eye tracking for input control. So-called *eye typing* uses an on-screen keyboard. The user looks at soft keys, fixating for a pre-scribed dwell time to make a selection. An example setup using an *iView X RED-III* eye tracking device by SensoMotoric Instruments (www.smivision.com) is shown in Figure 2.13a. Figure 2.13b shows a sequence of fixations and saccades (a scan-path) for one user while entering a phrase of text (Majaranta, MacKenzie, Aula, and Räihä, 2006). Straight lines indicate saccades. Circles indicate fixations, with the diameter indicating the duration of the fixation. Bear in mind that the fixations here are conscious, deliberate acts for controlling a computer interface. This is different from the fixations shown in Figure 2.7, where the user was simply viewing content on a web page. In Figure 2.13b, the interaction includes numerous fixations meeting the required dwell time criterion to select soft keys. There is also a fixation (with two corresponding saccades) to view the typed text.

2.5 The brain

The brain is the most complex biological structure known. With billions of neurons, the brain provides humans with a multitude of capacities and resources, including pondering, remembering, recalling, reasoning, deciding, and communicating. While sensors (human inputs) and responders (human outputs) are nicely mirrored, it is the brain that connects them. Without sensing or experiencing the environment, the brain would have little to do. However, upon experiencing the environment through sensors, the brain's task begins.

2.5.1 Perception

Perception, the first stage of processing in the brain, occurs when sensory signals are received as input from the environment. It is at the perceptual stage that associations and meanings take shape. An auditory stimulus is perceived as harmonious or discordant. A smell is pleasurable or abhorrent. A visual scene is familiar or strange. Touch something and the surface is smooth or rough, hot or cold. With associations and meaning attached to sensory input, humans are vastly superior to the machines they interact with:

> People excel at perception, at creativity, at the ability to go beyond the information given, making sense of otherwise chaotic events. We often have to interpret events far beyond the information available, and our ability to do this efficiently and effortlessly, usually without even being aware that we are doing so, greatly adds to our ability to function.
>
> **(Norman, 1988, p. 136)**

Since the late 19th century, perception has been studied in a specialized area of experimental psychology known as *psychophysics*. Psychophysics examines the relationship between human perception and physical phenomena. In a psychophysics experiment, a human is presented with a physical stimulus and is then asked about the sensation that was felt or perceived. The link is between a measurable property of a real-world phenomenon that stimulates a human sense and the human's subjective interpretation of the phenomenon. A common experimental goal is to measure the *just noticeable difference* (JND) in a stimulus. A human subject is presented with two stimuli, one after the other. The stimuli differ in a physical property, such as frequency or intensity, and the subject is asked if the stimuli are the same or different. The task is repeated over a series of trials with random variations in the magnitude of the difference in the physical property manipulated. Below a

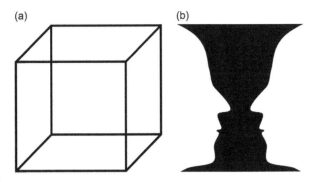

FIGURE 2.14

Ambiguous images: (a) Necker cube. (b) Rubin vase.

certain threshold, the difference between the two stimuli is so small that it is not perceived by the subject. This threshold is the JND. JND has been highly researched for all the human senses and in a variety of contexts. Does the JND depend on the absolute magnitude of the stimuli (e.g., high intensity stimuli versus low intensity stimuli)? Does the JND on one property (e.g., intensity) depend on the absolute value of a second property (e.g., frequency)? Does the JND depend on age, gender, or other property of the human? These are basic research questions that, on the surface, seem far afield from the sort of research likely to bear on human-computer interfaces. But over time and with new research extending results from previous research, there is indeed an application to HCI. For example, basic research in psychophysics is used in algorithms for audio compression in MP3 audio encoding.

Another property of perception is ambiguity—the human ability to develop multiple interpretations of a sensory input. Ambiguous images provide a demonstration of this ability for the visual sense. Figure 2.14a shows the Necker wireframe cube. Is the top-right corner on the front surface or the back surface? Figure 2.14b shows the Rubin vase. Is the image a vase or two faces? The very fact that we sense ambiguity in these images reveals our perceptual ability to go beyond the information given.

Related to ambiguity is illusion, the deception of common sense. Figure 2.15a shows Ponzo lines. The two black lines are the same length; however, the black line near the bottom of the illustration appears shorter because of the three-dimensional perspective. Müller-Lyer arrows are shown in Figure 2.15b. In comparing the straight-line segments in the two arrows, the one in the top arrow appears longer when in fact both are the same length. Our intuition has betrayed us.

If illusions are possible in visual stimuli, it is reasonable to expect illusions in the other senses. An example of an auditory illusion is the Shepard musical scale. It is perceived by humans to rise or fall continuously, yet it somehow stays the same. A variation is a continuous musical tone known as the Shepard-Risset glissando—a tone that continually rises in pitch while also continuing to stay at the same pitch. Figure 2.16 illustrates this illusion. Each vertical line represents a sine

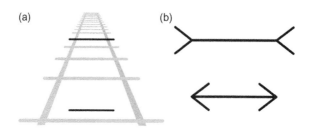

FIGURE 2.15

Visual illusion: (a) Ponzo lines. (b) Müller-Lyer arrows.

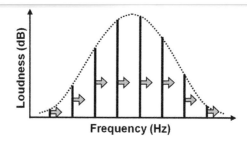

FIGURE 2.16

Auditory illusion. A collection of equally spaced sine waves rise in frequency. The human hears a tone that rises but stays the same.

wave. The height of each line is the perceived loudness of the sine wave. Each wave is displaced from its neighbor by the same frequency; thus, the waves are harmonics of a musical note with a base frequency equal to the displacement. This is the frequency of the single tone that a human perceives. If the sine waves collectively rise in frequency (block arrows in the figure), there is a sense that the tone is rising. Yet because the sine waves are equally spaced, there is a competing sense that the tone remains the same (because the frequency perceived is the distance between harmonics). Sine waves at the high end of the frequency distribution fade out, while new sine waves enter at the low end. Examples of the Shepard scale and the Shepard-Risset glissando can be heard on *YouTube*.

Tactile or *haptic* illusions also exist. A well-documented example is the "phantom limb." Humans who have lost a limb through amputation often continue to sense that the limb is present and that it moves along with other body parts as it did before amputation (Halligan, Zemen, and Berger, 1999).

Beyond perception, sensory stimuli are integrated into a myriad of other experiences to yield ideas, decisions, strategies, actions, and so on. The ability to excel at these higher-level capabilities is what propels humans to the top tier in classification schemes for living organisms. By and large it is the human ability to think and reason that affords this special position.

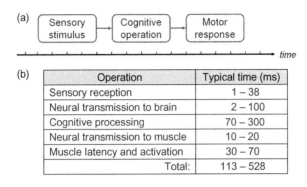

FIGURE 2.17

Cognitive operation in a reaction time task: (a) Problem schematic. (b) Sequence of operations (Bailey, 1996, p. 41).

2.5.2 **Cognition**

Among the brain's vital faculties is cognition—the human process of conscious intellectual activity, such as thinking, reasoning, and deciding. Cognition spans many fields—from neurology to linguistics to anthropology—and, not surprisingly, there are competing views on the scope of cognition. Does cognition include social processes, or is it more narrowly concerned with deliberate goal-driven acts such as problem solving? It is beyond the reach of this book to unravel the many views of cognition. The task is altogether too great and in any case is aptly done in other references, many of them in human factors (e.g., B. H. Kantowitz and Sorkin, 1983; Salvendy, 1987; Wickens, 1987).

Sensory phenomena such as sound and light are easy to study because they exist in the physical world. Instruments abound for recording and measuring the presence and magnitude of sensory signals. Cognition occurs within the human brain, so studying cognition presents special challenges. For example, it is not possible to directly measure the time it takes for a human to make a decision. When does the measurement begin and end? Where is it measured? On what input is the human deciding? Through what output is the decision conveyed? The latter two questions speak to a sensory stimulus and a motor response that bracket the cognitive operation. Figure 2.17a illustrates this. Since sensory stimuli and motor responses are observable and measurable, the figure conveys, in a rough sense, how to measure a cognitive operation. Still, there are challenges. If the sensory stimulus is visual, the retina converts the light to neural impulses that are transmitted to the brain for perceptual processing. This takes time. So the beginning of the cognitive operation is not precisely known. Similarly, if the motor response involves a finger pressing a button, neural associations for the response are developed in the brain with nerve signals transmitted to the hand before movement begins. So the precise ending of the cognitive operation is also unknown. This sequence of events is shown in Figure 2.17b, noting the operations and the typical time for each step. The most remarkable observation here is the wide range of values—an indication of the difficulty in pin-pointing where and how the measurements are made. Despite these challenges, techniques exist for measuring the duration of cognitive operations. These are discussed shortly.

The range of cognitive operations applicable to Figure 2.17 is substantial. While driving a car, the decision to depress a brake pedal in response to a changing signal light is simple enough. Similar scenarios abound in HCI. While using a mobile phone, one might decide to press the REJECT CALL key in response to an incoming call. While reading the morning news online, one might decide to click the CLOSE button on a popup ad. While editing a document, one might switch to e-mail in response to an audio alert of a new message. These examples involve a sensory stimulus, a cognitive operation, and a motor response, respectively.

Other decisions are more complicated. While playing the card game 21 (aka Blackjack), perhaps online[3], if a card is drawn and the hand then totals 16, the decision to draw another card is likely to produce a cognitive pause. What is the chance the next card will bring the hand above 21? Which cards 6 to KING are already dealt? Clearly, the decision in this scenario goes beyond the information in the sensory stimulus. There are strategies to consider, as well as the human ability to remember and recall past events—cards previously dealt. This ability leads us to another major function of the brain—memory.

2.5.3 Memory

Memory is the human ability to store, retain, and recall information. The capacity of our memory is remarkable. Experiences, whether from a few days ago or from decades past, are collected together in the brain's vast repository known as *long-term memory*. Interestingly enough, there are similarities between memory in the brain and memory in a computer. Computer memory often includes separate areas for data and code. In the brain, memory is similarly organized. A declarative/explicit area stores information about events in time and objects in the external world. This is similar to a data space. An implicit/procedural area in the brain's memory stores information about how to use objects or how to do things. This is similar to a code space.[4]

Within long-term memory is an active area for *short-term memory* or *working memory*. The contents of working memory are active and readily available for access. The amount of such memory is small, about seven units, depending on the task and the methodology for measurement. A study of short-term memory was

---

[3]The parenthetic "perhaps online" is included as a reminder that many activities humans do in the physical world have a counterpart in computing, often on the Internet.

[4]The reader is asked to take a cautious and loose view of the analogy between human memory and computer memory. Attempts to formulate analogies from computers to humans are fraught with problems. Cognitive scientists, for example, frequently speak of human cognition in terms of operators, operands, cycles, registers, and the like, and build and test models that fit their analogies. Such *reverse anthropomorphism*, while tempting and convenient, is unlikely to reflect the true inner workings of human biology.

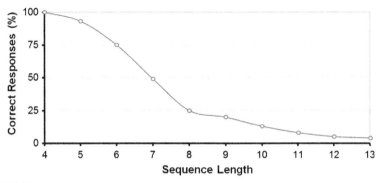

FIGURE 2.18

Results of a test of short-term memory.

published in 1956 in a classic essay by Miller, aptly titled "The Magic Number Seven, Plus or Minus Two: Some Limits on our Capacity for Processing Information" (G. A. Miller, 1956).[5] Miller reviewed a large number of studies on the absolute judgment of stimuli, such as pitch in an auditory stimulus or salt concentration in water in a taste stimulus. Humans are typically able to distinguish about seven levels of a uni-dimensional stimulus.[6]

Miller extended this work to human memory, describing an experiment where participants were presented with a sequence of items and then asked to recall the items. He found that the human ability with such tasks is, similarly, about seven items (±2). A simple demonstration of Miller's thesis is shown in Figure 2.18. For this "mini-experiment," log sheets were distributed to students in a class on human-computer interaction ($n \approx 60$). The instructor dictated sequences of random digits, with sequences varying in length from four digits to 13 digits. After each dictation, students copied the sequence from short-term memory onto the log sheet. The percentage of correct responses by sequence length is shown in the figure. At length seven the number of correct responses was about 50 percent. At lengths five and nine the values were about 90 percent and 20 percent, respectively.[7] See also student exercise 2-2 at the end of this chapter.

---

[5] Miller's classic work is referred to as an *essay* rather than a *research paper*. The essay is casual in style and, consequently, written in the first person; for example, "I am simply pointing to the obvious fact that…" (G. A. Miller, 1956, p. 93). Research papers, on the other hand, are generally plain in style and avoid first-person narratives (cf. "This points to the fact that…").

[6] The human ability to distinguish levels is greater if the stimulus is multidimensional; that is, the stimulus contains two or more independent attributes, such as a sound that varies in pitch and intensity.

[7] A response was deemed correct only if all the items were correctly recalled. For the longer sequences, many responses were "mostly correct." For example, at sequence length = 7, many of the responses had five or six items correct.

Miller extended his work by revealing and analyzing a simple but powerful process within the brain: our ability to associate multiple items as one. So-called *chunking* is a process whereby humans group a series of low-level items into a single high-level item. He described an example using binary digits. For example, a series of 16 bits, such as 1000101101110010, would be extremely difficult to commit to memory. If, however, the bits are collected into groups of four and chunked into decimal digits, the pattern is much easier to remember: 1000101101110010→1000, 1011, 0111, 0010→8, 11, 7, 2. Card et al. (1983, 36) give the example of BSCBMICRA. At nine units, the letter sequence is beyond the ability of most people to repeat back. But the sequence is similar to the following three groups of three-letter sequences: CBS IBM RCA. Shown like this, the sequence contains three chunks and is relatively easy to remember provided the person can perform the recoding rapidly enough. The process of chunking is mostly informal and unstructured. Humans intuitively build up chunked structures recursively and hierarchically, leading to complex organizations of memory in the brain.

2.6 Language

Language—the mental faculty that allows humans to communicate—is universally available to virtually all humans. Remarkably, language as speech is available without effort. Children learn to speak and understand speech without conscious effort as they grow and develop. Writing, as a codification of language, is a much more recent phenomenon. Learning to write demands effort, considerable effort, spanning years of study and practice. Daniels and Bright distinguish language and writing as follows: "Humankind is defined by language; but civilization is defined by writing." (Daniels and Bright, 1996, p. 1). These words are a reminder that the cultural and technological status associated with civilization is enabled by systems of writing. Indeed, the term *prehistory*, as applied to humans, dates from the arrival of human-like beings, millions of years ago, to the emergence of writing. It is writing that presaged *recorded history*, beginning a mere six thousand years ago.

In HCI, our interest in language is primarily in systems of writing and in the technology that enables communication in a written form. *Text* is the written material on a page or display. How it gets there is a topic that intrigues and challenges HCI researchers, as well as the engineers and designers who create products that support text creation, or text entry. Although text entry is hugely important in HCI, our interest here is language itself in a written form.

One way to characterize and study a language in its written form is through a corpus—a large collection of text samples gathered from diverse and representative sources such as newspapers, books, e-mails, and magazines. Of course, it is not possible for a corpus to broadly yet precisely represent a language. The sampling process brings limitations: During what timeframe were the samples written? In what country? In what region of the country? On what topics are the samples focused and who wrote them? A well-known corpus is the British National Corpus

Word Rank	English	French	German	Finnish	SMS English	SMS Pinyin
1	the	de	der	ja	u	wo (我)
2	of	la	die	on	i	ni (你)
3	and	et	und	ei	to	le (了)
4	a	le	in	että	me	de (的)
5	in	à	den	oli	at	bu (不)
...	...	...	...	...	...	...
1000	top	ceci	konkurrenz	muista	ps	jiu (舅)
1001	truth	mari	stieg	paikalla	quit	tie (贴)
1002	balance	solution	notwendig	varaa	rice	ji (即)
1003	heard	expliquer	sogenannte	vie	sailing	jiao (角)
1004	speech	pluie	fahren	seuran	sale	ku (裤)
...	...	...	...	...	...	...

FIGURE 2.19

Sample words from word-frequency lists in various languages.

(BNC), which includes samples totaling 100 million words.[8] The sources are written in British English and are from the late 20th century. So analyses gleaned from the BNC, while generally applicable to English, may not precisely apply, for example, to American English, to present day English, or to the language of teenagers sending text messages.

To facilitate study and analysis, a corpus is sometimes reduced to a word-frequency list, which tabulates unique words and their frequencies in the corpus. One such reduction of the BNC includes about 64,000 unique words with frequencies totaling 90 million (Silfverberg, MacKenzie, and Korhonen, 2000). Only words occurring three or more times in the original corpus are included. The most frequent word is *the*, representing about 6.8 percent of all words.

Figure 2.19 includes excerpts from several corpora, showing the five most frequently used words and the words ranked from 1000 to 1004. The English entries are from the British National Corpus. There are additional columns for French (New, Pallier, Brysbaert, and Ferrand, 2004), German (Sporka et al., 2011), Finnish, SMS English, and SMS Pinyin (Y. Liu and Räihä, 2010). The Finnish entries are from a database of text from a popular newspaper in Finland, *Turun Sanomat*. The SMS English entries are from a collection of about 10,000 text messages, mostly from students at the University of Singapore.[9] SMS text messaging is a good example of the dynamic and context-sensitive nature of language. Efforts to characterize SMS English are prone to the limitations noted above. Note that there is no overlap in the entries 1–5 under English and SMS English.

The right-hand column in Figure 2.19 is for SMS Pinyin. Pinyin has been the standard coding system since 1958, using the Latin alphabet for Mandarin Chinese characters. The entries are pinyin marks, not words. Each mark maps to the Chinese

---

[8] See www.natcorp.ox.ac.uk.
[9] Available at www.comp.nus.edu.sg/~rpnlpir/smsCorpus.

(a) | Th std ws flld wth th rch dr f rss,
nd whn th lght smmr wnd strrd mdst th
trs f th grdn, thr cm thrgh th pn
dr th hvy scnt f th llc, r th mr
dlct prfm f th pnk-flwrng thrn.

(b) | Th std ws flld wth th rch odr of rss,
and whn th lght smmr wnd strrd amdst th
trs of th grdn, thr cm thrgh th opn
dr th hvy scnt of th llc, or th mr
dlct prfm of th pnk-flwrng thrn.

(c) | The studio was filled with the rich odour of roses,
and when the light summer wind stirred amidst the
trees of the garden, there came through the open
door the heavy scent of the lilac, or the more
delicate perfume of the pink-flowering thorn.

FIGURE 2.20

First paragraph of Oscar Wilde's *The Picture of Dorian Gray*: (a) Vowels removed.
(b) Vowels intact at beginning of words. (c) Original.

character shown in parentheses. The entries are from a corpus of 630,000 text messages containing over nine million Chinese characters.

A notable feature of some corpora is part-of-speech (POS) tagging, where words are tagged by their category, such as noun, verb, and adjective. Importantly, the part of speech is contextual, reflecting a word's use in the original text. For example, *paint* is sometimes a verb (*Children* paint *with passion*), sometimes a noun (*The* paint *is dry*). POS tagging can be important in predictive systems where knowing a word's POS limits the possibilities for the next word (Gong, Tarasewich, and MacKenzie, 2008).

2.6.1 Redundancy in language

Native speakers of a language innately possess an immense understanding of the statistics of the language. We automatically insert words that are omitted or obscured (*ham and* ____ *sandwich*). We anticipate words (*a picture is worth a thousand* ____), letters (*questio_*), or entire phrases (*to be or* ___ __ __). We might wonder: since humans can fill in missing letters or words, perhaps the unneeded portions can be omitted. Let's consider this further. The example in Figure 2.20 gives three variations of a paragraph of text. The original excerpt contains 243 characters. In part (a), all 71 vowels are removed, thus shortening the text by 29.2 percent. Many words are easily guessed (e.g., smmr→summer, thrgh→through) and with some effort the gist of the text is apparent. It has something to do with summer [smmr], gardens [grdn], and scent [scnt]. Part (b) is similar except the first letter of each word is intact, even if it is a vowel. Still, 62 vowels are missing. The meaning

(a)	My smmr hols wr CWOT. B4, we used 2go2 NY 2C my bro, his GF & thr 3 :- kids FTF. ILNY, it's a gr8 plc.	(b)	My summer holidays were a complete waste of time. Before, we used to go to New York to see my brother, his girlfriend and their three screaming kids face to face. I love New York. It's a great place.

FIGURE 2.21

Shortening English: (a) SMS shorthand. (b) Standard English.

is slightly easier to decipher. The original text is given in (c). It is the first paragraph from Oscar Wilde's *The Picture of Dorian Gray*.

There are other examples, as above, where portions of text are removed, yet comprehension remains. SMS text messaging is a well-documented example. In addition to removing characters, recoding is often used. There are numerous techniques employed, such as using sound (th@s→that's, gr8→great) or invented acronyms (w→with, gf→girlfriend, x→times) (Grinter and Eldridge, 2003). One anecdote tells of a 13-year-old student who submitted an entire essay written in SMS shorthand.[10] Although the teacher was not impressed, the student's rationale was direct and honest: it is easier to write in shorthand than in standard English. An example from the essay is shown in Figure 2.21. Part (a) gives the shortened text. There are 26 words and 102 characters (including spaces). The expanded text in (b) contains 39 words and 199 characters. The reduction is dramatic: 48.7 percent fewer characters in the SMS shorthand. Of course, there are differences between this example and Figure 2.20. For instance, in this example, punctuation and digits are introduced for recoding. As well, the shortened message is tailored to the language of a particular community of users. It is likely the 13-year-old's teacher was not of that community.

There is, unfortunately, a more insidious side to redundancy in written text. A common fault in writing is the presence of superfluous words, with their eradication promoted in many books on writing style. Strunk and White's Rule 17 is Omit Needless Words, and advises reducing, for example, "he is a man who" to "he," or "this is a subject that" to "this subject" (Strunk and White, 2000, p. 23). Tips on writing style are given in Chapter 8.

2.6.2 Entropy in language

If redundancy in language is what we inherently know, entropy is what we don't know—the uncertainty about forthcoming letters, words, phrases, ideas, concepts, and so on. Clearly, redundancy and entropy are related: If we remove what we know, what remains is what we don't know. A demonstration of redundancy and entropy in written English was provided in the 1950s by Shannon in a letter-guessing experiment (Shannon, 1951). (See Figure 2.22.) The experiment proceeds as follows. The participant is asked to guess the letters in a phrase, starting at the

---

[10]news.bbc.co.uk/2/hi/uk_news/2814235.stm.

```
THE ROOM WAS NOT VERY LIGHT A SMALL OBLONG

----ROO------NOT-V-----I------SM----OB----


READING LAMP ON THE DESK SHED GLOW ON

REA----------O------D----SHED-GLO--O-


POLISHED WOOD BUT LESS ON THE SHABBY RED CARPET

P-L-S-----O---BU--L-S--O-------SH----RE--C-----
```

FIGURE 2.22

Shannon's letter-guessing experiment.

(Adapted from Shannon, 1951)

beginning. As guessing proceeds, the phrase is revealed to the participant, letter by letter. The results are recorded as shown in the line below each phrase in the figure. A dash ("-") is a correct guess; a letter is an incorrect guess. Shannon called the second line the "reduced text." In terms of redundancy and entropy, a dash represents redundancy (what is known), while a letter represents entropy (what is not known). Among the interesting observations in Figure 2.22 is that errors are more common at the beginning of words, less common as words progress. The statistical nature of the language and the participant's inherent understanding of the language facilitate guessing within words.

The letter-guessing experiment in Figure 2.22 is more than a curiosity. Shannon was motivated to quantify the entropy of English in information-theoretic terms. He pointed out, for example, that both lines in each phrase-pair contain the same information in that it is possible, with a good statistical model, to recover the first line from the second. Because of the redundancy in printed English (viz. the dashes), a communications system need only transmit the reduced text. The original text can be recovered using the statistical model. Shannon also demonstrated how to compute the entropy of printed English. Considering letter frequencies alone, the entropy is about 4.25 bits per letter.[11] Considering previous letters, the entropy is reduced because there is less uncertainty about forthcoming letters. Considering long range statistical effects (up to 100 letters), Shannon estimated the entropy of printed English at about one bit per letter with a corresponding redundancy of about 75 percent.

See also student exercise 2-2 at the end of this chapter.

2.7 Human performance

Humans use their sensors, brain, and responders to do things. When the three elements work together to achieve a goal, human performance arises. Whether the

---

[11] The data set and calculation are given in Chapter 7 (see Figure 7.19).

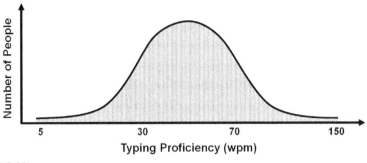

FIGURE 2.23

Variability of people in performing a task such as typing.

action is tying shoelaces, folding clothes, searching the Internet, or entering a text message on a mobile phone, human performance is present. Better performance is typically associated with faster or more accurate behavior, and this leads to a fundamental property of human performance—the *speed-accuracy trade-off*: go faster and errors increase; slow down and accuracy improves. Reported in academic papers dating back more than a century (see Swensson, 1972, for a review), mundane and proverbial ("Haste makes waste"), and steeped in common sense (we instinctively slow down to avoid errors), it is hard to imagine a more banal feature of human performance. Clearly, research on a new interface or interaction technique that seeks to determine the speed in doing a task must consider accuracy as well.

Humans position themselves on the speed-accuracy trade-off in a manner that is both comfortable and consistent with their goals. Sometimes we act with haste, even recklessly; at other times we act with great attention to detail. Furthermore, we may act in the presence of a secondary task, such as listening to the radio, conversing with a friend, or driving a car. Clearly, context plays an important role, as do the limits and capabilities of the sensors, the brain, and the responders.

With human performance, we begin to see complexities and challenges in HCI that are absent in traditional sciences such as physics and chemistry. Humans bring diversity and variability, and these characteristics bring imprecision and uncertainty. Some humans perform tasks better than others. As well, a particular human may perform a task better in one context and environment than when performing the same task in a different context and environment. Furthermore, if that same human performs the same task repeatedly in the same context and environment, the outcome will likely vary.

Human diversity in performing tasks is sometimes illustrated in a distribution, as in Figure 2.23. Here the distribution reveals the number of people performing a task (*y*-axis) versus their proficiency in doing it (*x*-axis). The example assumes computer users as the population and illustrates typing on a conventional computer keyboard as the task. Most people fall somewhere in the middle of the distribution.

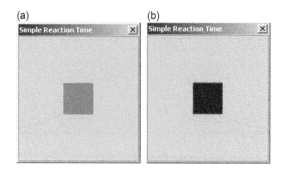

FIGURE 2.24

Simple reaction time: (a) The user fixates on the grey box. (b) After a delay, the box turns red whereupon the user presses a key as quickly as possible.

Typing speeds here are in the range of, say, 30–70 words per minute. Some people are slower, some faster. However, a small number of people will be exceedingly fast, say, 150 words per minute or faster. Yet others, also a small number, exhibit difficulty in achieving even a modest speed, such as 5 words per minute, equivalent to one word every 12 seconds.

2.7.1 Reaction time

One of the most primitive manifestations of human performance is *simple reaction time*, defined as the delay between the occurrence of a single fixed stimulus and the initiation of a response assigned to it (Fitts and Posner, 1968, p. 95). An example is pressing a button in response to the onset of a stimulus light. The task involves the three elements of the human shown in Figure 2.17. The cognitive operation is trivial, so the task is relatively easy to study. While the apparatus in experimental settings is usually simple, humans react to more complex apparatus all the time, in everyday pursuits and in a variety of contexts, such as reacting to the ring of a phone, to a traffic light, or to water in a bath (hot!). These three examples all involve a motor response. But the sensory stimuli differ. The ring of a phone is an auditory stimulus; a changing traffic light is a visual stimulus; hot water touching the skin is a tactile stimulus. It is known that simple reaction times differ according to the stimulus source, with approximate values of 150 ms (auditory), 200 ms (visual), 300 ms (smell), and 700 ms (pain) (Bailey, 1996, p. 41).

To explore reaction times further, a Java-based application was developed to experimentally test and demonstrate several reaction time tasks.[12] (See also Appendix A.) After describing each task, the results of an experiment are presented. For *simple reaction*, the interface is shown in Figure 2.24. A trial begins with the

---

[12] The software, a detailed API, and related files are in ReactionTimeExperiment.zip, available on this book's website.

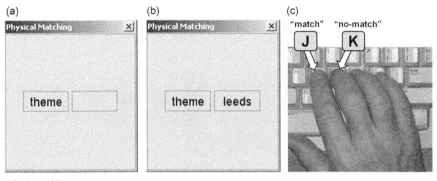

FIGURE 2.25

Physical matching: (a) Initial stimulus. (b) After a delay, a second stimulus appears. (c) Setup.

appearance of a grey box in a GUI window. Following a delay, the box turns red (color is not apparent in grayscale print). This is the sensory stimulus. The user's goal is to press a key on the system keyboard as quickly as possible after the stimulus appears. The delay between the grey box appearing and the box turning red is randomized to prevent the user from anticipating the onset of the stimulus.

The software implements three extensions of simple reaction tasks: physical matching, name matching, and class matching. Each adds a layer of complexity to the cognitive operation. The tasks were modeled after descriptions by Card et al. (1983, 65–71). For *physical matching*, the user is presented with a five-letter word as an initial stimulus. After a delay a second stimulus appears, also a five-letter word. The user responds as quickly as possible by pressing one of two keys: a "match" key if the second stimulus matches the first stimulus, or a "no-match" key if the second stimulus differs from the first stimulus. Matches occur with 50 percent probability. An example experimental setup is shown in Figure 2.25.

Obviously, physical matching is more complicated than simple reaction, since the user must compare the stimulus to a code stored in working memory. There are many examples of similar tasks in HCI, such as entering text on a mobile phone using predictive input (*T9*). While entering a word, the user has in her or his mind an intended word. This is the initial stimulus. With the last keystroke, the system presents a word. This is the second stimulus. If the presented word matches the intended word, the user presses 0 to accept the word. If the presented word does not match the intended word, the user presses * to retrieve the next alternative word matching the key sequence. (Details vary depending on the phone.)

Name matching is the same as physical matching except the words vary in appearance: uppercase or lowercase, mono-spaced or sans serif, plain or bold, 18 point or 20 point. A match is deemed to occur if the words are the same, regardless of the look of the fonts. See Figure 2.26. Name matching should take longer than physical matching because "the user must now wait until the visual code has been

(a)   (b)

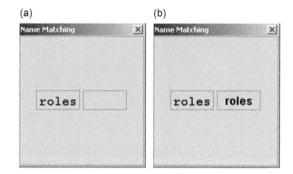

FIGURE 2.26

Name matching: (a) Initial stimulus. (b) Second stimulus.

(a)   (b)

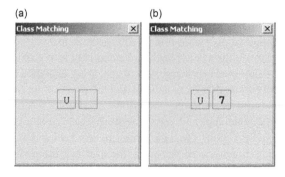

FIGURE 2.27

Class matching: (a) Initial stimulus. (b) Second stimulus.

recognized and an abstract code representing the name of the letter is available"
(Card et al., 1983, p. 69).

For *class matching*, the initial stimulus contains a letter or digit. After a delay a
second stimulus appears, also containing a letter or digit. The font is mono-spaced
or sans serif, plain or italic, 18 point or 20 point. A match is deemed to occur if
both symbols are of the same class; that is, both are letters or both are digits. Class
matching takes longer still, because "the user has to make multiple references to
long-term memory" (Card et al., 1983, p. 70). To avoid confusion, 0 (digit) and O
(letter) are not included, nor are 1 (digit) and I (letter). (See Figure 2.27.)

The interfaces described above were tested in the lab component of a course on
HCI. Fourteen students served as participants and performed three blocks of ten trials
for each condition. The first block was considered practice and was discarded. To offset learning effects, participants were divided into two groups of equal size. One group

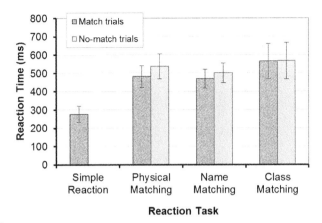

FIGURE 2.28

Results of an experiment comparing several reaction tasks. Error bars show ±1 *SD*.

preformed the simple reaction task first, followed in order by the physical, name, and class matching tasks. The other group performed the tasks in the reverse order.

The results are shown in Figure 2.28. The mean time for simple reaction was 276 ms. This value is nicely positioned in the 113 to 528 ms range noted earlier for reaction time tasks (see Figure 2.17). Note that the time measurement began with the arrival of the second stimulus and ended with the key event registered in the software when a key was pressed; thus, the measurement includes the time for the motor response.

Physical matching took about twice as long as simple reaction, depending on whether the second stimulus was a match (482 ms) or a no-match (538 ms). Interestingly enough, name matching did not take longer than physical matching. One explanation is that the words in the name-matching task had insufficient variability in appearance to require additional cognitive processing. Class matching was the hardest of the tasks, with means of about 565 ms for both the match and no-match conditions.

Choice reaction is yet another type of reaction time task. In this case, the user has *n* stimuli, such as lights, and *n* responders, such as switches. There is a one for one correspondence between stimulus and response. Choice reaction time is discussed in Chapter 7 on modeling.

2.7.2 **Visual search**

A variation on reaction time is *visual search*. Here, the user scans a collection of items, searching for a desired item. Obviously, the time increases with the number of items to scan. The software described above includes a mode for visual search, with the search space configurable for 1, 2, 4, 8, 16, or 32 items. An example for $N=16$ is shown in Figure 2.29. The initial stimulus is a single letter. After a random

(a)   (b)

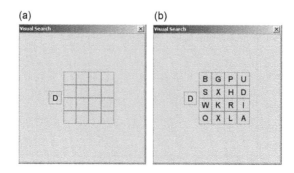

FIGURE 2.29

Visual search: (a) Initial stimulus. (b) After a delay a collection of letters appears.

delay of two to five seconds, the squares on the right are populated with letters selected at random. The initial stimulus appears on the right with 50 percent probability. The user presses a "match" or "no-match" key, as appropriate.

A small experiment was conducted with the same 14 students from the experiment described above, using a similar procedure. The results are shown in Figure 2.30 in two forms. In (a), reaction time (RT) versus number of items (N) is plotted. Each marker reveals the mean of $14 \times (10 + 10) = 280$ trials. The markers are connected and a linear regression line is superimposed. At $R^2 = .9929$, the regression model is an excellent fit. Clearly, there is a linear relationship between reaction time in a visual search task and the number of items to scan. This is well known in the HCI literature, particularly from research on menu selection (e.g., Cockburn, Gutwin, and Greenberg, 2007; Hornof and Kieras, 1997; Landauer and Nachbar, 1985). For this experiment,

$$RT = 498 + 41 \times N \, \text{ms} \tag{1}$$

$N=1$ is a special case since there is only one item to scan. This reduces the task to physical matching. The task is slightly different than in the physical matching experiment, since the user is matching a letter rather than a word. Nevertheless, the result is consistent with the physical matching result in Figure 2.28 $(RT \approx 500 \, \text{ms})$.

In Figure 2.30b, the results are given separately for the match trials and the no-match trials. The no-match trials take longer. The reason is simple. If the initial stimulus is not present, an exhaustive search is required to determine such before pressing the no-match key. If the initial stimulus is present, the user presses the match key immediately when the initial stimulus is located in the right-side stimuli. The effect only surfaces at $N=16$ and $N=32$, however.

Before moving on, here is an interesting reaction time situation, and it bears directly on the title of this section, Human Performance. Consider an athlete competing in the 100 meter dash in the Olympics. Sometimes at the beginning of a race there is a "false start." The definition of a false start is rather interesting: a false start occurs if an athlete reacts to the starter's pistol before it is sounded *or within*

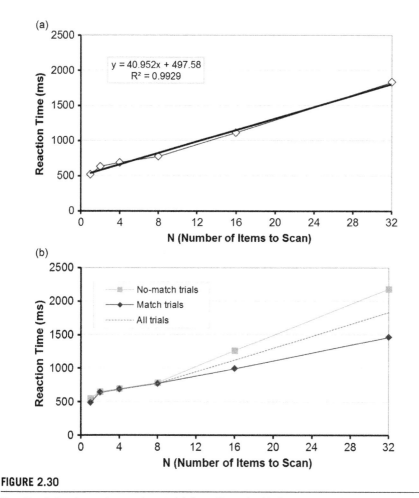

FIGURE 2.30

Results of visual search experiment: (a) Overall result with linear regression model.
(b) Results by match and no-match trials.

100 ms after.[13] Clearly, an athlete who reacts before the starter's pistol sounds is anticipating, not reacting. Interesting in the definition, however, is the criterion that a false start has occurred if the athlete reacts within 100 ms *after* the starter's pistol is sounded. One hundred milliseconds is precariously close to the lower bound on reaction time, which is cited in Figure 2.17 as 113 ms. Card et al. peg the lower bound at 105 ms (Card et al., 1983, p. 66). World records are set, and gold medals won, by humans at the extreme tails of the normal distribution. Is it possible that

---

[13] Rule 161.2 of the International Association of Athletics Federations (IAAF) deems a false start to occur "when the reaction time is less than 100/1000ths of a second." See www.iaaf.org/mm/Document/imported/42192.pdf (107).

a false start is declared occasionally, very occasionally, when none occurred (e.g., honestly *reacting* 95 ms after the starter's pistol is fired)? There are slight differences between the lower-bound reaction times cited above and the false-start scenario, however. The values cited are for pressing a key with a finger in response to a visual stimulus. The motor response signals in the 100 meter dash must travel farther to reach the feet. This tends to lengthen the reaction time. Also, the stimulus in the 100 meter dash is auditory, not visual. Auditory reaction time is less than visual reaction time, so this tends to shorten the reaction time. Nevertheless, the example illustrates the application of low-level research in experimental psychology to human performance and to the design of human-machine systems.

2.7.3 Skilled behavior

The response time tasks in the previous section are simple: a sensory stimulus initiates a simple cognitive operation, which is followed by a simple motor response. It takes just a few trials to get comfortable with the task and with additional practice there is little if any improvement in performance. However, in many tasks, human performance improves considerably and continuously with practice. For such tasks, the phenomenon of learning and improving is so pronounced that the most endearing property of the task is the progression in performance and the level of performance achieved, according to a criterion such as speed, accuracy, degree of success, and so on. *Skilled behavior*, then, is a property of human behavior whereby human performance necessarily improves through practice. Examples include playing darts, playing chess and, in computing scenarios, gaming or programming. One's ability to do these tasks is likely to bear significantly on the amount of practice done.

The examples just cited were chosen for a reason. They delineate two categories of skilled behavior: sensory-motor skill and mental skill (Welford, 1968, p. 21). Proficiency in darts or gaming is likely to emphasize sensory-motor skill, while proficiency in chess or computer programming is likely to emphasize mental skill. Of course, there is no dichotomy. All skilled behavior requires mental faculties, such as perception, decision, and judgment. Similarly, even the most contemplative of skilled tasks requires coordinated, overt action by the hands or other organs.

While tasks such as gaming and computer programming may focus on sensory-motor skill or mental skill, respectively, other tasks involve considerable elements of both. Consider a physician performing minimally invasive surgery, as is common for abdominal procedures. To access the abdominal area, a camera and a light mounted at the end of a laparoscope are inserted through a small incision, with the image displayed on an overhead monitor. Tools are inserted through other incisions for convenient access to an internal organ. The surgeon views the monitor and manipulates the tools to grasp and cut tissue. In Figure 2.31a, the tips of the surgeon's tools for grasping (left) and cutting (top) are shown as they appear on a monitor during a cholecystectomy, or gallbladder removal. The tools are manually operated, external to the patient. Figure 2.31b shows examples of such tools in a training simulator. The tools are complex instruments. Note, for example, that the tips of the tools

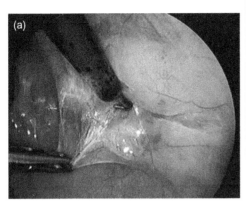

FIGURE 2.31

Sensory-motor skill combined with mental skill during laparoscopic surgery: (a) Tips of tools for grasping and cutting. (b) Exterior view of tools and monitor in a training simulator.

(Photos courtesy of the Centre of Excellence for Simulation Education and Innovation at Vancouver General Hospital)

articulate, or bend, thus providing an additional degree of freedom for the surgeon (Martinec, Gatta, Zheng, Denk, and Swanstrom, 2009). Clearly, the human-machine interaction involves both sensory-motor skill (operating the tools while viewing a monitor) and mental skill (knowing what to do and the strategy for doing it).

One way to study skilled behavior is to record and chart the progression of skill over a period of time. The level of skill is measured in a dependent variable, such as speed, accuracy, or some variation of these. The time element is typically a convenient procedural unit such as trial iteration, block or session number, or a temporal unit such as minutes, hours, days, months, or years. Measuring and modeling the progression of skill is common in HCI research, particularly where users confront a new interface or interaction technique. The methodology for evaluating skilled behavior is presented in Chapter 5 (see Longitudinal Studies) with the mathematical steps for modeling presented in Chapter 7 (see Skill Acquisition). See also student exercise 2-4 at the end of this chapter.

2.7.4 **Attention**

Texting while driving. It's hard to imagine a more provocative theme to open this discussion on attention. Although driving a car is relatively easy, even the most experienced driver is a potential killer if he or she chooses to read and send text messages while driving. The problem lies in one's inability to attend to both tasks simultaneously. Much like the bottleneck posed by working memory (7 ± 2 items), the human ability to attend is also limited. But what is the limit? More fundamentally, what is attention? Which tasks require attention? Which do not? How is human performance impacted? According to one view, attention is a property of human behavior that occurs when a person who is attending to one thing cannot attend to another (Keele, 1973, p. 4). Typing, for example, requires attention because while typing we cannot engage in conversation. On the other hand, walking requires very little attention since we can think, converse, and do other things while walking. One way to study attention is to observe and measure humans performing two tasks separately and then to repeat the procedure with the two tasks performed simultaneously. A task with performance that degrades in the simultaneous case is said to require attention.

Attention is often studied along two themes: *divided attention* and *selected attention* (B. H. Kantowitz and Sorkin, 1983, p. 179). Divided attention is the process of concentrating on and doing more than one task at time. Texting while driving is an example, and the effect is obvious enough. In other cases, divided attention poses no problem, as in walking and talking. Selected attention (aka *focused attention*) is attending to one task to the exclusion of others. For example, we converse with a friend in a crowded noise-filled room while blocking out extraneous chatter. But there are limits. In that same conversation we are occasionally unable to recall words just spoken because our attention drifted away or was pulled away by a distraction. Selective attention, then, is the human ability to ignore extraneous events and to maintain focus on a primary task. One theory of selective attention holds that our ability to selectively attend bears on the importance of the events to the individual. A person listening to a speech is likely to stop listening if the person's name is spoken from another location (Keele, 1973, p. 140). One's own name is intrinsically important and is likely to intrude on the ability to selectively attend to the speech. Clearly, importance is subjective. Wickens gives an example of an airplane crash where the flight crew were preoccupied with a malfunction in the cockpit that had no bearing on the safety of the flight (Wickens, 1987, p. 249). The crew attended to the malfunction while failing to notice critical altimeter readings showing that the airplane was gradually descending to the ground. The malfunction was of salient importance to the flight crew.

The distinction between divided and selected attention is often explained in terms of channels (Wickens, 1987, p. 254). Events in a single channel (e.g., visual, auditory, motor) are processed in parallel, whereas events in different channels are processed in serial. When processing events in parallel (single channel) one event may intrude on the ability to focus attention on another event. When processing events in serial (different channels), we strive to focus on one event to the exclusion of others or to divide attention in a convenient manner between the channels.

Analyzing accidents is an important theme in human factors, as the aviation example above illustrates, and there is no shortage of incidents. Accidents on the road, in the air, on the seas, or in industry are numerous and in many cases the cause is at least partly attributable to the human element—to distractions or to selectively attending to inappropriate events. One such accident involving a driver and a cyclist occurred because a Tamagotchi digital pet distracted the driver.[14] Evidently, the pet developed a dire need for "food" and was distressed: *bleep, bleep, bleep, bleep, bleep*. The call of the pet was of salient importance to the driver, with a horrific and fatal outcome (Casey, 2006, pp. 255–259). More likely today, it is the call of the mobile phone that brings danger. The statistics are shocking, yet unsurprising—a 23-fold increase in the risk of collision while texting (Richtel, 2009).

Attention has relevance in HCI in for example, office environments where interruptions that demand task switching affect productivity (Czerwinski, Horvitz, and Wilhite, 2004). The mobile age has brought a milieu of issues bearing on attention. Not only are attention resources limited, these resources are engaged while users are on the move. There is a shift toward immediate, brief tasks that demand constant vigilance and user availability, with increasingly demanding expectations in response times. So-called psychosocial tasks compete for and deplete attention resources, with evidence pointing to an eventual breakdown of fluency in the interaction (Oulasvirta, Tamminen, Roto, and Kuorelahti, 2005).

2.7.5 Human error

Human error can be examined from many perspectives. In HCI experiments testing new interfaces or interaction techniques, errors are an important metric for performance. An error is a discrete event in a task, or trial, where the outcome is incorrect, having deviated from the correct and desired outcome. The events are logged and analyzed as a component of human performance, along with task completion time and other measurable properties of the interaction. Typically, errors are reported as the ratio of incorrectly completed trials to all trials, and are often reported as a percent ($\times 100$). Sometimes accuracy is reported—the ratio of correctly completed trials to all trials.

Two examples for computing tasks are shown in Figure 2.32. A GUI target selection task is shown on the left in two forms. The top image shows the goal: moving a tracking symbol from a starting position to a target and ending with a select operation. The bottom image shows an error, since the final selection was outside the target. A text entry task is shown on the right. The goal of entering the word *quickly* is shown correctly done at the top. The bottom image shows an error, since the word was entered incorrectly.

Mishaps and miscues in human performance are many. Often, a simple categorization of the outcome of a task as correct or incorrect falls short of fully capturing the behavior. We need look no further than Figure 2.32 for examples. Not only were the results of the tasks on the bottom erroneous in a discrete sense, there were additional behaviors that deviated from perfect execution of the tasks. For the target selection error, the tracking symbol veered off the direct path to the target. For the text entry error, it appears that at least part of the word was correctly entered.

Taking a broader perspective, human error is often studied by examining how and why errors occur. Once again, Figure 2.32 provides insight. In the erroneous

---

[14]Ample descriptions of the Tamagotchi are found in various online sources (search using "Tamagotchi").

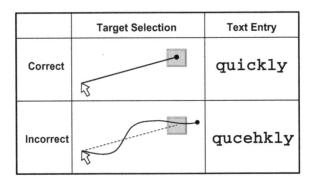

FIGURE 2.32

Common computing tasks completed correctly (*top*) and incorrectly (*bottom*).

target selection task, was there a control problem with the input device? Was the device's gain setting too sensitive? Was the device a mouse, a touchpad, an eye tracker, a game controller, or some other input control? Note as well that the tracking symbol entered then exited the target. Was there a problem with the final target acquisition in the task? In the erroneous text entry task, if input involved a keyboard, were errors due to the user pressing keys adjacent to correct keys? Were the keys too small? If entry involved gestural input using a finger or stylus on a digitizing surface, did the user enter the wrong gesture or an ill-formed gesture? Was the digitizing surface too small, awkwardly positioned, or unstable? Clearly, there are many questions that arise in developing a full understanding of how and why errors occur. Note as well that the questions above are not simply about the human; they also question aspects of the device and the interaction.

An even broader perspective in analyzing errors may question the environmental circumstances coincident with the tasks. Were users disadvantaged due to noise, vibration, lighting, or other environmental conditions? Were users walking or performing a secondary task? Were they distracted by the presence of other people, as might occur in a social setting?

Human factors researchers often examine human error as a factor in industrial accidents where the outcome causes substantial damage or loss of life. Such events rarely occur simply because a human operator presses the wrong button, or commits an interaction error with the system or interface. Usually, the failures are systemic— the result of a confluence of events, many having little to do with the human.

To the extent that a significant accident is determined to have resulted from *human error*, a deeper analysis is often more revealing. Casey's retelling of dozens of such accidents leads to the conclusion that the failures are often *design-induced errors* (Casey, 1998, p. 2006). This point is re-cast as follows: if a human operator mistakenly flicks the wrong switch or enters an incorrect value, and the action results in a serious accident, is the failure due to human error? Partly so, perhaps, but clearly the accident is enabled by the design of whatever he or she is operating. A design that can lead to catastrophic outcomes purely on the basis of an operator's interaction error is a faulty design. For safety-critical systems, interaction errors by an operator must be considered and accounted for. Such errors are not only possible, they are, in time, likely. Designs of safety-critical systems must accommodate such vagaries in human behavior.

STUDENT EXERCISES

2-1. Penfield's motor homunculus in Figure 2.9 illustrates the area in the cerebral cortex devoted to human responders. The sketch includes solid bars corresponding to the cortical area for each responder. The length of each bar is a quantitative indicator. Reverse engineer the motor homunculus to determine the length of each bar. The general idea is shown below for the toes and ankles.

	A	B	C	D	E	F	G	H
1	Responder	x1	y1	x2	y2	dx	dy	Length
2	Toes	52	153	55	111	-3	42	42.1
3	Ankle	56	106	64	58	-8	48	48.7

The shaded cells contain values digitized from an image processing application. The *toes* bar, for example, extends from (52, 153) to (55, 111). Using the Pythagorean theorem, the length is 42.1 pixels. Of course, the scale and units are arbitrary. Evidently, there is about 15.7 percent more cortical area devoted to the ankle than to the toes. See above. This is also evident in the figure.

For all responders, digitize the endpoints of the corresponding bars and enter the values in a spreadsheet, as above. Create a bar chart showing the relative amounts of cortical area for each responder. It might be useful to collect together the values for the leg, arm, and head, with each shown as the sum of contributing responders. Write a brief report discussing the motor homunculus and the empirical data for the various responders.

2-2. Conduct a small experiment on memory recall as follows. Find an old discarded keyboard and remove the key tops for the letters (below left). Using a drawing application, create and print an outline of the letter portion of a Qwerty keyboard (below right). Find five computer users (participants). Ask each one to position the key tops in the printout. Limit the time for the task to three minutes. Record the number of key tops correctly positioned. (Suggestion: Photograph the result and do the analysis afterward.)

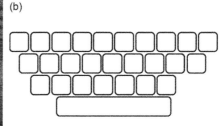

Then assess each participant's typing style and typing speed as follows. Open a blank document in an editor and enter the phrase "the quick brown fox jumps over the lazy dog." On the next line, ask the participant to correctly type the same phrase. Measure and record the time in seconds. Repeat five times. For each participant, note and record whether the typing style is *touch* or *hunt-and-peck*. Enter the data into a spreadsheet. Convert the time to enter the phrase (t, in seconds) to typing speed (s, in words per minute) using $s = (43/5)/(t/60)$. Write a brief report on your findings for the *number of key tops correctly positioned*. Consider participants overall as well as *by typing speed* and *by typing style*. Discuss other relevant observations.

2-3. Conduct a small experiment on redundancy and entropy in written English, similar to Shannon's letter guessing experiment described earlier (see Figure 2.22). Use 5–10 participants. For the experiment, use the `LetterGuessingExperiment` software provided on this book's website. Use five trials (phrases) for each participant. The setup dialog and a screen snap of the experiment procedure are shown below:

(a)   (b)

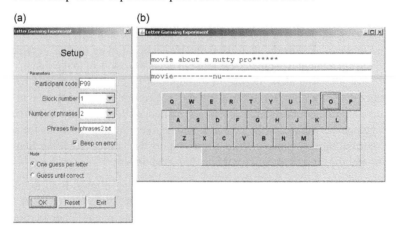

Data collection is automated in the software. Analyze the results for the number of letters correctly guessed (redundancy) and the number incorrectly guessed (entropy). Examine the results overall and by participants. Investigate, as well, whether the responses differ according to the position of letters in words and in phrases. Write a brief report on your findings.

2-4. Construct a 2D chart on skilled behavior showing sensory-motor skill on one axis and mental skill on the other. For both axes, add the label *little* near the origin, and *lots* near the end. An example of a similar chart is given in Figure 3.46. Add markers in the chart showing at least five computing skills. Position the markers according to the relative emphasis on sensory-motor skill and mental skill in each task. Write a brief report, describing each skill and rationalizing the position of the marker in the chart. For guidance, see the discussion in this chapter on skilled behavior. For further guidance, read the discussion in Chapter 7 on descriptive models.

2-5. Conduct a small experiment on gestural input, human performance, and human error using the GraffitiExperiment software on this book's website. There is both a *Windows* version and an *Android* version. Recruit about 10 participants. Divide the participants into two groups and use a different input method for each group. Consider using a mouse and touch-pad (*Windows*) or a finger and stylus (*Android*). The software uses *Graffiti* gestures for text entry. For the experiment, the participants are to enter the alphabet 10 times. The setup dialog and a screen snap of the experimental procedure are shown below for *Windows* (top) and for *Android* (bottom) .

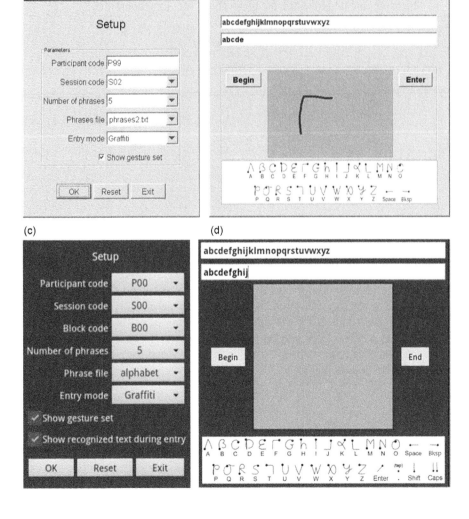

One of the options in the setup dialog is "Phrases file." Use alphabet.txt. Set the "Number of phrases" to 10. Leave "Show gesture set" checked. The gestures are viewable in the experiment screen (see above). Participants may correct errors using the BACKSPACE stroke (←). However, instruct participants not to attempt more than three corrections per symbol.

Data collection is automated. Consult the API for complete details. Analyze the data to reveal the progress over the 10 trials for both groups of participants. Analyze the entry speed (wpm), error rate (%), and keystrokes per char (*KSPC*). (A "keystroke," here, is a gesture stroke.) Write a brief report on your findings.

2-6. Conduct a small experiment on human reaction time using the ReactionTimeExperiment software provided on this book's website. Recruit about 10 participants. The setup dialog is shown below. Examples of the experimental procedure are given above (see Reaction Time).

Consider modifying the software in some way, such using words instead of letters for the visual search task, or using an auditory stimulus instead of a visual stimulus for the simple reaction time task. The modification can serve as a point of comparison (e.g., visual search for words versus letters, or reaction time to an auditory stimulus versus a visual stimulus). Write a brief report on your findings.

Interaction Elements

Interaction occurs when a human performs a task using computing technology of some sort. The "performs a task" aspect forms the interaction. The task is often goal-oriented, such as sending e-mail, burning a CD, programming a thermostat, or entering a destination in a global positioning system (GPS). But sometimes there is no specific goal. Just browsing the web or chatting with friends on a social networking site is sufficient to qualify as a task. If the user is engaged in any activity with computing technology, interaction is taking place.

In this chapter, elements of human-computer interaction are examined. The topics do not comprehensively span the field of HCI. Instead, the topics are selective and focus on low-level aspects of interaction. Most of the tasks are situated in the cognitive band in Newell's *Time Scale of Human Action* presented in Chapter 2. The human systems at work are deliberate acts ($\approx$100 ms), operations ($\approx$1 s), and unit tasks ($\approx$10 s). With durations ranging from 100 ms to 10 s, the tasks are well suited to empirical research. In fact, most experimental research in HCI is directed at tasks of this sort. Due to the brevity of the tasks, extraneous behaviors are easy to control. Thus, experiments with high *internal validity* are possible. (Internal validity is discussed in the next chapter.) Although it is possible to experimentally study higher-level tasks—those in the rational social bands—difficulties arise due to the duration of the tasks. Operations in these bands take from minutes to months (see Figure 2.1), and therefore often include extraneous behaviors such as pausing, task switching, pondering, decision-making, and secondary and unrelated tasks. Although such behaviors are germane to the HCI experience, they present challenges for experimental study; therefore, we focus on interaction elements in the cognitive band.

At a stripped-down level, interaction involves humans using their sensors and responders to monitor and control devices, machines, and systems that include computing technology. We saw a typical human factors view of this in the Chapter 2 (see Figure 2.2). The internal states of both the human and the machine interact in a closed-loop system through controls and displays (the machine side) and motor-sensory behaviors (the human side). By convention, the terms *input* and *output* are with respect to the machine; so inputs, or input devices, are inputs to the machine that are controlled or manipulated by human outputs. Most commonly, human outputs are limbs—the fingers, hands, arms, legs, and feet—but speech, articulated sounds, eye motions, blinks, breath, electrical body signals, and so on can also serve as human outputs. Some of these communication channels are extremely important for disabled users.

There is a long history of human factors research following the classical view that focuses on "knobs and dials" (Chapanis, 1965; Van Cott and Kinkade, 1972). Using responders, the human operator manipulates controls or knobs, perhaps with a goal in mind, while engaging senses to perceive the status of a system on displays or dials.[1] This work is important in HCI, too. Relevant examples are numerous, particularly from tasks when things don't quite go as planned: terminating an application on a computer while intending only to minimize a window, putting food in a microwave oven and heating it for three seconds instead of three minutes, or terminating a call on a mobile phone while intending only to adjust the volume. These are all knobs and dials issues, and they perplex and frustrate us, even today.

We begin with the basic properties of human input to computers (the knobs or controls) and the responses produced (the dials or displays). The conventional desktop computer system is a convenient input/output system in which to frame these discussions. Although the issues have been highly researched over the years, the interactions in desktop computing are relevant in newer domains, such a mobile computing, virtual environments, surface computing, tangible computing, wearable computing, gaming, and so on.

3.1 Hard controls and soft controls

Before computers infiltrated every aspect of our homes and workplaces, displays and controls tended to be physical single-purpose devices. Controls like joysticks, switches, arrays of switches, push buttons, keys, keyboards, mice, steering wheels, handles, knobs, levers, and so on arrived through an involved process of design, engineering, and manufacturing. Once built, they were fixed for life. This meant their behaviors were constrained to a small set of relationships with the displays they accompanied. Even an aircraft's cockpit had a relatively small number of controls and displays. Because they were physical and single-purpose, there was a limited set of relationships that existed between them.

The advent of computers with software, graphical displays, and point-and-click interactions changed this. Through *soft interfaces*, the way humans interact with technology changed, and changed everywhere. The malleability of a display, through software, brings unlimited possibilities to a relatively small physical space. The result is *soft controls*. A soft control can be born out of little more than a programmer's whim—a few lines of computer code and a quick round or two of code-compile-test—all done between the morning coffee break and lunch. Before you

---

[1]*Displays* as used here is any form of computer output. This includes visual as well as auditory and tactile displays.

know it, there is a new button on a toolbar, a new "Options . . . " popup dialog, or a new drawing mode invoked with CTRL-*something*. The possibilities are limitless.[2]

Human-computer interfaces contain lots of controls. Most are soft controls manipulated by physical controls (the mouse or keyboard). Desktop computer applications, for example, have thousands of control-display arrangements. Every conceivable action one might make with a soft control that produces a displayed response on the system is an example. Controls invoke different responses (displays) depending on the context, so the combinations multiply rapidly.

The distinction between controls and displays is blurred with soft controls. Since a soft control is rendered on a display through software, its size, shape, or appearance can change dynamically to convey information to the user. Thus, soft controls often have properties of displays. Toolbar buttons and widgets are typical examples. Figure 3.1 shows an example from the word processor used to create this chapter. The image was captured with the cursor, or I-beam, positioned inside *this*. The image contains three combo boxes and seven buttons. Each is both a control and a display. The combo boxes reveal that the style is Body Text, the font is Times, and the font size is 12 point. The buttons are toggle buttons, revealing the state of the text at the insertion point. The text is italicized, underlined, left justified.

A scrollbar slider, or elevator, is another example[3] (See Figure 3.2.). The slider is both a control and a display. As a control, it is moved to change the view in the document. As a display, its size reveals the magnitude of the view relative to the entire document and its position reveals the position of the view within the document. Most soft controls are also displays.

Soft controls need little space. Figure 3.3 shows a small area of a GUI application. It is only 30 square centimeters, but look: it contains a bewildering array of soft controls—more than 20. Or are they displays? Each is a world unto itself. Each identifies or suggests its purpose by its shape, its position, a label, or an icon. Each of these soft controls is manipulated by a hard control, by clicking. Or is it double-clicking? Or is it SHIFT-clicking? Or is it dragging? What about right-clicking? What about keyboard access? And there are presumptions that somehow it all makes sense to the user. Each control is also precariously close to a neighbor. Many users of this application, Microsoft Word, will invest thousands of hours working this

FIGURE 3.1

Many soft controls are also displays.

---

[2]Of the programmer's whimsical role in creating overly complex and unusable interfaces, Cooper is even less kind (Cooper, 1999, pp. 1–246). Others also note the undue influence of technical staff. In one case, management's inability to challenge the judgment of engineering staff is cited as contributing to the failure of an entire project (D. K. Smith and Alexander, 1988, p. 160).

[3]The scrollbar slider has a variety of names, depending on the platform, including thumb, box, knob, scroller, wiper, and grip.

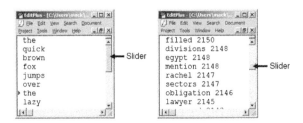

FIGURE 3.2

A scrollbar slider is both a control and a display.

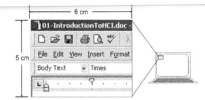

FIGURE 3.3

A small physical space on a graphical display. There are more than 20 soft controls and displays in a 30-square-centimeters area. A single user action can initiate a complete redefinition of the space.

30-square-centimeters interface. The users are, by all accounts, experts. Yet thousands of times users, even expert users, commit errors working in this same space. Sometimes they act in haste. At other times they're just not sure what to do. It's a complex space, this 30 square centimeters. And all it takes is one user action—a key press or button click—and the entire 30 square centimeters is morphed into a completely different interface. See student exercise 3-1 at the end of this chapter.

The hard-control/soft-control distinction is similar to the idea of *space multiplexing* versus *time multiplexing* (Buxton, 1983). With space multiplexing, there is a dedicated physical control for each parameter that is controlled. Each control has a separate physical location. With time multiplexing, there are fewer controls than parameters, and so a single device (e.g., a small region of a display) is reconfigured to control different parameters at different stages of an operation.

In the next section, we examine controls and displays in terms of their spatial relationships. We begin with hard controls such as a mouse, and typical displays such as are found on desktop computer systems.

3.2 Control-display relationships

When a user grasps a computer mouse and moves it to the right, the cursor on the system's display moves to the right. This *control-display relationship* is not something users think much about. This is human-computer interaction as it should be—where the relationship between what a user does and what is experienced is natural, seamless, intuitive, and efficient. Control-display relationships are sometimes called *mappings*, since the relationships attribute how a controller property maps to a display property.

The mouse/cursor example describes a *spatial relationship*. There are also *dynamic relationships*, describing how a controller affects the speed of the response, and *physical relationships*, describing whether the response is to a movement or a force in the controller. We will examine each of these in this section, beginning with spatial relationships.

3.2.1 **Spatial relationships**

The mouse-cursor spatial relationship described above is illustrated in Figure 3.4a. The mapping is *congruent* because there is an exact spatial correspondence between the controller input and the display output. Move the mouse right, and the cursor moves right. The situation in Figure 3.4b is different. Move the mouse "forward" and the cursor moves "up." As with side-to-side movement, users likely don't think much about this. Yet the first time someone encounters a mouse, there is likely some uncertainty on how it works. What does it do? What is it controlling? Where is the effect seen? No doubt, the spatial relationship between mouse and cursor is learned very quickly.[4] I will say more about learned versus natural relationships later.

It is useful at this juncture to introduce labels to further examine the spatial mappings between input controls and output displays. Figure 3.5a and Figure 3.5b show the display and mouse pad surfaces in a Cartesian coordinate space with x-, y-, and z-axes.[5] Left-right motion is along the x-axis. Up-down motion is along the y-axis. Forward-backward motion is along the z-axis. Of course, a cursor cannot move along the z-axis, nor is mouse motion sensed on the y-axis. The arrows show positive motion along each axis.

The mouse-to-cursor mapping is shown in Figure 3.5c. Here we see the slight disjoint noted above. Mouse x-axis motion maps to cursor x-axis motion, but mouse

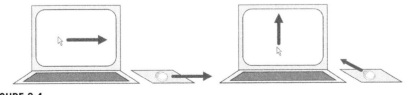

FIGURE 3.4

Control-display relationships for a mouse and cursor.

---

[4] A student once told me of his experience teaching his mother how to use a computer. At one point he told his mother to move the cursor "up" to the menu bar. She raised the mouse "up" off the mousepad.
[5] The choice of labels is, of course, arbitrary.

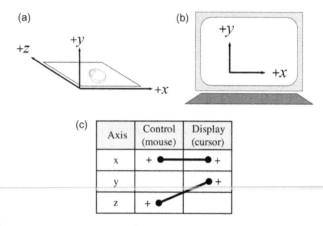

FIGURE 3.5

Axis labels. (a) Control space. (b) Display space. (c) Control-display mapping for a mouse and cursor.

z-axis motion maps to cursor y-axis motion. The plus (+) symbols indicate that positive motion of the control yields positive motion in the display along each axis.

The y-axis cursor motion is an example of a *transformed spatial mapping*. In this case the transformation is 90°, if viewed along the y-z plane. We might expect an effect on user performance in the presence of a spatial transformation, and that is the case. Aiming error is known to be higher for 90° to 135° transformations and lower for 0° or 180° transformations (Cunningham, 1989). It is also known that adaptation occurs for all transformations, in a few as 50 trials (Wigdor, Shen, Forlines, and Balakrishnan, 2006). So while initial exposure to a mouse might pose a problem (and yield inaccurate pointing), with practice the relationship is learned and accuracy improves.

Describing mouse-cursor mappings in a three-dimensional (3D) space, as above, invites a deeper analysis of other control-display relationships. This is justified at the very least because HCI is more than desktop interaction. Whether using a thumb-controlled wheel to scroll through a calendar on a personal digital assistant (PDA) or using a handheld controller to annihilate the enemy in a first-person shooter game, the relationship between what we do and what we get is of the utmost importance in designing interfaces and interaction techniques that are efficient and transparent.

Now consider scrolling the view of an image or document. A scroll pane includes scrollbars with sliders to move the view. Interaction involves manipulating a physical controller, such as a mouse (a hard control), to move a pointer to the slider (a soft control) and acquiring it with a button-down action. The slider is then dragged up or down to produce a change in the view. This scenario adds a third tier to the control-display mappings. Figure 3.6a shows a mouse and an image of a map displayed in a GUI window. Scrollbars with sliders appear to the right and (a)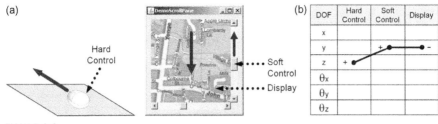

(b)

DOF	Hard Control	Soft Control	Display
x			
y		+	−
z	+		
θx			
θy			
θz			

FIGURE 3.6

A three-tier control-display relationship: (a) Moving the hard control forward moves the soft control up, which in turn moves the display view down. (b) Control-display mappings.

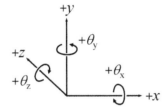

FIGURE 3.7

Axis labels for a three-dimensional space.

on the bottom of the window. There is a spatial transformation between the hard control and soft control and between the soft control and the view on the display. (See Figure 3.6b.)

Most computer users are adept at scrolling through documents and have no trouble with the spatial transformations illustrated in Figure 3.6. The +/− reversal in the control-display relationship along the z-axis is interesting, however. What if the relationship between the soft control (scrollbar slider) and the display (map image) were reversed? Would this be okay? Yes, but the relationship would have to be learned.

The next step in examining spatial relationships is to expand the 3D space to include rotation about each axis. This is shown in Figure 3.7 using *theta* (θ) to designate angle or rotation. The arrows indicate positive rotation, corresponding to clockwise movement as viewed looking out from the origin along each axis. In all, there are six parameters, or *degrees of freedom* (DOF). Degrees of freedom means that each parameter may be manipulated independently of the others. So to fully place an object in 3D space, six parameters are required: three for the object's *position* in space (*x, y, z*), and three for the object's *orientation* in space (θ_x, θ_y, θ_z). In aeronautics, the rotation terms are known as pitch (θ_x), roll (θ_z), and yaw (θ_y).

Figure 3.8a shows an example of 3D interaction where congruence is fully attained (see also Zimmerman, Lanier, Blanchard, Bryson, and Harvill, 1987). Of course the depth, or z-axis, is simulated on the display. Nevertheless, the figure illustrates the goal of facile 6 DOF interaction. The figure shows a 6 DOF input glove (a controller) in exact spatial correspondence with a simulated glove on the

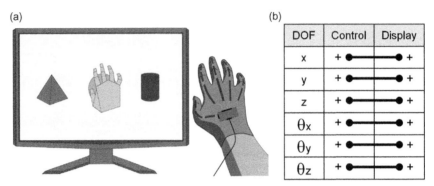

(a)   (b)

DOF	Control	Display
x	+ ●——●	+
y	+ ●——●	+
z	+ ●——●	+
θx	+ ●——●	+
θy	+ ●——●	+
θz	+ ●——●	+

FIGURE 3.8

Spatial congruence in 3D: (a) 6 DOF input controller and 6 DOF display (sketch courtesy of Bartosz Bajer). (b) 6 DOF control-display correspondence.

display. The fluidity of the interaction is clearly evident: The mappings are congruent for all 6 DOF, as illustrated in Figure 3.8b.

Most interactive systems support a subset of the 6 DOF available in 3D. And in most cases, there are spatial transformations that encumber the user with small challenges to learn and overcome, like the mouse-cursor interaction noted earlier. Rotation is a challenge since traditional controllers, such as a mouse, only sense translation along the *x*-axis and *z*-axis. Control-display spatial congruence is not possible, so creative mappings are needed to facilitate interaction. The typical solution is modes, which we examine in more detail later. For the moment, consider Street View in Google Maps, which provides panoramic views of streets in major cities around the world.[6] A street scene showing the city hall in Toronto is seen in Figure 3.9a along with facsimiles of the controls for viewpoint control. The most common manipulations are *panning*, *zooming*, and *positioning*. Panning involves rotating the camera view left-right and up-down. Zooming involves changing the magnification of the view. Positioning is a change in the camera position. In the case of Google Street View, the camera position is constrained to points along the street from which the images were captured. So, while it is possible to zoom in to the city hall, it is not possible to walk toward it.

Scene manipulations are supported through a variety of interactions using the keyboard or mouse. One way to pan with the mouse is to drag the image—position the pointer anywhere on the image, press and hold the primary mouse button, then move the pointer. Left-right, or *x*-axis, linear movement of the mouse effects rotation of the scene about the *y*-axis. Forward-backward, or *z*-axis, linear movement of the mouse rotates the scene about the *x*-axis. These mappings are illustrated in Figure 3.9b. Although the mappings look convoluted, the interaction is reasonably simple (i.e., quickly learned).

[6]http://maps.google.com/streetview.

(a)
(b)

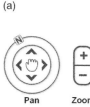

Pan   Zoom

DOF	Control	Display
x	+	
y		
z	+	
θx		+
θy		−
θz		

FIGURE 3.9

Rotating a 3D scene: (a) Street scene in Toronto with pan and zoom controls. (b) Mapping of mouse control for panning if the scene is dragged.

Another way to pan with the mouse is through the soft control labeled Pan in the figure. Clicking an arrow effects a discrete pan in the expected direction. Left-right continuous panning is possible by dragging the circle that surrounds the arrows. This interaction is tricky and of questionable merit. It requires a tight coupling of left-right, up-down linear movement of the mouse *and* it requires the user's visual attention—on the soft control! Of course, the user would prefer to look at the scene.

Zooming is performed by clicking on + and − soft controls seen in the figure. The effect is to zoom the view in and out along the z-axis. It is interesting to consider zooming via z-axis movement of the mouse, since the result is a spatially congruent control-display mapping.[7] Unfortunately, z-axis mouse movement is committed to x-axis scene rotation (i.e., up-down panning; see Figure 3.9b). Perhaps a modifier key, such as SHIFT, could be used to map mouse z-axis movement to z-axis zooming.

Another congruent mapping to consider is using y-axis rotation of the mouse to control y-axis rotation of the camera to create left-right panning. Y-axis rotation amounts to rotating the mouse on the mouse pad or desktop surface. Of course, such movement is not sensed. But with some careful reengineering it can be (as discussed later in this chapter).

Using y-axis rotation is a potentially interesting and new interaction technique. It suggests an interaction worth investigating through empirical research. Can user interaction with Google Street View be improved using other input controllers or other mappings? If so, how is a conjectured improvement evaluated? What tasks and user performance measurements are relevant? The spatial mappings between input controls and output displays are numerous in HCI, and the relationships are often complex. These complexities invite thinking about the problem space, searching out new and potentially facile interactions, and then testing and comparing them through experimental research. See also student exercise 3-2 at the end of this chapter.

---

[7]Zooming is possible using the mouse wheel, but the detents in the wheel motion make the interaction feel jerky.

3.2.2 CD gain and transfer function

There is more to mouse-cursor movement than spatial mappings. Another property is *CD gain*, which represents the amount of movement in a display object, such as a cursor, for a given amount of movement in a control.[8] For example, if a mouse is moved three cm and the cursor also moves three cm, then the CD gain is 1. If the cursor moves six cm, the CD gain is 6/3 = 2. CD gain for a mouse and cursor is typically set in a control panel, as seen in Figure 3.10. Moving the slider to the "slow" end of the scale reduces CD gain, meaning more controller movement is required for each unit of cursor movement.

Often the relationship between controller motion and cursor motion is non-linear and uses a *power function*. In this case, the amount of cursor motion depends on the velocity of mouse motion as well as controller motion. This is enabled in Figure 3.10 by selecting "Enhance pointer precision." If the mouse moves quickly, CD gain increases. If the mouse moves slowly, CD gain decreases. Lowering the CD gain for slow controller movements is useful to enhance the precision of target selection at the end of a point-select operation. The term *transfer function* is sometimes used since non-linear relationships are more elaborate. To ensure the cursor is responsive to mouse movement, with no perceivable delay, the software implementation of a non-linear relationship typically uses a lookup table to map controller movement to display movement. See also student exercise 3-3 at the end of this chapter.

Research on optimizing CD gain dates back to at least the 1940s, when the first electronic joysticks were developed (Jenkins and Connor, 1949). The problem of optimizing is trickier than it seems, however. Varying CD gain evokes a trade-off between gross positioning time (getting to the vicinity of a target) and fine positioning time (final acquisition). (See Figure 3.11.) In a simplistic sense, the optimal setting is that which minimizes the combined gross and fine positioning times. However, this may be confounded with a potentially non-optimal error rate at the CD gain setting yielding a minimal overall positioning time. Other factors such as display size or scale (independent of the CD gain setting) also bring into question the optimization of this common input device parameter (Arnault and Greenstein, 1990; Blanch, Guiard, and Beaudouin-Lafon, 2004).

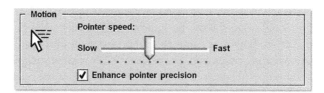

FIGURE 3.10

Controlling the CD gain (pointer speed) from the mouse control panel.

---

[8]CD gain is sometimes called C:D ratio. A CD gain of 2 is equivalent to a C:D ratio of 1:2; that is, one unit of control (mouse) movement yielding two units of display (cursor) movement.

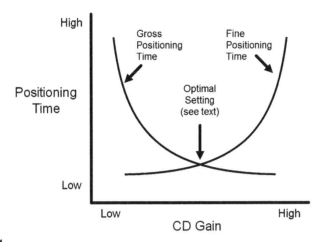

FIGURE 3.11

Trade-off between gross positioning time and fine positioning time as a function of CD gain.

Over the past 20 to 30 years, CD gain has been highly researched as it applies to interaction with GUIs on desktop computing systems (e.g., Barrett, Selker, Rutledge, and Olyha, 1995; Buck, 1980; Jellinek and Card, 1990; B. H. Kantowitz and G. C. Elvers, 1988). The majority of studies found that significant performance benefits are not achieved by adjusting CD gain. One challenge in optimizing CD gain is in defining optimal performance. Is the goal to maximize speed (viz. minimize positioning time) or to maximize accuracy? The goal of optimizing *both* speed and accuracy is problematic, because of the speed-accuracy trade-off. What improves speed tends to worsen accuracy, and vice versus. A useful metric that combines speed and accuracy is Fitts' throughput, but the calculation of throughput is subject to considerable variation in the literature, and this exacerbates assimilating research results into a comprehensive understanding of CD gain and human performance.

Optimizing CD gain is of continuing interest today, although the focus is often in different settings, such very large displays (Kobayashi and Igarashi, 2008; McCallum and Irani, 2009), very small displays (D. Harrison and Hudson, 2009), accessible computing (Wobbrock, Fogarty, Shih-Yen, Kimuro, and Harada, 2009), remote pointing (Konig, Gerken, Dierdorf, and Reiterer, 2009), and 3D interaction (Argelaguet and Andujar, 2008). In each of the examples just cited, the research brought a new idea to the problem of tuning the relationship between an input control and interaction on an output display. Since human performance is the main criterion for optimization, research on CD gain is well suited to empirical enquiry and experimentation. See also student exercise 3-4 at the end of this chapter.

3.2.3 Latency

Human interaction with computers is a two-way structure. As participants in a closed-loop system, we issue commands through input controllers and receive responses on output displays. Subsequent input depends on the latest output. Not surprisingly, human performance and the interaction experience are adversely affected when feedback is delayed. The delay between an input action and the corresponding response on a display is called *latency* or *lag*. Fortunately, latency is negligible in many interactive computing tasks, such as typing or cursor positioning.

The opposite extreme is remote manipulation, where the human operator is physically displaced from the machine under control. The latency may be due to mechanical linkages or to transmission delays in the communications channel. For example, in controlling a space vehicle on a distant moon or planet (as viewed on a display), transmission delays—latency—are on the order of several minutes or longer.

Latency is often present with Internet connections: click on a link and wait a few seconds or longer for a page to appear. The research issues here are more about user experience and frustration than about human performance. Frustration is reduced, for example, if the interface includes feedback informing the user that the network is processing the request (Bouch, Kuchinsky, and Bhatti, 2000).

Virtual reality relies heavily on the tracking of hand, head, or body motion in a simulated 3D environment. The pretense of reality requires a tight link between the user's view of the environment and the actions—usually hand, head, or body motions—that set the view. When changes in the environment lag behind input motions, the loss of fidelity is dramatic.

Latency is attributable to properties of input devices, output devices, and software. Input devices are usually sampled at fixed rates in the range of 10 to 60 samples per second. At 60 Hz sampling, for example, an input movement may not be sensed for $1/60\,s = 0.01667\,s = 16.67\,ms$. Latency increases further due to software overhead—a loose expression for a variety of system-related factors. Communication modes, network configurations, number crunching, and application software all contribute to it. Latency will increase dramatically when output requires substantial computation for graphics rendering. A display frame rate of 10 Hz is considered minimal to achieve real-time animation. Since the construction of the frame begins only once the position is known, the potential for parallel processing is limited. Using standard double buffering (where the frame is presented only once fully drawn), there is 100 ms minimum latency to the start of the frame display interval and a latency of 150 ms to the middle of the frame display interval.

From the points above, we can infer that it is not possible to accurately measure latency from within the target system. Using software to log timestamps for input and output operations within a system misses the actions and responses at the human interface. To reflect the user's experience as a whole, a proper latency measurement is done externally (Roberts, Duckworth, Moore, Wolff, and O'Hare, 2009; Steed, 2008). Teather et al. (2009) describe a pendulum apparatus for measuring latency. The input controller swings in front of the output display with a high-speed camera recording the temporal relationship between input motion and the output response.

Latency in virtual reality is associated mostly with 6 DOF tracking devices attached to the hand, head, or body as well as the latency caused by the low frame

---

[9] www.polhemus.com.

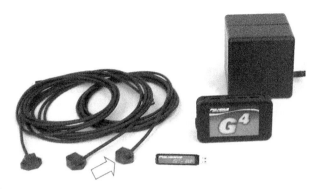

FIGURE 3.12

Polhemus G^4™ 6 DOF tracking system. The 6 DOF sensor is identified by the arrow.

(Photo courtesy of Polhemus)

rates. Typical tracking devices include the Polhemus G^4™ (Figure 3.12)[9] and the Ascension *MotionStar*.[10] These devices and their interfaces transmit six degree-of-freedom position and orientation data to the host computer at a high rate while acting in concert with competing processes in the complete virtual reality (VR) environment. Maintaining negligible latency is usually not possible. The Polhemus G^4™, for example, is sampled at 120 Hz, meaning one sample every $1/120\,s = 0.00833\,s = 8.33\,ms$. According to the device specification, latency is less than 10 ms, meaning the three position and three orientation coordinates are available no later than 10 ms after each sample. Of course, this only applies to the input sub-system. From an HCI perspective, this value is irrelevant. The user experiences the system as a whole.

Although latency is known as a compromising parameter in VR systems (Liang, Shaw, and Green, 1991), and its effect on human performance is considerable, the evidence for this is mostly anecdotal. On intuitive grounds, Pausch noted that low-latency is significantly more important than high-quality graphics or stereoscope (Pausch, 1991). His low-end VR system emphasized presence (i.e., low latency) over output graphics by maintaining seven screen updates per second with wire-frame images. In an experiment with force feedback, Brooks et al. (1990) concluded that screen updates are needed 15 times per second minimum to maintain the illusion of continuous change in the force sensed. Even at this rate, subjects noted the "sponginess of the feel". Others cite motion sickness as a by-product of lag with head-mounted displays (Draper, Viire, Furness, and Gawron, 2001; Foley, van Dam, Feiner, and Hughes, 1987; Laurel, 1991; Roberts et al., 2009).

Empirical measurements of the effect of latency on human performance are rare. There was some research in the 1960s (e.g., Gibbs, 1962, Sheridan, and Ferrell, 1968) on the design of controllers for remote manipulation systems; however, the latency tested was extremely long (up to several seconds). In one instance the apparatus was mechanical (Sheridan and Ferrell, 1968) and in another latency

---

[10]www.ascension-tech.com.

was programmed as an exponential time constant preventing the cursor from fully reaching a target unless a deliberate overshoot was programmed (Gibbs, 1962). In both cases movement time increases due to latency were dramatic—well in excess of the amount of latency. Since latency is on the order of a few hundred milliseconds in VR, its effect on human performance is less apparent.

MacKenzie and Ware (1993) systematically introduced latency in a system and measured the effect on human performance in simple point-select tasks. With 75 ms latency, movement time increased by 16 percent and error rate by 36 percent. At 225 ms the effect was dramatic, with movement time increasing by 64 percent and error rate by 214 percent.

3.2.4 Property sensed and order of control

When a human engages an input controller, the dialog involves actions such as touching, tapping, grasping, moving, pushing, flicking, and squeezing. The input controller senses the interaction and coverts a *property sensed* into data that are transmitted to the host computer for processing. For pointing devices, the most common properties sensed are *position*, *displacement*, and *force*. In this section, we examine both the property sensed and the way the property is used to control an object or view on an output display. Does the property sensed control the position or the velocity of the object or view? This question speaks to the *order of control*, which I present shortly.

With a graphics tablet, touchpad, or touchscreen, the property sensed is the position of a stylus or a finger on a digitizing surface. Position is sensed as an *absolute* coordinate at the point of contact along the x-axis and z-axis. (Discussions here assume the coordinate system in Figure 3.7.) A mouse is different. It is not possible to know where a mouse is situated on a mousepad or desktop. With a mouse, the property sensed is the *displacement*—the amount of movement along the x-axis and z-axis. Each sample is reported *relative* to the last sample. Touchpads in notebook computers typically operate in mouse-emulation mode. Even though the property sensed is the absolute position of the finger on the touchpad surface, the value is reported to the host in relative terms—the amount of finger displacement relative to the last sample. Graphics tablets typically support either absolute or relative modes of reporting.

The most common orders of control are position-control (aka zero-order control) and velocity-control (aka first-order control) (Zhai, 1995, p. 4). With position-control, the sensed property of the input device controls the position of the object or view on a display. With velocity-control, the sense property controls the velocity of the object or view. A mouse is a position-control input device, since mouse displacement controls the position of the cursor.

Order of control is often associated with joysticks. Joysticks are either *isotonic* or *isometric*. With an isotonic joystick, the user manipulates the stick handle, which, in turn, swivels about a pivot-point. The property sensed is the movement of the stick. Isotonic joysticks are also called *displacement joysticks*. The output signal represents the position of the stick as the amount of displacement (i.e., rotation) from the neutral or home position, about the x- and z-axes. An example is the

(a)   (b)

FIGURE 3.13

Joysticks: (a) Isotonic (displacement sensing).[11] (b) Isometric (force sensing).

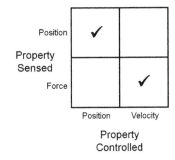

FIGURE 3.14

Order of control mapping for property sensed versus property controlled. Checks indicate the preferred mappings.

Premium II from Kraft Systems, a common joystick for computer games in the 1980s. (See Figure 3.13a.)

With an isometric joystick, the stick does not move. The property sensed is the force applied to the stick. The output signal represents the amount of force along the x-axis and z-axis. An example is the joystick between the G, H, and B keys on many notebook computer keyboards. (See Figure 3.13b.)

The order-of-control mappings for isotonic (position sensing) and isometric (force sensing) joysticks are illustrated in Figure 3.14. These possibilities raise the question of performance: Which mappings are best in terms of speed and accuracy for common point-select tasks? Kantowitz and Elvers (1988) evaluated an isometric joystick in both position-control and velocity-control modes. Velocity-control performed best. A full investigation of the possibilities in Figure 3.14 requires evaluation with two independent variables: property sensed and property controlled. In other words, both position-sensing and force-sensing input controllers must be tested in both position-control and velocity-control modes. Zhai conducted such an

---

[11] From the Buxton Collection (http://research.microsoft.com).

(a)

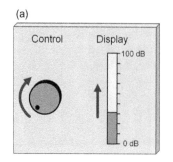

(b)

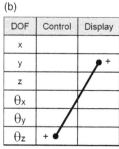

FIGURE 3.15

A control-display relationship. Learned or natural?

experiment and observed that position control is best for a position-sensing device and that velocity control is best for a force-sensing device (1995, 35). These mappings are indicated with check marks in the figure.

3.3 Natural versus learned relationships

Comments were offered above on the need for users to learn a control-display relationship. (The need arises when there is a spatial transformation between the control motion and the display response.) It is worth examining, then, whether some relationships are more natural than others. Consider the example in Figure 3.15a. Rotating the control produces linear movement in a reading on a display. The arrows show clockwise control motion producing upward display motion. As seen in Figure 3.15b, there is a spatial transformation between control and display. Is the relationship natural? Is it simple, intuitive, and easy? Both arrows in the figure point *up*, so perhaps the relationship is natural. However, if the curved arrow were positioned on the right of the control, rather than on the left, it would point down. So the relationship would then appear backward. The real question, then, is not about the arrows, but whether there is a natural relationship between clockwise motion of a control and linear motion on a display. The answer is *no*. It is a learned relationship. It might seem simple, intuitive, and easy, but it is a learned relationship.

One might argue that turning a rotary dial "clockwise" should produce an "increase" in a parameter. But this is true only if it supports the user's *expectation*. If the relationship is expected and considered correct by a majority of people within a population, such as a cultural, ethnic, or geographic group, then the relationship holds; it is accepted and considered natural by that population. In this case, it is more accurately a *population stereotype* (B. H. Kantowitz and Sorkin, 1983, p. 325) or *cultural standard* (Norman, 1988, p. 23). The relationship is considered natural for a population, but still, it is a learned relationship.

Referring again to Figure 3.15, would placing the rotary control on the opposite side of the display make a difference? According to "Warrick's principle," the display indicator should move in the same direction as the nearest point on the control (B. H. Kantowitz and Sorkin, 1983, p. 330). In this case, the mapping in Figure 3.15 is, in fact, wrong! Warrick's principle is an example of applied ergonomics, with little basis in human sensory-perceptual cognition. Wherever there is a spatial transformation, the ensuing relationship—no matter how easy we accept it or adapt to it—is learned, not natural. In the case of Warrick's principle, we might further inquire whether the principle applies equally to left-handed and right-handed users. Regardless, the best possible scenario is spatial congruence, which for a linear display implies using a sliding or linear control. This is shown in Figure 3.16. Upward movement in the control handle produces upward movement in the display reading.

Here's another example. Consider the control (switch) and display (light bulb) in Figure 3.17. There is no spatial meaning to the state of the light bulb (it is either on or off), yet the question remains: is there a natural relationship between the control and the display? As the switch is shown, is the light on or off? Your answer is influenced by where you live. If you live in the United Kingdom, the light is off. If you live in the United States or Canada, the light is on.

A tenable physical analogy is difficult to form in some situations. There is no physical analogy between the position of a switch (up, down) and the state of a light (on, off). Given a consistent recurring implementation within a geographical region, a population stereotype will emerge, even in the absence a physical analogy. And that's what happens with the switch-light interaction. People in different

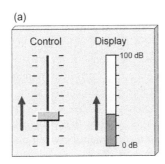

FIGURE 3.16

Spatial congruence: (a) Control and display. (b) Mapping.

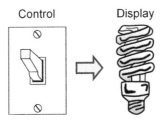

FIGURE 3.17

Culture plays a role. Is the display on or off?

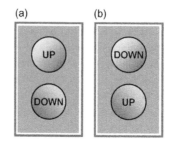

FIGURE 3.18

Button arrangements for an elevator control panel. (a) Correct. (b) Incorrect.

geographic regions have experienced and learned it differently. What is accepted in one region may differ from what is accepted in another.

If there is a physical contradiction, then the situation is different. Consider elevators (in buildings, not scrollbars). Early elevators didn't have buttons to specify floors; they only had UP and DOWN buttons. Consider the two arrangements for the button controls shown in Figure 3.18. Clearly the arrangement in (a) is superior. When the UP control is pressed, the display (the elevator) moves UP. The stimulus (control) and response (display) are compatible beyond doubt. In (b) the position of the controls is reversed. Clearly, there is an incompatibility between the stimulus and the response. This situation is different from the scroll pane example given in Figure 3.6 because there is no physical analogy to help the user (can you think of one?). If all elevator control panels had the arrangement in Figure 3.18b, would a population stereotype emerge, as with the light switch example? Well, sort of. People would learn the relationship, because they must. But they would make more errors than if the relationship was based on a correct physical mapping. This particular point has been the subject of considerable experimental testing, dating back to the 1950s (Fitts and Seeger, 1953). See also Newell (1990, 276–278) and Kantowitz and Sorkin (1983, 323–331). The gist of this work is that people take longer and commit more errors if there is a physical misalignment between displays and controls, or between controls and the responses they effect.

This work is important to HCI at the very least to highlight the challenges in designing human-computer systems. The physical analogies that human factors engineers seek out and exploit in designing better systems are few and far between in human-computer interfaces. Sure, there are physical relationships like "mouse right, cursor right," but considering the diversity of people's interactions with computers, the tasks with physical analogies are the exception. For example, what is the physical analogy for "file save"? Human-computer interfaces require a different way of thinking. Users need help—a lot of help. The use of metaphor is often helpful.

3.4 Mental models and metaphor

There is more to learning or adapting than simply experiencing. One of the most common ways to learn and adapt is through *physical analogy* (Norman, 1988, p. 23) or *metaphor* (Carroll and Thomas, 1982). Once we latch on to a physical under-standing of an interaction based on experience, it all makes sense. We've expe-rienced it, we know it, it seems natural. With a scroll pane, moving the slider up moves the *view* up. If the relationship were reversed, moving the slider up would move the *content* up. We could easily develop a physical sense of slider up → view up or slider up → content up. The up-up in each expression demonstrates the importance of finding a spatially congruent physical understanding. These two analogies require opposite control-display relationships, but either is fine and we could work with one just as easily as with the other, provided implementations were consistent across applications and platforms.

Physical analogies and metaphors are examples of the more general concept of *mental models*, also known as *conceptual models*. Mental models are common in HCI. The idea is simple enough: "What is the user's mental model of . . . ?" An association with human experience is required. HCI's first mental model was per-haps that of the office or desktop. The desktop metaphor helped users understand the graphical user interface. Today it is hard to imagine the pre-GUI era, but in the late 1970s and early 1980s, the GUI was strange. It required a new way of thinking. Designers exploited the metaphor of the office or desktop to give users a jump-start on the interface (Johnson et al., 1989). And it worked. Rather than learning some-thing new and unfamiliar, users could act out with concepts already understood: documents, folders, filing cabinets, trashcans, the top of the desk, pointing, select-ing, dragging, dropping, and so on. This is the essence of mental models.

Implementation models are to be avoided. These are systems that impose on the user a set of interactions that follow the inner workings of an application. Cooper and Reimann give the example of a software-based fax product where the user is paced through a series of agonizing details and dialogs (Cooper and Riemann, 2003, p. 25). Interaction follows an implementation model, rather than the user's mental model of how to send a fax. The user is prompted for information when it is convenient for the program to receive it, not when it makes sense to the user. Users often have pre-existing experiences with artifacts like faxes, calendars, media players, and so on. It is desirable to exploit these at every opportunity in designing a software-based product. Let's examine a few other examples in human-computer interfaces.

Toolbars in GUIs are fertile ground for mental models. To keep the buttons small and of a consistent size, they are adorned with an icon rather than a label. An icon is a pictorial representation. In HCI, icons trigger a mental image in the user's mind, a clue to a real-world experience that is similar to the action associated with the button or tool. Icons in drawing and painting applications provide good exam-ples. Figure 3.19a shows the Tool Palette in Corel's *Paint Shop Pro*, a painting and image manipulation application.[12] The palette contains 21 buttons, each displaying an icon. Each button is associated with a function and its icon is carefully chosen to elicit the association in the user's mind. Some are clear, like the magnifying glass or the paintbrush. Some are less clear. Have a look. Can you tell what action is

---

[12] www.jasc.com.

(a) (b)

FIGURE 3.19

Icons create associations. (a) Array of toolbar buttons from Corel's *Paint Shop Pro*.
(b) Tooltip help for "Picture Tube" icon.

associated with each button? Probably not. But users of this application likely know the meaning of most of these buttons.

Preparing this example gave me pause to consider my own experience with this toolbar. I use this application frequently, yet some of the buttons are entirely strange to me. In 1991 Apple introduced a method to help users like me. Hover the mouse pointer over a GUI button and a field pops up providing a terse elaboration on the button's purpose. Apple called the popups *balloons*, although today they are more commonly known as *tooltips* or *screen tips*. Figure 3.19b gives an example for a button in *Paint Shop Pro*. Apparently, the button's purpose is related to a picture tube. I'm still in the dark, but I take solace in knowing that I am just a typical user: "Each user learns the smallest set of features that he needs to get his work done, and he abandons the rest." (Cooper, 1999, p. 33)

Another example of mental models are a compass and a clock face as metaphors for direction. Most users have an ingrained understanding of a compass and a clock. The inherent labels can serve as mental models for direction. Once there is an understanding that a metaphor is present, the user has a mental model and uses it efficiently and accurately for direction: *north*, for straight ahead or up, *west* for left, and so on. As an HCI example, Lindeman et al. (2005) used the mental model of a compass to help virtual reality users navigate a building. Users wore a vibro-tactile belt with eight actuators positioned according to compass directions. They were able to navigate the virtual building using a mental model of the compass. There is also a long history in HCI of using a compass metaphor for stylus gestures with pie menus (Callahan et al., 1988) and marking menus (G. P. Kurtenbach, Sellen, and Buxton, 1993; Li, Hinckley, Guan, and Landay, 2005).

With twelve divisions, a clock provides finer granularity than a compass ("obstacle ahead at 2 o'clock!"). Examples in HCI include numeric entry (Goldstein, Chincholle, and Backström, 2000; Isokoski and Käki, 2002; McQueen, MacKenzie, and Zhang, 1995) and locating people and objects in an environment (Sáenz and Sánchez, 2009; A. Sellen, Eardley, Iazdl, and Harper, 2006). Using a clock metaphor for numeric entry with a stylus is shown in Figure 3.20. Instead of scripting numbers using Roman characters, the numbers are entered using straight-line strokes. The direction of the stroke is the number's position on a clock face. In a longitudinal study, McQueen et al. (1995) found that numeric entry was about

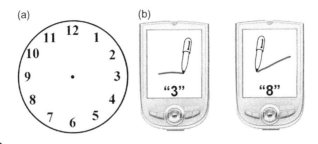

FIGURE 3.20

Mental model example: (a) Clock face. (b) Numeric entry with a stylus.

24 percent faster using straight-line strokes compared to handwritten digits. The 12 o'clock position was used for 0. The 10 o'clock and 11 o'clock positions were reserved for system commands.

Sáenz and Sánchez describe a system to assist the blind (Sáenz and Sánchez, 2009) using the clock metaphor. Users carried a mobile locating device that provided spoken audio information about the location of nearby objects (see Figure 3.21a). For the metaphor to work, the user is assumed to be facing the 12 o'clock position. The system allowed users to navigate a building eyes-free (Figure 3.21b). Users could request position and orientation information from the locator. Auditory responses were provided using the clock metaphor and a text-to-speech module (e.g., "door at 3 o'clock"). A similar interface is Rümelin et al.'s *NaviRadar* (Rümelin, Rukzio, and Hardy, 2012), which uses tactile feedback rather that auditory feedback. Although not specifically using the clock metaphor, *NaviRadar* leverages users' spatial sense of their surroundings to aid navigation. Users receive combinations of long and short vibratory pulses to indicate direction (Figure 3.21c). Although the patterns must be learned, the system is simple and avoids auditory feedback, which may be impractical in some situations.

The systems described by Sáenz and Sánchez (2009) and Rümelin et al. (2012) have similar aims yet were presented and evaluated in different ways. Sáenz and Sánchez emphasized and described the system architecture in detail. Although this is of interest to some in the HCI community, from the user's perspective the system architecture is irrelevant. A user test was reported, but the evaluation was not experimental. There were no independent or dependent variables. Users performed tasks with the system and then responded to questionnaire items, expressing their level of agreement to assertions such as "The software was motivating," or "I like the sounds in the software." While qualitative assessments are an essential component of any evaluation, the navigation and locating aides described in this work are well suited to experimental testing. Alternative implementations, even minor modifications to the interface, are potential independent variables. Speed (e.g., the time to complete tasks) and accuracy (e.g., the number of wrong turns, retries, direction changes, wall collisions) are potential dependent variables.

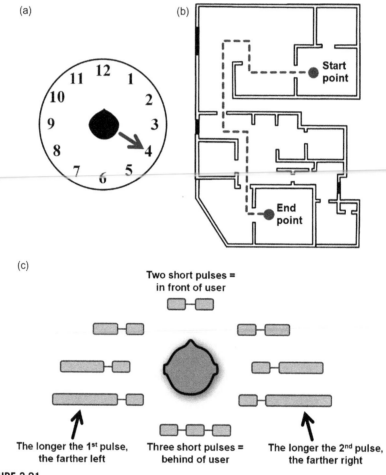

FIGURE 3.21

Spatial metaphor: (a) Auditory feedback provides information for locating objects, such as "object at 4 o'clock." (b) Navigation task. (c) NaviRadar.

(Source: b, adapted from Sáenz and Sánchez, 2009; c, adapted from Rumelin et al., 2012)

Rümelin et al. (2012) took an empirical approach to system tests. Their research included both the technical details of *NaviRadar* and an evaluation in a formal experiment with independent variables, dependent variables, and so on. The main independent variable included different intensities, durations, and rhythms in the tactile pulses. Since their approach was empirical, valuable analyses were possible. They reported, for example, the deviation of indicated and reported directions and how this varied according to direction and the type of tactile information given. Their approach enables other researchers to study the strengths and weaknesses in *NaviRadar* in empirical terms and consider methods of improvement.

3.5 **Modes**

A common and sometimes frustrating property of user interfaces is modes. A mode is "a functioning arrangement or condition." The soft controls in Figure 3.3 demonstrate modes, since every new application brings a new functioning arrangement of controls and displays. Usually, though, modes are viewed in a more limited sense, such as lowercase mode versus uppercase mode. Either way, it is a simple fact that systems of all stripes have modes.

We confront modes everywhere, often without realizing it. For example, office phones have modes: light=*on* means *message waiting*. Electric staplers have modes: LED=*on* means *add staples*. Complex physical systems, such as lawn mowers, stoves, traffic intersections, washing machines, and so on, are more challenging. If computers are involved, all bets are off. For example, some lights at traffic intersections—under computer control—include a time-of-day mode to control the advance green signal. There is an advance green signal, but only during rush hours. Or is it non-rush hours? Traffic flow may improve, but other problems may arise, such as pedestrians or motorists incorrectly anticipating a mode.

For interactive systems, challenges with modes occur because there are fewer controls than tasks. A computer keyboard is an example. A standard desktop keyboard has about 100 keys, yet can produce more than 800 key variations, using the modes afforded by modifier keys such as SHIFT, CTRL, and ALT. For example, a key might produce *a* in one mode and *A* in another. (See Figure 3.22a.) Most users are fully aware of a keyboard's shift mode. Keyboards for European languages, such as German, include three modes for some keys. (See Figure 3.22b.) No doubt, local users are comfortable with the arrangement; however, operating such a keyboard for the first time is a challenge. Still, mode problems with standard keyboards do arise. An example is when CAPS LOCK mode is on, which we'll visit later.

Is it over-reaching to ascribe modes to the A key on a keyboard? Not at all. Taking a research perspective in HCI involves finding simple ways to explain the complex. Having modes assigned to keys on a computer keyboard is worth thinking about. Taking a broad view of modes, or other elements of HCI, is a powerful approach to developing a comprehensive understanding that includes the intricate, the common, and the banal. This idea underpins *descriptive models*, where the goal is to delineate and categorize a problem space. Descriptive models are described in more detail in Chapter 7 (Modeling Interaction).

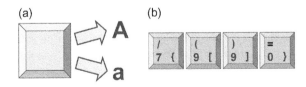

FIGURE 3.22

Keys and modes. (a) Key with two modes. (b) Keys on a German keyboard with three modes.

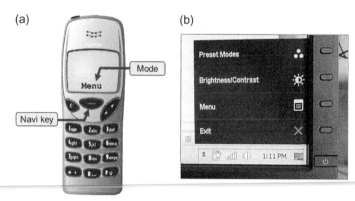

FIGURE 3.23

Physical keys with modes. (a) Navi key on the Nokia *3210* mobile phone. (b) Image adjust buttons on an LCD monitor.

Function keys have many modes. Help for Microsoft Word lists six interpretations of the F9 key. Pressed alone, it means "update selected fields." With combinations of SHIFT, CTRL, and ALT, there are five additional interpretations.

Some mobile phones have physical keys with modes. The idea first appeared in 1997 as the Navi key, introduced by Nokia (Lindholm, Keinonen, and Kiljander, 2003, p. 24). The Nokia *3210* implementation is shown in Figure 3.23a. The Navi key was embossed with only a blue horizontal line, leaving its interpretation unclear. The trick—novel at the time—was a creative use of the display. The current action (mode) of the Navi key was revealed by the word on the display immediately above the key, so the possibilities exploded. A quick look in the *3210* User Guide reveals at least 14 interpretations of the Navi key: Menu, Select, Answer, Call, End, OK, Options, Assign, Send, Read, Use, View, List, Snooze, and Yes. The word displayed above the key provided *feedback*—a feature that is crucial for systems with modes. The close proximity of the display (the word) with the control (the Navi key) alerted the user of the current mode of the Navi key and the action associated with pressing the key.

A contemporary version of the same concept is shown in Figure 3.23b. The figure shows a portion of an LCD computer monitor. There are four physical buttons above the power button (right side of image). In a general sense the buttons are used to adjust the image or configure the display; however, no purpose is indicated. Press any button and a set of associations appears on the left, superimposed on the display. Since the associations are created in software, the purpose of the buttons can change with the context of use.

If we combine the ideas above with the earlier discussion on soft controls, there is the possibility of a *mode model for keys*. Physical keys on standard keyboards are *hard keys*. They have a few modes. The Navi key and the image adjust buttons just described are *soft-hard* keys, since they involve both a physical key and a definition of the key created through software. They have lots of modes. The small regions on GUIs, shown in Figure 3.3, are the full embodiment of *soft keys*. Their size, shape, location, and function are entirely malleable. Soft keys have an infinite number of modes.

Designing modeless interactions is sometimes viewed as desirable (Ishii and Ullmer, 1997). But the truth is, modes can't be avoided in most cases. A car, for example, has at least three transmission modes: neutral, drive, and reverse. Good luck designing a modeless car.[13] The same is true of computer systems where modes are unavoidable, as demonstrated above. From a design perspective, the main issues with modes are (a) changing modes, and (b) feedback, or making the mode apparent to the user. Let's examine each of these.

Figure 3.24a shows five soft controls for switching view modes in Microsoft PowerPoint. The controls persist on the display, so they are discoverable. They are clearly apparent to the user. That's good. Furthermore, tooltips (as per Figure 3.19b) lie in wait to help the user, if necessary. Also good. Changing modes is a simple matter of clicking the desired soft button. It's all quite simple, and it works reasonably well. But still problems lurk. For example, with five view modes, there are $5 \times 4 = 20$ mode transitions. Most of these transitions are accomplished using the soft buttons shown in Figure 3.24a. However, transitioning from Slide Show mode to another mode cannot be done with the soft buttons, because they are hidden during Slide Show mode. The user must press the ESC key on the system's keyboard. Pressing ESC transitions from Slide Show mode to the previous mode. While many users know this, not all do. Can you think of an occasion when you were stuck in a mode and had to take a drastic measure to get out of it, like exiting an application or, worse yet, restarting the system?[14] Probably.

Small devices such as mobile phones, media players, watches, radios, and thermostats are more limited. They have a small display, if any, and just a few physical controls, but have lots of modes. Figure 3.24b demonstrates the method of switching modes on a sport watch. The buttons are physical, but there are only five. Changing modes requires cycling through the modes using a single button.

Making the mode apparent to the user is a long-standing principle in user interface design. The issue is the quality of feedback to the user. Shneiderman advises to "offer informative feedback" (2005, 74). Norman argues to "make things visible" (1988, 17–25). Obviously, problems arise if the user doesn't know what mode or state the system is in. A classic example is the *vi* editor in the *unix* operating system. There are two modes: command mode and insert mode. The application is launched in command mode. This is interesting in itself. If a user launches *vi* and immediately types *hello*, look out! The letters typed are interpreted as commands. The first key the user must type is *i* to enter insert mode. Hitting the ESC key switches back to command mode. (See Figure 3.25a.) Remarkably, there is no feedback marking the current mode, nor the transition between modes. Consequently, the *vi* editor is susceptible to mode errors, a phenomenon that is well documented in the HCI literature (e.g., Brewster, Wright, and Edwards, 1994; Norman, 1983; Poller and Garter, 1984; A. J. Sellen, Kurtenbach, and Buxton, 1992).

---

[13] Actually, it is possible, but the result is a separate car for each mode.

[14] Applications that include a full screen view mode typically use ESC to transition out of full screen mode. But this is not always the case. Users of Mozilla Firefox are invited to investigate this.

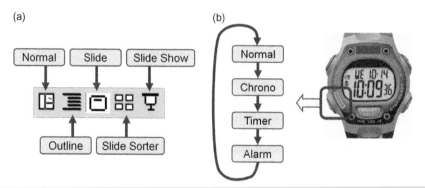

FIGURE 3.24

Changing modes: (a) Dedicated soft buttons on Microsoft PowerPoint change the view mode. (b) A single physical button on a sport watch cycles through watch modes.

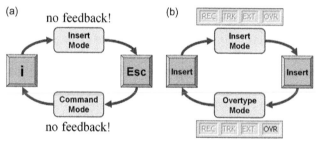

FIGURE 3.25

Changing modes and mode visibility: (a) *vi* editor. (b) Microsoft Word.

The text editor *vi* is a legacy application emblematic of pre-GUI text-based command-line interaction. Most *vi* users were computer specialists—expert users. GUI-based systems necessitate a higher standard of usability, since they are targeted at a broad base of users, many of whom are not computer professionals per se. This point was argued in Chapter 1. Yet problems still exist. Similar to the *vi* example is Insert versus Overtype mode in Microsoft Word. (See Figure 3.25b.) Word's default mode is Insert. In Insert mode, typed text appears within existing text. In Overtype mode, typed text overwrites existing text. There are two problems with this system: changing modes and mode visibility. Changing modes uses the INSERT key. Simple enough, but a quick look at keyboard images reveals considerable variability in the location of the Insert key.[15] Seems the INSERT key is not important enough to have entrenched itself in a consistent location. And for good reason. Many users rarely, if ever, use this key. Furthermore, Insert is sometimes on a key with modes. In

---

[15] Many keyboard layouts can be found at http://images.google.com. The INSERT key may appear (a) along the top row of function keys, (b) in the numeric keypad, (c) in the block above the arrow keys, or (d) along the bottom row in the main keyboard.

"normal mode" the key means one thing (perhaps Insert); in "function-lock mode," it means something else. So the INSERT key may be pressed by accident, if there is confusion on the current mode of the key. This amounts to a "mode within a mode." So changing modes is a potential problem with the INSERT key. Mode visibility is also a problem. There is feedback (see Figure 3.25b), but it is in a small display along the bottom of the screen. It is so subtle that many users are not likely to notice it. Furthermore, a user who inadvertently enters Overtype mode may not have a linguistic association of overtype with the problem they are experiencing. What is OVR? This is an example of a *gulf of evaluation*—a disconnect between what the system provides and what the user intends and expects (Norman, 1988, p. 51).[16]

From an empirical research perspective, it is worth thinking about ways to improve interaction that involves modes. Feedback is the critical issue. Can audio feedback improve a user's awareness of mode transitions? Can a larger visual indication help, and if so, what are the trade-offs? Is mode awareness improved if a large visual indication appears in the center of the screen when a mode is entered, and then shrinks to a small persistent mode display at the bottom of the screen? See also student exercises 3-5 and 3-6 at the end of this chapter.

Modes are common in graphics and 3D interaction. Consider the control-display operations in Figure 3.26. In (a) the hand + mouse movement combines side-to-side and forward-backward motion. The object manipulated on the display moves similarly. Of course, the hand + mouse motion is on the desktop, or x-z plane, while the object motion is on the display, or x-y plane, using the labeling in Figure 3.5. Despite the spatial incongruence, users are accustomed to this (learned) relationship. In Figure 3.26b the hand + mouse action includes a sweeping or rotating motion. There is an additional deficiency here. Note that the final position of the triangle is the same in (a) and (b). Yet the hand + mouse movements were different. Let's examine this in more detail.

If the user wanted the triangle to move with the hand + mouse, then there is a breakdown in the interaction. This occurs because of a gap between the capabilities of 2D pointing devices, such as a mouse, and the characteristics of a 2D surface. The typical fix is a *rotate mode*. To rotate the triangle in a typical graphics application, a few steps are involved: (1) select the triangle, (2) select the application's rotate tool, (3) acquire a handle on the triangle, (4) drag the handle. This is shown in Figure 3.27. Part (a) shows the Microsoft PowerPoint rotate tool, with instructions below on using it. Part (b) shows the triangle being rotated. Side-to-side x-axis motion or forward-backward z-axis motion of the mouse rotates the triangle. There is clearly a disconnect. We manage, but the interaction is awkward and difficult. For one, translation of the triangle is prevented while in rotate mode. This control-display relationship is anything but natural.

---

[16]User frustration with Insert versus Overtype mode in Microsoft Word is a well-worn discussion in online help forums. With Office 2010, the insert key is disabled by default but is enabled through a setting in the Options | Advanced dialog box. If enabled, the INSERT key toggles between Insert mode and Overtype mode; however, there is no feedback indicating the current mode.

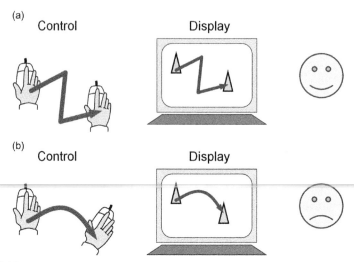

FIGURE 3.26

Two-dimensional movement with the hand + mouse: (a) x and y displacement only. (b) z-axis rotation of the hand + mouse is not sensed, so the object on the display undergoes x and y displacement only.

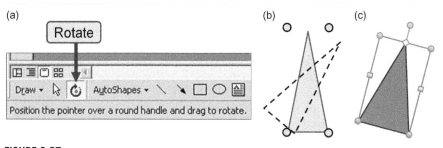

FIGURE 3.27

Rotate mode: (a) Microsoft PowerPoint's rotate tool is selected, with instructions below on using it. (b) The selected triangle enters rotate mode. The x and y displacement of the mouse with the button down (dragging) is used to rotate the triangle. (c) Newer version of PowerPoint. Rotate handle appears when triangle is selected.

In newer versions of PowerPoint, a rotate handle appears whenever an object is selected. (See Figure 3.27c.) This eliminates the need for a rotate mode. However, the control-display relationships are the same—one mapping for rotation, a separate mapping for translation.

Another way to eliminate the rotate mode in 2D is to reengineer a mouse to sense rotation. Several configurations are possible. Almeida and Cubaud (2006) glued two small mice together. (See Figure 3.28a.) MacKenzie et al. (1997) put the mechanical and electrical components of two mice into a single chassis. (See

(a)   (b)   (c)

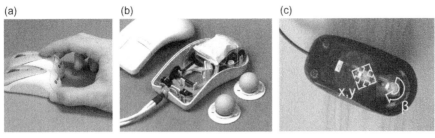

FIGURE 3.28

Mouse configurations sensing rotation: (a) Two small mice glued together (Almeida and Cubaud, 2006). (b) The components from two mice assembled in a single chassis (MacKenzie et al., 1997). (c) Optical mouse with additional camera for rotation.

(Source: a, photo courtesy of Rodrigo Almeida; c, Hannagan and Regenbrecht, 2008; Photo courtesy of Holger Regenbrecht)

Figure 3.28b.) Contemporary designs are more likely to use camera technology. Hannagan and Regenbrecht's (2008) *TwistMouse* is an example. (See Figure 3.28c.) The latter two configurations are advantageous from the user's perspective, since the device has the look and feel of a conventional mouse. For all the examples in Figure 3.28, the prototype is equivalent to two mice and requires a custom driver to handle both data streams. If the device is maneuvered with x- and z-axis displacement only, the two data streams are the same. If movement includes y-axis rotation, the two data streams are slightly different. With a little trigonometry, the driver is able to produce y-axis rotation data coincident with x- and z-axis translation. Thus, an acquired object can undergo translation and rotation at the same time.

There are interesting design issues for 3 DOF mice. Usually the extra DOF is not needed; the rotation data can be ignored most of the time. When a task requires both translation and rotation, a modifier key can engage the third DOF. This in itself is interesting. Recall that this analysis began as an effort to eliminate the rotate mode in graphics applications. Yet the solution includes modes: a 2 DOF translate-only mode and a 3 DOF translate + rotate mode.

Another challenge is in accommodating the biomechanics of the lower arm. It is difficult to effect the required wrist movement if an on-screen object is rotated through a wide angle, such as 200 degrees. A solution is to use another modifier key to amplify the angular mapping of mouse rotation. This is somewhat analogous to CD gain, except the gain is applied to rotation. Hinckley et al. (1999) take a different approach. Their system is camera-based, with a mouse pad serving as the ground plane for the camera image. They propose a two-handed technique: one hand manipulates and rotates the mouse, while the other hand counter-rotates the mouse pad. Large rotation angles are thereby possible.

Although 3 DOF mice demo well, a complete bottom-up redesign is necessary for deployment as a product. Today's optical mice are well suited to this. Since the built-in camera captures 2D images (e.g., 18 × 18) of the desktop surface at 1,000+

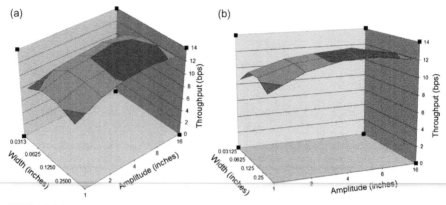

FIGURE 3.29

Two views of the same data in the same chart. 3D rotation is performed by dragging a handle (small black square) with the mouse.

frames per second, it should be relatively easy to determine the rotational component of mouse movement without a second camera (as used in the TwistMouse; see Figure 3.28c). However, turning such initiatives into products is easier said than done. Besides re-engineering the hardware and firmware, a new driver protocol is needed (with y-axis rotation data) along with modifications to applications to effectively use the full potential of 3 DOF data.

The situation is more complicated in 3D environments, since there are six degrees of freedom (see Figure 3.7). If the input controller has fewer than six degrees of freedom, then modes are needed to fully access the environment. A particularly unnatural interaction is shown in Figure 3.29. The figure shows a 3D data plot.[17] (It is known as a "surface chart" in Microsoft *Excel*.) Part (a) shows one view. To alter the view, the chart is selected. Handles (small black squares) appear and rotate mode is entered. A handle is acquired and dragged with the mouse, much like the 2D rotation presented above. A rotated view of the data is shown in part (b). But the interaction is clumsy. Rotation about two axes is supported, but it is extremely difficult to control. One is never quite sure what effect a particular mouse movement will produce. Interaction degrades to trial and error.

Desktop systems are simply inappropriate for this sort of interaction. If 3D is the goal, then a more sophisticated setup is needed. Typically, different or additional devices are used to provide more natural control-display relationships. These systems may include a head-mounted display and a 6 DOF motion tracker to provide an improved view of 3D objects in 3D space. Not only is the head position tracked with six degrees of freedom, the image provided to each eye is altered slightly to provide depth cues, making the virtual scene appear three-dimensional.

---

[17]The data are from the pin-transfer task in Fitts', 1954 paper (Fitts, 1954, Table 3). Fitts includes a hand-drawn 3D plot similar to that shown here (Fitts, 1954, Figure 4).

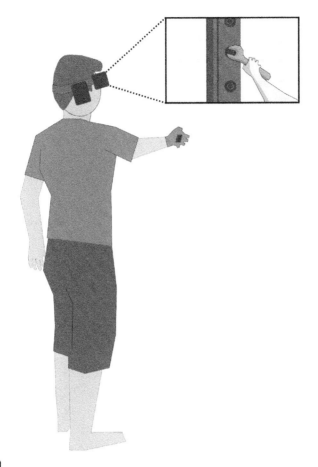

FIGURE 3.30

A head-mounted display along with 6 DOF head and hand trackers provides 3D viewing and control.

(Sketch courtesy of Bartosz Bajer)

With the addition of a 6 DOF hand tracker, more powerful 3D control is possible. An example setup is shown in Figure 3.30 (see also Garau et al., 2003).

3.6 More about degrees of freedom

The research literature in HCI has numerous examples of devices engineered to provide additional sensing capabilities. The *Rockin'Mouse* is a 4 DOF mouse with a rounded bottom (Balakrishnan, Baudel, Kurtenbach, and Fitzmaurice, 1997). It senses planar *x-z* movement, like a regular mouse, but also senses rocking side-to-side (Θ_z) and to-and-fro (Θ_x) rotation. (See Figure 3.31.)

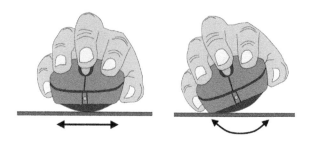

FIGURE 3.31

The Rockin'Mouse works like a mouse but also senses side-to-side (θ_z) rotation (shown) and forward-backward (θ_x) rotation. (Balakrishnan et al., 1997). Rotation about the y-axis is not sensed.

(Sketch courtesy of Bartosz Bajer)

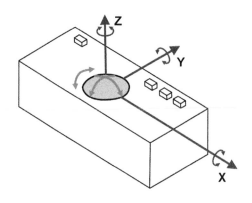

FIGURE 3.32

Three-axis trackball.

(Adapted from Evans et al., 1981)

The prototype operated on the surface of a tablet. A cordless sensor was mounted in the center of the Rockin'Mouse. The sensor was extracted from the tablet's stylus. From the tablet's perspective, the Rockin'Mouse is a stylus. From the user's perspective, it looks and feels like a mouse, except for the rounded body. The tablet senses and reports the x and z positions of the sensor as well as tilt (Θ_x and Θ_z). Balakrishnan et al. (1997) evaluated the Rockin'Mouse in a 3D positioning task using tilt for the up-down movement of the object. In the mouse comparison condition, participants had to select a handle on the object to switch movement modes. Overall, the Rockin'Mouse was about 30 percent faster than the standard mouse.

Evans et al. (1981) describe a three-axis trackball that senses rotation about each of the x-, y-, and z-axes. (See Figure 3.32.) Even though the usual operation of a trackball is x-y planar control of a cursor, the ball rotates, so the labeling of the degrees of freedom in Figure 3.32 is appropriate. A device like this would likely perform quite well in controlling the view of the 3D surface plot in Figure 3.29.

FIGURE 3.33

Etch-A-Sketch children's toy with separate controls for the *x* and *y* degrees of freedom.[18]

Of course, it is relatively easy to include modes, allowing the trackball to also operate in mouse-emulation mode.

There is more to degrees of freedom than simply counting them. It is important to consider the relationship between device properties, such as degrees of freedom, and task requirements. Jacob et al. (1994) speak of the *integrality* and *separability* of the degrees of freedom. With a regular mouse, controlling one degree of freedom in isolation of the other is difficult. Consider drawing a horizontal line with a mouse using the drawing mode of an application. The task is difficult because the *x* and *y* degrees of freedom are integrated. Of course, degrees of freedom can be separated. A classic example for *x-y* positioning is the children's toy *Etch-A-Sketch* introduced in the 1950s by the Ohio Art Company. (See Figure 3.33.) There are separate 1 DOF controllers to move the drawing instrument along the *x-* and *y*-axes. Drawing a horizontal line is easy. Drawing a diagonal line is a challenge, however. See Buxton (1986) for additional discussion on input using the Etch-A-Sketch and other toys.

Another example for *x-y* positioning is the wheel mouse, released in 1996 as Microsoft's *IntelliMouse*. (See Figure 3.34a.) The rotating wheel gives the mouse an extra—and separate—degree of freedom. A less successful version was Mouse System's *ProAgio*, released about a year earlier. (See Figure 3.34b.) Even earlier was Venolia's *Roller Mouse* (1993), presented at the annual ACM *SIGCHI* conference in 1993. (See Figure 3.34c.) The Roller Mouse had two wheels. The primary intention with the Roller Mouse was to control the many, and often separate, degrees of freedom in 3D graphics applications.

Additional but separate degrees of freedom are evident in Balakrishnan and Patel's *PadMouse* (1998). (See Figure 3.35a.) A touchpad was added to the surface of a regular mouse. The intent was to support pie menu access with gestures on the touchpad while the mouse operated as usual, controlling an on-screen cursor.

---

[18] From the Buxton Collection (http://research.microsoft.com).

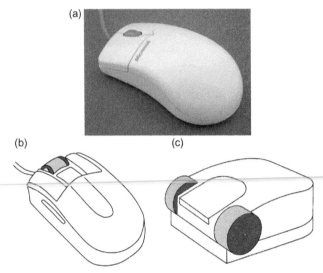

FIGURE 3.34

Wheel mice: (a) Microsoft's Intellimouse. (b) Mouse Systems' ProAgio. (c) *Roller Mouse* research prototype.

(Source: b, adapted from Gillick and Lam, 1996; c, adapted from Venolia and Ishikawa, 1994)

Clearly, combining interaction in this manner requires separating the degrees of freedom for pie menu access and cursor control.

Silfverberg et al. (2003) describe a display screen that allows the displayed image to be zoomed and panned by two touch sensors positioned underneath the device (See Figure 3.34b.). An obvious advantage is that occlusion is avoided since the fingers act below the display. Also, the 1 DOF zooming and 2 DOF panning operations are separated and thus do not interfere.

Villar et al. (2009) describe a variety of mouse configurations instrumented to detect touch, including *multi-touch*. The devices use infrared (IR) transmitters that inject light into the edge of an acrylic surface. An IR camera below the surface receives an image of the surface. When fingers contact the surface, the light is scattered at the points of contact. Image processing software determines the location and pressure of the points of contact. Some of the device configurations are shown in Figure 3.36. The devices support multi-touch gestures as well as regular mouse operations.

One configuration for touch detection is the CapMouse (second from left in Figure 3.36). It uses a capacitive sensor rather than an IR transmitter and camera. The setup is similar to Balakrishnan and Patel's PadMouse (Figure 3.35a), except the touch-sensing surface is contoured and seamlessly integrates with the device chassis.

The message in this section is that degrees of freedom (DOF) is a property that spans a rich complement of tasks and interaction techniques. User interactions are

(a)

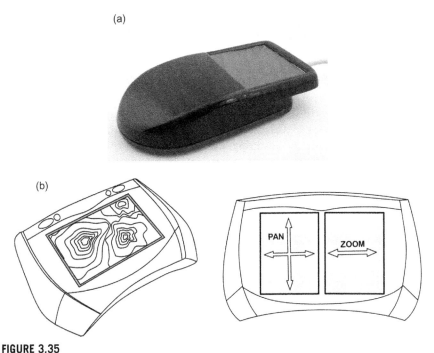

(b)

FIGURE 3.35

Adding degrees of freedom with a touchpad: (a) PadMouse (Balakrishnan and Patel, 1998).[19] (b) Zooming and panning display screen (Silfverberg, Korhonen, and MacKenzie, 2003), top view (*left*), bottom view (*right*).

FIGURE 3.36

Multi-touch sensing input devices (Villar et al., 2009).

(Photo courtesy of Nicolas Villar)

plentiful, and they are juxtaposed in complex ways, such as overlapping, sequential, and in parallel. The degrees of freedom in the interactions merit deeper consideration. Opportunities for empirical research are plentiful. Let's move on to the unique interactions in the world of mobile computing.

---

[19]From the Buxton Collection (http://research.microsoft.com).

3.7 Mobile context

Mobile computing dates to the 1980s, with the emergence of pocket organizers and personal digital assistants (PDAs). This was followed in the early 1990s with the first pen-based tablet computers and mobile phones supporting text messaging. The 2007 release of the Apple iPhone was a significant event from a user interface standpoint. With the arrival of the iPhone and follow-on products, such as touch-based tablet computers, the landscape of HCI experienced a dramatic shift. Pressing keys on small keyboards or gesturing with a stylus gave way to finger actions: swiping, flicking, pinching, tapping, and so on. Furthermore, devices in this genre include additional components to enhance the user experience. Cameras, light sensors, vibro-tactile actuators, accelerometers, gyroscopes, GPS receivers, and so on work together in broadening the experience for users. With the prefix "smart," these devices are full-fledged media players, providing unprecedented connectivity to users through both Third Generation (3G) and Internet access.

Many of the interaction elements noted above for desktop environments don't even exist in the mobile context. This follows from the distinction between indirect input and direct input. Cursor control using a mouse or touchpad is an example of *indirect input* because the system response is spatially displaced from the input device. Finger input on a touch-sensitive display uses *direct input* because the system response is located at the point of touch. On a touch-sensitive display, a cursor or on-screen tracking symbol is not needed. Properties like control-display mappings and CD gain do not exist for direct input. Mouse-based systems, on the other hand, *require* an on-screen tracking symbol such as a cursor or pointer. Of course, this is a by-product of indirect input. Direct touch input is the full embodiment of WYSIWYG interaction – *what you see is what you get*. A simple example on a tablet computer appears in Figure 3.37. A slider to control screen brightness appears on the tablet's display (left). The finger interacts directly with the slider (right).

FIGURE 3.37

Example of direct input: A slider GUI element to control the display brightness (*expanded, left*) is engaged directly by the user's finger (*right*).

However, direct touch input has an unfortunate side effect: precise pixel-level selection is difficult. On a desktop system, the tip of the on-screen pointer visually identifies the selection point. With touchscreens, users typically do not know, and cannot control, the precise location of the contact point. There are two reasons: (1) the finger occludes the location of contact, and (2) finger contact forms an area, not a point. These issues are sometimes called the "fat finger problem" (Wigdor, Forlines, Baudisch, Barnwell, and Shen, 2007) and follow from the physiology of the human finger. The size and shape of the contact area varies from user to user and also by usage patterns, such as the force applied or the reach of the arm.

New technologies bring possibilities, which in turn bring challenges. With challenges come ideas for solutions. Early research on touchscreens focused on their use in information kiosks. Improving the precision of pointing was a key challenge. How can occlusion and precision be accommodated for touch input? Are there alternate methods to consider and, if so, which ones perform better? These are the sorts of questions that underpin empirical research in HCI. One of the earliest selection enhancements for touchscreens was the *offset cursor* presented by Potter et al. (1988) at the ACM SIGCHI conference in 1988.[20] When the finger contacts the display surface, a crosshair cursor appears just above the fingertip. The user maneuvers his or her finger along the display surface, positions the cursor within a selectable target, then lifts the finger to select the target. Potter et al. called the method *take-off selection*. They described an experimental evaluation to compare take-off selection with two alternate methods, *first-contact*, where selection occurs immediately when the contact point enters a target, and *land-on*, where selection occurs only if the initial contact point is on a target. Of the three methods, they found take-off most accurate, but first-contact fastest. The main point here is that Potter et al. chose a methodology that was both empirical and experimental to present and evaluate a novel interaction method and to compare it with alternatives.

Variations on Potter et al.'s offset cursor combined with take-off selection are seen in contemporary touchscreen devices. The most recognizable is perhaps the soft keyboard on the Apple *iPhone*. Figure 3.38a shows a portion of the keyboard, including the D key. In Figure 3.38b, the user's finger is in contact with the D key. The key is occluded. However, an offset animation alerts the user that the D key is tentatively selected. The user may slide his or her finger to another key or lift the finger to enter D.

Yet another difference between touch input and mouse input is the ability of touch-sensing technologies to sense multiple contact points. Indeed, multi-touch is one of the most provocative interaction techniques to enter mainstream computing in recent years. An example is shown in Figure 3.39 where a map is maneuvered by a sliding gesture, then resized with a two-finger reverse pinching gesture.

---

[20]Unfortunately, an image of the offset cursor in use was not included in the cited paper or in related papers. However, a video by Sears and Shneiderman from 1991 shows the offset cursor. (Search YouTube using "1991_touchscreenkeyboards.mpg.")

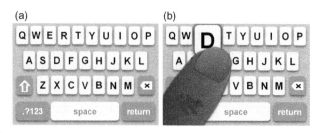

FIGURE 3.38

Enhancing touchscreen selection: (a) Apple iPhone soft keyboard. (b) User finger on D key. Selection occurs on finger lift.

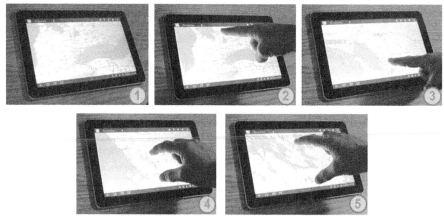

FIGURE 3.39

Touch example: A map image (1) is moved by touching the map (2) and dragging the finger (3). The image is zoomed in by touching with two fingers (4) and widening the distance between the fingers (5).

Multi-touch does not end at two points of contact. Recent devices can sense several contact points. Figure 3.40a is a multi-touch demonstration on a Samsung Galaxy Tab 10.1 running the Android 3.1 operating system. Ten contact points are sensed. Although the thumb contacts are partly occluded in the image, ten contact points are apparent. They appear as large colored circles. Beginning with the pinkie contact on the right, the circles follow the color coding for numbers on electronic resistors: black (0), brown (1), red (2), orange (3), yellow (4), green (5), blue (6), violet (7), grey (8), and white (9).

It is easy to imagine applications for input using multiple contacts points (>2). A simple example is the piano keyboard in Figure 3.40b. This was suggested as early as 1985 as an application of the multi-touch input system described by Lee et al. (1985). Lee et al.'s system also sensed pressure (as do contemporary touch-sensitive displays). With added pressure data, both the pitch and loudness of notes

(a)

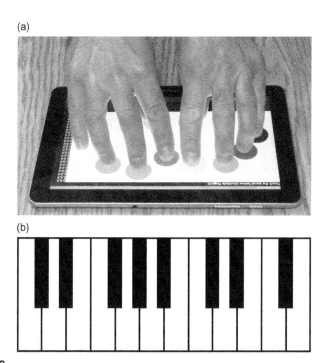

(b)

FIGURE 3.40

Multi-touch demonstration: (a) Ten contact points are sensed. Markers, beginning with the user's pinkie finger on the right, follow the color codes for electronic resistors. (b) Piano keyboard application.

can be controlled upon finger contact. Multi-touch piano keyboard applications are readily downloadable for Android tablets.

Besides the use of multi-touch, today's mobile devices include a host of additional components. A good example is the accelerometer. The technology has matured in terms of pricing, size, data speed, precision, and power consumption to the point where accelerometers are now a standard component in most touchscreen phones and tablet computers. An accelerometer allows the angle or tilt of the device to be sensed. Tilt as an input primitive has entered the mainstream of interaction techniques in mobile computing.

Early research on tilt, dating to the 1990s, examined its potential for tasks such as document scrolling (Bartlett, 2000; B. Harrison et al., 1998; Small and Ishii, 1997), panning and zooming (Small and Ishii, 1997), menu navigation (Rekimoto, 1996), and changing screen orientation (Hinckley, Pierce, Sinclair, and Horvitz, 2000). As with any new technology, research initially focused on what can be done rather than on how well it can be done. The focus was on the technology and its integration in prototype devices. Test results with users tended to be anecdotal, not empirical. In fact, tilt is a user input primitive that is well suited to empirical inquiry. For each of the tasks just cited, several input methods either currently exist or can be envisioned as alternatives. Implementing the tasks using tilt is novel and exciting. But how well can the tasks be executed? How does tilt input compare to alternative methods in terms of human performance? What aspects of tilt influence human performance? These questions are well suited to empirical inquiry. One such evaluation for tilt has recently been completed. The evaluation tested four settings of tilt gain: 25, 50, 100, 200 (MacKenzie and Teather, 2012).[21] The experiment used a position-select task similar to the multi-direction task in ISO 9241-9 (ISO 2000; Soukoreff and MacKenzie, 2004). Results suggest that performance is best (i.e., lower task completion time, higher throughput) for a tilt gain setting in the range of 50 to 100.

Another interesting application of accelerometer input is a *spatially aware display*. In this case, a view on the display moves as the device moves, as sensed by the accelerometer. (See Figure 3.41.) A variety of new issues arise. For planar 2D movement, the interaction is straightforward. But what if the device rotates, or moves in and out. How should the view change? Is the interaction fluid and natural? These issues are well-suited to empirical inquiry. Experimental studies of spatially aware displays are reported by Fitzmaurice (1993), Rohs and Oulasvirta (2008), Cao et al. (2008), and others.

If there is one observation that emerges from the annual ACM SIGCHI conference, it is that the pace of innovation in HCI is increasing. New technologies and new ideas for interactions are plentiful and they are emerging quickly. They are often presented, like tilt was initially, as possibilities. Prototypes, demos, videos, posters, work-in-progress contributions, and so on, get the ideas out there. But sooner or later, plausible ideas need testing with users. Testing that is empirical and experimental is recommended. The results will add to the knowledge base that engineers and designers draw upon in bringing to market new and cool products.

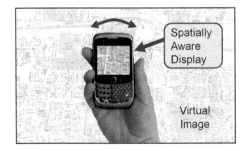

FIGURE 3.41

Spatially aware display. As the device moves, the view into the virtual image moves.

---

[21] Tilt gain is a multiplier that maps the magnitude of device tilt (degrees) to the velocity of an object on the display (pixels per second).

3.8 **Interaction errors**

Most of analyses in this chapter are directed at the physical properties of the human-machine interface, such as degrees of freedom in 2D or 3D or spatial and temporal relationships between input controllers and output displays. Human performance, although elaborated in Chapter 2, has not entered into discussions here, except through secondary observations that certain interactions are better, worse, awkward, or unintuitive. At the end of the day, however, human performance is what counts. Physical properties, although instructive and essential, are secondary. Put another way, human performance is like food, while physical properties are like plates and bowls. It is good and nutritious food that we strive for.

Empirical research in HCI is largely about finding the physical properties and combinations that improve and enhance human performance. We conclude this chapter on interaction elements with comments on that nagging aspect of human performance that frustrates users: interaction errors. Although the time to complete a task can enhance or hinder by degree, errors only hinder. Absence of errors is, for the most part, invisible. As it turns out, errors—interaction errors—are germane to the HCI experience. The big errors are the easy ones—they get fixed. It is the small errors that are interesting.

As the field of HCI matures, a common view that emerges is that the difficult problems (in desktop computing) are solved, and now researchers should focus on new frontiers: mobility, surface computing, ubiquitous computing, online social networking, gaming, and so on. This view is partially correct. Yes, the emerging themes are exciting and fertile ground for HCI research, and many frustrating UI problems from the old days are gone. But desktop computing is still fraught with problems, lots of them. Let's examine a few of these. Although the examples below are from desktop computing, there are counterparts in mobile computing. See also student exercise 3-8 at the end of this chapter.

The four examples developed in the following discussion were chosen for a specific reason. There is a progression between them. In severity, they range from serious problems causing loss of information to innocuous problems that most users rarely think about and may not even notice. In frequency, they range from rarely, if ever, occurring any more, to occurring perhaps multiple times every minute while users engage in computing activities. The big, bad problems are well-traveled in the literature, with many excellent sources providing deep analyses on what went wrong and why (e.g., Casey, 1998, 2006; Cooper, 1999; Johnson, 2007;

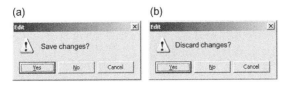

FIGURE 3.42

HCI has come a long way: (a) Today's UIs consistently use the same, predictable dialog to alert the user to a potential loss of information. (b) Legacy dialog rarely (if ever) seen today.

B. H. Kantowitz and Sorkin, 1983; Norman, 1988). While the big problems get lots of attention, and generally get fixed, the little ones tend to linger. We'll see the effect shortly. Let's begin with one of the big problems.

Most users have, at some point, lost information while working on their computers. Instead of saving new work, it was mistakenly discarded, overwritten, or lost in some way. Is there any user who has not experienced this? Of course, nearly everyone has a story of losing data in some silly way. Perhaps there was a distraction. Perhaps they just didn't know what happened. It doesn't matter. It happened. An example is shown in Figure 3.42. A dialog box pops up and the user responds a little too quickly. Press ENTER with the "Save changes?" dialog box (Figure 3.42a) and all is well, but the same response with the "Discard changes?" dialog box spells disaster (Figure 3.42b). The information is lost. This scenario, told by Cooper (1999, 14), is a clear and serious UI design flaw. The alert reader will quickly retort, "Yes, but if the 'Discard changes?' dialog box defaults to 'No,' the information is safe." But that misses the point. The point is that a user expectation is broken. Broken expectations sooner or later cause errors.

Today, systems and applications consistently use the "Save changes?" dialog box in Figure 3.42a. With time and experience, user expectations emerge and congeal. The "Save changes?" dialog box is expected, so we act without hesitating and all is well. But new users have no experiences, no expectations. They will develop them sure enough, but there will be some scars along the way. Fortunately, serious flaws like the "Discard changes?" dialog box are rare in desktop applications today.

The following is another error to consider. If prompted to enter a password, and CAPS_LOCK mode is in effect, logging on will fail and the password must be reentered. The user may not know that CAPS_LOCK is on. Perhaps a key-stroking error occurred. The password is reentered, slowly and correctly, with the CAPS_LOCK mode still in effect. Oops! Commit the same error a third time and further log-on attempts may be blocked. This is not as serious as losing information by pressing ENTER in response to a renegade dialog box, but still, this is an interaction error. Or is it a design flaw? It is completely unnecessary, it is a nuisance, it slows our interaction, and it is easy to correct. Today, many systems have corrected this problem (Figure 3.43a), while others have not (Figure 3.43b).

The CAPS_LOCK error is not so bad. But it's bad enough that it occasionally receives enough attention to be the beneficiary of the few extra lines of code necessary to pop up a CAPS_LOCK alert.

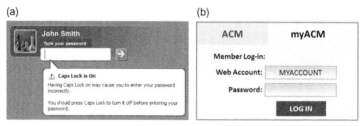

FIGURE 3.43

Entering a password: (a) Many systems alert the user if CAPS_LOCK is on. (b) Others do not.

Let's examine another small problem. In editing a document, suppose the user wishes move some text to another location in the document. The task is easy. With the pointer positioned at the beginning of the text, the user presses and holds the primary mouse button and begins dragging. But the text spans several lines and extends past the viewable region. As the dragging extent approaches the edge of the viewable region, the user is venturing into a difficult situation. The interaction is about to change dramatically. (See Figure 3.44.) Within the viewable region, the interaction is position-control—the displacement of the mouse pointer controls the *position* of the dragging extent. As soon as the mouse pointer moves outside the viewable region, scrolling begins and the interaction becomes velocity-control—the displacement of the mouse pointer now controls the *velocity* of the dragging extent. User beware!

Once in velocity-control mode, it is anyone's guess what will happen. This is a design flaw. A quick check of several applications while working on this example revealed dramatically different responses to the transition from position control to velocity control. In one case, scrolling was so fast that the dragging region extended to the end of the document in less time than the user could react ($\approx 200\,\text{ms}$). In another case, the velocity of scrolling was controllable but frustratingly slow. Can you think of a way to improve this interaction? A two-handed approach, perhaps. Any technique that gets the job done and allows the user to develop an expectation of the interaction is an improvement. Perhaps there is some empirical research waiting in this area.

Whether the velocity-control is too sensitive or too sluggish really doesn't matter. What matters is that the user experience is broken or awkward. Any pretense to the interaction being facile, seamless, or transparent is gone. The user will recover, and no information will be lost, but the interaction has degraded to error recovery. This is a design error or, at the very least, a design-induced error. Let's move on to a very minor error.

When an application or a dialog box is active, one of the UI components has focus and receives an event from the keyboard if a key is pressed. For buttons,

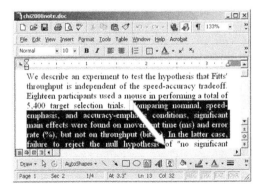

FIGURE 3.44

On the brink of hyper-speed scrolling. As the mouse pointer is dragged toward the edge of the viewable region, the user is precipitously close to losing control over the speed of dragging.

focus is usually indicated with a dashed border (see "Yes" button in Figure 3.42). For input fields, it is usually indicated with a flashing insertion bar ("|"). "Focus advancement" refers to the progression of focus from one UI component to the next. There is wide-spread inconsistency in current applications in the way UI widgets acquire and lose focus and in the way focus advances from one component to the next. The user is in trouble most of the time. Here is a quick example. When a login dialog box pops up, can you immediately begin to enter your username and password? Sometimes yes, sometimes no. In the latter case, the entry field does not have focus. The user must click in the field with the mouse pointer or press TAB to advance the focus point to the input field. Figure 3.43 provides examples. Both are real interfaces. The username field in (a) appears with focus; the same field in (b) appears without focus. The point is simply that users don't know. This is a small problem (or is it an interaction error?), but it is entirely common. Focus uncertainty is everywhere in today's user interfaces. Here is another, more specific example:

Many online activities, such as reserving an airline ticket or booking a vacation, require a user to enter data into a form. The input fields often require very specific information, such as a two-digit month, a seven-digit account number, and so on. When the information is entered, does focus advance automatically or is a user action required? Usually, we just don't know. So we remain "on guard." Figure 3.45 gives a real example from a typical login dialog box. The user is first requested to enter an account number. Account numbers are nine digits long, in three three-digit segments. After seeing the dialog box, the user looks at the keyboard and begins entering: 9, 8, 0, and then what? Chances are the user is looking at the keyboard while entering the numeric account number. Even though the user can enter the entire nine digits at once, interaction is halted after the first three-digit group because the user doesn't know if the focus will automatically advance to the next field. There are no expectations here, because this example of GUI interaction has not evolved and stabilized to a consistent pattern. Data entry fields have not reached the evolutionary status of, for example, dialog boxes for saving versus discarding changes (Figure 3.42a). The user either acts, with an approximately 50 percent likelihood of committing an error, or pauses to attend to the display (*Has the focus advanced to the next field?*).

Strictly speaking, there is no gulf of evaluation here. Although not shown in the figure, the insertion point is present. After entering *980*, the insertion point is either after the *0* in the first field, if focus did not advance, or at the beginning of the next field, if focus advanced. So the system does indeed "provide a physical

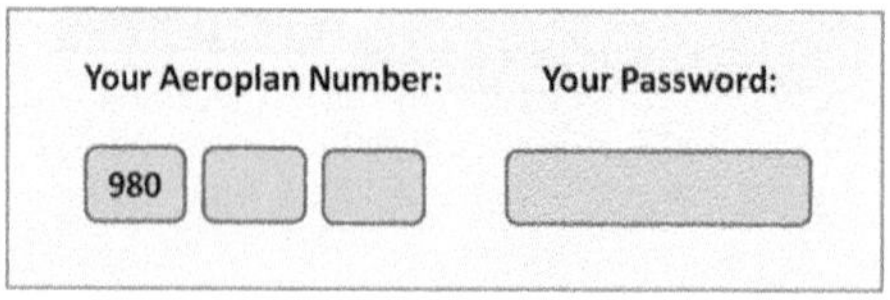

FIGURE 3.45

Inconsistent focus advancement keeps the user on guard. "What do I do next?"

representation that can be perceived and that is directly interpretable in terms of the intentions and expectations of the person" (Norman, 1988, p. 51). That's not good enough. The user's attention is on the keyboard while the physical presentation is on the system's display. The disconnect is small, but nevertheless, a shift in the user's attention is required.

The absence of expectations keeps the user on guard. The user is often never quite sure what to do or what to expect. The result is a slight increase in the attention demanded during interaction, which produces a slight decrease in transparency. Instead of engaging in the task, attention is diverted to the needs of the computer. The user is like a wood carver who sharpens tools rather than creates works of art.

Where the consequences of errors are small, such as an extra button click or a gaze shift, errors tend to linger. For the most part, these errors aren't on anyone's radar. The programmers who build the applications have bigger problems to focus on, like working on their checklist of new features to add to version 2.0 of the application before an impending deadline.[22] The little errors persist. Often, programmers' discretion rules the day (Cooper, 1999, p. 47). An interaction scenario that makes sense to the programmer is likely to percolate through to the final product, particularly if it is just a simple thing like focus advancement. Do programmers ever discuss the nuances of focus advancement in building a GUI? Perhaps. But was the discussion framed in terms of the impact on the attention or gaze shifts imposed on the user? Not likely.

Each time a user shifts his or her attention (e.g., from the keyboard to the display and back), the cost is two gaze shifts. Each gaze shift, or saccade, takes from 70 to 700 ms (Card et al., 1983, p. 28).[23] These little bits of interaction add up. They are the fine-grained details—the microstructures and microstrategies used by, or imposed on, the user. "Microstrategies focus on what designers would regard as the mundane aspects of interface design; the ways in which subtle features of interactive technology influence the ways in which users perform tasks" (W. D. Gray and Boehm-Davis, 2000, p. 322). Designers might view these fine-grained details as a mundane sidebar to the bigger goal, but the reality is different. Details are everything. User experiences exist as collections of microstrategies. Whether booking a vacation online or just hanging out with friends on a social networking site, big actions are collections of little actions. To the extent possible, user actions form the experience, our experience. It is unfortunate that they often exist simply to serve the needs of the computer or application.

---

[22] The reader who detects a modicum of sarcasm here is referred to Cooper (1999, 47–48 and elsewhere) for a full frontal assault on the insidious nature of feature bloat in software applications. The reference to version 2.0 of a nameless application is in deference to Johnson's second edition of his successful book where the same tone appears in the title: *GUI Bloopers 2.0*. For a more sober and academic look at software bloat, feature creep, and the like, see McGrenere and Moore (2000).

[23] An eye movement involves both a saccade and fixation. A saccade—the actual movement of the eye—is fast, about 30 ms. Fixations takes longer as they involve perceiving the new stimulus and cognitive processing of the stimulus.

Another reason little errors tend to linger is that they are often deemed *user errors*, not design, programming, or system errors. These errors, like most, are more correctly called *design-induced errors* (Casey, 2006, p. 12). They occur "when designers of products, systems, or services fail to account for the characteristics and capabilities of people and the vagaries of human behavior" (Casey, 1998, p. 11). We should all do a little better.

Figure 3.46 illustrates a tradeoff between the cost of errors and the frequency of errors. There is no solid ground here, so it's just a sketch. The four errors described above are shown. The claim is that high-cost errors occur with low frequency. They receive a lot of attention and they get dealt with. As systems mature and the big errors get fixed, designers shift their efforts to fixing less costly errors, like the CAPS_LOCK design-induced error, or consistently implementing velocity-controlled scrolling. Over time, more and more systems include reasonable and appropriate implementations of these interactions. Divergence in the implementations diminishes and, taken as a whole, there is an industry-wide coalescing toward the same consistent implementation (e.g., a popup alert for CAPS_LOCK). The ground is set for user expectation to take hold.

Of the errors noted in Figure 3.46, discard changes is ancient history (in computing terms), CAPS_LOCK is still a problem but is improving, scrolling frenzy is much more controlled in new applications, and focus uncertainty is, well, a mess. The cost is minor, but the error happens frequently.

In many ways, the little errors are the most interesting, because they slip past designers and programmers. A little self-observation and reflection goes a long way here. Observe little errors that you encounter. What were you trying to do? Did it work the first time, just as expected? Small interactions are revealing. What were your hands and eyes doing? Were your interactions quick and natural, or were there unnecessary or awkward steps? Could a slight reworking of the interaction help? Could an attention shift be averted with the judicious use of auditory or tactile feedback? Is there a "ready for input" auditory signal that could sound when an input field receives focus? Could this reduce the need for an attention shift? Would this improve user performance? Would it improve the user experience? Would users like it, or would it be annoying? The little possibilities add up. Think of them as opportunities for empirical research in HCI.

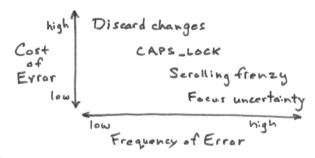

FIGURE 3.46

Trade-off between the cost of errors and the frequency of errors.

STUDENT EXERCISES

3-1. Conduct a small experiment on icon recognition, as follows. Find 15 computer users (participants) and enquire as to their computer experience. Find users with a range of computing experience (e.g., less than 10 hours per week, more than 25 hours per week. Preferably, find an equal number of participants for each experience level.) Prepare a handout sheet with the six toolbar buttons (soft controls) seen in Figure 3.3a. The general idea is shown below:

> **Icon Recognition**
>
> Participant initials:_____
> Weekly computer usage:
> ☐ <10 hrs   ☐ 10-25 hrs   ☐ >25 hrs
>
> Please indicate the purpose/meaning of the following icons:
>
> ☐ _____
> ☐ _____
> ☐ _____
> ☐ _____
> ☐ _____
> ☐ _____

Ask each participant to identify the purpose of the buttons. Record the responses. Write a brief report on the findings, showing and discussing the responses for participants overall and for participants by button and by experience level.

3-2. Conduct a small experiment on panning and zooming using Google Street View. Devise three tasks and measure users' performance using different input methods (e.g., keyboard versus mouse or touchpad versus mouse). As an example task, see Figure 3.9a. For this example, a reasonable task is to pan and zoom to the clock tower (right side of image), determine the time on the clock, then pan and zoom back to the starting position. User performance may be measured in a variety of ways, such as task completion time, accuracy in the final scene position, number of steps or corrective actions, etc. Use five participants. Write a brief report on your observations and measurements.

3-3. Conduct a small experiment to measure the CD gain of the mouse and cursor on a computer system. Build an apparatus, perhaps using wooden blocks, with an opening for a mouse, as below:

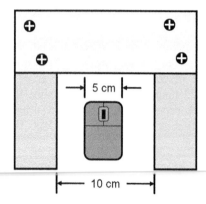

Measure the width of the opening and the mouse, as shown above, and determine the span of mouse movement in the opening. Set the pointer speed in the control panel to the center of the slider position (see below). Position the system pointer (cursor) near the left side of the display and position the mouse on the left side of the opening. Move the mouse at a nominal speed across the opening. Measure and record the amount of pointer movement on the display. Repeat five times. Repeat the above exercise for slow and fast mouse movement. Also repeat for two other pointer speed settings in the control panel (below left) and for two pointer precision settings (below right). Tailor according to the control panel options on the computer system used.

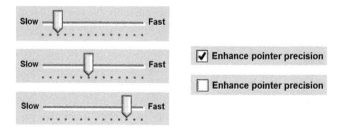

The total number of measurements is 90 (five repetitions × three mouse movement speeds × three pointer speed settings × two enhanced pointer precision settings). Write a brief report on your observations and measurements.

3-4. Conduct a small experiment investigating speed and accuracy in cursor positioning as a function of CD gain. Find five computer users (participants). Prepare a computer system as follows. Set the pointer speed in the system control panel to the middle position (see exercise 3-3 above). Open any application in full screen mode (below left). Click the Restore Down button. Position the window by dragging the title bar so that the button (now Maximize) is about 15 cm away from the initial position (below right).

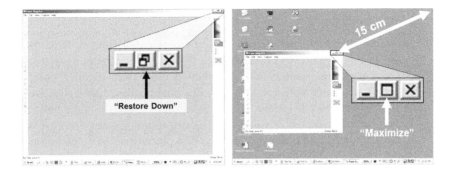

Ask the participants to use the mouse (or other pointing device) to alternately restore down and maximize the window ten times. Measure and record the time to do the task. Observe and record behaviors (e.g., miss-selections) that represent accuracy. Repeat using a lower pointer speed setting and again with a higher setting. Write a brief report on your observations and measurements.

3-5. Conduct a small experiment on mode switching, as follows. Find five computer users (participants) who are familiar with Microsoft PowerPoint. Seat them in front of a computer system with a set of slides open in PowerPoint in Slide View mode (aka Normal mode). Have each participant do the following two tasks. First, ask them to use the system's pointing device to switch modes (e.g., to Outline mode or to Slide Sorter mode). Record the time to do the task and whether they used the buttons or menu method (buttons method = soft buttons on the display; menu method = View pull-down menu or ribbon). Return the mode to Slide/Normal. Second, ask them to again change the mode, but this time tell them to use another method, without telling them what the other method is. Write a brief report on your observations.

3-6. Conduct a small experiment on mode switching, as follows. Find five computer users (participants) who are familiar with Microsoft Word. Open a text document and switch the mode to Overtype (see Figure 3.25b and related discussion).[24] Do this without the participants seeing what you did. Ask each participant to insert a word somewhere in the document. Write a brief report on your observations.

3-7. Many companies use the World Wide Web to sell their products (e.g., amazon.com). To assist users in making purchases, these sites often use a metaphor borrowed from the user experience in a grocery store. What is this metaphor? With reference to at least two such websites, discuss the implementation of the metaphor. Describe the metaphor's presentation and the

---

[24]For Office 2007 or Office 2010, Insert mode must first be enabled. Go to File → Options →Advanced → Editing Options and check "Use the Insert key to control overtype mode."

actions supported. Use screen snapshots or other aides to support the analysis. Present your findings in a brief report or in a slide show presentation.

3-8. Consider the trade-off between the cost of errors and the frequency of errors shown in Figure 3.46. The examples are from desktop computing. For each of the four errors, identify a corresponding error from mobile computing using a touchscreen device such as a smartphone or tablet computer. "Corresponding," in this sense, refers to the level of severity in the error, not to the interaction per se. Position the errors in a similar chart and develop a discussion to justify the choice of error and its placement in the chart. Present your findings in a brief report or in a slide show presentation.

Scientific Foundations

In the last chapter, we examined a variety of interaction topics in HCI. By and large, the research methodology for studying these topics is empirical and scientific. Ideas are conceived, developed, and implemented and then framed as hypotheses that are tested in experiments. This chapter presents the enabling features of this methodology. Our goal is to establish the what, why, and how of research, with a focus on research that is both empirical and experimental. While much of the discussion is general, the examples are directed at HCI. We begin with the terminology surrounding research and empirical research.

4.1 What is research?

Research means different things to different people. "Being a researcher" or "conducting research" carries a certain elevated status in universities, colleges, and corporations. Consequently, the term research is bantered around in a myriad of situations. Often, the word is used simply to add weight to an assertion ("Our research shows that ..."). While writing an early draft of this chapter, a television ad for an Internet service provider was airing in southern Ontario. The ad proclaimed, "Independent research proves [name_of_product] is the fastest and most reliable—period."[1] One might wonder about the nature of the research, or of the independence and impartiality of the work. Of course, forwarding assertions to promote facts, observations, hypotheses, and the like is often the goal. But what is research? Surely, it is more than just a word to add force to a statement or opinion. To rise above conjecture, we demand evidence—evidence meeting a standard of credibility such that the statement is beyond dispute. Providing such credibility is the goal of research.

Returning to the word itself, research has at least three definitions. First, conducting research can be an exercise as simple as *careful or diligent search.*[2] So carefully searching one's garden to find and remove weeds meets one standard of

---

[1] Advertisement by Rogers Communications Inc. airing on television in southern Ontario during the winter of 2008/2009.

[2] www.merriam-webster.com.

conducting research. Or perhaps one undertakes a search on a computer to locate all files modified on a certain date. That's research. It's not the stuff of MSc or PhD theses, but it meets one definition of research.

The second definition of research is *collecting information about a particular subject*. So surveying voters to collect information on political opinions is conducting research. In HCI we might observe people interacting with an interface and collect information about their interactions, such as the number of times they consulted the manual, clicked the wrong button, retried an operation, or uttered an expletive. That's research.

The third definition is more elaborate: *research is investigation or experimentation aimed at the discovery and interpretation of facts and revision of accepted theories or laws in light of new facts.*

In this definition we find several key elements of research that motivate discussions in this book. We find the idea of *experimentation*. Conducting experiments is a central activity in a lot of HCI research. I will say more about this in the next chapter. In HCI research, an experiment is sometimes called a *user study*. The methodology is sometimes formal, sometimes ad hoc. A formal and standardized methodology is generally preferred because it brings consistency to a body of work and facilitates the review and comparison of research from different studies. One objective of this book is to promote the use of a consistent methodology for experimental research in HCI.

To be fair, the title of this book changed a few times on the way to press. Is the book about *experimental research*? Well, yes, a lot of it is, but there are important forms of HCI research that are non-experimental. So as not to exclude these, the focus shifted to *empirical research*, a broader term that encompasses both experimental and non-experimental methodologies. Among the latter is building and testing models of interaction, which we examine formally in Chapter 7.

Returning to research, the third definition speaks of *facts*. Facts are the building blocks of evidence, and it is evidence we seek in experimental research. For example, we might observe that a user committed three errors while entering a command with an interface. That's a fact. Of course, context is important. Did the user have prior experience with the interface, or with similar interfaces? Was the user a child or a computer expert? Perhaps we observed and counted the errors committed by a group of users while interacting with two different interfaces over a period of time. If they committed 15 percent more errors with one interface than with the other, the facts are more compelling (but, again, context is important). Collectively, the facts form an outward sign leading to evidence—evidence that one interface is better, or less error prone, than the other. Evidence testing is presented in more detail in Chapter 6, Hypothesis Testing. Note that *prove* or *proof* is not used here. In HCI research we don't prove things; we gather facts and formulate and test evidence.

The third definition mentions *theories* and *laws*. Theory has two common meanings. In the sense of Darwin's *theory of evolution* or Einstein's *theory of relativity*, the term theory is synonymous with *hypothesis*. In fact, one definition of theory is simply "a hypothesis assumed for the sake of argument or investigation." Of course, through experimentation, these theories advanced beyond argument and investigation. The stringent demands of scientific inquiry confirmed the hypotheses of these great scientists. When confirmed through research, a theory becomes a *scientifically accepted body of principles that explain phenomena.*

A *law* is different from a theory. A law is more specific, more constraining, more formal, more binding. In the most exacting terms, a law is a relationship or phenomenon that is "invariable under given conditions." Because variability is germane to human behavior, laws are of questionable relevance to HCI. Of course, HCI has laws. Take HCI's best-known law as an example. *Fitts' law* refers to a body of work, originally in human motor behavior (Fitts, 1954), but now widely used in HCI. Fitts' work pertained to rapid-aimed movements, such as rapidly moving a cursor to an object and selecting it in a graphical user interface. Fitts himself never proposed a law. He proposed a model of human motor behavior. And by all accounts, that's what Fitts' law is—a model, a behavioral, descriptive, and predictive model. It includes equations and such for predicting the time to do point-select tasks. It is a law only in that other researchers took up the label as a celebration of the generality and importance of Fitts' seminal work. We should all be so lucky. Fitts' law is presented in more detail in Chapter 7.

Research, according to the third definition, involves *discovery, interpretation*, and *revision*. Discovery is obvious enough. That's what we do—look for, or discover, things that are new and useful. Perhaps the discovery is a new style of interface or a new interaction technique. Interpretation and revision are central to research. Research does not proceed in a vacuum. Today's research builds on what is already known or assumed. We interpret what is known; we revise and extend through discovery.

There are additional characteristics of research that are not encompassed in the dictionary definitions. Let's examine a few of these.

4.1.1 Research must be published

Publication is the final step in research. It is also an essential step. Never has this rung as true as in the edict *publish or perish*. Researchers, particularly in academia, must publish. A weak or insufficient list of publications might spell disappointment when applying for research funds or for a tenure-track professorship at a university. Consequently, developing the skill to publish begins as a graduate student and continues throughout one's career as a researcher, whether in academia or industry. The details and challenges in writing research papers are elaborated in Chapter 8.

Publishing is crucial, and for good reason. Until it is published, the knowledge gained through research cannot achieve its critical purpose—to extend, refine, or revise the existing body of knowledge in the field. This is so important that publication bearing a high standard of scrutiny is required. Not just any publication, but publication in archived peer-reviewed journals or conference proceedings. Research results are "written up," submitted, and reviewed for their integrity, relevance, and contribution. The review is by peers—other researchers doing similar work. Are the results novel and useful? Does the evidence support the conclusions? Is there a contribution to the field? Does the methodology meet the expected standards for research? If these questions are satisfactorily answered, the work has a good chance of acceptance and publication. Congratulations. In the end, the work is published and archived. *Archived* implies the work is added to the collection of related work accessible to other researchers throughout the world. This is the "existing body of knowledge" referred to earlier. The final step is complete.

Research results are sometimes developed into bona fide inventions. If an individual or a company wishes to profit from their invention, then patenting is an option. The invention is disclosed in a patent application, which also describes previous related work (prior art), how the invention addresses a need, and the best mode of implementation. If the application is successful, the patent is granted and the inventor or company thereafter owns the rights to the invention. If another company wishes to use the invention for commercial purpose, they must enter into a license agreement with the patent holder. This side note is included only to make a small point: a patent is a publication. By patenting, the individual or company is not only retaining ownership of the invention but is also making it public through publication of the patent. Thus, patents meet the must-publish criterion for research.

4.1.2 Citations, references, impact

Imagine the World Wide Web without hyperlinks. Web pages would live in isolation, without connections between them. Hyperlinks provide the essential pathways that connect web pages to other web pages, thus providing structure and cohesion to a topic or theme. Similarly, it is hard to imagine the world's body of published research without *citations* and *references*. Citations, like hyperlinks, connect research papers to other research papers. Through citations, a body of research takes shape. The insights and lessons of early research inform and guide later research. The citation itself is just an abbreviated tag that appears in the body of a paper, for example, "... as noted in earlier research (Smith and Jones, 2003)" or "... as confirmed by Green et al. [5]." These two examples are formatted differently and follow the requirements of the conference or journal. The citation is expanded into a full bibliographic entry in the reference list at the end of the paper. Formatting of citations and references is discussed in Chapter 8.

Citations serve many purposes, including supporting intellectual honesty. By citing previous work, researchers acknowledge that their ideas continue, extend, or refine those in earlier research. Citations are also important to back up assertions that are otherwise questionable, for example, "the number of tablet computer users worldwide now exceeds two billion [9]." In the Results section of a research paper, citations are used to compare the current results with those from earlier research, for example, "the mean time to formulate a search query was about 15 percent less than the time reported by Smith and Jones [5]."

Figure 4.1 provides a schematic of a collection of research papers. Citations are shown as arrows. It incorporates a timeline, so all arrows point to the left, to earlier

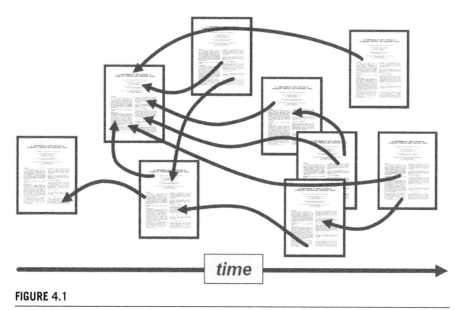

FIGURE 4.1

A collection of research papers with citations to earlier papers.

papers. One of the papers seems to have quite a few citations to it. The number of citations to a research paper is a measure of the paper's *impact*. If many researchers cite a single paper, there is a good chance the work described in the cited paper is both of high quality and significant to the field. This point is often echoed in academic circles: "The only objective and transparent metric that is highly correlated with the quality of a paper is the number of citations."[3] Interestingly enough, citation counts are only recently easily available. Before services like Google Scholar emerged, citation counts were difficult to obtain.

Since citation counts are available for individual papers, they are also easy to compile for individual researchers. Thus, impact can be assessed for researchers as well as for papers. The most accepted single measure of the impact of a researcher's publication record is the *H-index*. If a researcher's publications are ordered by the number of citations to each paper, the H-index is the point where the rank equals the number of citations. In other words, a researcher with H-index $= n$ has n publications each with n or more citations. Physicist J. Hirsch first proposed the H-index in 2005 (Hirsch, 2005). H-index quantifies in a single number both research productivity (number of publications) and overall impact of a body of work (number of citations). Some of the strengths and weaknesses of the H-index, as a measure of impact, are elaborated elsewhere (MacKenzie, 2009a).

---

[3] Dianne Murray, General Editor, *Interacting with Computers*. Posted to chi-announcements@acm.org on Oct 8, 2008.

4.1.3 **Research must be reproducible**

Research that cannot be replicated is useless. Achieving an expected standard of reproducibility, or repeatability, is therefore crucial. This is one reason for advancing a standardized methodology: it enforces a process for conducting and writing about the research that ensures sufficient detail is included to allow the results to be replicated. If skilled researchers care to test the claims, they will find sufficient guidance in the methodology to reproduce, or replicate, the original research. This is an essential characteristic of research.

Many great advances in science and research pertain to methodology. A significant contribution by Louis Pasteur (1822–1895), for example, was his use of a consistent methodology for his research in microbiology (Day and Gastel, 2006, pp. 8–9). Pasteur's experimental findings on germs and diseases were, at the time, controversial. As Pasteur realized, the best way to fend off skepticism was to empower critics—other scientists—to see for themselves. Thus, he adopted a methodology that included a standardized and meticulous description of the materials and procedure. This allowed his experiments and findings to be replicated. A researcher questioning a result could redo the experiment and therefore verify or refute the result. This was a crucial advance in science. Today, reviewers of manuscripts submitted for publication are often asked to critique the work on this very point: "Is the work replicable?" "No" spells certain rejection.

One of the most cited papers in publishing history is a method paper. Lowry et al.'s, 1951 paper "Protein Measurement With the Folin Phenol Reagent" has garnered in excess of 200,000 citations (Lowry, Rosenbrough, Farr, and Randall, 1951).[4] The paper describes a method for measuring proteins in fluids. In style, the paper reads much like a recipe. The method is easy to read, easy to follow, and, importantly, easy to reproduce.

4.1.4 **Research versus engineering versus design**

There are many ways to distinguish research from engineering and design. Researchers often work closely with engineers and designers, but the skills and contributions each brings are different. Engineers and designers are in the business of building things. They create products that strive to bring together the best in *form* (design emphasis) and *function* (engineering emphasis). One can imagine that there is certain tension, even a trade-off, between form and function. Finding the right balance is key. However, sometimes the balance tips one way or the other. When this occurs, the result is a product or a feature that achieves one (form or function) at the expense of the other. An example is shown in Figure 4.2a. The image shows part of a notebook computer, manufactured by a well-known computer company. By most accounts, it is a typical notebook computer. The image shows part of the keyboard and the built-in pointing device, a touchpad. The touchpad design (or is it engineering?) is interesting. It is seamlessly embedded in the system chassis.

---

[4] See http://scholar.google.com.

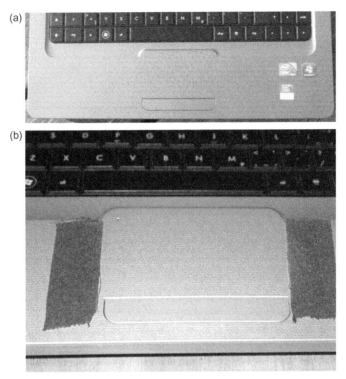

FIGURE 4.2

Form trumping function: (a) Notebook computer. (b) Duct tape provides tactile feedback indicating the edge of the touchpad.

The look is elegant—smooth, shiny, metallic. But something is wrong. Because the mounting is seamless and smooth, tactile feedback at the sides of the touchpad is missing. While positioning a cursor, the user has no sense of when his or her finger reaches the edge of the touchpad, except by observing that the cursor ceases to move. This is an example of form trumping function. One user's solution is shown in Figure 4.2b. Duct tape added on each side of the touchpad provides the all-important tactile feedback.[5]

Engineers and designers work in the world of products. The focus is on designing complete systems or products. Research is different. Research tends to be narrowly focused. Small ideas are conceived of, prototyped, tested, then advanced or discarded. New ideas build on previous ideas and, sooner or later, good ideas are refined into the building blocks—the materials and processes—that find their way into products. But research questions are generally small in scope. Research tends to be incremental, not monumental.

---

[5] For an amusing example of function trumping form, visit Google Images using "Rube Goldberg simple alarm clock."

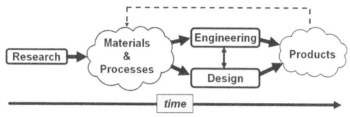

FIGURE 4.3

Timeline for research, engineering, and design.

Engineers and designers also work with prototypes, but the prototype is used to assess alternatives at a relatively late stage: as part of product development. A researcher's prototype is an early mock-up of an idea, and is unlikely to directly appear in a product. Yet the idea of using prototypes to inform or assess is remarkably similar, whether for research or for product development. The following characterization by Tim Brown (CEO of design firm IDEO) is directed at designers, but is well aligned with the use of prototypes for research:

> *Prototypes should command only as much time, effort, and investment as are needed to generate useful feedback and evolve an idea. The more "finished" a prototype seems, the less likely its creators will be to pay attention to and profit from feedback. The goal of prototyping isn't to finish. It is to learn about the strengths and weaknesses of the idea and to identify new directions that further prototypes might take (Brown, 2008, p. 3).*

One facet of research that differentiates it from engineering and design is the timeline. Research precedes engineering and design. Furthermore, the march forward for research is at a slower pace, without the shackles of deadlines. Figure 4.3 shows the timeline for research, engineering, and design. Products are the stuff of deadlines. Designers and engineers work within the corporate world, developing products that sell, and hopefully sell well. The raw materials for engineers and designers are materials and processes that already exist (dashed line in Figure 4.3) or emerge through research.

The computer mouse is a good example. It is a hugely successful product that, in many ways, defines a generation of computing, post 1981, when the Xerox Star was introduced. But in the 1960s the mouse was just an idea. As a prototype it worked well as an input controller to maneuver a tracking symbol on a graphics display. Engelbart's invention (English et al., 1967) took nearly 20 years to be engineered and designed into a successful product.

Similar stories are heard today. Apple Computer Inc., long known as a leader in innovation, is always building a better mousetrap. An example is the *iPhone*, introduced in June, 2007. And, evidently, the world has beaten a path to Apple's door.[6] Notably, "with the iPhone, Apple successfully brought together decades

---

[6]The entire quotation is "Build a better mousetrap and the world will beat a path to your door" and is attributed to American essayist Ralph Waldo Emerson (1803–1882).

of research" (Selker, 2008). Many of the raw materials of this successful product came by way of low-level research, undertaken well before Apple's engineers and designers set forth on their successfully journey. Among the iPhone's interaction novelties is a two-finger *pinch* gesture for zooming in and out. New? Perhaps, but Apple's engineers and designers no doubt were guided or inspired by research that came before them. For example, multi-touch gestures date back to at least the 1980s (Buxton, Hill, and Rowley, 1985; Hauptmann, 1989). What about changing the aspect ratio of the display when the device is tilted? New? Perhaps not. Tilt, as an interaction technique for user interfaces, dates back to the 1990s (B. Harrison et al., 1998; Hinckley et al., 2000; Rekimoto, 1996). These are just two examples of research ideas that, taken alone, are small scale. While engineers and designers strive to build better systems or products, in the broadest sense, researchers provide the raw materials and processes engineers and designers work with: stronger steel for bridges, a better mouse for pointing, a better algorithm for a search engine, a more natural touch interface for mobile phones.

4.2 **What is empirical research?**

By prefixing research with *empirical*, some powerful new ideas are added. According to one definition, empirical means *originating in or based on observation or experience*. Simple enough. Another definition holds that empirical means *relying on experience or observation alone, often without due regard for system and theory*. This is interesting. These words suggest researchers should be guided by direct observations and experiences about phenomena, without prejudice to, or even consideration of, existing theories. This powerful idea is a guiding principle in science—not to be blinded by preconceptions. Here's an example. Prior to the 15th century, there was a prevailing *system* or *theory* that celestial bodies revolved around the earth. The Polish scientist Nicolas Copernicus (1473–1543) found evidence to the contrary. His work was empirical. It was based on observation without bias toward, influence by, or due regard to, existing theory. He observed, he collected data, he looked for patterns and relationships in the data, and he found evidence within the data that cut across contemporary thinking. His empirical evidence led to one of the great achievements in modern science—a heliocentric cosmology that placed the sun, rather than the earth, at the center of the solar system. Now that's a nice *discovery* (see the third definition of research at the beginning of this chapter). In HCI and other fields of research, discoveries are usually more modest.

By another definition, empirical means *capable of being verified or disproved by observation or experiment*. These are strong words. An HCI research initiative is framed by hypotheses—assertions about the merits of an interface or an interaction technique. The assertions must be sufficiently clear and narrow to enable verification or disproval by gathering and testing evidence. This means using language in an assertion that speaks directly to empirical, observable, quantifiable aspects of the interaction. I will expand on this later in this chapter in the discussion on research questions.

4.3 Research methods

There are three common approaches, or methods, for conducting research in HCI and other disciplines in the natural and social sciences: the *observational method*, the *experimental method*, and the *correlational method*. All three are empirical as they are based on observation or experience. But there are differences and these follow from the objectives of the research and from the expertise and style of the researcher. Let's examine each method.

4.3.1 Observational method

Observation is the starting point for this method. In conducting empirical research in HCI, it is essential to observe humans interacting with computers or computer-embedded technology of some sort. The observational method encompasses a collection of common techniques used in HCI research. These include interviews, field investigations, contextual inquiries, case studies, field studies, focus groups, think aloud protocols, storytelling, walkthroughs, cultural probes, and so on. The approach tends to be qualitative rather than quantitative. As a result, observational methods achieve *relevance* while sacrificing *precision* (Sheskin, 2011, p. 76). Behaviors are studied by directly observing phenomena in a natural setting, as opposed to crafting constrained behaviors in an artificial laboratory setting. Real world phenomena are high in relevance, but lack the precision available in controlled laboratory experiments.

Observational methods are generally concerned with discovering and explaining the reasons underlying human behavior. In HCI, this is the *why* or *how* of the interaction, as opposed to the *what*, *where*, or *when*. The methods focus on human thought, feeling, attitude, emotion, passion, sensation, reflection, expression, sentiment, opinion, mood, outlook, manner, style, approach, strategy, and so on. These human qualities can be studied through observational methods, but they are difficult to measure. The observations are more likely to involve note-taking, photographs, videos, or audio recordings rather than measurement. Measurements, if gathered, tend to use categorical data or simple counts of phenomena. Put another way, observational methods tend to examine and record the quality of interaction rather than quantifiable human performance.

4.3.2 Experimental method

With the experimental method (also called the *scientific method*), knowledge is acquired through controlled experiments conducted in laboratory settings. Acquiring knowledge may imply gathering new knowledge, but it may also mean studying existing knowledge for the purpose of verifying, refuting, correcting, integrating, or extending. In the relevance-precision dichotomy, it is clear where controlled experiments lie. Since the tasks are artificial and occur in a controlled laboratory setting, relevance is diminished. However, the control inherent in the methodology brings precision, since extraneous factors—the diversity and chaos of the real world—are reduced or eliminated.

A controlled experiment requires at least two variables: a *manipulated variable* and a *response variable*. In HCI, the manipulated variable is typically a property of an interface or interaction technique that is presented to participants in different configurations. Manipulating the variable simply refers to systematically exposing participants to different configurations of the interface or interaction technique. To qualify as a controlled experiment, at least two configurations are required. Thus, comparison is germane to the experimental method. This point deserves further elaboration. In HCI, we often hear of a system or design undergoing a "usability evaluation" or "user testing." Although these terms often have different meanings in different contexts, such evaluations or tests generally do not follow the experimental method. The reason is simple: there is no manipulated variable. This is mentioned only to distinguish a usability evaluation from a *user study*. Undertaking a user study typically implies conducting a controlled experiment where different configurations of a system are tested and compared. A "usability evaluation," on the other hand, usually involves assessing a single user interface for strengths and weaknesses. The evaluation might qualify as research ("collecting information about a particular subject"), but it is not experimental research. I will return to this point shortly. A manipulated variable is also called an *independent variable* or *factor*.

A response variable is a property of human behavior that is observable, quantifiable, and measurable. The most common response variable is time, often called *task completion time* or some variation thereof. Given a task, how long do participants take to do the task under each of the configurations tested? There are, of course, a multitude of other behaviors that qualify as response variables. Which ones are used depend on the characteristics of the interface or interaction technique studied in the research. A response variable is also called a *dependent variable*. Independent variables and dependent variables are explored in greater detail in Chapter 5.

HCI experiments involve humans, so the methodology employed is borrowed from experimental psychology, a field with a long history of research involving humans. In a sense, HCI is the beneficiary of this more mature field. The circumstances manipulated in a psychology experiment are often quite different from those manipulated in an HCI experiment, however. HCI is narrowly focused on the interaction between humans and computing technology, while experimental psychology covers a much broader range of the human experience.

It is naïve to think we can simply choose to focus on the experimental method and ignore qualities of interaction that are outside the scope of the experimental procedure. A full and proper user study—an experiment with human participants—involves more than just measuring and analyzing human performance. We engage observational methods by soliciting comments, thoughts, and opinions from participants. Even though a task may be performed quickly and with little or no error, if participants experience fatigue, frustration, discomfort, or another *quality* of interaction, we want to know about it. These qualities of interaction may not appear in the numbers, but they cannot be ignored.

One final point about the experimental method deserves mention. A controlled experiment, if designed and conducted properly, often allows a powerful form of conclusion to be drawn from the data and analyses. The relationship between the independent variable and the dependent variable is one of *cause and effect*; that is, the manipulations in the interface or interaction techniques are said to have *caused* the observed differences in the response variable. This point is elaborated in greater detail shortly. Cause-and-effect conclusions are not possible in research using the observational method or the correlational method.

4.3.3 Correlational method

The correlational method involves looking for relationships between variables. For example, a researcher might be interested in knowing if users' privacy settings in a social networking application are related to their personality, IQ, level of education, employment status, age, gender, income, and so on. Data are collected on each item (privacy settings, personality, etc.) and then relationships are examined. For example, it might be apparent in the data that users with certain personality traits tend to use more stringent privacy settings than users with other personality traits.

The correlational method is characterized by quantification since the magnitude of variables must be ascertained (e.g., age, income, number of privacy settings). For nominal-scale variables, categories are established (e.g., personality type, gender). The data may be collected through a variety of methods, such as observation, interviews, on-line surveys, questionnaires, or measurement. Correlational methods often accompany experimental methods, if questionnaires are included in the experimental procedure. Do the measurements on response variables suggest relationships by gender, by age, by level of experience, and so on?

Correlational methods provide a balance between relevance and precision. Since the data were not collected in a controlled setting, precision is sacrificed. However, data collected using informal techniques, such as interviews, bring relevance—a connection to real-life experiences. Finally, the data obtained using correlational methods are circumstantial, not causal. I will return to this point shortly.

This book is primarily directed at the experimental method for HCI research. However, it is clear in the discussions above that the experimental method will often include observational methods and correlational methods.

4.4 Observe and measure

Let's return to the foundation of empirical research: observation.

4.4.1 Observation

The starting point for empirical research in HCI is to observe humans interacting with computers. But how are observations made? There are two possibilities. Either another human is the observer or an apparatus is the observer. A human observer is the experimenter or investigator, not the human interacting with the computer. Observation is the precursor to *measurement*, and if the investigator is the observer, then measurements are collected manually. This could involve using a log sheet or notebook to jot down the number of events of interest observed. Events of interest might include the number of times the user clicked a button or moved his or her hand from the keyboard to the mouse. It might involve observing users in a public space and counting those who are using mobile phones in a certain way, for example, while walking, while driving, or while paying for groceries at a checkout counter. The observations may be broken down by gender or some other attribute of interest.

Manual observation could also involve timing by hand the duration of activities, such as the time to type a phrase of text or the time to enter a search query. One can imagine the difficulty in manually gathering measurements as just described, not to mention the inaccuracy in the measurements. Nevertheless, manual timing is useful for preliminary testing, sometimes called *pilot testing*.

More often in empirical research, the task of observing is delegated to the apparatus—the computer. Of course, this is a challenge in some situations. As an example, if the interaction is with a digital sports watch or automated teller machine (ATM), it is not possible to embed data collection software in the apparatus. Even if the apparatus is a conventional desktop computer, some behaviors of interest are difficult to detect. For example, consider measuring the number of times the user's attention switches from the display to the keyboard while doing a task. The computer is not capable of detecting this behavior. In this case, perhaps an eye tracking apparatus or camera could be used, but that adds complexity to the experimental apparatus. Another example is clutching with a mouse—lifting and repositioning the device. The data transmitted from a mouse to a host computer do not include information on clutching, so a conventional host system is not capable of observing and recording this behavior. Again, some additional apparatus or sensing technology may be devised, but this complicates the apparatus. Or a human observer can be used. So depending on the behaviors of interest, some ingenuity might be required to build an apparatus and collect the appropriate measurements.

If the apparatus includes custom software implementing an interface or interaction technique, then it is usually straightforward to record events such as key presses, mouse movement, selections, finger touches, or finger swipes and the associated timestamps. These data are stored in a file for follow-up analyses.

4.4.2 Measurement scales

Observation alone is of limited value. Consider observations about rain and flowers. In some locales, there is ample rain but very few flowers in April. This is followed by less rain and a full-blown field of flowers in May. The observations may inspire anecdote (*April showers bring May flowers*), but a serious examination of patterns for rain and flowers requires measurement. In this case, an observer located in a garden would observe, measure, and record the amount of rain and

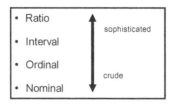

FIGURE 4.4

Scales of measurement: nominal, ordinal, interval, and ratio. Nominal measurements are considered simple, while ratio measurements are sophisticated.

the number of flowers in bloom. The measurements might be recorded each day during April and May, perhaps by several observers in several gardens. The measurements are collected, together with the means, tallied by month and analyzed for "significant differences" (see Chapter 6). With measurement, anecdotes turn to empirical evidence. The observer is now in a position to quantify the amount of rain and the number of flowers in bloom, separately for April and May. The added value of measurement is essential for science. In the words of engineer and physicist Lord Kelvin (1824–1907), after whom the Kelvin scale of temperature is named, "[Without measurement] your knowledge of it is of a meager and unsatisfactory kind."[7]

As elaborated in many textbooks on statistics, there are four scales of measurement: nominal, ordinal, interval, and ratio. Organizing this discussion by these four scales will help. Figure 4.4 shows the scales along a continuum with nominal scale measurements as the least sophisticated and ratio-scale measurements as the most sophisticated. This follows from the types of computations possible with each measurement, as elaborated below.

The nature, limitations, and abilities of each scale determine the sort of information and analyses possible in a research setting. Each is briefly defined below.

4.4.3 Nominal

A measurement on the nominal scale involves arbitrarily assigning a code to an attribute or a category. The measurement is so arbitrary that the code needn't be a number (although it could be). Examples are automobile license plate numbers, codes for postal zones, job classifications, military ranks, etc. Clearly, mathematical manipulations on nominal data are meaningless. It is nonsense, for example, to

---

[7]The exact and full quote, according to several online sources, is "When you can measure what you are speaking about, and express it in numbers, you know something about it; but when you cannot measure it, when you cannot express it in numbers, your knowledge of it is of a meager and unsatisfactory kind; it may be the beginning of knowledge, but you have scarcely, in your thoughts, advanced it to the stage of science."

compute the mean of several license plate numbers. Nominal data identify mutually exclusive categories. Membership or exclusivity is meaningful, but little else. The only relationship that holds is equivalence, which exists between entities in the same class. Nominal data are also called *categorical data.*

If we are interested in knowing whether males and females differ in their use of mobile phones, we might begin our investigation by observing people and assigning each a code of "M" for male, "F" for female. Here, the attribute is gender and the code is M or F. If we are interested in handedness, we might observe the writing habits of users and assign codes of "LH" for left-handers and "RH" for right-handers. If we are interested in scrolling strategies, we might observe users interacting with a GUI application and categorize them according to their scrolling methods, for example as "MW" for mouse wheel, "CD" for clicking and dragging the scrollbar, or "KB" for keyboard.

Nominal data are often used with frequencies or counts—the number of occurrences of each attribute. In this case, our research is likely concerned with the difference in the counts between categories: "Are males or females more likely to …?", "Do left handers or right handers have more difficulty with …?", or "Are Mac or PC users more inclined to …?" Bear in mind that while the attribute is categorical, the count is a ratio-scale measurement (discussed shortly).

Here is an example of nominal scale attributes using real data. Attendees of an HCI research course were dispatched to several locations on a university campus. Their task was to observe, categorize, and count students walking between classes. Each student was categorized by gender (male, female) and by whether he or she was using a mobile phone (not using, using). The results are shown in Figure 4.5. A total of 1,527 students were observed. The split by gender was roughly equal (51.1% male, 48.9% female). By mobile phone usage, 13.1 percent of the students (200) were observed using their mobile phone while walking.

The research question in Figure 4.5 is a follows: are males or females more likely to use a mobile phone as they walk about a university campus? I will demonstrate how to answer this question in Chapter 6 on Hypothesis Testing.

Gender	Mobile Phone Usage		Total	%
	Not Using	Using		
Male	683	98	781	51.1%
Female	644	102	746	48.9%
Total	1327	200	1527	
%	86.9%	13.1%		

FIGURE 4.5

Two examples of nominal scale data: gender (male, female) and mobile phone usage (not using, using).

How many email messages do you receive each day?

1. None (I don't use email)
2. 1-5 per day
3. 6-25 per day
4. 26-100 per day
5. More than 100 per day

FIGURE 4.6

Example of a questionnaire item soliciting an ordinal response.

4.4.4 Ordinal data

Ordinal scale measurements provide an order or ranking to an attribute. The attribute can be any characteristic or circumstance of interest. For example, users might be asked to try three global positioning systems (GPS) for a period of time and then rank the systems by preference: first choice, second choice, third choice. Or users could be asked to consider properties of a mobile phone such as price, features, cool-appeal, and usability, and then order the features by personal importance. One user might choose usability (first), cool-appeal (second), price (third), and then features (fourth). The main limitation of ordinal data is that the interval is not intrinsically equal between successive points on the scale. In the example just cited, there is no innate sense of how much more important usability is over cool-appeal or whether the difference is greater or less than that between, for example, cool-appeal and price.

If we are interested in studying users' e-mail habits, we might use a questionnaire to collect data. Figure 4.6 gives an example of a questionnaire item soliciting ordinal data. There are five rankings according to the number of e-mail messages received per day. It is a matter of choice whether to solicit data in this manner or, in the alternative, to ask for an estimate of the number of e-mail messages received per day. It will depend on how the data are used and analyzed.

Ordinal data are slightly more sophisticated than nominal data since comparisons of *greater than* or *less than* are possible. However, it is not valid to compute the mean of ordinal data.

4.4.5 Interval data

Moving up in sophistication, interval data have equal distances between adjacent values. However, there is no absolute zero. The classic example of interval data is temperature measured on the Fahrenheit or Celsius scale. Unlike ordinal data, it is meaningful to compute the mean of interval data, for example, the mean mid-day temperature during the month of July. Ratios of interval data are not meaningful, however. For example, one cannot say that 20°C is twice as warm as 10°C.

In HCI, interval data are commonly used in questionnaires where a response on a linear scale is solicited. An example is a Likert Scale (see Figure 4.7), where verbal responses are given a numeric code. In the example, verbal responses are

Please indicate your level of agreement with the following statements.					
	Strongly disagree	Mildly disagree	Neutral	Mildly agree	Strongly agree
It is safe to talk on a mobile phone while driving.	1	2	3	4	5
It is safe to read a text message on a mobile phone while driving.	1	2	3	4	5
It is safe to compose a text message on a mobile phone while driving.	1	2	3	4	5

FIGURE 4.7

A set of questionnaire items organized in a Likert Scale. The responses are examples of interval scale data.

symmetric about a neutral, central value with the gradations between responses more or less equal. It is this last quality—equal gradations between responses—that validates calculating the mean of the responses across multiple respondents.

There is some disagreement among researchers on the assumption of equal gradations between the items in Figure 4.7. Do respondents perceive the difference between, say, 1 and 2 (strongly disagree and mildly disagree) the same as the difference between, say, 2 and 3 (mildly disagree and neutral)? Attaching verbal tags to numbers is likely to bring qualitative and highly personal interpretations to the responses. There is evidence that respondents perceive items at the extremes of the scale as farther apart than items in the center (Kaptein, Nass, and Markopoulos, 2010). Nevertheless, the graduation between responses is much more similar here than between the five ordinal responses in Figure 4.6. One remedy for non-equal gradations in Likert-scale response items is simply to instruct respondents to interpret the items as equally spaced.

Examples of Likert Scale questionnaire items in HCI research papers are as follows: Bickmore and Picard, 2004; Dautenhahn et al., 2006; Garau et al., 2003; Guy, Ur, Ronen, Perer, and Jacovi, 2011; Wobbrock, Chau, and Myers, 2007.

4.4.6 Ratio data

Ratio-scale measurements are the most sophisticated of the four scales of measurement. Ratio data have an absolute zero and support a myriad of calculations to summarize, compare, and test the data. Ratio data can be added, subtracted, multiplied, divided; means, standard deviations, and variances can be computed. In HCI, the most common ratio-scale measurement is time—the time to complete a task. But generally, all physical measurements are also ratio-scale, such as the distance or velocity of a cursor as it moves across a display, the force applied by a finger on a touchscreen, and so on. Many social variables are also ratio-scale, such as a user's age or years of computer experience.

Another common ratio-scale measurement is count (noted above). Often in HCI research, we count the number of occurrences of certain human activities, such as the number of button clicks, the number of corrective button clicks, the number of characters entered, the number of incorrect characters entered, the number of times an option is selected, the number of gaze shifts, the number of hand movements between the mouse and keyboard, the number of task retries, the number of words in a search query, etc. Although we tend to give time special attention, it too is a count—the number of seconds or minutes elapsed as an activity takes place. These are all ratio-scale measurements.

The expressive nature of a count is improved through *normalization*; that is, expressing the value as a count *per something*. So for example, knowing that a 10-word phrase was entered in 30 seconds is less revealing than knowing that the rate of entry was 10/0.5 = 20 words per minute (wpm). The main benefit of normalizing counts is to improve comparisons. It is easy to compare 20 wpm for one method with 23 wpm for another method—the latter method is faster. It is much harder to compare 10 words entered in 30 seconds for one method with 14 words entered in 47 seconds for another method.

As another example, let's say two errors were committed while entering a 50-character phrase of text. Reporting the occurrence of two errors reveals very little, unless we also know the length of the phrase. Even so, comparisons with results from another study are difficult. (What if the other study used phrases of different lengths?) However, if the result is reported as a 2/50 = 4% error rate, there is an immediate sense of the meaning, magnitude, and relevance of the human performance measured, and as convention has it, the other study likely reported error rates in much the same way. So where possible, normalize counts to make the measurements more meaningful and to facilitate comparisons.

An example in the literature is an experiment comparing five different text entry methods (Magerkurth and Stenzel, 2003). For speed, results were reported in "words per minute" (that's fine); however, for accuracy, results were reported as the number of errors committed. Novice participants, for example, committed 24 errors while using multi-tap (Magerkurth and Stenzel, 2003, Table 2). While this number is useful for comparing results within the experiment, it provides no insight as to how the results compare with those in related research. The results would be more enlightening if normalized for the amount of text entered and reported as an "error rate (%)," computed as the number of character errors divided by the total number of characters entered times 100.

4.5 **Research questions**

In HCI, we conduct experimental research to answer (and raise!) questions about a new or existing user interface or interaction technique. Often the questions pertain to the relationship between two variables, where one variable is a circumstance or condition that is manipulated (an interface property) and the other is an observed and measured behavioral response (task performance).

The notion of posing or answering questions seems simple enough, but this is tricky because of the human element. Unlike an algorithm operating on a data set, where the time to search, sort, or whatever is the same with each try, people exhibit variability in their actions. This is true both from person to person and for a single person repeating a task. The result is always different! This variability affects the confidence with which we can answer *research questions*. To gauge the confidence of our answers, we use statistical techniques, as presented in Chapter 6, Hypothesis Testing.

Research questions emerge from an inquisitive process. The researcher has an idea and wishes to see if it has merit. Initial thoughts are fluid and informal:

- Is it viable?
- Is it as good as or better than current practice?
- What are its strengths and weaknesses?
- Which of several alternatives is best?
- What are the human performance limits and capabilities?
- Does it work well for novices, for experts?
- How much practice is required to become proficient?

These questions are unquestionably relevant, since they capture a researcher's thinking at the early stages of a research project. However, the questions above suffer a serious deficiency: They are not testable. The goal, then, is to move forward from the loose and informal questions above to questions more suitable for empirical and experimental enquiry.

I'll use an example to show how this is done. Perhaps a researcher is interested in text entry on touchscreen phones. Texting is something people do a lot. The researcher is experienced with the Qwerty soft keyboard on touchscreen phones, but finds it error prone and slow. Having thought about the problem for a while, an idea emerges for a new technique for entering text. Perhaps it's a good idea. Perhaps it's really good, better than the basic Qwerty soft keyboard (QSK). Being motivated to do research in HCI, the researcher builds a prototype of the entry technique and fiddles with the implementation until it works fine. The researcher decides to undertake some experimental research to evaluate the idea. What are the research questions? Perhaps the following capture the researcher's thinking:

- Is the new technique any good?
- Is the new technique better than QSK?

- Is the new technique faster than QSK?
- Is the new technique faster than QSK after a bit of practice?
- Is the measured entry speed (in words per minute) higher for the new technique than for a QSK after one hour of use?

From top to bottom, the questions are progressively narrower and more focused. Expressions like "any good" or "better than," although well intentioned, are problematic for research. Remember observation and measurement? How does one measure "better than"? Farther down the list, the questions address qualities that are more easily observed and measured. Furthermore, since they are expressed across alternative designs, comparisons are possible. The last question speaks very specifically to entry speed measured in words per minute, to a comparison between two methods, and to a criterion for practice. This is a testable research question.

4.6 Internal validity and external validity

At this juncture we are in a position to consider two important properties of experimental research: *internal validity* and *external validity*. I'll use the research questions above to frame the discussion. Two of the questions appear in the plot in Figure 4.8. The x-axis is labeled Breadth of Question or, alternatively, External Validity. The y-axis is labeled Accuracy of Answer or, alternatively, Internal Validity.

The question

> Is the new technique better than QSK?

is positioned as high in breadth (that's good!) yet answerable with low accuracy (that's bad!). As already noted, this question is not testable in an empirical sense. Attempts to answer it directly are fraught with problems, because we lack a methodology to observe and measure "better than" (even though finding better interfaces is the final goal).

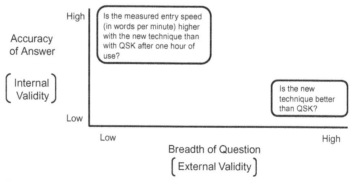

FIGURE 4.8

Graphical comparison of Internal Validity and External Validity.

The other, more detailed question

> Is the measured entry speed (in words per minute) higher with
> the new technique than with QSK after one hour of use?

is positioned as low in breadth (that's bad!) yet answerable with high accuracy
(that's good!). The question is testable, which means we can craft a methodology
to answer it through observation and measurement. Unfortunately, the narrow scope
of the question brings different problems. Focusing on entry speed is fine, but what
about other aspects of the interaction? What about accuracy, effort, comfort, cognitive load, user satisfaction, practical use of the technique, and so on? The question
excludes consideration of these, hence the low breadth rating.

The alternative labels for the axes in Figure 4.8 are internal validity and external
validity. In fact, the figure was designed to set up discussion on these important
terms in experimental research.

Internal validity (definition) is the extent to which an effect observed is due
to the test conditions. For the example, an *effect* is simply the difference in entry
speed between the new technique and QSK. If we conduct an experiment to measure and compare the entry speed for the two techniques, we want confidence that
the difference observed was actually due to inherent differences between the techniques. Internal validity captures this confidence. Perhaps the difference was due
to something else, such as variability in the responses of the participants in the
study. Humans differ. Some people are predisposed to be meticulous, while others
are carefree, even reckless. Furthermore, human behavior—individually or between
people—can change from one moment to the next, for no obvious reason. Were
some participants tested early in the day, others late in the day? Were there any distractions, interruptions, or other environmental changes during testing? Suffice it to
say that any source of variation beyond that due to the inherent properties of the test
conditions tends to compromise internal validity. High internal validity means the
effect observed really exists.

External validity (definition) is the extent to which experimental results are
generalizable to other people and other situations. *Generalizable* clearly speaks to
breadth in Figure 4.8. To the extent the research pursues broadly framed questions,
the results tend to be broadly applicable. But there is more. Research results that
apply to "other people" imply that the participants involved were representative of a
larger intended population. If the experiment used 18- to 25-year-old computer literate college students, the results might generalize to middle-aged computer literate
professionals. But they might not generalize to middle-aged people without computer experience. And they likely would not apply to the elderly, to children, or to
users with certain disabilities. In experimental research, random sampling is important for generalizability; that is, the participants selected for testing were drawn at
random from the desired population.

Generalizable to "other situations" means the experimental *environment* and
procedures were representative of real world situations where the interface or

FIGURE 4.9

There is tension between internal validity and external validity. Improving one comes at the expense of the other.

(Sketch courtesy of Bartosz Bajer)

technique will be used. If the research studied the usability of a GPS system for taxi drivers or delivery personnel and the experiment was conducted in a quiet, secluded research lab, there may be a problem with external validity. Perhaps a different experimental environment should be considered. Research on text entry where participants enter predetermined text phrases with no punctuation symbols, no uppercase characters, and without any ability to correct mistakes, may have problem with external validity. Again, a different experimental procedure should be considered.

The scenarios above are overly dogmatic. Experiment design is an exercise in compromise. While speaking in the strictest terms about high internal validity and high external validity, in practice one is achieved at the expense of the other, as characterized in Figure 4.9.

To appreciate the tension between internal and external validity, two additional examples are presented. The first pertains to the experimental environment. Consider an experiment that compares two remote pointing devices for presentation systems. To improve external validity, the experimental environment mimics expected usage. Participants are tested in a large room with a large presentation-size display, they stand, and they are positioned a few meters from the display. The other participants are engaged to act as an audience by attending and sitting around tables in the room during testing. There is no doubt this environment improves external validity. But what about internal validity? Some participants may be distracted or intimidated by the audience. Others might have a tendency to show off, impress, or act out. Such behaviors introduce sources of variation outside the realm of the devices under test, and thereby compromise internal validity. So our effort to improve external validity through environmental considerations may negatively impact internal validity.

A second example pertains to the experimental procedure. Consider an experiment comparing two methods of text entry. In an attempt to improve external validity, participants are instructed to enter whatever text they think of. The text may include punctuation symbols and uppercase and lowercase characters, and participants can edit the text and correct errors as they go. Again, external validity is improved since this is what people normally do when entering text. However, internal validity is compromised because behaviors are introduced that are not directly related to the text entry techniques—behaviors such as pondering (What should

I enter next?) and fiddling with commands (How do I move the cursor back and make a correction? How is overtype mode invoked?). Furthermore, since participants generate the text, errors are difficult to record since there is no "source text" with which to compare the entered text. So here again we see the compromise. The desire to improve external validity through procedural considerations may negatively impact internal validity.

Unfortunately, there is no universal remedy for the tension between internal and external validity. At the very least, one must acknowledge the limitations. Formulating conclusions that are broader than what the results suggest is sure to raise the ire of reviewers. We can strive for the best of both worlds with a simple approach, however. Posing multiple narrow (testable) questions that cover the range of outcomes influencing the broader (untestable) questions will increase both internal and external validity. For example, a technique that is fast, accurate, easy to learn, easy to remember, and considered comfortable and enjoyable by users is generally better. Usually there is a positive correlation between the testable and untestable questions; i.e., participants generally find one UI better than another if it is faster and more accurate, takes fewer steps, is more enjoyable, is more comfortable, and so on.

Before moving on, it is worth mentioning *ecological validity*, a term closely related to external validity. The main distinction is in how the terms are used. Ecological validity refers to the methodology (using materials, tasks, and situations typical of the real world), whereas external validity refers to the outcome (obtaining results that generalize to a broad range of people and situations).

4.7 Comparative evaluations

Evaluating new ideas for user interfaces or interaction techniques is central to research in human-computer interaction. However, evaluations in HCI sometimes focus on a single idea or interface. The idea is conceived, designed, implemented, and evaluated—but not compared. The research component of such an evaluation is questionable. Or, to the extent the exercise is labeled research, it is more aligned with the second definition of research noted earlier: "collecting information about a particular subject."

From a research perspective, our third definition is more appealing, since it includes the ideas of experimentation, discovery, and developing theories of interaction. Certainly, more meaningful and insightful results are obtained if a *comparative evaluation* is performed. In other words, a new user interface or interaction technique is designed and implemented and then compared with one or more alternative designs to determine which is faster, more accurate, less confusing, more preferred by users, etc. The alternatives may be variations in the new design, an established design (a baseline condition), or some combination of the two. In fact, the testable research questions above are crafted as comparisons (e.g., "Is Method A faster than Method B for …?"), and for good reason. A controlled experiment must include at least one independent variable and the independent variable must have at

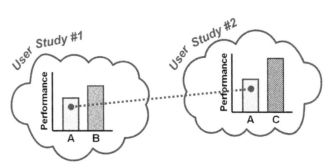

FIGURE 4.10

Including a baseline condition serves as a check on the methodology and facilitates the comparison of results between user studies.

least two levels or test conditions. Comparison, then, is inherent in research following the experimental method discussed earlier. The design of HCI experiments is elaborated further in Chapter 5.

The idea of including an established design as a baseline condition is particularly appealing. There are two benefits. First, the baseline condition serves as a check on the methodology. Baseline conditions are well traveled in the research literature, so results in a new experiment are expected to align with previous results. Second, the baseline condition allows results to be compared with other studies. The general idea is shown in Figure 4.10. The results from two hypothetical user studies are shown. Both user studies are comparative evaluations and both include condition A as a baseline. Provided the methodology was more or less the same, the performance results in the two studies should be the same or similar for the baseline condition. This serves not only as a check on the methodology but also facilitates comparisons between the two user studies. A quick look at the charts suggests that condition C out-performs condition B. This is an interesting observation because condition C was evaluated in one study, condition B in another.

Consider the idea cited earlier of comparing two remote pointing devices for presentation systems. Such a study would benefit by including a conventional mouse as a baseline condition.[8] If the results for the mouse are consistent with those found in other studies, then the methodology was probably okay, and the results for the remote pointing devices are likely valid. Furthermore, conclusions can often be expressed in terms of the known baseline condition, for example, "Device A was found to be about 8 percent slower than a conventional mouse."

The value in conducting a comparative study was studied in research by Tohidi et al. (2006), who tested the hypothesis that a comparative evaluation yields more insight than a one-of evaluation. In their study, participants were assigned to groups and were asked to manually perform simple tasks with climate control interfaces

---

[8]The example cited earlier on remote pointing devices included a conventional mouse as a baseline condition (MacKenzie and Jusoh, 2001).

(i.e., thermostats). There were three different interfaces tested. Some of the participants interacted with just one interface, while others did the same tasks with all three interfaces. The participants interacting with all three interfaces consistently found more problems and were more critical of the interfaces. They were also less prone to inflate their subjective ratings. While this experiment was fully qualitative—human performance was not measured or quantified—the message is the same: a comparative evaluation yields more valuable and insightful results than a single-interface evaluation.

4.8 **Relationships: circumstantial and causal**

I noted above that looking for and explaining interesting relationships is part of what we do in HCI research. Often a controlled experiment is designed and conducted specifically for this purpose, and if done properly a particular type of conclusion is possible. We can often say that the condition manipulated in the experiment *caused* the changes in the human responses that were observed and measured. This is a *cause-and-effect relationship*, or simply a *causal relationship*.

In HCI, the variable manipulated is often a nominal-scale attribute of an interface, such as device, entry method, feedback modality, selection technique, menu depth, button layout, and so on. The variable measured is typically a ratio-scale human behavior, such as task completion time, error rate, or the number of button clicks, scrolling events, gaze shifts, etc.

Finding a causal relationship in an HCI experiment yields a powerful conclusion. If the human response measured is vital in HCI, such as the time it takes to do a common task, then knowing that a condition tested in the experiment reduces this time is a valuable outcome. If the condition is an implementation of a novel idea and it was compared with current practice, there may indeed be reason to celebrate. Not only has a causal relationship been found, but the new idea improves on existing practice. This is the sort of outcome that adds valuable knowledge to the discipline; it moves the state of the art forward.[9] This is what HCI research is all about!

Finding a relationship does not necessarily mean a causal relationship exists. Many relationships are *circumstantial*. They exist, and they can be observed, measured, and quantified. But they are not causal, and any attempt to express the relationship as such is wrong. The classic example is the relationship between smoking and cancer. Suppose a research study tracks the habits and health of a large number of people over many years. This is an example of the correlational method of research mentioned earlier. In the end, a relationship is found between smoking and cancer: cancer is more prevalent in the people who smoked. Is it correct to conclude from the study that smoking *causes* cancer? No. The relationship observed is

---

[9]Reporting a non-significant outcome is also important, particularly if there is reason to believe a test condition might improve an interface or interaction technique. Reporting a non-significant outcome means that, at the very least, other researchers needn't pursue the idea further.

circumstantial, not causal. Consider this: when the data are examined more closely, it is discovered that the tendency to develop cancer is also related to other variables in the data set. It seems the people who developed cancer also tended to drink more alcohol, eat more fatty foods, sleep less, listen to rock music, and so on. Perhaps it was the increased consumption of alcohol that caused the cancer, or the consumption of fatty foods, or something else. The relationship is circumstantial, not causal. This is not to say that *circumstantial relationships* are not useful. Looking for and finding a circumstantial relationship is often the first step in further research, in part because it is relatively easy to collect data and look for circumstantial relationships.

Causal relationships emerge from controlled experiments. Looking for a causal relationship requires a study where, among other things, participants are selected randomly from a population and are randomly assigned to test conditions. A random assignment ensures that each group of participants is the same or similar in all respects except for the conditions under which each group is tested. Thus, the differences that emerge are more likely due to (*caused by*) the test conditions than to environmental or other circumstances. Sometimes participants are balanced into groups where the participants in each group are screened so that the groups are equal in terms of other relevant attributes. For example, an experiment testing two input controllers for games could randomly assign participants to groups or balance the groups to ensure the range of gaming experience is approximately equal.

Here is an HCI example similar to the smoking versus cancer example: A researcher is interested in comparing multi-tap and predictive input (*T9*) for text entry on a mobile phone. The researcher ventures into the world and approaches mobile phone users, asking for five minutes of their time. Many agree. They answer a few questions about experience and usage habits, including their preferred method of entering text messages. Fifteen multi-tap users and 15 *T9* users are found. The users are asked to enter a prescribed phrase of text while they are timed. Back in the lab, the data are analyzed. Evidently, the *T9* users were faster, entering at a rate of 18 words per minute, compared to 12 words per minute for the multi-tap users. That's 50 percent faster for the *T9* users! What is the conclusion? There is a relationship between method of entry and text entry speed; however, the relationship is circumstantial, not causal. It is reasonable to report what was done and what was found, but it is wrong to venture beyond what the methodology gives. Concluding from this simple study that *T9* is faster than multi-tap would be wrong. Upon inspecting the data more closely, it is discovered that the *T9* users tended to be more tech-savvy: they reported considerably more experience using mobile phones, and also reported sending considerably more text messages per day than the multi-tap users who, by and large, said they didn't like sending text messages and did so very infrequently.[10] So the difference observed may be due to prior experience and usage habits, rather than to inherent differences in the text entry methods. If there is a genuine interest in determining if one text entry method

---

[10] Although it is more difficult to determine, perhaps technically savvy users were more willing to participate in the study. Perhaps the users who declined to participate were predominantly multi-tap users.

is faster than another, a controlled experiment is required. This is the topic of the next chapter.

One final point deserves mention. Cause and effect conclusions are not possible in certain types of controlled experiments. If the variable manipulated is a *naturally occurring attribute* of participants, then cause and effect conclusions are unreliable. Examples of naturally occurring attributes include gender (female, male), personality (extrovert, introvert), handedness (left, right), first language (e.g., English, French, Spanish), political viewpoint (left, right), and so on. These attributes are legitimate independent variables, but they cannot be manipulated, which is to say, they cannot be assigned to participants. In such cases, a cause and effect conclusion is not valid because is not possible to avoid confounding variables (defined in Chapter 5). Being a male, being an extrovert, being left-handed, and so on always brings forth other attributes that systematically vary across levels of the independent variable. Cause and effect conclusions are unreliable in these cases because it is not possible to know whether the experimental effect was due to the independent variable or to the confounding variable.

4.9 **Research topics**

Most HCI research is not about designing products. It's not even about designing applications for products. In fact, it's not even about design or products. Research in HCI, like in most fields, tends to nip away at the edges. The march forward tends to be incremental. The truth is, most new research ideas tend to build on existing ideas and do so in modest ways. A small improvement to this, a little change to that. When big changes do arise, they usually involve bringing to market, through engineering and design, ideas that already exist in the research literature. Examples are the finger flick and two-finger gestures used on touchscreen phones. Most users likely encountered these for the first time with the Apple iPhone. The gestures seem like bold new advances in interaction, but, of course, they are not. The flick gesture dates at least to the 1960s. Flicks are clearly seen in use with a light pen in the videos of Sutherland's Sketchpad, viewable on YouTube. They are used to terminate a drawing command. Two-finger gestures date at least to the 1970s. Figure 4.11 shows Herot and Weinzapfel's (1978) two-finger gesture used to rotate a virtual knob on a touch-sensitive display. As reported, the knob can be rotated to within 5 degrees of a target position. So what might seem like a bold new advance is often a matter of good engineering and design, using ideas that already exist.

Finding a *research topic* is often the most challenging step for graduate students in HCI (and other fields). The expression "ABD" for "all but dissertation" is a sad reminder of this predicament. Graduate students sometimes find themselves in a position of having finished all degree requirements (e.g., coursework, a teaching practicum) without nailing down the big topic for dissertation research. Students might be surprised to learn that seasoned researchers in universities and industry also struggle for that next big idea. Akin to writer's block, the harder one tries, the

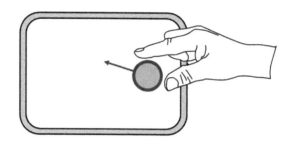

FIGURE 4.11

A two-finger gesture on a touch-sensitive display is used to rotate a virtual knob.

(Adapted from Herot and Weinzapfel, 1978)

less likely is the idea to appear. I will present four tips to overcome "researcher's block" later in this section. First, I present a few observations on ideas and how and where they arise.

4.9.1 Ideas

In the halcyon days after World War II, there was an American television show, a situation comedy, or sitcom, called *The Many Loves of Dobie Gillis* (1959–1963). Much like *Seinfeld* many years later, the show was largely about, well, nothing. Dobie's leisurely life mostly focused on getting rich or on endearing a beautiful woman to his heart. Each episode began with an idea, a scheme. The opening scene often placed Dobie on a park bench beside *The Thinker*, the bronze and marble statue by French sculptor Auguste Rodin (1840–1917). (See Figure 4.12.) After some pensive moments by the statue, Dobie's idea, his scheme, would come to him. It would be nice if research ideas in HCI were similarly available and with such assurance as were Dobie's ideas. That they are not is no cause for concern, however. Dobie's plans usually failed miserably, so we might question his approach to formulating his plans. Is it possible that *The Thinker*, in his pose, is more likely to inspire writer's block than the idea so desperately sought? The answer may be *yes*, but there is little science here. We are dealing with human thought, inspiration, creativity, and a milieu of other human qualities that are poorly understood, at best.

If working hard to find a good idea doesn't work, perhaps a better approach is to relax and just get on with one's day. This seems to have worked for the ancient Greek scholar Archimedes (287–212 BC) who is said to have effortlessly come upon a brilliant idea as a solution to a problem. As a scientist, Archimedes was called upon to determine if King Hiero's crown was pure gold or if it was compromised with a lesser alloy. One solution was to melt the crown, separating the constituent parts. This would destroy the crown–not a good idea. Archimedes' idea was simple, and he is said to have discovered it while taking a bath. Yes, taking a bath, rather than sitting for hours in *The Thinker*'s pose. He realized–in an instant– that the volume of water displaced as he entered the bathtub must equal the volume

FIGURE 4.12

Rodin's *The Thinker* often appeared in the opening scenes of the American sitcom *The Many Loves of Dobie Gillis.*

of his body. Immersing the crown in water would similarly yield the crown's volume, and this, combined with the crown's weight, would reveal the crown's density. If the density of the crown equaled the known density of gold, the King's crown was pure gold–problem solved. According to the legend, Archimedes was so elated at his moment of revelation that he jumped from his bath and ran nude about the streets of Syracuse shouting "Eureka!" ("I found it!").

While legends make good stories, we are not likely to be as fortunate as Archimedes in finding a good idea for an HCI research topic. Inspiration is not always the result of single moment of revelation. It is often gradual, with sources unknown or without a conscious and recognizable connection to the problem. Recall Vannevar Bush's memex, described in the opening chapter of this book. Memex was a concept. It was never built, even though Bush described the interaction with memex in considerable detail. We know memex today as hypertext and the World Wide Web. But where and how did Bush get his idea? The starting point is having a problem to solve. The problem of interest to Bush was coping with ever-expanding volumes of information. Scientists like Bush needed a convenient way to access this information. But how? It seems Bush's inspiration for memex came from… Let's pause for a moment, lest we infer Bush was engaged in a structured approach to problem solving. It is not likely that Bush went to work one morning intent on solving the problem of information access. More than likely, the idea came without deliberate effort. It may have come flittingly, in an instant, or gradually, over days, weeks, or months. Who knows? What is known, however, is that the idea did not arise from nothing. Ideas come from the human experience. This is why in HCI we often read about things like "knowledge in the head and knowledge in the world"

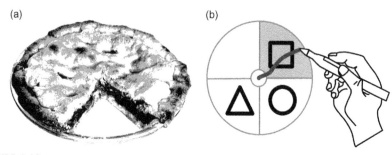

(a)   (b)

FIGURE 4.13

Pie menus in HCI: (a) The inspiration? (b) HCI example.

(Adapted from G. Kurtenbach, 1993)

(Norman, 1988, ch. 3) or metaphor and analogy (Carroll and Thomas, 1982). The context for inspiration is the human experience. So what was the source of Bush's inspiration for memex? The answer is in Bush's article, and also in Chapter 1.

Are there other examples relevant to HCI? Sure. Twitter co-founder Jack Dorsey is said to have come up with the idea for the popular micro-blogging site while sitting on a children's slide in a park eating Mexican food.[11] What about pie menus in graphical user interfaces? Pie menus, as an alternative to linear menus, were first proposed by Don Hopkins at the University of Maryland in 1988 (cited in Callahan et al., 1988). We might wonder about the source of Hopkins' inspiration (see Figure 4.13).

See also student exercises 4-2 and 4-3 at the end of this chapter.

4.9.2 Finding a topic

It is no small feat to find an interesting research topic. In the following paragraphs, four tips are offered on finding a topic suitable for research. As with the earlier discussion on the cost and frequency of errors (see Figure 3-46), there is little science to offer here. The ideas follow from personal experience and from working with students and other researchers in HCI.

4.9.3 Tip #1: Think small!

At a conference recently, I had an interesting conversation with a student. He was a graduate student in HCI. "Have you found a topic for your research," I asked. "Not really," he said. He had a topic, but only in a broad sense. Seems his supervisor had funding for a large research project related to aviation. The topic, in a general sense, was to develop an improved user interface for an air traffic control system. He was stuck. Where to begin? Did I have any ideas for him? Well, actually, no I didn't. Who wouldn't be stuck? The task of developing a UI for an air traffic control system is huge. Furthermore, the project mostly involves engineering and

---

[11] *New York Times* Oct 30, 2010, p BU1.

design. Where is the research in designing an improved system of any sort? What are the research questions? What are the experimental variables? Unfortunately, graduate students are often saddled with similar big problems because a supervisor's funding source requires it. The rest of our discussion focused on narrowing the problem—in a big way. Not to some definable sub-system, but to a small aspect of the interface or interaction. The smaller, the better.

The point above is to think small. On finding that big idea, the advice is… forget it. Once you shed that innate desire to find something really significant and important, it's amazing what will follow. If you have a small idea, something that seems a little useful, it's probably worth pursuing as a research project. Pursue it and the next thing you know, three or four related interaction improvements come to mind. Soon enough, there's a dissertation topic in the works. So don't hesitate to think small.

4.9.4 Tip #2: Replicate!

An effective way to get started on research is to replicate an existing experiment from the HCI literature. This seems odd. Where is the research in simply replicating what has already been done? Of course, there is none. But there is a trick. Having taught HCI courses many times over many years, I know that students frequently get stuck finding a topic for the course's research project. Students frequently approach me for suggestions. If I have an idea that seems relevant to the student's interests, I'll suggest it. Quite often (usually!) I don't have any particular idea. If nothing comes to mind, I take another approach. The student is advised just to study the HCI literature—research papers from the CHI proceedings, for example— and find some experimental research on a topic of interest. Then just replicate the experiment. Is that okay, I am asked. Sure, no problem.

The trick is in the path to replicating. Replicating a research experiment requires a lot of work. The process of studying a research paper and precisely determining what was done, then implementing it, testing it, debugging it, doing an experiment around it, and so on will empower the student—the researcher—with a deep understanding of the issues, much deeper than simply reading the paper. This moves the line forward. The stage is set. Quite often, a new idea, a new twist, emerges. But it is important not to *require* something new. The pressure in that may backfire. Something new may emerge, but this might not happen until late in the process, or after the experiment is finished. So it is important to avoid a requirement for novelty. This is difficult, because it is germane to the human condition to strive for something new. Self-doubt may bring the process to a standstill. So keep the expectations low. A small tweak here, a little change there. Good enough. No pressure. Just replicate. You may be surprised with the outcome.

4.9.5 Tip #3: Know the literature!

It might seem obvious, but the process of reviewing research papers on a topic of interest is an excellent way to develop ideas for research projects. The starting point is identifying the topic in a general sense. If one finds gaming of interest, then gaming is the topic. If one finds social networking of interest, then that's the topic. From there the task is to search out and aggressively study and analyze all published research on the topic. If there are too many publications, then narrow the topic. What, in particular, is the interest in gaming or social networking? Continue the search. Use Google Scholar, the ACM Digital Library, or whatever resource is conveniently available. Download all the papers, store them, organize them, study them, make notes, then open a spreadsheet file and start tabulating features from the papers. In the rows, identify the papers. In the columns, tabulate aspects of the interface or interaction technique, conditions tested, results obtained, and so on. Organize the table in whatever manner seems reasonable.

The process is chaotic at first. Where to begin? What are the issues? The task is daunting, at the very least, because of the divergence in reporting methods. But that's the point. The gain is in the process—bringing shape and structure to the chaos. The table will grow as more papers are found and analyzed. There are examples of such tables in published papers, albeit in a condensed summary form. Figure 4.14 shows an example from a research paper on text entry using small keyboards. The table amounts to a mini literature review. Although the table is neat and tidy, don't be fooled. It emerged from a difficult and chaotic process of reviewing a collection of papers and finding common and relevant issues. The collection of notes in the right-hand column is evidence of the difficulty. This column is like a disclaimer, pointing out issues that complicate comparisons of the data in the other columns.

Are there research topics lurking within Figure 4.14? Probably. But the point is the process, not the product. Building such a table shapes the research area into relevant categories of inquiry. Similar tables are found in other research papers (e.g., Figure 11 and Figure 12 in MacKenzie, 1992; Table 3 and Table 4 in Soukoreff and MacKenzie, 2004). See also student exercise 4-4 at the end of this chapter.

4.9.6 Tip #4: Think inside the box!

The common expression "think outside the box" is a challenge to all. The idea is to dispense with accepted beliefs and assumptions (in the box) and to think in a new way that assumes nothing and challenges everything. However, there is a problem with the challenge. Contemporary, tech-savvy people, clever as they are, often believe they in fact do think outside the box, and that it is everyone else who is confined to life in the box. With this view, the challenge is lost before starting. If there is anything useful in tip #4, it begins with an unsavory precept: You are inside the box! All is not lost, however. Thinking inside the box, then, is thinking about and challenging one's own experiences—the experiences inside the box. The idea is simple. Just get on with your day, but at every juncture, every interaction, think and question. What happened? Why did it happen? Is there an alternative? Play the

Study (1st author)	Number of Keys[a]	Direct/Indirect	Scanning	Number of Participants	Speed[b] (wpm)	Notes
Bellman [2]	5	Indirect	No	11	11	4 cursors keys + SELECT key. Error rates not reported. No error correction method.
Dunlop [4]	4	Direct	No	12	8.90	4 letter keys + SPACE key. Error rates reported as "very low."
Dunlop [5]	4	Direct	No	20	12	4 letter keys + 1 key for SPACE/NEXT. Error rates not reported. No error correction method.
Tanaka-Ishii [25]	3	Direct	No	8	12+	4 letters keys 4 keys for editing, and selecting. 5 hours training. Error rates not reported. Errors corrected using CLEAR key.
Gong [7]	3	Direct	No	32	8.01	3 letter keys + two additional keys. Error rate = 2.1%. Errors corrected using DELETE key.
MacKenzie [16]	3	Indirect	No	10	9.61	2 cursor keys + SELECT key. Error rate = 2.2%. No error correction method.
Baljko [1]	2	Indirect	Yes	12	3.08	1 SELECT key + BACKSPACE key. 43 virtual keys. RC scanning. Same phrase entered 4 times. Error rate = 18.5%. Scanning interval = 750 ms.
Simpson [24]	1	Indirect	Yes	4	4.48	1 SELECT key. 26 virtual keys. RC scanning. Excluded trials with selection errors or missed selections. No error correction. Scanning interval = 525 ms at end of study.
Koester [10]	1	Indirect	Yes	3	7.2	1 SELECT key. 33 virtual keys. RC scanning with word prediction. Dictionary size not given. Virtual BACKSPACE key. 10 blocks of trials. Error rates not reported. Included trials with selection errors or missed selections. Fastest participant: 8.4 wpm.

a For "direct" entry, the value is the number of letter keys. For "indirect" entry, the value is the total number of keys.
b The entry speed cited is the highest of the values reported in each source, taken from the last block if multiple blocks.

FIGURE 4.14

Table showing papers (rows) and relevant conditions or results (columns) from research papers on text entry using small keyboards.

(From MacKenzie, 2009b, Table 1; consult for full details on studies cited)

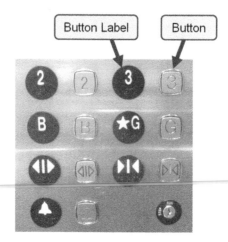

FIGURE 4.15

Elevator control panel. The button label is more prominent than the button.

role of both a participant (this is unavoidable) and an observer. Observe others, of course, but more importantly observe yourself. You are in the box, but have a look, study, and reconsider.

Here's an example, which on the surface seems trivial (but see tip #1). Recently, while at work at York University, I was walking to my class on Human-Computer Interaction. Being a bit late, I was in a hurry. The class was in a nearby building on the third floor and I was carrying some equipment. I entered the elevator and pushed the button—the wrong button. Apparently, for each floor the control panel has both a button label and a button. (See Figure 4.15.) I pushed the button label instead of the button. A second later I pushed the button, and my journey continued. End of story.

Of course, there is more. Why did I push the wrong button? Yes, I was in a hurry, but that's not the full reason. With a white number on a black background, the floor is identified more prominently by the button label than by the button. And the button label is round, like a button. On the button, the number is recessed in the metal and is barely visible. The error was minor, only a *slip* (right intention, wrong action; see Norman, 1988, ch. 5). Is there a research topic in this? Perhaps. Perhaps not. But experiencing, observing, and thinking about one's interactions with technology can generate ideas and promote a humbling yet questioning frame of thinking—thinking that moves forward into research topics. The truth is, I have numerous moments like this every day (and so do you!). Most amount to nothing, but the small foibles in interacting with technology are intriguing and worth thinking about.

In this chapter, we have examined the scientific foundations for research in human-computer interaction. With this, the next challenge is in designing and conducting experiments using human participants (users) to evaluate new ideas for user interfaces and interaction techniques. We explore these topics in Chapter 5.

STUDENT EXERCISES

4-1. Examine some published papers in HCI and find examples where results were reported as a raw count (e.g., number of errors) rather than as a count *per something* (e.g., percent errors). Find three examples and write a brief report (or prepare a brief presentation) detailing how the results were reported and the weakness or limitation in the method. Propose a better way to report the same results. Use charts or graphs where appropriate.

4-2. What, in Vannevar Bush's "human experience," formed the inspiration for memex? (If needed, review Bush's essay "As We May Think," or see the discussion in Chapter 1.) What are the similarities between his inspiration and memex?

4-3. A *fisheye lens* or *fisheye view* is a tool or concept in HCI whereby high-value information is presented in greater detail than low-value information. Furnas first introduced the idea in 1986 (Furnas, 1986). Although the motivation was to improve the visualization of large data sets, such as programs or databases, Furnas' idea came from something altogether different. What was Furnas' inspiration for fisheye views? Write a brief report describing the analogy offered by Furnas. Include in your report three examples of fisheye lenses, as described and implemented in subsequent research, noting in particular the background motivation.

4-4. Here are some research themes: 3D gaming, mobile phone use while driving, privacy in social networking, location-aware user interfaces, tactile feedback in pointing and selecting, multi-touch tabletop interaction. Choose one of these topics (or another) and build a table similar to that in Figure 4.14. Narrow the topic, if necessary (e.g., mobile phone *texting* while driving), and find at least five relevant research papers to include in the table. Organize the table identifying the papers in the rows and methods, relevant themes, and findings in the columns. Write a brief report about the table. Include citations and references to the selected papers.

4-5. In Chapter 3, we used a 2D plot to illustrate the trade-off between the frequency of errors (*x*-axis) and the cost of errors (*y*-axis) (see Figure 3.46). The plot was just a sketch, since the analysis was informal. In this chapter, we discussed another trade-off, that between form and function. The trade-off is shown below, drawn in a similar way for the same reason. Two juice squeezers are positioned in the plot according to their suggested form and function.

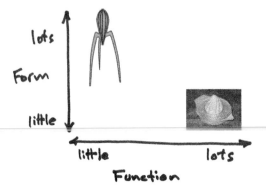

Find three examples of artifacts, each with two implementations (e.g., two juice squeezers are shown above) and position them in the form versus function 2D plot. Ensure at least one of the artifacts is computer-based and at least one is not computer-based. Write a brief report describing the artifacts and implementations and rationalizing their placement in the chart.

Designing HCI Experiments

5

Learning how to design and conduct an experiment with human participants is a skill required of all researchers in human-computer interaction. In this chapter I describe the core details of designing and conducting HCI experiments.

One way to think about experiment design is through a signal and noise metaphor. In the metaphor, we divide our observations and measurements into two components: signal and noise. (See Figure 5.1.) The source shows a time series. A slight upward trend is apparent; however, the variability or noise in the source makes this difficult to detect. If we separate the source into components for signal and noise, the trend in the signal is clear.

In HCI experiments, the signal is related to a variable of interest, such as input device, feedback mode, or an interaction technique under investigation. The noise is everything else—the random influences. These include environmental circumstances such as temperature, lighting, background noise, a wobbly chair, or glare on the computer screen. The people or participants in the experiment are also a source of noise or variability. Some participants may be having a good day, while others are having a bad day. Some people are predisposed to behave in a certain manner; others behave differently. The process of designing an experiment is one of enhancing the signal while reducing the noise. This is done by carefully considering the setup of the experiment in terms of the variables manipulated and measured, the variables controlled, the procedures, the tasks, and so on. Collectively, these properties of an experiment establish the methodology for the research.

5.1 What methodology?

The term *method* or *methodology* refers to the way an experiment is designed and carried out. This involves deciding on the people (participants), the hardware and software (materials or apparatus), the tasks, the order of tasks, the procedure for briefing and preparing the participants, the variables, the data collected and analyzed, and so on. Having a sound methodology is critical. On this point, Allen Newell did not hesitate: "Science is method. Everything else is commentary."[1]

[1] This quote from Allen Newell was cited and elaborated on by Stuart Card in an invited talk at the ACM's SIGCHI conference in Austin, Texas (May 10, 2012).

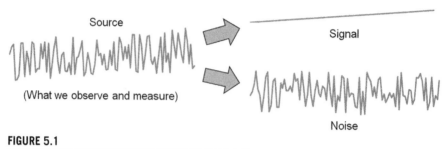

Source

(What we observe and measure)

Signal

Noise

FIGURE 5.1

Signal-to-noise conceptualization of experiment design.

These are strong words. Why did Newell apply such forceful yet narrow language to a topic as broad as science? The reason is that Newell, and others, understand that methodology is the bedrock of science. If the methodology is weak or flawed, there is no science forthcoming. What remains is little else than commentary.

In the preceding chapter, I advocated the use of a standardized methodology to strengthen experimental research. The flip side is that an ad hoc, or made-up, methodology weakens research. There is little sense in contriving a methodology simply because it seems like a good way to test or demonstrate an idea. So what is the appropriate methodology for research in human-computer interaction? The discussions that follow pertain only to experimental research and in particular to *factorial experiments*, where participants are exposed to levels of factors (test conditions) while their behavior (human performance) is observed and measured. By and large, the methodology is plucked from one of HCI's parent disciplines: experimental psychology.

Just as the Association for Computing Machinery (ACM) is the dominant organization overseeing computer science and related special interests such as HCI, the American Psychological Association (APA) is the dominant organization overseeing experimental psychology. Their *Publication Manual of the American Psychological Association*, first published in 1929, is a valuable resource for researchers undertaking experimental research involving human participants (APA, 2010). The manual, now in its sixth edition, is used by over 1,000 journals across many disciplines (Belia, Fidler, Williams, and Cumming, 2005). These include HCI journals. The APA guidelines are recommended by journals such as the ACM's *Transactions on Computer-Human Interaction* (*TOCHI*) (ACM, 2012) and Taylor and Francis's *Human-Computer Interaction* (Taylor and Francis, 2012). The APA *Publication Manual* is about more than publishing style; the manual lays out many methodological issues, such as naming and referring to independent and dependent variables, recruiting participants, reporting the results of statistical tests, and so on. Also the important link between research and publication is reflected in the title.

Another resource is psychologist David Martin's *Doing Psychology Experiments*, now in its sixth edition (D. W. Martin, 2004). Martin's approach is refreshing and entertaining, more cookbook-like than academic. All the core details are there, with examples that teach and amuse.

The proceedings of the ACM SIGCHI's annual conference (CHI) are also an excellent resource. CHI papers are easily viewed and downloaded from the ACM Digital Library. Of course, many research papers in the CHI proceedings do not present experimental research. And that's fine. HCI is multidisciplinary. The research methods brought to bear on human interaction with technology are equally diverse. However, of those papers that do present a *user study*—an experiment with human participants—there are, unfortunately, many where the methodology is ad hoc. The additional burden of weaving one's way through an unfamiliar methodology while simultaneously trying to understand a new and potentially interesting idea makes studying these papers difficult. But there are many CHI papers that stick to the standard methodology for experiments with human participants. It is relatively easy to spot examples. If the paper has a section called Method or Methodology and the first sub-section within is called Participants, there is a good chance the paper and the research it describes follow the standards for experimental research as laid out in this chapter. Examples from the CHI proceedings include the following: Aula, Khan, and Guan, 2010; Chin and Fu, 2010; Chin, Fu, and Kannampallil, 2009; Duggan and Payne, 2008; Gajos, Wobbrock, and Weld, 2008; Kammerer, Nairn, Pirolli, and Chi, 2009; Majaranta, Ahola, and Špakov, 2009; Räihä and Špakov, 2009; Sjölie et al., 2010; Sun, Zhang, Wiedenbeck, and Chintakovid, 2006; Tohidi et al., 2006; Wobbrock et al., 2009.

5.2 **Ethics approval**

One crucial step that precedes the design of every HCI experiment is *ethics approval*. Since HCI research involves humans, "researchers must respect the safety, welfare, and dignity of human participants in their research and treat them equally and fairly."[2] The approval process is governed by the institution or funding agency overseeing the research. At this author's institution, research projects must be approved by the Human Participant Review Committee (HRPC). Other committee names commonly used are the Institutional Review Board (IRB), Ethics Review Committee (ERC), and so on.

Typically, the review committee serves to ensure a number of ethical guidelines are acknowledged and adhered to. These include the right of the participant to be informed of the following:

- The nature of the research (hypotheses, goals and objectives, etc.)
- The research methodology (e.g., medical procedures, questionnaires, participant observation, etc.)
- Any risks or benefits

---

[2] www.yorku.ca/research/support/ethics/humans.html.

- The right not to participate, not to answer any questions, and/or to terminate participation at any time without prejudice (e.g., without academic penalty, withdrawal of remuneration, etc.)
- The right to anonymity and confidentiality

Details will vary according to local guidelines. Special attention is usually given for vulnerable participants, such as pregnant women, children, or the elderly. The basis for approving the research, where human participants are involved, is in achieving a balance between the risks to participants and the benefits to society.

5.3 Experiment design

Experiment design is the process of bringing together all the pieces necessary to test hypotheses on a user interface or interaction technique. It involves deciding on and defining which variables to use, what tasks and procedure to use, how many participants to use and how to solicit them, and so on.

One of the most difficult steps in designing an HCI experiment is just getting started. Ideas about a novel interface or interaction technique take shape well before thoughts of doing an experiment. There may even be an existing prototype that implements a research idea. Perhaps there is no prototype—yet. Regardless, there is an idea about an interface or interaction technique, and it seems new and interesting. Doing an experiment to test the idea seems like a good idea, but it is difficult transitioning from the creative and exciting work of developing a novel idea to the somewhat mechanical and mundane work of doing an experiment. Here is a question that will focus the mind more than any other in getting off and running with an HCI experiment: *what are the experimental variables?*

This seems like an odd place to begin. After all, experimental variables are in a distant world from the creative effort invested thus far. Well, not really. Thinking about experimental variables is an excellent exercise. Here's why. The process forces us to transition from well-intentioned, broad yet untestable questions (e.g., *Is my idea any good?*) to narrower yet testable questions (e.g., *Can a task be performed more quickly with my new interface than with an existing interface?*). If necessary, review the discussion in the preceding chapter on research questions and internal and external validity.

Thinking about experimental variables forces us to craft narrow and testable questions. The two most important experimental variables are *independent variables* and *dependent variables*. In fact, these variables are found within the example question in the preceding paragraph. Expressions like "more quickly" or "fewer steps" capture the essence of dependent variables: human behaviors that are measured. The expression "with my new interface than with an existing interface" captures the essence of an independent variable: an interface that is compared with an alternative interface. In fact, a testable research question inherently expresses the relationship between an independent variable and a dependent variable. Let's examine these two variables in more detail.

5.4 **Independent variables**

An *independent variable* is a circumstance or characteristic that is manipulated or systematically controlled to a change in a human response while the user is interacting with a computer. An independent variable is also called a *factor*. Experiments designed with independent variables are often called *factorial experiments*. The variable is manipulated across multiple (at least two) levels of the circumstance or characteristic. The variable is "independent" because it is independent of participant behavior, which means there is nothing a participant can do to influence an independent variable.

The variable manipulated is typically a nominal-scale attribute, often related to a property of an interface. Review any HCI research paper that presents a factorial experiment and examples of independent variables are easily found. They are anything that might affect users' proficiency in using a computer system. Examples include device (with levels mouse, trackball, and stylus) (MacKenzie, Sellen, and Buxton, 1991), feedback modality (with levels auditory, visual, and tactile) (Akamatsu et al., 1995), display size (with levels large and small) (Dillon, Richardson, and Mcknight, 1990), display type (with levels CRT and LCD) (MacKenzie and Riddersma, 1994), cross-display technique (with levels stitching, mouse ether, and ether + halo) (Nacenta, Regan, Mandry, and Gutwin, 2008), transfer function (with levels constant gain and pointer acceleration) (Casiez, Vogel, Pan, and Chaillou, 2007), tree visualization (with levels traditional, list, and multi-column) (Song, Kim, Lee, and Seo, 2010), and navigation technique (with levels standard pan and zoom versus PolyZoom) (Javed, Ghani, and Elmqvist, 2012). These variables are easy to manipulate because they are attributes of the apparatus (i.e., the computer or software). The idea of "manipulating" simply refers to systematically giving one interface, then another, to participants as part of the experimental procedure.

However, an independent variable can be many things besides an attribute of a computer system. It can be characteristics of humans, such as age (Chin and Fu, 2010; Chin et al., 2009), gender (male, female) (Sun et al., 2006; Zanbaka, Goolkasian, and Hodges, 2006), handedness (left handed, right handed) (Kabbash et al., 1993; Peters and Ivanoff, 1999), expertise in assessing web pages (expert, novice) (Brajnik, Yesilada, and Harper, 2011), body position (standing, sitting, walking), preferred operating system (Windows, Mac OS, Linux), first language (e.g., English, French, Chinese), political viewpoint (left, right), religious viewpoint, highest level of education, income, height, weight, hair color, shoe size, and so on. It is not clear that these human characteristics necessarily relate to HCI, but who knows.

Note that human characteristics such as gender or first language are *naturally occurring attributes*. Although such attributes are legitimate independent variables, they cannot be "manipulated" in the same way as an attribute of an interface.

An independent variable can also be an environmental circumstance, such as background noise (quiet, noisy), room lighting (sun, incandescent, fluorescent), vibration level (calm, in a car, in a train), and so on.

Here are two tips to consider. First, when formulating an independent variable, express it both in terms of the circumstance or characteristic itself as well as the levels of the circumstance or characteristic chosen for testing. (The levels of an independent variable are often called *test conditions*.) So we might have an independent variable called *interaction stance* with levels *sitting*, *standing*, and *walking*. This might seem like an odd point; however, in reading HCI research papers, it is surprising how often an independent variable is not explicitly named. For example, if an experiment seeks to determine whether a certain PDA task is performed better using audio versus tactile feedback, it is important to separately name both the independent variable (e.g., *feedback modality*) and the levels (*audio*, *tactile*).

The second tip is related to the first: Once the name of the independent variable and the names of the levels are decided, stick with these terms consistently throughout a paper. These terms hold special meaning within the experiment and any deviation in form is potentially confusing to the reader. Switching to terms like interaction position (cf. interaction stance), upright (cf. standing), sound (cf. audio), or vibration (cf. tactile) is potentially confusing. Is this a minor, nit-picky point? No. At times, it is a struggle to follow the discussions in a research paper. The fault often lies in the write-up, not in one's ability to follow or understand. The onus is on the researcher writing up the results of his or her work to deliver the rationale, methodology, results, discussion, and conclusions in the clearest way possible. Writing in a straightforward, consistent, and concise voice cannot be overemphasized. Further tips on writing for clarity are elaborated in Chapter 8.

Although it is reasonable to design and conduct an HCI experiment with a single independent variable, experiments often have more than one independent variable. Since considerable work is invested in designing and executing an experiment, there is a tendency to pack in as many independent variables as possible, so that more research questions are posed and, presumably, answered. However, including too many variables may compromise the entire experiment. With every additional independent variable, more effects exist between the variables. Figure 5.2 illustrates.

A design with a single independent variable includes a *main effect*, but no *interaction effects*. A design with two independent variables includes two main effects and one interaction effect, for a total of three effects. The interaction effect is a *two-way interaction*, since it is between two independent variables. For example, an experiment with independent variables Device and Task includes main effects for

Independent variables	Effects					Total
	Main	2-way	3-way	4-way	5-way	
1	1	-	-	-	-	1
2	2	1	-	-	-	3
3	3	3	1	-	-	7
4	4	6	3	1	-	14
5	5	10	6	3	1	25

FIGURE 5.2

The number of effects (main and interaction) increases as the number of independent variables increases.

Device and Task as well as a Device × Task interaction effect. As a reminder, the effect is *on the dependent variable*. The interpretation of interaction effects is discussed in Chapter 6 on Hypothesis Testing.

Once a third independent variable is introduced, the situation worsens: there are seven effects! With four and five independent variables, there are 14 and 25 effects, respectively. Too many variables! It is difficult to find meaningful interpretations for all the effects where there are so many. Furthermore, variability in the human responses is added with each independent variable, so all may be lost if too many variables are included. Interaction effects that are three-way or higher are extremely difficult to interpret and are best avoided. A good design, then, is one that limits the number of independent variables to one or two, three at most.[3]

5.5 **Dependent variables**

A *dependent variable* is a measured human behavior. In HCI the most common dependent variables relate to speed and accuracy, with speed often reported in its reciprocal form, time—task completion time. Accuracy is often reported as the percentage of trials or other actions performed correctly or incorrectly. In the latter case, accuracy is called errors or error rate. The *dependent* in dependent variable refers to the variable being dependent on the human. The measurements *depend on* what the participant does. If the dependent variable is, for example, task completion time, then clearly the measurements are highly dependent on the participant's behavior.

Besides speed and accuracy, a myriad of other dependent variables are used in HCI experiments. Others include preparation time, action time, throughput, gaze shifts, mouse-to-keyboard hand transitions, presses of BACKSPACE, target re-entries, retries, key actions, gaze shifts, wobduls, etc. The possibilities are limitless.

Now, if you are wondering about "wobduls," then you're probably following the discussion. So what is a wobdul? Well, nothing, really. It's just a made-up word. It is mentioned only to highlight something important in dependent variables: Any observable, measurable aspect of human behavior is a potential dependent variable. Provided the behavior has the ability to differentiate performance between two test conditions in a way that might shed light on the strengths or weaknesses of one condition over another, then it is a legitimate dependent variable. So when it comes to dependent variables, it is acceptable to "roll your own." Of course, it is essential to clearly define all dependent variables to ensure the research can be replicated.

An example of a novel dependent variable is "negative facial expressions" defined by Duh et al. (2008) in a comparative evaluation of three mobile phones used for gaming. Participants were videotaped playing games on different mobile

---

[3]We should add that additional independent variables are sometimes added simply to ensure the procedure covers a representative range of behaviors. For example, a Fitts' law experiment primarily interested in device and task might also include movement distance and target size as independent variables—the latter two included to ensure the task encompasses a typical range of target selection conditions (MacKenzie et al., 1991).

phones. A post-test analysis of the videotape was performed to count negative facial expressions such as frowns, confusion, frustration, and head shakes. The counts were entered in an analysis of variance to determine whether participants had different degrees of difficulty with any of the interfaces.

Another example is "read text events." In pilot testing a system using an eye tracker for text entry (eye typing), it was observed that users frequently shifted their point of gaze from the on-screen keyboard to the typed text to monitor their progress (Majaranta et al., 2006). Furthermore, there was a sense that this behavior was particularly prominent for one of the test conditions. Thus RTE (read text events) was defined and used as a dependent variable. The same research also used "re-focus events" (RFE) as a dependent variable. RFE was defined as the number of times a participant refocuses on a key to select it.

Unless one is investigating mobile phone gaming or eye typing, it is unlikely negative facial expressions, read text events, or refocus events are used as dependent variables. They are mentioned only to emphasize the merit in defining, measuring, and analyzing any human behavior that might expose differences in the interfaces or interaction techniques under investigation.

As with independent variables, it is often helpful to name the variable separately from its units. For example, in a text entry experiment there is likely a dependent variable called *text entry speed* with units "words per minute." Experiments on computer pointing devices often use a Fitts' law paradigm for testing. There is typically a dependent variable named *throughput* with units "bits per second." The most common dependent variable is *task completion time* with units "seconds" or "milliseconds." If the measurement is a simple count of events, there is no unit per se.

When contriving a dependent variable, it is important to consider how the measurements are gathered and the data collected, organized, and stored. The most efficient method is to design the experimental software to gather the measurements based on time stamps, key presses, or other interactions detectable through software events. The data should be organized and stored in a manner that facilitates follow-up analyses. Figure 5.3 shows an example for a text entry experiment. There are two data files. The first contains timestamps and key presses, while the second summarizes entry of a complete phrase, one line per phrase.

The data files in Figure 5.3 were created through the software that implements the user interface or interaction technique. Pilot testing is crucial. Often, pilot testing is considered a rough test of the user interface—with modifications added to get the interaction right. And that's true. But pilot testing is also important to ensure the data collected are correct and available in an appropriate format for follow-on analyses. So pilot test the experiment software and perform preliminary analyses on the data collected. A spreadsheet application is often sufficient for this.

To facilitate follow-up analyses, the data should also include codes to identify the participants and test conditions. Typically, this information is contained in additional columns in the data or in the filenames. For example, the filename for the data in Figure 5.3a is TextInputHuffman-P01-D99-B06-S01.sd1 and identifies the

(a)
```
my bike has a flat tire
my bike has a flat tire
16 3
891 2
1797 3 m
3656 2
4188 1
4672 2 y
5750 3
5938 3 [Space]
6813 3
6984 2
7219 0
8656 3 b
```

(b)
```
min_keystrokes,keystrokes,presented_characters,transcribed_characters, ...
55, 59, 23, 23, 29.45, 0, 9.37, 0.0, 2.5652173913043477, 93.22033898305085
61, 65, 26, 26, 30.28, 0, 10.3, 0.0, 2.5, 93.84615384615384
85, 85, 33, 33, 48.59, 0, 8.15, 0.0, 2.5757575757575757, 100.0
67, 71, 28, 28, 33.92, 0, 9.91, 0.0, 2.5357142857142856, 94.36619718309859
61, 70, 24, 24, 39.44, 0, 7.3, 0.0, 2.9166666666666665, 87.14285714285714
```

FIGURE 5.3

Example data files from a text entry experiment: (a) The summary data one (sd1) file contains timestamps and keystroke data. (b) The summary data two (sd2) file contains one line for each phrase of entry.

experiment (TextInputHuffman), the participant (P01), the device (D99), the block (B06) and the session (S01). The suffix is "sd1" for "summary data one." Note that the sd2 file in Figure 5.3b is comma-delimited to facilitate importing and contains a header line identifying the data in each column below.

If the experiment is conducted using a commercial product, it is often impossible to collect data through custom experimental software. Participants are observed externally, rather than through software. In such cases, *data collection* is problematic and requires a creative approach. Methods include manual timing by the experimenter, using a log sheet and pencil to record events, or taking photos or screen snaps of the interaction as entry proceeds. A photo is useful, for example, if results are visible on the display at the end of a trial. Videotaping is another option, but follow-up analyses of video data are time consuming. Companies such as Noldus (www.noldus.com) offer complete systems for videotaping interaction and performing post hoc timeline analyses.

5.6 **Other variables**

Besides independent and dependent variables, there are three other variables: control, random, and confounding. These receive considerably less attention and are rarely mentioned in research papers. Nevertheless, understanding each is important for experimental research.

5.6.1 **Control variables**

There are many circumstances or factors that (a) might influence a dependent variable but (b) are not under investigation. These need to be accommodated in some manner. One way is to control them—to treat them as *control variables*. Examples include room lighting, room temperature, background noise, display size, mouse shape, mouse cursor speed, keyboard angle, chair height, and so on. Mostly, researchers don't think about these conditions. But they exist and they might influence a dependent variable. Controlling them means that they are fixed at a nominal setting during the experiment so they don't interfere. But they might interfere if set at an extreme value. If the background noise level is very high or if the room is too cold, these factors might influence the outcome. Allowing such circumstances to exist at a fixed nominal value is typical in experiment research. The circumstances are treated as control variables.

Sometimes it is desirable to control characteristics of the participants. The type of interface or the objectives of the research might necessitate testing participants with certain attributes, for example, right-handed participants, participants with 20/20 vision, or participants with certain experience. Having lots of control variables reduces the variability in the measured behaviors but yields results that are less generalizable.

5.6.2 **Random variables**

Instead of controlling all circumstances or factors, some might be allowed to vary randomly. Such circumstances are *random variables*. There is a *cost* since more variability is introduced in the measures, but there is a *benefit* since results are more generalizable.

Typically, random variables pertain to characteristics of the participants, including biometrics (e.g., height, weight, hand size, grip strength), social disposition (e.g., conscientious, relaxed, nervous), or even genetics (e.g., gender, IQ). Generally, these characteristics are allowed to vary at random.

Before proceeding, it is worth summarizing the trade-off noted above for control and random variables. The comparison is best presented when juxtaposed with the experimental properties of internal validity and external validity, as discussed in the preceding chapter. Figure 5.4 shows the trade-off.

5.6.3 **Confounding variables**

Any circumstance or condition that changes systematically with an independent variable is a *confounding variable*. Unlike control or random variables, confounding variables are usually problematic in experimental research. Is the effect observed due to the independent variable or to the confounding variable? Researchers must attune to the possible presence of a confounding variable and eliminate it, adjust for it, or consider it in some way. Otherwise, the effects observed may be incorrectly interpreted.

Variable	Advantage	Disadvantage
Random	Improves external validity by using a variety of situations and people.	Compromises internal validity by introducing additional variability in the measured behaviours.
Control	Improves internal validity since variability due to a controlled circumstance is eliminated	Compromises external validity by limiting responses to specific situations and people.

FIGURE 5.4

Relationship between random and control variables and internal and external validity.

As an example, consider an experiment seeking to determine if there is an effect of camera distance on human performance using an eye tracker for computer control. In the experiment, camera distance—the independent variable—has two levels, near and far. For the near condition, a small camera (A) is mounted on a bracket attached to the user's eye glasses. For the far condition, an expensive eye tracking system is used with the camera (B) positioned above the system's display. Here, camera is a confounding variable since it varies systematically across the levels of the independent variable: camera A for the near condition and camera B for the far condition. If the experiment shows a significant effect of camera distance on human performance, there is the possibility that the effect has nothing to do with camera distance. Perhaps the effect is simply the result of using one camera for the near condition and a different camera for the far condition. The confound is avoided by using the same camera (and same system) in both the near and far conditions. Another possibility is simply to rename the independent variable. The new name could be "setup," with levels "near setup" and "far setup." The new labels acknowledge that the independent variable encompasses multiple facets of the interface, in this case, camera distance, camera, and system. The distinction is important if for no other reason than to ensure the conclusions speak accurately to the different setups, rather than to camera distance alone.

Confounding variables are sometimes found in Fitts' law experiments. Most Fitts' law experiments use a target selection task with movement amplitude (A) and target width (W) as independent variables. Fitts' original experiment is a typical example. He used a stylus-tapping task with four levels each for movement amplitude ($A = 0.25, 0.5, 1.0,$ and 2.0 inches) and target width ($W = 2, 4, 8,$ and 16 inches) (Fitts, 1954).[4] Fitts went beyond simple target selection, however. He argued by analogy with information theory and electronic communications that A and W are like signal and noise, respectively, and that each task carries information in *bits*. He proposed an *index of difficulty* (*ID*) as a measure in bits of the information content of a task: $ID = \log_2(2A/W)$. Although the majority of Fitts' law experiments treat A and W as independent variables, sometimes A and *ID* are treated as independent variables (e.g., Gan and Hoffmann, 1988). Consider the example in Figure 5.5a. There are two independent variables, A with levels 4, 8, 16, and 32 cm, and *ID* with

---

[4]See also section 7.7.7, Fitts' law.

(a)

ID	Amplitude (pixels)			
(bits)	16	32	64	128
1	*	*	*	*
2	*	*	*	*
3	*	*	*	*
4	*	*	*	*

(b)

ID	Amplitude (pixels)			
(bits)	16	32	64	128
1	16	32	64	128
2	8	16	32	64
3	4	8	16	32
4	2	4	8	16

(c)

W	Amplitude (pixels)			
(pixels)	16	32	64	128
2	*			
4	*	*		
8	*	*	*	
16	*	*	*	*
32		*	*	*
64			*	*
128				*

FIGURE 5.5

Fitts' law experiment with *A* and *ID* as independent variables: (a) Yellow cells (*) show the test conditions. (b) Numbers in yellow cells show the target width, revealing a confounding variable. (c) Same design showing test conditions by *A* and *W*.

levels 1, 2, 3, and 4 bits, yielding $4 \times 4 = 16$ test conditions (shaded/yellow cells in the figure). To achieve the necessary *ID* for each *A*, target width must vary. The top-left cell, for example, requires $W = 2A/2^{ID} = (2 \times 16)/2^1 = 16$ cm. The target width for each condition is added in Figure 5.5b. Do you see the confound? As *ID* increases, *W* decreases. Target width (*W*) is a confounding variable. If the experiment reveals a significant effect of *ID*, is the effect due to *ID* or to *W*?[5] To further illustrate, Figure 5.5c shows the same design, but reveals the conditions by movement amplitude (*A*) and target width (*W*).

As another example, consider an experiment with "interaction technique" as an independent variable with three levels, A, B, and C. Assume, further, that there were 12 participants and all were tested on A, then B, then C. Clearly, performance might improve due to practice. Practice, in this case, is a confounding variable because it changes systematically with interaction technique. Participants had just a little practice for A, a bit more for B, still more for C. If performance was best for C, it would be nice to conclude that C is better than A or B. However, perhaps performance was better simply because participants benefited from practice on

[5] It can be argued that a traditional Fitts' law design, using *A* and *W* as independent variables, is similarly flawed because it contains *ID* as a confounding variable. However, this is a weak argument: *A* and *W* are primitive characteristics of the task whereas *ID* is a contrived variable, calculated from *A* and *W*.

A and B prior to testing on C. One way to accommodate practice as a confounding variable is to counterbalance the order of presenting the test conditions to participants (see section 5.11).

Here is another example: Two search engine interfaces are compared, Google versus "new." If all participants have prior experience with Google but no experience with the new interface, then *prior experience* is a confounding variable. This might be unavoidable, as it is difficult to find participants without experience with the Google search engine. As long as the effect of prior experience is noted and acknowledged, then this isn't a problem. Of course, the effect may be due to the confound, not to the test conditions.

A similar confound may occur in text entry experiments where, for example, a new keyboard layout is compared with a Qwerty layout. A fair comparison would require participants having the same level of experience with both layouts. But of course it is difficult to find participants unfamiliar with the Qwerty layout. Thus the Qwerty layout is certain to have an advantage, at least initially. In such cases, it is worth considering a longitudinal design, where the layouts are compared over a prolonged period to see if the new keyboard layout has the potential to overcome Qwerty with practice.

5.7 Task and procedure

Let's revisit the definition of an independent variable: "a circumstance or characteristic that is manipulated or systematically controlled to *elicit a change in a human response* while the user is interacting with a computer." Emphasis is added to "elicit a change in a human response." When participants are given a test condition, they are asked to do a task while their performance is measured. Later, they are given a different test condition—another level of the independent variable—and asked to do the task again. Clearly, the choice of task is important.

There are two objectives in designing a good task: *represent* and *discriminate*. A good task is representative of the activities people do with the interface. A task that is similar to actual or expected usage will improve the external validity of the research–the ability to generalize results to other people and other situations. A good task is also one that can discriminate the test conditions. Obviously, there is something in the interaction that differentiates the test conditions, otherwise there is no research to conduct. A good task must attune to the points of differentiation in order to elicit behavioral responses that expose benefits or problems among the test conditions. This should surface as a difference in the measured responses across the test conditions. A difference might occur if the interfaces or interaction techniques are sufficiently distinct in the way the task is performed.

Often, the choice of a task is self-evident. If the research idea is a graphical method for inserting functions in a spreadsheet, a good task is inserting functions into a spreadsheet—using the graphical method versus the traditional typing method. If the research idea is an auditory feedback technique while programming a GPS device, a good task is programming a destination in a GPS device—aided with auditory feedback versus visual feedback.

Making a task representative of actual usage will improve external validity, but there is a downside. The more representative the task, the more the task is likely to include behaviors not directly related to the interface or interaction method under test. Such behaviors are likely to compromise the ability of the task to discriminate among the test conditions. There is nothing sinister in this. It is simply a reflection of the complex way humans go about their business while using computers. When we enter text, we also think about what to enter. We might pause, think, enter something, think again, change our minds, delete something, enter some more, and so on. This is actual usage. If the research goal is to evaluate a new text entry method, a task that mimics actual usage is fraught with problems. Actual usage includes secondary tasks—lots of them. If the task involves, for example, measuring text entry speed in words per minute, the measurement is seriously compromised if tasks unrelated to the entry method are present.

While using a task that is representative of actual usage may improve external validity, the downside is a decrease in internal validity. Recall that high internal validity means the effects observed (i.e., the differences in means on a dependent variable) are due to the test conditions. The additional sources of variation introduced by secondary tasks reduce the likelihood that the differences observed are actually due to, or caused by, the test conditions. The differences may simply be artifacts of the secondary tasks. Furthermore, the additional variation may bring forth a non-significant statistical result. This is unfortunate if indeed there are inherent differences between the test conditions—differences that should have produced a statistically significant outcome.

The best task is one that is natural yet focuses on the core aspects of the interaction: the points of differentiation between the test conditions. Points of similarly, while true to actual usage, introduce variability. Consider two different text entry techniques being compared in an experimental evaluation. If the techniques include the same method of capitalization, then capitalization does not serve to discriminate the techniques and can be excluded from the experimental task. Including capitalization will improve external validity but will also compromise internal validity due to the added variability.

The tasks considered above are mostly performance-based or skill-based. Sometimes an independent variable necessitates using a knowledge-based task. For example, if the research is comparing two search methods, a reasonable task is to locate an item of information in a database or on the Internet (e.g., "Find the date of birth of Albert Einstein."). Performance is still measured; however, the participant acquires knowledge of the task goal and, therefore, is precluded from further exposure to the same task. This is a problem if the independent variable is assigned within-subjects (discussed below). When the participant is tested with the other search method, the task must be changed (e.g., "Find the date of birth of William Shakespeare."). This is tricky, since the new task must be more or less the same (so the search methods can be compared), but also different enough so that the participant does not benefit from exposure to the earlier, similar task.

The experimental procedure includes the task but also the instructions, demonstration, or practice given to the participants. The procedure encompasses everything that the participant did or was exposed to. If a questionnaire was administered before or after testing, it is also part of the experimental procedure and deserves due consideration and explanation in the write-up of the experiment.

5.8 Participants

Researchers often assume that their results apply to people who were not tested. Applying results to people other than those who were tested is possible; however, two conditions are required. First, the people actually tested must be members of the same population of people to whom results are assumed to hold. For example, results are unlikely to apply to children if the participants in the experiment were drawn exclusively from the local university campus. Second, a sufficient number of participants must be tested. This requirement has more to do with statistical testing than with the similarly of participants to the population.[6] Within any population, or any sample drawn from a population, variability is present. When performance data are gathered on participants, the variability in the measurements affects the likelihood of obtaining statistically significant results. Increasing the number of participants (large n) increases the likelihood of achieving statistically significant results.

In view of the point above, we might ask: How many participants should be used in an experiment? Although the answer might seem peculiar, it goes something like this: use the same number of participants as in similar research (D. W. Martin, 2004, p. 234). Using more participants seems like a good idea, but there is a downside. If there truly is an inherent difference in two conditions, then it is always possible to achieve statistical significance—if enough participants are used. Sometimes the inherent difference is slight, and therein lies the problem. To explain, here is a research question to consider: *Is there a speed difference between left-handed and right-handed users in performing point-select tasks using a mouse?* There may be a slight difference, but it likely would surface only if a very large number of left- and right-handed participants were tested. Use enough participants and statistically significant results will appear. But the difference may be small and of no practical value. Therein lies the problem of using a large number of participants: statistically significant results for a difference of no practical significance.

The converse is also problematic. If not enough participants are used, statistical significance may fail to appear. There might be a substantial experimental effect, but the variance combined with a small sample size (not enough participants) might prevent statistical significance from appearing.

It is possible to compute the power of statistical tests and thereby determine the number of participants required. The analysis may be done *a priori*—before an

---

[6] Participants drawn from a population are, by definition, similar to the population, since they (collectively) define the population.

experiment is conducted. In practice, *a priori* power analysis is rarely done because it hinges on knowing the variance in a sample before the data are collected.[7] The recommendation, again, is to study published research. If an experiment similar to that contemplated reported statistically significant results with 12 participants, then 12 participants is a good choice.

In HCI, we often hear of researchers doing *usability evaluation* or *usability testing*. These exercises often seek to assess a prototype system with users to determine problems with the interface. Such evaluations are typically not organized as factorial experiments. So the question of how many participants is not relevant in a statistical sense. In usability evaluations, it is known that a small number of participants is sufficient to expose a high percentage of the problems in an interface. There is evidence that about five participants (often usability experts) are sufficient to expose about 80 percent of the usability problems (Lewis, 1994; Nielsen, 1994).

It is worth reflecting on the term *participants*. When referring specifically to the experiment, use the term participants (e.g., "all participants exhibited a high error rate").[8] General comments on the topic or conclusions drawn may use other terms (e.g., "these results suggest that users are less likely to...").

When recruiting participants, it is important to consider how the participants are selected. Are they solicited by word of mouth, through an e-mail list, using a notice posted on a wall, or through some other means? Ideally, participants are drawn at random from a population. In practice, this is rarely done, in part because of the need to obtain participants that are close by and available. More typically, participants are solicited from a convenient pool of individuals (e.g., members in the workplace, children at a school, or students from the local university campus). Strictly speaking, convenience sampling compromises the external validity of the research, since the true population is somewhat narrower than the desired population.

To help identify the population, participants are typically given a brief questionnaire (discussed shortly) at the beginning or end of the experiment to gather demographic data, such as age and gender. Other information relevant to the research is gathered, such as daily computer usage or experience with certain applications, devices, or products.

HCI experiments often require participants with specific skills. Perhaps a filtering process is used to ensure only appropriate participants are used. For example, an experiment investigating a new gaming input device might want a participant pool with specific skills, such a minimum of 15 hours per week playing computer games. Or perhaps participants without gaming experience are desired. Whatever the case, the selection criteria should be clear and should be stated in the write-up of the methodology, in a section labeled "Participants."

---

[7]Computing power in advance of an experiment also requires the researcher to know the size of the experimental effect (the difference in the means on the dependent variable) that is deemed relevant. Usually, the researcher simply wants to know if there is a statistically significant difference without committing in advance to a particular difference being of practical significance.

[8]According to the APA guidelines, the term *subjects* is also acceptable (APA, 2010, p. 73).

Depending on the agency or institution overseeing the research, participants are usually required to sign a consent form prior to testing. The goal is to ensure participants know that their participation is voluntary, that they will incur no physical or psychological harm, that they can withdraw at any time, and that their privacy, anonymity, and confidentiality will be protected.

5.9 **Questionnaire design**

Questionnaires are a part of most HCI experiments. They have two purposes. One is to gather information on demographics (age, gender, etc.) and experience with related technology. Another is to solicit participants' opinions on the devices or interaction tasks with which they are tested.

Questionnaires are the primary instrument for survey research, a form of research seeking to solicit a large number of people for their opinions and behaviors on a subject such as politics, spending habits, or use of technology. Such questionnaires are often lengthy, spanning several pages. Questionnaires administered in HCI experiments are usually more modest, taking just a few minutes to complete.

Questions may be posed in several ways, depending on the nature of the information sought and how it is to be used. Let's look at a few examples. Closed-ended questions are convenient, since they constrain a participant's response to small set of options. The following are examples of close-ended questions:

Do you use a GPS device while driving?   ☐ yes ☐ no

Which browser do you use?
☐ Mozilla *Firefox*   ☐ Google *Chrome*
☐ Microsoft *IE*   ☐ Other (_____)

The question above includes an open-ended category, "Other." Of course, the entire question could be open-ended, as shown here:

Which browser do you use? _____

Closed-end questions simplify follow-on analyses, since it is straightforward to tally counts of responses.

It is usually important to know the gender and age of participants, since this helps identify the population. Age can be solicited as an open-ended ratio-scale response, as seen here:

Please indicate your age:_____

Collected in this manner, the mean and standard deviation are easily calculated. Ratio-scale responses are also useful in looking for relationships in data. For example, if the same questionnaire also included a ratio-scale item on the number of text messages sent per day, then it is possible to determine if the responses are correlated (e.g., *Is the number of text messages sent per day related to age?*). Age can also be solicited as an ordinal response, as in this example:

```
Please indicate your age.
   ☐ < 20      ☐ 20-29      ☐ 30-39
   ☐ 40-49     ☐ 50-59      ☐ 60+
```

In this case, the counts in each category are tabulated. Such data are particularly useful if there is a large number of respondents. However, ordinal data are inherently lower quality than ratio-scale data, since it is not possible to compute the mean or standard deviation.

Questionnaires are also used at the end of an experiment to obtain participants' opinions and feelings about the interfaces or interaction techniques. Items are often formatted using a Likert scale (see Figure 4.7) to facilitate summarizing and analyzing the responses. One example is the NASA-TLX (task load index), which assesses perceived workload on six subscales: mental demand, physical demand, temporal demand, performance, effort, and frustration (Hart and Staveland, 1988). A questionnaire on frustration may be presented as follows:

```
Frustration: I felt a high level of insecurity, discouragement,
irritation, stress, or annoyance.
          1    2    3    4    5    6    7
       Strongly          Neutral         Strongly
       disagree                            agree
```

The ISO 9241-9 standard for non-keyboard input devices includes a questionnaire with 12 items to assess the comfort and fatigue experienced by participants (ISO 2000). The items are similar to those in the NASA-TLX but are generally directed to interaction with devices such as mice, joysticks, or eye trackers. The items may be tailored according to the device under test. For example, an evaluation of an eye tracker for computer control might include a questionnaire with the following response choices (see also Zhang and MacKenzie, 2007):

```
Eye fatigue:
          1    2    3    4    5    6    7
        Very                            Very
        high                            low
```

Note that the preferred response is 7, whereas the preferred response in the NASA-TLX example is 1. In the event the mean is computed over several response items, it is important that the items are consistently constructed.

5.10 **Within-subjects and between-subjects**

The administering of test conditions (levels of a factor) is either *within-subjects* or *between-subjects*. If each participant is tested on each level, the assignment is within-subjects. Within-subjects is also called *repeated measures*, because the measurements on each test condition are repeated for each participant. If each participant is tested on only one level, the assignment is between-subjects. For a *between-subjects design*, a separate group of participants is used for each test condition. Figure 5.6 provides a simple illustration of the difference between a within-subjects assignment and a between-subjects assignment. The figure assumes a single factor with three levels: A, B, and C. Figure 5.6a shows a within-subjects assignment because each participant is tested on all three levels of the factor (but see section 5.11, Counterbalancing). Figure 5.6b shows a between-subjects assignment, since each participant is tested on only one level of the factor. There are three groups of participants, with two participants in each group.

Clearly, there is a trade-off. For a between-subjects design, each participant is tested on only one level of a factor; therefore, more participants are needed to obtain the same number of observations (Figure 5.6b). For a *within-subjects design*, each participant is tested on all levels of a factor. Fewer participants are needed; however, more testing is required for each participant (Figure 5.6a). Given this trade-off, it is reasonable to ask: is it better to assign a factor within-subjects or between-subjects? Let's examine the possibilities.

Sometimes a factor must be between-subjects. For example, if the research is investigating whether males or females are more adept at texting, the experiment probably involves entering text messages on a mobile phone. The independent variable is gender with two levels, male and female. The variable gender is between-subjects. Clearly, there is no choice. A participant cannot be male for half the testing, then female for the other half! Another example is handedness. Research investigating performance differences between left-handed and right-handed users requires a group of left-handed participants and a group of right-handed participants. Handedness, then, is a between-subjects factor. There is no choice.

Sometimes a factor must be within-subjects. The most obvious example is practice, since the acquisition of skill occurs within people, not between people. Practice is usually investigated by testing participants over multiple blocks of trials.

(a)

Participant	Test Condition		
1	A	B	C
2	A	B	C

(b)

Participant	Test Condition
1	A
2	A
3	B
4	B
5	C
6	C

FIGURE 5.6

Assigning test conditions to participants: (a) Within-subjects. (b) Between-subjects.

For such designs, block is an independent variable, or factor, and there are multiple levels, such as block 1, block 2, block 3, and so on. Clearly, block is within-subjects since each participant is exposed to multiple blocks of testing. There is no choice.

Sometimes there is a choice. An important trade-off was noted above. That is, a within-subjects design requires fewer participants but requires more testing for each participant. There is a significant advantage to using fewer participants, since recruiting, scheduling, briefing, demonstrating, practicing, and so on is easier if there are fewer participants.

Another advantage of a within-subjects design is that the variance due to participants' predispositions will be approximately the same across test conditions. Predisposition, here, refers to any aspect of a participant's personality, mental condition, or physical condition that might influence performance. In other words, a participant who is predisposed to be meticulous (or sloppy!) is likely to carry their disposition in the same manner across the test conditions. For a between-subjects design, there are more participants and, therefore, more variability due to inherent differences between participants.

Yet another advantage of within-subjects designs is that it is not necessary to balance groups of participants—because there is only one group! Between-subjects designs include a separate group of participants for each test condition. In this case, balancing is needed to ensure the groups are more or less equal in terms of characteristics that might introduce bias in the measurements. Balancing is typically done through random assignment, but may also be done by explicitly placing participants in groups according to reasonable criteria (e.g., ensuring levels of computer experience are similar among the groups).

Because of the three advantages just cited, experiments in HCI tend to favor within-subjects designs over between-subjects designs.

However, there is an advantage to a between-subjects design. Between-subjects designs avoid interference between test conditions. Interference, here, refers to conflict that arises when a participant is exposed to one test condition and then switches to another test condition. As an example, consider an experiment that seeks to measure touch-typing speed with two keyboards. The motor skill acquired while learning to touch type with one keyboard is likely to adversely affect touch-typing with the other keyboard. Clearly, participants cannot "unlearn" one condition before testing on another condition. A between-subjects design avoids this because each participant is tested on one, and only one, of the keyboards. If the interference is likely to be minimal, or if it can be mitigated with a few warm-up trials, then the benefit of a between-subjects design is diminished and a within-subjects design is the best choice. In fact the majority of factors that appear in HCI experiments are like this, so levels of factors tend to be assigned within-subjects. I will say more about interference in the next section.

It is worth noting that in many areas of research, within-subjects designs are rarely used. Research testing new drugs, for example, would not use a within-subjects design because of the potential for interference effects. Between-subjects designs are typically used.

For an experiment with two factors it is possible to assign the levels of one factor within-subjects and the levels of the other factor between-subjects. This is a *mixed design*. Consider the example of an experiment seeking to compare learning of a text entry method between left-handed and right-handed users. The experiment has two factors: Block is within-subjects with perhaps 10 levels (block 1, block 2 … block 10) and handedness is between-subjects with two levels (left, right).

5.11 Order effects, counterbalancing, and latin squares

When the levels of a factor (test conditions) are assigned within-subjects, participants are tested with one condition, then another condition, and so on. In such cases, interference between the test conditions may result due to the order of testing, as noted above. In most within-subjects designs, it is possible—in fact, likely—that participants' performance will improve as they progress from one test condition to the next. Thus participants may perform better on the second condition simply because they benefited from practice on the first. They become familiar with the apparatus and procedure, and they are learning to do the task more effectively. Practice, then, is a confounding variable, because the amount of practice increases systematically from one condition to the next. This is referred to as a *practice effect* or a *learning effect*. Although less common in HCI experiments, it is also possible that performance will worsen on conditions that follow other conditions. This may follow from mental or physical fatigue—a *fatigue effect*. In a general sense, then, the phenomenon is an *order effect* or *sequence effect* and may surface either as improved performance or degraded performance, depending on the nature of the task, the inherent properties of the test conditions, and the order of testing conditions in a within-subjects design.

If the goal of the experiment is to compare the test conditions to determine which is better (in terms of performance on a dependent variable), then the confounding influence of practice seriously compromises the comparison. The most common method of compensating for an order effect is to divide participants into groups and administer the conditions in a different order for each group. The compensatory ordering of test conditions to offset practice effects is called *counterbalancing*.

In the simplest case of a factor with two levels, say, A and B, participants are divided into two groups. If there are 12 participants overall, then Group 1 has 6 participants and Group 2 has 6 participants. Group 1 is tested first on condition A, then on condition B. Group 2 is given the test conditions in the reverse order. This is the simplest case of a *Latin square*. In general, a Latin square is an $n \times n$ table filled with n different symbols (e.g., A, B, C, and so on) positioned such that each symbol occurs exactly once in each row and each column.[9] Some examples of Latin square tables are shown in Figure 5.7. Look carefully and the pattern is easily seen.

---

[9]The name "Latin" in Latin square refers to the habit of Swiss mathematician Leonhard Euler (1707–1783), who used Latin symbols in exploring the properties of multiplication tables.

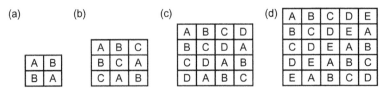

FIGURE 5.7

Latin squares: (a) 2 × 2. (b) 3 × 3. (c) 4 × 4. (d) 5 × 5.

(a)

A	B	D	C
B	C	A	D
C	D	B	A
D	A	C	B

(b)

A	B	F	C	E	D
B	C	A	D	F	E
C	D	B	E	A	F
D	E	C	F	B	A
E	F	D	A	C	B
F	A	E	B	D	C

FIGURE 5.8

Balanced Latin squares where each condition precedes and follows other conditions an equal number of times: (a) 4 × 4. (b) 6 × 6.

The first column is in order, starting at A. Entries in the rows are in order, with wrap around.

A deficiency in Latin squares of order 3 and higher is that conditions precede and follow other conditions an unequal number of times. In the 4 × 4 Latin square, for example, B follows A three times, but A follows B only once. Thus an A-B sequence effect, if present, is not fully compensated for. A solution to this is a balanced Latin square, which can be constructed for even-order tables. Figure 5.8 shows 4 × 4 and 6 × 6 balanced Latin squares. The pattern is a bit peculiar. The first column is in order, starting at A. The top row has the sequence, A, B, n, C, $n-1$, D, $n-2$, etc. Entries in the second and subsequent columns are in order, with wrap around.

When designing a within-subjects counterbalanced experiment, the number of levels of the factor must divide equally into the number of participants. If a factor has three levels, then the experiment requires multiple-of-3 participants; for example, 9, 12, or 15 participants. If there are 12 participants, then there are three groups with 4 participants per group. The conditions are assigned to Group 1 in order ABC, to Group 2 in order BCA, and to Group 3 in order CAB (see Figure 5.7b). Let's explore this design with a hypothetical example.

An experimenter seeks to determine if three editing methods (A, B, C) differ in the time required for common editing tasks. For the evaluation, the following task is used:[10]

> Replace one 5-letter word with another, starting one line away.

---

[10] This is the same as task T1 described by Card, Moran, and Newell in an experiment to validate the keystroke-level model (KLM) (Card et al., 1980).

Participant	Test Condition			Group	Mean	SD
	A	B	C			
1	12.98	16.91	12.19			
2	14.84	16.03	14.01	1	14.7	1.84
3	16.74	15.15	15.19			
4	16.59	14.43	11.12			
5	18.37	13.16	10.72			
6	15.17	13.09	12.83	2	14.6	2.46
7	14.68	17.66	15.26			
8	16.01	17.04	11.14			
9	14.83	12.89	14.37			
10	14.37	13.98	12.91	3	14.4	1.88
11	14.40	19.12	11.59			
12	13.70	16.17	14.31			
Mean	15.2	15.5	13.0			
SD	1.48	2.01	1.63			

FIGURE 5.9

Hypothetical data for an experiment with one within-subjects factor having three levels (A, B, C). Values are the mean task completion time(s) for five repetitions of an editing task.

The following three editing methods are compared (descriptions are approximate):

Method A: arrow keys, BACKSPACE, type
Method B: search and replace dialog
Method C: point and double click with the mouse, type

Twelve participants are recruited. To counterbalance for learning effects, participants are divided into three groups with the tasks administered according to a Latin square (see Figure 5.7b). Each participant does the task five times with one editing method, then again with the second editing method, then again with the third. The mean task completion time for each participant using each editing method is tabulated. (See Figure 5.9.) Overall means and standard deviations are also shown for each editing method and for each group. Note that the left-to-right order of the test conditions in the figure applies only to Group 1. The order for Group 2 was BCA and for Group 3 CAB (see Figure 5.7b).

At 13.0 s, the mouse method (C) was fastest. The arrow-key method (A) was 17.4 percent slower at 15.2 s, while the search-and-replace method (B) was 19.3 percent slower at 15.5 s. (Testing for statistical significance in the differences is discussed in the next chapter.) Evidently, counterbalancing worked, as the group means are very close, within 0.3 s. The tabulated data in Figure 5.9 are not typically provided in a research report. More likely, the results are presented in a chart, similar to that in Figure 5.10.

Although counterbalancing worked in the above hypothetical example, there is a potential problem for the 3 × 3 Latin square. Note in Figure 5.7b that B follows A twice, but A follows B only once. So there is an imbalance. This cannot be avoided in Latin squares with an odd number of conditions. One solution in this case is to counterbalance by using all sequences. The 3 × 3 case is shown in Figure 5.11.

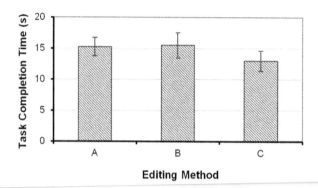

FIGURE 5.10

Task completion time(s) by editing method for the data in Figure 5.9. Error bars show ±1 *SD*.

A	B	C
A	C	B
B	C	A
B	A	C
C	A	B
C	B	A

FIGURE 5.11

Counterbalancing an odd number of conditions using all (*n!*) combinations.

There are 3! = 6 combinations. Balancing is complete (e.g., B follows A three times, A follows B three times). MacKenzie and Isokoski (2008) used such an arrangement in an experiment with 18 participants, assigning 3 participants to each order.

Yet another way to offset learning effects is to randomize the order of conditions. This is most appropriate where (a) the task is very brief, (b) there are many repetitions of the task, and (c) there are many test conditions. For example, experiments that use point-select tasks often include movement direction, movement distance, or target size as factors (Figure 5.12).

The test conditions in Figure 5.12 might appear as factors in an experiment even though the experiment is primarily directed at something else. For example, research comparing the performance of different pointing devices might include device as a factor with, say, three levels (mouse, trackball, stylus). Movement direction, movement distance, and target size might be varied to ensure the tasks cover a typical range of conditions. Treating these conditions as factors ensures they are handled in a systematic manner. To ensure equal treatment, the conditions are chosen at random without replacement. Once all conditions have been used, the process may repeat if multiple blocks of trials are desired.

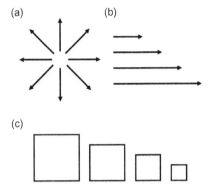

FIGURE 5.12

Test conditions suitable for random assignment: (a) Movement direction. (b) Movement distance. (c) Target size.

5.12 **Group effects and asymmetric skill transfer**

If the learning effect is the same from condition to condition in a within-subjects design, then the group means on a dependent variable should be approximately equal.[11] This was demonstrated above (see Figure 5.9). In other words, the advantage due to practice for a condition tested later in the experiment is offset equally by the disadvantage when the same condition is tested earlier in the experiment. That's the point of counterbalancing. However, there are occasions where different effects appear for one order (e.g., A→B) compared to another (e.g., B→A). In such cases there may be a *group effect*—differences across groups in the mean scores on a dependent variable. When this occurs, it is a problem. In essence, counterbalancing did not work. A group effect is typically due to *asymmetric skill transfer*— differences in the amount of improvement, depending on the order of testing.

We could develop an example of asymmetric skill transfer with hypothetical data, as with the counterbalancing example above; however, there is an example data set in a research report where an asymmetric transfer effect is evident. The example provides a nice visualization of the effect, plus an opportunity to understand why asymmetric skill transfer occurs. So we'll use that data. The experiment compared two types of scanning keyboards for text entry (Koester and Levine, 1994a). Scanning keyboards use an on-screen virtual keyboard and a single key or switch for input. Rows of keys are highlighted one by one (scanned). When the row bearing the desired letter is highlighted, it is selected. Scanning enters the row and advances left to right. When the key bearing the desired letter is highlighted it is selected and the letter is added to the text message. Scanning keyboards provided a convenient text entry method for many users with a physical disability.

---

[11] There is likely some difference, but the difference should not be statistically significant.

(a)

```
  _  E  A  R  D  U
  T  N  S  F  W  B
  O  H  C  P  V  J
  I  M  Y  K  Q  ,
  L  G  X  Z  .  "
  <  r     q
```

```
  _  E  A  R  D  U      1: the_
  T  N  S  F  W  B      2: of_
  O  H  C  P  V  J      3: an_
  I  M  Y  K  Q  ,      4: a_
  L  G  X  Z  .  "      5: in_
  <  bw r     q         6: to_
```

(b)

| Testing Half | | Group |
First (Trials 1-10)	Second (Trials 11-20)	
20.42	27.12	
22.68	28.39	
23.41	32.50	
25.22	32.12	
26.62	35.94	1
28.82	37.66	
30.38	39.07	
31.66	35.64	
32.11	42.76	
34.31	41.06	
19.47	24.97	
19.42	27.27	
22.05	29.34	
23.03	31.45	
24.82	33.46	2
26.53	33.08	
28.59	34.30	
26.78	35.82	
31.09	36.57	
31.07	37.43	

FIGURE 5.13

Experiment comparing two scanning keyboards: (a) Letters-only keyboard (LO, *top*) and letters plus word prediction keyboard (L + WP, *bottom*). (b) Results for entry speed in characters per minute (cpm). Shaded cells are for the LO keyboard.

The experiment compared a letters-only (LO) scanning keyboard with a similar keyboard that added word prediction (L + WP). The keyboards are shown in Figure 5.13a. Six participants entered 20 phrases of text, 10 with one keyboard, followed by 10 with the other. To compensate for learning effects, counterbalancing was used. Participants were divided into two groups. Group 1 entering text with the LO keyboard first, then with the L + WP keyboard. Group 2 used the keyboards in the reverse order. Although not usually provided in a report, the results were given in a table showing the entry speed in characters per minute (cpm). The data are repro-duced in Figure 5.13b as they appeared in the original report (Koester and Levine, 1994a, Table 2). The two columns show the sequence of testing: first half, then sec-ond half. The shaded and un-shaded cells show the results for the LO and L + WP keyboards respectively, thus revealing the counterbalanced order.

There are at least three ways to summarize the data in Figure 5.13b. The overall result showing the difference between the LO and L + WP keyboards is shown in the left-side chart in Figure 5.14. Clearly, there was very little difference between the two keyboards: 30.0 cpm for the LO keyboard versus 30.3 cpm for the L + WP keyboard. The L + WP keyboard was just 1 percent faster. The error bars are large, mostly due to the improvement from trial to trial, as seen in Figure 5.13b.

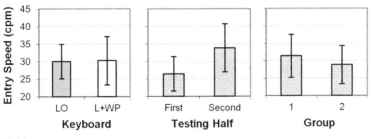

FIGURE 5.14

Three ways to summarize the results in Figure 5.13b, by keyboard (*left*), by testing half (*center*), and by group (*right*). Error bars show ±1 *SD*.

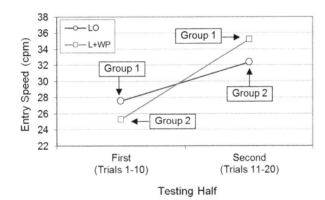

FIGURE 5.15

Demonstration of asymmetric skill transfer. The chart uses the data in Figure 5.13b.

The center chart in Figure 5.14 shows another view of the results, comparing the first half and second half of testing. A learning effect is clearly seen. The overall entry speed was 26.4 cpm in the first half of testing (trials 1 to 10) and 33.8 cpm, or 28 percent higher, in the second half of testing (trials 11 to 20). Learning is fully expected, so this result is not surprising.

Now consider the right-side chart in Figure 5.14. Counterbalancing only works if the *order effects* are the same or similar. This implies that the performance benefit of an LO→L + WP order is the same as the performance benefit of an L + WP→LO order. If so, the group means will be approximately equal. (This was demonstrated earlier in the counterbalancing example; see Figure 5.9). The right-side chart in Figure 5.14 reveals a different story. The mean for Group 1 was 31.4 cpm. The mean for Group 2 was lower at 28.8 cpm. For some reason, there was an 8 percent performance disadvantage for Group 2. This is an example of asymmetric skill transfer. Figure 5.15 illustrates. The figure reduces the data in Figure 5.13b to four points, one for each quadrant of 10 trials. Asymmetry is clearly seen in the cross-over of the lines connecting the LO points and L + WP points between the first half and second half of testing.

If counterbalancing had worked, the lines in Figure 5.15 would be approximately parallel. They are not parallel because of the asymmetry in the LO→L + WP order versus the L + WP→LO order. Asymmetric skill transfer is usually explainable by considering the test conditions or the experimental procedure. For this experiment, the effect occurs because of the inherent differences in entering text with the letters-only (LO) keyboard versus entering text with the letters plus word prediction (L + WP) keyboard. In fact, this example provides an excellent opportunity to understand why asymmetric skill transfer sometimes occurs. Here is the explanation. The L + WP keyboard is an enhanced version of the LO keyboard. The basic method of entering letters is the same with both keyboards; however, the L + WP keyboard adds word-prediction, allowing words to be entered before all letters in the word are entered. It is very likely that entering text first with the LO keyboard served as excellent practice for the more difficult subsequent task of entering text with the L + WP keyboard. To appreciate this, examine the two points labeled Group 1 in Figure 5.15. Group 1 participants performed better overall because they were tested initially with the easier LO keyboard before moving on the enhanced L + WP keyboard. Group 2 participants fared less well because they were tested initially on the more difficult L + WP keyboard.

The simplest way to avoid asymmetric skill transfer is to use a between-subjects design. Clearly, if participants are exposed to only one test condition, they cannot experience skill transfer from another test condition. There are other possibilities, such as having participants practice on a condition prior to data collection. The practice trials seek to overcome the benefit of practice in the earlier condition, so that the measured performance accurately reflects the inherent properties of the test condition. It is not clear that this would work in the example. Participants cannot "unlearn."

In the end, the performance difference between the LO and L + WP keyboards remains an outstanding research question. The practice effect (28%) was much greater than the group effect (8%), so it is difficult to say whether word prediction in the L + WP keyboard offers a performance advantage. Clearly, there is a *benefit* with the L + WP keyboard, because words can be entered before all the letters are entered. However, there is also a *cost*, since users must attend to the on-going prediction process, and this slows entry. To determine whether the costs outweigh the benefits in the long run, a longitudinal study is required. This is examined in the next section.

5.13 Longitudinal studies

The preceding discussion focused on the confounding influence of learning in experiments where an independent variable is assigned within-subjects. Learning effects—more generally, order effects—are problematic and must be accommodated in some way, such as counterbalancing. However, sometimes the research

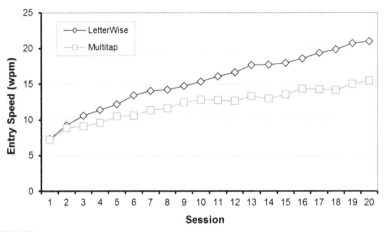

FIGURE 5.16

Example of a longitudinal study. Two text entry methods were tested and compared over 20 sessions of input. Each session involved about 30 minutes of text entry.

has a particular interest in learning, or the acquisition of skill. In this case, the experimental procedure involves testing users over a prolonged period while their improvement in performance is measured. Instead of eliminating learning, the research seeks to observe it and measure it. An experimental evaluation where participants practice over a prolonged period is called a *longitudinal study*.

In a longitudinal study, "amount of practice" is an independent variable. Participants perform the task over multiple units of testing while their improvement with practice is observed and measured. Each unit of testing is a level of the independent variable. Various names are used for the independent variable, but a typical example is *Session* with levels Session 1, Session 2, Session 3, and so on. An example is an experiment comparing two text entry methods for mobile phones: multi-tap and *LetterWise* (MacKenzie, Kober, Smith, Jones, and Skepner, 2001). For English text entry, LetterWise requires an average of 44 percent fewer keystrokes than does multi-tap. However, a performance benefit might not appear immediately, since users must learn the technique. Furthermore, learning occurs with both methods, as participants become familiar with the experimental procedure and task. However, it was felt that the reduction in keystrokes with LetterWise would eventually produce higher text entry speeds. To test this, a longitudinal study was conducted, with entry method assigned between-subjects. The results are shown in Figure 5.16. Indeed, the conjectured improvement with practice was observed. Initial entry speeds were about 7.3 wpm for both methods in Session 1. With practice, both methods improved; however, the improvement was greater with LetterWise because of the ability to produce English text with fewer keystrokes on average. By Session 20, text entry speed with LetterWise was 21.0 wpm, about 36 percent higher than the rate of 15.5 wpm for multi-tap.

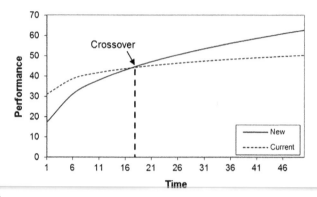

FIGURE 5.17

Crossover point. With practice, human performance with a new interaction technique may eventually exceed human performance using a current technique.

(From MacKenzie and Zhang, 1999)

Performance trends in longitudinal studies, as shown in Figure 5.15, are often accompanied by an equation and best-fitting curve demonstrating the *power law of learning*. Examples are given in Chapter 7, section 7.2.5 (Skill Acquisition).

In many situations, the goal of a longitudinal study is to compare the viability of a new technique against current practice. Here, current practice is any conventional interaction that is quantifiable using a performance measure. Examples include text entry, editing, pointing, selecting, searching, panning, zooming, rotating, drawing, scrolling, menu access, and so on. If users are experienced with a current interaction technique, then relatively poorer initial performance is expected with the new technique. But as learning progresses, the performance trends may eventually cross over, wherein performance with the new technique exceeds that with current practice. This is illustrated in Figure 5.17.

As an example, consider the ubiquitous Qwerty keyboard. Although improved designs have been proposed, users experienced with a Qwerty keyboard are unlikely to demonstrate an immediate improvement in performance with an alternative design. Considerable practice may be required before performance on the new keyboard exceeds that with the Qwerty keyboard. The Dvorak simplified keyboard (DSK), for example, has been demonstrated in longitudinal studies to provide a speed advantage over Qwerty (see Noyes, 1983 for a review). Yet Qwerty remains the dominant form factor for computer keyboards. From a practical standpoint, learning a new technique bears a *cost*, since performance is initially superior with the current technique. However, after the crossover point is reached, the new technique provides a *benefit*, since performance is superior compared to current practice. The cost-benefit trade-off is shown in Figure 5.18.

Despite the long-term benefits evident in Figure 5.18, new technologies often languish in the margins while established but less-optimal designs continue to dominate the marketplace. Evidently, the benefits are often insufficient to overcome the costs.

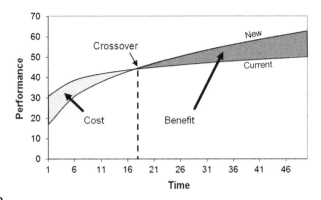

FIGURE 5.18

Cost-benefit progression in learning a new interaction technique where there is existing skill with current practice.

With respect to the Qwerty debate, there are two such costs. One is the cost of manufacturing and retooling. Keyboards are electro-mechanical devices, so new designs require ground-up reengineering and new manufacturing materials and procedures. This is expensive. The other cost lies in overcoming user perceptions and attitudes. By and large, users are change-adverse: they are reluctant to give up habits they have acquired and are comfortable with. Simply put, users are "unwilling to change to a new keyboard layout because of the retraining required" (Noyes, 1983, p. 278).

One interesting example is a soft or virtual keyboard, as commonly used on touchscreen phones or personal digital assistants (PDAs). Input is typically with a finger or stylus. Most such keyboards use the Qwerty letter arrangement. However, since the keyboard is created in software, there is no retooling cost associated with an alternative design. Thus there is arguably a better chance for an optimized design to enter the marketplace. One idea to increase text entry speed is to rearrange letters with common letters clustered near the center of the layout and less common letters pushed to the perimeter. The increase in speed results from the reduction in finger or stylus movement. However, since users are unfamiliar with the optimized letter arrangement, performance is initially poor (while they get accustomed to the letter arrangement). If learning the new technique is likely to take several hours or more, then the evaluation requires a longitudinal study, where users are tested over multiple sessions of input. Eventually, the crossover point may appear. This idea is explored further in Chapter 7, section 7.2.5 (Skill Acquisition).

5.14 Running the experiment

When the experiment is designed, the apparatus built and tested, the participants recruited and scheduled, then testing begins. But wait! Are you sure the time to begin has arrived? It is always useful to have a pilot test (yes, one more pilot test) with one or two participants. This will help smooth out the protocol for briefing and preparing the participants. It will serve as a check on the amount of time needed for each participant. If the testing is scheduled for one hour, it is important that all the testing combined with briefing, practicing, etc., comfortably fit into one hour. A final tweak to the protocol may be necessary. Better now than to have regrets later on.

So the experiment begins. The experimenter greets each participant, introduces the experiment, and usually asks the participants to sign consent forms. Often, a brief questionnaire is administered to gather demographic data and information on the participants' related experience. This should take just a few minutes. The apparatus is revealed, the task explained and demonstrated. Practice trials are allowed, as appropriate.

An important aspect of the experiment is the instructions given to participants. Of course, the instructions depend on the nature of the experiment and the task. For most interaction tasks, the participant is expected to proceed quickly and accurately. These terms—quickly and accurately—are subject to interpretation, as well as to the capabilities of participants. What is reasonably quick for one participant may be unattainable by another. Performing tasks reasonably quick and with high accuracy, but at a rate comfortable to the individual, is usually the goal. Whatever the case, the instructions must be carefully considered and must be given to all participants in the same manner. If a participant asks for clarification, caution must be exercised in elaborating on the instructions. Any additional explanation that might motivate a participant to act differently from other participants is to be avoided.

The experimenter plays a special role as the public face of the experiment. It is important that the experimenter portrays himself or herself as neutral. Participants should not feel they are under pressure to produce a specific outcome. Deliberately attempting to perform better on one test condition compared to another is to be avoided. Also, participants should not sense a particular attitude in the experimenter. An overly attentive experimenter may make the participant nervous. Similarly, the experimenter should avoid conveying indifference or disregard. If the experimenter conveys a sense of not caring, the participant may very well act with little regard to his or her performance. A neutral manner is preferred.

STUDENT EXERCISES

5-1. It was noted above that independent variables in research papers are sometimes identified without being given a name. Review some experimental research papers in HCI and find three examples of this. Propose a name for the independent variable and give examples of how to improve the paper, properly identifying both the name of the variable and the levels of the variable. Examine how the independent variables and the levels of the independent variables (test conditions) were referred to in the paper. Point out any inconsistencies.

5-2. Review some HCI experimental research papers and find three examples where an independent variable was assigned between-subjects. Briefly describe the rationale.

5-3. Find an example of an HCI paper describing an experiment that included three (or more) independent variables. Construct a chart similar to Figure 5.2, labeling the independent variables. Indicate which effects were studied and which effects (if any) were not studied.

5-4. Users and computers (Part I). Design and administer a simple questionnaire to about 25 computer users. Solicit four items of information: gender, age, hours per day using a computer, and preferred brand of computer (Mac versus PC). Use a ratio-scale questionnaire item to solicit the respondent's age. Write a brief report on the findings. This exercise continues in Chapter 6 (Part II) and Chapter 7 (Part III).

5-5. Find an example of an HCI paper describing a longitudinal study. (Preferably, find an example not cited in this book.) Write a brief report describing the testing procedure. Over what period of time did testing extend, and how were the trials organized? Identify the main independent variable (and levels) and discuss how it was administered. Note features such as counterbalancing, within-subjects or between-subjects assignment, and whether practice trials were administered.

Hypothesis Testing

6

At a cocktail party, it is advisable to avoid discussions on religion or politics. The reason, of course, is that people's opinions on these thorny topics are often both strong and divergent. Let's add statistics to the list. Few topics raise more controversy than the application of statistical techniques to the data and hypotheses in experimental research. Fortunately, the reader is not dragged into the debate here.[1] Instead, the approach in this chapter is to describe and present a few useful statistical tools and techniques as they are typically used in HCI research. In the pages ahead I will work hard to minimize theory and controversy while maximizing practical value.

Statistical procedures for hypothesis testing come in two flavors: *parametric tests* and *non-parametric tests*. Both are examined in this chapter. The distinguishing feature is that parametric tests operate on data from a probability distribution, such as the normal distribution or the *t*-distribution, whereas non-parametric tests are "distribution free," which is to say, they make no assumption about the distribution of the underlying data. A useful way to distinguish parametric tests versus non-parametric tests is by the level or scale of measurement in the data being tested (Sheskin, 2011, p. 109; Siegel, 1957, Table 1). Figure 6.1 illustrates. The figure shows the four scales of measurement discussed in Chapter 4 (see section 4.4.2) with ratio data as the most sophisticated and nominal data as the least sophisticated.

Parametric tests are applicable to ratio data and interval data, although they are most commonly used with ratio data. The analysis of variance (ANOVA), discussed in detail in this chapter, is the most widely used parametric procedure.

---

[1] Many of the footnotes in this chapter add detail and rigor to the discussions, which, taken alone, are intended to explain in the simplest way possible. Readers new to statistical techniques for hypothesis testing are invited to ignore these footnotes, at least initially. No doubt, readers with statistical training will place a discerning eye on the footnotes. While the footnotes add detail, the presentation as a whole is introductory. Many topics are omitted or only briefly presented, such as assumptions and tests on the distribution of data and the corrections and alternative techniques to apply when assumptions are violated. The best sources for these topics are the user manuals and guides that accompany advanced statistical tools, such as *SPSS*, *SAS*, or *R*. A notable comprehensive source is Sheskin's *Handbook of Parametric and Non-parametric Statistical Procedures* (Sheskin, 2011).

Measurement Scale	Defining Relations	Examples of Appropriate Statistics	Appropriate Statistical Tests
Nominal	• Equivalence	• Mode • Frequency	• Non-parametric tests
Ordinal	• Equivalence • Order	• Median • Percentile	
Interval	• Equivalence • Order • Ratio of intervals	• Mean • Standard deviation	• Parametric tests • Non-parametric tests
Ratio	• Equivalence • Order • Ratio of intervals • Ratio of values	• Geometric mean • Coefficient of variation	

FIGURE 6.1

Measurement scales of data, properties of data, and appropriate statistical tests.

For experimental research in HCI, ratio data are typically human performance measurements such as the time, speed, or accuracy in doing tasks, or counts for events such as key presses, finger flicks, gaze shifts, or target re-entries. Non-parametric tests are applicable to any scale of data, although they are most commonly used for nominal or ordinal data. The non-parametric procedures examined in this chapter include the chi-square (χ^2) test for nominal data and the Mann-Whitney U, Wilcoxon Signed Rank, Kruskal-Wallis, and Friedman tests for ordinal data. Typically, the data used in non-parametric tests are nominal categories, questionnaire responses, rating scores, or assessments on a scale. There is limited use of non-parametric tests for ratio data, a topic we will return to later in this chapter.

Since non-parametric tests are deemed relevant to all four measurement scales (see right-hand column in Figure 6.1), they are more generally applicable than parametric tests. However, by the criterion of power, parametric tests are superior to non-parametric tests. This is a by-product of the strong assumptions and requirements of parametric tests. Provided the assumptions are reasonably well adhered to, parametric tests bring greater ability (power) to draw correct conclusions in the statistical tests undertaken.

The largest part of this chapter is directed at the ANOVA. However, most researchers who use an ANOVA have little understanding of the calculations and assumptions underpinning the "F-test" in the ANOVA. And that's fine. Understanding what the test means, how to do it, and how to interpret and explain it is important, however. Therefore our approach here is more cookbook-like than academic.

6.1 Analysis of variance

An ANOVA, or F-test, is the main statistical procedure for hypothesis testing in factorial experiments. The majority of HCI research papers that describe experiments include the results of an ANOVA, giving an F-statistic, the degrees of freedom for the F-statistic, and the associated p value (explained later). The ANOVA result is typically reported in parentheses as support for a statement indicating whether or not the outcome of the test was statistically significant.

An ANOVA determines if an independent variable—the test conditions—had a significant impact on a dependent variable—the measured responses. The ANOVA determines this by partitioning the variance in the observations on a dependent variable into components attributable to the variance. The "components attributable" are the test conditions (factors and levels) and the participants. If the variance across levels of a factor is large relative to all the remaining variance (other factors and the participants), it is often possible to conclude that the distinguishing properties of the factor—features in the test conditions—*caused* the observed differences in the measurements on the dependent variable. If so, the factor is said to have had a statistically significant effect on the dependent variable.

There are different ways to set up an ANOVA, depending on the design of the experiment. This discussion begins with a simple one-factor design with two test conditions. I then progress to a one-factor design with four test conditions. A post hoc comparisons test is often used if there are more than two test conditions, and I give an example of such a test as well. I then discuss more complex designs with two or more factors, each having two or more levels.

The initial examples assume a within-subjects assignment of test conditions to participants. This means that each participant is tested on all levels of a factor. Some designs have test conditions assigned between-subjects, meaning a separate group of participants is recruited and assigned to each test condition. A few examples of between-subjects ANOVAs are also given.

6.1.1 Why analyze the variance?

I noted earlier that research questions are usually comparative. Typically, the goal is to compare two or more interfaces or interaction techniques to determine which is better. By "better" I mean superior performance on one or more dependent variables, such as task completion time, error rate, task re-tries, presses of the BACKSPACE key, target re-entries, and so on. It is interesting that the test is called analysis of *variance* yet we are more concerned with overall performance:

> Does it take less time to complete a task using Method A rather than Method B?

The question above refers to time—the overall, average, or mean time that was observed and measured. The mean is calculated for each test condition over multiple users and often over multiple trials of a representative task. In some situations, multiple trials of a task are administered to investigate learning effects (see Chapter 4, Longitudinal Studies), but often the idea of using multiple trials is just to obtain stable and representative measurements. Nevertheless, it is the difference in the means, not the variances, that interests us. Note that while the above research question is certainly important, the statistical question pursued is not a question at all. It is a statement known as the *null hypothesis*:

> There is no difference in the mean time to complete a task using Method A vs. Method B.

There is an assumption of "no difference," which is a reasonable starting point. The ANOVA tests the data to determine the likelihood of the null hypothesis being true (tenable) or false (rejected). In most cases, the researcher seeks to reject the null hypothesis. By convention, a statistically significant result means there is little likelihood the null hypothesis is true. The conclusion in such case is that (a) there is a difference in the means, (b) the difference is statistically significant, and (c) the difference was caused by distinguishable properties in the test conditions. Let's see how this is done.

Consider a hypothetical experiment where 10 participants perform a few repetitions of a task using two interaction techniques. The techniques could be anything; for example, use of a mouse versus a keyboard. A task is chosen that is representative of common interactions, yet likely to expose inherent differences. An example for mouse versus keyboard interaction might be selecting options in a hierarchical menu. For this discussion, I will keep it simple and refer to the techniques as Method A and Method B. Bear in mind that the experiment has a single factor (Interaction Method) with two levels (Method A and Method B).

Performance is measured on a dependent variable such as task completion time (in seconds) and the means are computed for each participant over a few trials. Then the means are computed for each method. Two example outcomes for this hypothetical experiment are shown in the bar charts in Figure 6.2.

The mean task completion times are the same in Figure 6.2a and Figure 6.2b; however, the annotations proclaim vastly different outcomes. In Figure 6.2a, the difference in the means is statistically significant. This implies that in all likelihood the difference observed was real and was due to distinguishing properties of Method A versus Method B. Simply put, Method A is faster than Method B. Do the test again, and there is a pretty good chance the result will be similar.

In Figure 6.2b, the difference in the means is *not* statistically significant. This implies the difference in the means is likely due to chance. There is no reasonable basis to suggest that either method is faster than the other. Do the test again and the outcome could very well be reversed. Despite the dramatically different interpretations, the two examples seem the same: a task completion time of 4.5 seconds for Method A versus 5.5 seconds for Method B. How is this? The answer lies in the variability in the observations—the variance. Let's have a closer look.

Figure 6.3a gives the data for the simulation in Figure 6.2a as the mean task completion time (in seconds) for each participant for each method along with the

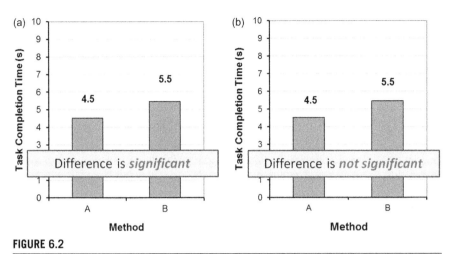

FIGURE 6.2

Difference in task completion time (in seconds) across two test conditions, Method A and Method B. Two hypothetical outcomes are shown: (a) The difference is statistically significant. (b) The difference is not statistically significant.

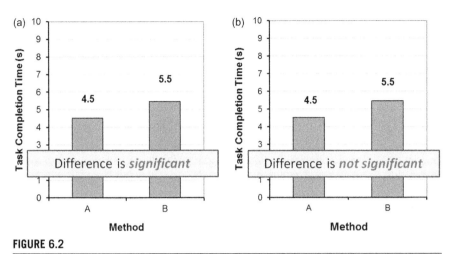

Participant	Method	
	A	B
1	5.3	5.7
2	3.6	4.8
3	5.2	5.1
4	3.6	4.5
5	4.6	6.0
6	4.1	6.8
7	4.0	6.0
8	4.8	4.6
9	5.2	5.5
10	5.1	5.6
Mean	4.5	5.5
SD	0.68	0.72

FIGURE 6.3

(a) Data for simulation in Figure 6.2a. (b) Bar chart with error bars showing ±1 standard deviation.

overall mean and standard deviation for each method. Figure 6.3b shows the corresponding bar chart embellished with error bars. The error bars show ±1 standard deviation in the means. Mathematically, the variance is the square of the standard deviation; however, it is more common in research papers to report standard deviations because the units of the standard deviation and the mean are the same ("seconds" in this case).

ANOVA Table for Task Completion Time (s)

	DF	Sum of Squares	Mean Square	F-Value	P-Value	Lambda	Power
Subject	9	5.080	.564				
Method	1	4.232	4.232	9.796	.0121	9.796	.804
Method * Subject	9	3.888	.432				

FIGURE 6.4

Analysis of variance table for data in Figure 6.3a.

The step-by-step process of doing an ANOVA on the data in Figure 6.3a depends on the statistics program used. Nevertheless, the result is a table similar to that shown in Figure 6.4.[2]

The most important statistic in the table is the "P-Value." This is the probability of obtaining the observed data if the null hypothesis is true. A low probability indicates that the differences in the means are unlikely to have occurred in view of the null hypothesis. A high probability indicates that the differences in the means may simply be due to chance. With $p = .0121$, there is a fairly low probability—less than 2 percent—that the difference is simply a chance outcome. In all likelihood, there is some inherent and distinguishing property of one or the other method that caused the difference. Note the term "caused" in the preceding sentence. One reason experimental research is so valuable is that conclusions of a cause-and-effect nature are possible.

It is a convention in experimental research that significance, in a statistical sense, requires p less than .05, or a 1 in 20 probability.[3] In other words, we consider the null hypothesis tenable unless there is a 1 in 20 chance or less that it is not. In addition to the probability, important statistics in the ANOVA are the F statistic (F-Value, the ratio of sample variances) and the degrees of freedom for the main effect (Method) and the residual effect (Method * Subject).[4] The relevant statistics come together in a statement that declares the outcome of the research question.

---

[2] The statistics program used is *StatView*, now marketed a *JMP* (jmp.com).

[3] The significance level is also called alpha (α). Alpha is the probability of committing a Type I error, or false positive. A Type I error occurs when the null hypothesis is incorrectly rejected. Beta (β) is the probability of committing a Type II error, or false negative. A Type II error occurs when the test fails to reject a false null hypothesis. These explanations are confusing because of the built-in assumption of "no difference" in the null hypothesis. Medical examples are more straightforward: A false positive (Type I error) occurs when a test indicates that a patient has a disease when in fact the patient does not. A false negative (Type II error) occurs when a test indicates that a patient does not have a disease when in fact the patient does.

[4] The F-statistic in Figure 6.4 is the ratio of the variance (mean square) for the Method to the Method * Subject: $4.232/0.432 = 9.796$. The numerator is the variance due to the effect of the methods, or test conditions. The denominator is all of the remaining variance. If there is no experimental effect, this ratio should be approximately 1. The amount F rises above 1 is an indication of the impact of the test conditions on the differences in the means observed across the test conditions. Statistical significance depends on the value of F, the degrees of freedom, and the threshold for p that is deemed significant.

The mean task completion time for Method A was 4.5 s. This was 20.1% less than the mean of 5.5 s observed for Method B. The difference was statistically significant ($F_{1,9} = 9.80$, $p < .05$).

FIGURE 6.5

Example of how to report the results of an analysis of variance in a research paper.

An example of how this might appear in a research paper for the hypothetical experiment is shown in Figure 6.5 (with F rounded to three significant figures).[5]

Note that the probability is not precisely cited. Instead, p is cited as less than a more conservative threshold from the set {.05, .01, .005, .001, .0005, .0001}. So p is cited as $p < .05$ rather than $p = .0121$.[6]

The language in Figure 6.5 includes both the means for the test conditions and an articulation of the difference in the means. The difference in the means is the *effect size.* The effect size is usually conveyed in HCI research in a statement giving the means and the absolute difference (one second, in this case) or the relative difference. In the example, the effect size is given as a relative difference: the task completion time for Method A was 20.1 percent less than that for Method B. Of course, whether the effect size is of practical significance is not within the scope of the ANOVA.[7]

F statistics are often poorly formatted in research papers, so it is worthwhile to pause for a moment and observe the following in the F statistic in Figure 6.5:

- Placed in parentheses
- Uppercase for F
- Lowercase for p
- Italics for F and p
- Space on both sides of the equal sign
- Space after the comma

---

[5]Lambda and Power in Figure 6.4 are generally not reported in research papers. Lambda is a measure of the non-centrality of the F distribution. Power, which ranges from 0 to 1, is the ability to detect an effect, if there is one. The closer to one, the more the experiment is likely to find an effect if one exists in the population. Power $> .80$ is generally considered acceptable; that is, if p is significant and power $> .80$, then it is likely that the effect found actually exists. Note that power $= 1 - \beta$ (see footnote 3).

[6]The APA's *Publication Manual* has a different recommendation: "When reporting p values, report exact p values (e.g., $p = .031$) to two or three decimal places. However, report p values less than .001 as $p < .001$." (APA 2010, 114) This practice is not (yet) generally followed in human-computer interaction.

[7]Here, and in most HCI research, the reported effect size is *unstandardized*. The unstandardized effect size is useful since it allows the practical importance of the results to be assessed and compared with other research using the same dependent variable. Statisticians generally prefer a *standardized* effect size, such as Cohen's d, which normalizes for the standard deviation in the sample. A standardized effect size is unitless and therefore is more difficult to interpret in terms of the magnitude of, and differences in, the measurements on the dependent variable. Generally, standardized effect sizes are not reported in HCI research, although there are exceptions (e.g., Banovic, Li, Dearman, Yatani, and Truong, 2011; MacDorman, Whalen, Ho, and Patel, 2011; Weisband and Kiesler, 1996).

- Space on both sides of the less than sign
- Degrees of freedom are subscript, plain, smaller font[8]
- Three or four significant figures for the F statistic
- No zero before the decimal point for the p statistic (because it is constrained between 0 and 1)[9]

For completeness, let's study the second example, the simulation in Figure 6.2b. The data and corresponding bar chart embellished with error bars are shown in Figure 6.6.

As noted earlier, the results for the second simulation are not statistically significant. A hint of this is the large error bars in Figure 6.6b. The ANOVA reveals and confirms the lack of significance with a high value in the p statistic. As evident by the P-value in Figure 6.7, there is about a 45 percent chance the difference in the

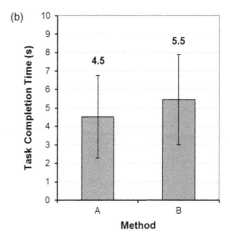

(a)

Participant	Method A	Method B
1	2.4	6.9
2	2.7	7.2
3	3.4	2.6
4	6.1	1.8
5	6.4	7.8
6	5.4	9.2
7	7.9	4.4
8	1.2	6.6
9	3.0	4.8
10	6.6	3.1
Mean	4.5	5.5
SD	2.23	2.45

FIGURE 6.6

(a) Data for simulation in Figure 6.2b. (b) Bar chart with error bars showing ±1 standard deviation.

ANOVA Table for Task Completion Time (s)

	DF	Sum of Squares	Mean Square	F-Value	P-Value	Lambda	Power
Subject	9	37.372	4.152				
Method	1	4.324	4.324	.626	.4491	.626	.107
Method * Subject	9	62.140	6.904				

FIGURE 6.7

Analysis of variance for data in Figure 6.3b.

---

[8] Alternatively, the degrees of freedom may be set in parentheses in a plain style. In this case, a space follows the comma.

[9] Some journals require a zero before the decimal point.

> The mean task completion times were 4.5 s for Method A and 5.5 s for Method B. As there was substantial variation in the observations across participants, the difference was not statistically significant as revealed in an analysis of variances ($F_{1,9} = 0.626$, ns).

FIGURE 6.8

Reporting a non-significant ANOVA result.

means is simply a chance outcome. Even though the means are the same as in the first simulation, there was such a large variation in the performance of participants that the difference in the means between the test conditions may simply be due to chance. Observe in Figure 6.6a, for example, that participant #8 completed the task in 1.2 seconds using Method A while participant #10 took 6.6 seconds. Evidently, there is something going on that falls outside the explanatory power of the two interaction methods under test.

In a research paper, non-significant results are also important to report. Figure 6.8 is an example for the second simulation. Bear in mind that a non-significant ANOVA does not imply that the null hypothesis is true (i.e., no difference in the means). A non-significant ANOVA simply indicates that the evidence is insufficient to reject the null hypothesis: The null hypothesis remains tenable.[10]

For non-significant results, the ANOVA result is reported in one of two ways. If F is less than 1, it is impossible for the effect to be significant, and in this case "ns," for "not significant," is substituted for p. If the F statistic is greater than 1 and p is greater than .05, the result does not meet the acceptable threshold for significance and p is reported as $p > .05$.

6.1.2 **More than two test conditions**

The example above involves one factor with two levels (test conditions).[11] In practice, a factor often has more than two levels. Although the idea is similar, an example is worthwhile. Figure 6.9 gives the data and bar chart for a hypothetical experiment where four user interfaces or interaction methods are compared. The data are the observed, measured responses on a dependent variable.

An ANOVA on the data produces the table in Figure 6.10. Right off, we see that p is less than .05, the accepted threshold for significance. Plainly put, there was a significant effect of Test Condition on the dependent variable ($F_{3,45} = 4.95$,

---

[10]Note that at .107 the power in Figure 6.7 is low. This implies that the ANOVA could not have found a significant difference even if one existed (for the given sample size, sample variance, and effect size). Power is generally low for non-significant ANOVAs and, with hindsight, could only have been higher had more participants been tested—often many more (>100). While there is some debate on the implication of this (e.g., Kaptein and Robertson, 2012), the conclusion that the null hypothesis *remains tenable* is valid irrespective of power.

[11]A *t* test is the same as an analysis of variance if only two test conditions are compared.

(a)

Participant	Test Condition			
	A	B	C	D
1	11	11	21	16
2	18	11	22	15
3	17	10	18	13
4	19	15	21	20
5	13	17	23	10
6	10	15	15	20
7	14	14	15	13
8	13	14	19	18
9	19	18	16	12
10	10	17	21	18
11	10	19	22	13
12	16	14	18	20
13	10	20	17	19
14	10	13	21	18
15	20	17	14	18
16	18	17	17	14
Mean	14.25	15.13	18.75	16.06
SD	3.84	2.94	2.89	3.23

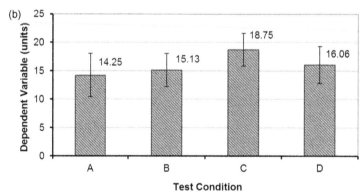

(b)

FIGURE 6.9

Experiment with four test conditions: (a) Data set. (b) Bar chart with error bars showing ± 1 standard deviation in the means.

ANOVA Table for Dependent Variable (units)

	DF	Sum of Squares	Mean Square	F-Value	P-Value	Lambda	Power
Subject	15	81.109	5.407				
Test Condition	3	182.172	60.724	4.954	.0047	14.862	.896
Test Condition * Subject	45	551.578	12.257				

FIGURE 6.10

ANOVA for data in Figure 6.9a.

Scheffe for Dependent Variable (units)
Effect: Test Condition
Significance Level: 5 %

	Mean Diff.	Crit. Diff.	P-Value	
A, B	-.875	3.302	.9003	
A, C	-4.500	3.302	.0032	S
A, D	-1.813	3.302	.4822	
B, C	-3.625	3.302	.0256	S
B, D	-.938	3.302	.8806	
C, D	2.688	3.302	.1520	

FIGURE 6.11

Scheffé post hoc comparisons test for data in Figure 6.9. "S" identifies comparisons that meet the $p < .05$ threshold for significance.

$p < .005$). In the parentheses, the relevant statistics are pulled from the table, as before. The degrees of freedom are different in this example. If n is the number of test conditions and m is the number of participants, then the degrees of freedom are $(n - 1)$ for the variance due to Test Condition and $(n - 1)(m - 1)$ for the variance due to Test Condition × Subject.

Since the P-value in the ANOVA table is .0047, there is less than a 0.5 percent chance the difference in the means is a chance outcome. In all likelihood, the difference was caused by inherent properties of one or more of the test conditions. In other words, the effect of the test conditions on the dependent variable was statistically significant.

6.1.3 Post hoc comparisons

The ANOVA in Figure 6.10 reveals only that at least one of the means is significantly different from at least one other mean. A quick glance at the bar chart in Figure 6.9b leaves us wondering which test conditions differ from which other test conditions. To determine this, a post hoc comparisons test is used. An example is the Scheffé test shown in Figure 6.11.[12] Among the four test conditions, six comparisons are possible. Of these, only the A-C and B-C comparisons are significant. In others words, the means are significantly different between test conditions A and C and between test conditions B and C. The other four comparisons did not meet the 5 percent threshold for significance.

Several HCI research papers using a Scheffé post hoc analysis include the following: Chen and Chien, 2005; Czerwinski et al., 1999; Fang, Chai, and Ferreira, 2009; Freeman, Norris, and Hyland, 2006; Kurihara, Vronay, and Igarashi, 2005; Kuzuoka, Kosaka, et al., 2004.

---

[12]Other post hoc comparison tests include Fisher PLSD, Bonferroni/Dunn, Dunnett, Tukey/Kramer, Games/Howell, Student-Newman-Keuls, and orthogonal contrasts. There are statistical assumptions inherent in each, but these are not discussed here.

(a)

Participant	Task Completion Time (s)	Handedness
1	23	L
2	19	L
3	22	L
4	21	L
5	23	L
6	20	L
7	25	L
8	23	L
9	17	R
10	19	R
11	16	R
12	21	R
13	23	R
14	20	R
15	22	R
16	21	R
Mean	20.9	
SD	2.38	

(b)

Handedness	Task Completion Time (s)	
	Mean	SD
Left	22.0	1.93
Right	19.9	2.42

(c)

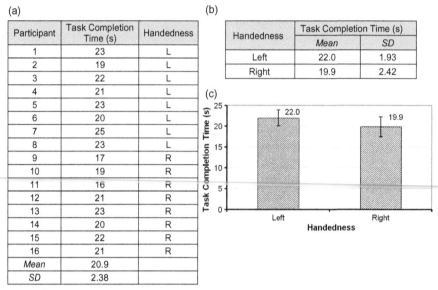

FIGURE 6.12

Experiment with handedness as a between-subjects factor: (a) Data used in the ANOVA. (b) Summary data showing handedness results. (c) Bar chart with error bars showing ±1 standard deviation about the means.

6.1.4 Between-subjects designs

The examples above assume a within-subjects design: each participant was tested on all test conditions (levels of the factor). While within-subjects designs are the most common in HCI, between-subjects designs are also used. When performing an ANOVA on the data for either design, it is important to set up the analysis properly, as the variances are partitioned differently for within-subjects data versus between-subjects data.

Let's consider an example experiment on the differences between left-handed and right-handed users in using a stylus to add calendar entries on a PDA. Depending on the screen layout, occlusion may occur when, for example, a left-handed user interacts with widgets on the right side of the display. Does the occlusion affect performance? Maybe. Maybe not. For the experiment, 16 participants were recruited. Handedness was a between-subjects factor with two levels: left handers, with 8 participants, and right handers, with 8 different participants. Each participant performed a few iterations of an "add calendar entry" task. The mean times to complete the task for each participant are tabulated in Figure 6.12a. While such tables are generally not provided in research papers, the data are given here to illustrate the organization for between-subjects ANOVAs. Most ANOVA applications operate on a matrix of data where the number of rows equals the number of participants, so the data in Figure 6.12a are organized in sixteen rows. The between-subjects factor is identified as an added column of nominal data

ANOVA Table for Task Completion Time (s)

	DF	Sum of Squares	Mean Square	F-Value	P-Value	Lambda	Power
Handedness	1	18.063	18.063	3.781	.0722	3.781	.429
Residual	14	66.875	4.777				

FIGURE 6.13

Between-subjects ANOVA for data in Figure 6.12a.

encoding the levels of the factor. "L" and "R" identify the participants who were left handers versus right handers.

Figure 6.12b summarizes the results by handedness, while Figure 6.12c presents the same information in a bar chart, as might appear in a research paper. The ANOVA is performed on the 16×2 matrix in the right two columns in Figure 6.12a. The result is shown in Figure 6.13. The degrees of freedom are $(n - 1)$ for the variance due to Handedness and $(m - n)$ for the variance due to the Residual.

Since the P-value in Figure 6.13 is greater than .05, the difference between left handers and right handers was not statistically significant. Even though there was about a 10 percent difference between the groups—22.0s for left handers, 19.9s for right handers—there was considerable variability in the observations. Based on the results of this experiment, we consider the null hypothesis tenable and conclude that there is no performance difference between left and right handed users in performing the add calendar entry task on the system under test.

6.1.5 Two-way analysis of variance

An experiment with two independent variables, or two factors, is called a "two-way design." For such experiments, the analysis of variance tests for the main effects of each factor on the dependent variable, as well as an interaction effect. A significant interaction effect means that the factors in combination influence, or have an effect on, the dependent variable. Let's see how these effects are revealed in a two-way analysis of variance.

If an experiment has two factors, there are three possibilities for assigning conditions to participants. The assignments may be within-subjects for both factors, between-subjects for both factors, or within-subjects for one factor and between-subjects for the other. Figure 6.14 gives the results for a hypothetical experiment with both factors assigned within-subjects. The factors are device, with three levels, and task, with two levels. The devices could be, for example, a mouse, a trackball, and a stylus, while the tasks could be, for example, point-select and drag-select.[13] But this isn't important here. For the example, each participant was tested on all three devices and with both tasks in a simple target acquisition task. In this case, the experiment is referred to as a "3 × 2 within-subjects design." We assume as well that the order of administering conditions was counterbalanced in some

---

[13] An example of an experiment with these conditions is found in a paper from the ACM SIGCHI conference proceedings (MacKenzie, Sellen, and Buxton, 1991).

(a)

Participant	Device 1		Device 2		Device 3	
	Task 1	Task 2	Task 1	Task 2	Task 1	Task 2
1	11	18	15	13	20	14
2	10	14	17	15	11	13
3	10	23	13	20	20	16
4	18	18	11	12	11	10
5	20	21	19	14	19	8
6	14	21	20	11	17	13
7	14	16	15	20	16	12
8	20	21	18	20	14	12
9	14	15	13	17	16	14
10	20	15	18	10	11	16
11	14	20	15	16	10	9
12	20	20	16	16	20	9
Mean	15.4	18.5	15.8	15.3	15.4	12.2
SD	4.01	2.94	2.69	3.50	3.92	2.69

(b)

	Task 1	Task 2	Mean
Device 1	15.4	18.5	17.0
Device 2	15.8	15.3	15.6
Device 3	15.4	12.2	13.8
Mean	15.6	15.3	15.4

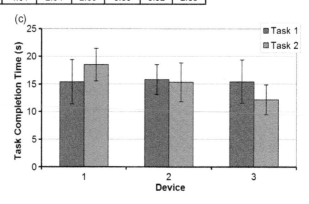

(c)

FIGURE 6.14

Hypothetical experiment with two within-subjects factors. The factors are device, with three levels, and task, with two levels: (a) Results by participant, device, and task. (b) Results by device and task. (c) Bar chart with error bars showing ±1 standard deviation about the means.

manner (see Chapter 5, section 5.11). The data show the measured responses on the dependent variable, task completion time, in seconds.

In Figure 6.14a, the data are given by participant, device, and task. Evidently, participant #12 performed task 2 with device 3 in nine seconds. The means and standard deviations are shown in the bottom rows, calculated across the 12 participants for each device-task condition. Figure 6.14b reorganizes the data to more clearly demonstrate the device and task effects. As seen, device 3 was the fastest, device 1 the slowest. Task 2 was performed slightly faster than task 1. Figure 6.14c shows the mean scores for each device and task in a bar chart, as might appear in a research paper. The error bars show ±1 standard deviation about the means.

While there were differences between the three devices and two tasks, there were also variations in the responses, as evident along the bottom row in Figure 6.14a. So the question remains: were the observed differences significant

ANOVA Table for Task Completion Time (s)

	DF	Sum of Squares	Mean Square	F-Value	P-Value	Lambda	Power
Subject	11	134.778	12.253				
Device	2	121.028	60.514	5.865	.0091	11.731	.831
Device * Subject	22	226.972	10.317				
Task	1	.889	.889	.076	.7875	.076	.057
Task * Subject	11	128.111	11.646				
Device * Task	2	121.028	60.514	5.435	.0121	10.869	.798
Device * Task * Subject	22	244.972	11.135				

FIGURE 6.15

Two-way analysis of variance for data in Figure 6.14a.

> The grand mean for task completion time was 15.4 seconds.
> Device 3 was the fastest at 13.8 seconds, while device 1 was the
> slowest at 17.0 seconds. The main effect of device on task
> completion time was statistically significant ($F_{2,22}$ = 5.865, p <.01).
> The task effect was modest, however. Task completion time was
> 15.6 seconds for task 1. Task 2 was slightly faster at 15.3
> seconds; however, the difference was not statistically significant
> ($F_{1,11}$ = 0.076, ns). The results by device and task are shown in
> Figure x. There was a significant Device × Task interaction effect
> ($F_{2,22}$ = 5.435, p < .05), which was due solely to the difference
> between device 1 task 2 and device 3 task 2, as determined by
> a Scheffé post hoc analysis.

FIGURE 6.16

Results of the two-way analysis of variance in Figure 6.15 as might appear in a research paper.

and attributable to inherent properties of the devices or tasks, or were the differences simply a chance outcome? This question is answered by an analysis of variance. The ANOVA is performed on the core 12 × 6 matrix in Figure 6.14a. In preparing the data for analysis, it is important to properly assign the factors and levels. As organized in Figure 6.14a, the columns are ordered by device, with task nested within device. The results are shown in Figure 6.15.

There are three results in Figure 6.15: the device main effect, the task main effect, and the device by task interaction effect. Let's see how these results are pulled from the analysis of variance table and presented in a research paper. An example is given in Figure 6.16.

It is a challenge to create interest in presenting statistical results. A reader who confronts a tedious, sterile recitation of statistic after statistic will quickly lose interest. The goal in reporting results is to selectively pull interesting and revealing measures and statistics from the large array of data that emerges in experimental research. Note in Figure 6.16 expressions like "difference was modest," "slightly faster," and "due solely to." These are minor embellishments intended to improve the readability of the results. Further discussion is needed to explain the results (e.g., "The improved performance with device 3 with task 2 is attributed to....").

It is, of course, the data that are important, not the statistics. Statistical tests help assess hypotheses, but they are not the results per se. Day and Gastel (2006, 63) further emphasize this point: "Generally, a lengthy description of statistical methods indicates that the writer has recently acquired this information and believes that the readers need similar enlightenment." Don't feel compelled to explain the analysis of variance, or any other statistical method. Give the results in terms of the data, with supporting statistical tests conveyed plainly and without elaboration.

6.1.6 ANOVA tool

A resource available on this book's website is a Java utility called Anova2. Anova2 is a command-line application that processes data in a text file and produces an ANOVA table on the console. The utility supports five designs:

- One-way with one within-subjects factor
- One-way with one between-subjects factor
- Two-way with two within-subjects factors
- Two-way with one within-subjects factor and one between-subjects factor
- Three-way with two within-subjects factors and one between-subjects factor

To illustrate the general operation of Anova2, Figure 6.17 shows the usage message if the program is run without arguments.

Although the API gives extensive instructions and examples, one example is included here. The file dix-example-10×2.txt contains the data shown in Figure 6.18. The data are from a hypothetical experiment on icon recognition, as described by Dix et al. (2004, 337). The single factor (F1) is icon design with two levels: natural and abstract. The data are the measurements for task completion time, the dependent variable. The first column contains the task completion times for the natural icons, the second column for the abstract icons. Each row contains the measurements for one participant. The hypothetical experiment used 10 participants.

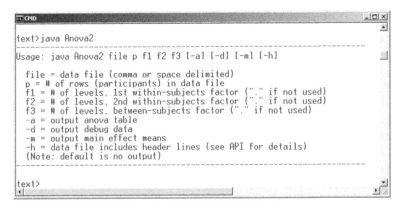

FIGURE 6.17

Usage message for Anova2.

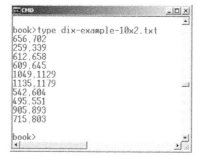

FIGURE 6.18

Data in file dix-example-10 × 2.txt.

```
CMD                                                      _□×
book>java Anova2 dix-example-10x2.txt 10 2 . . -a
=======================================================
Effect              df        SS            MS          F       p
-------------------------------------------------------
Participant          9    1231492.000    136832.444
F1                   1      13833.800     13833.800    33.359   2.7E-4
F1_x_Par             9       3732.200       414.689
=======================================================
book>
```

FIGURE 6.19

ANOVA table produced by `Anova2` for data in `dix-example-10x2.txt`.

The mean task completion times (not shown) are 697.7 s for the natural icons and 750.3 s for the abstract icons. Evidently the recognition time for the natural icons was 7.0 percent less than for the abstract icons. An analysis of variance determines if the difference was statistically significant or if it was likely due to chance. The analysis is initiated from the command-line and outputs an ANOVA table to the console. (See Figure 6.19.)

As seen in the table, and as might appear in a research paper, "The experiment revealed a significant effect of icon type on task completion time ($F_{1,9} = 33.36$, $p < .0005$)."

6.1.7 Counterbalancing and testing for a group effect

As noted in the previous chapter, if a factor is assigned within-subjects, learning effects must be offset between conditions. The most common way to do this is counterbalancing. For a single factor with two levels (A and B), this requires dividing the participants into two equal groups. One group (G1) is tested on A followed by B, while the other (G2) is tested on B followed by A. The goal is to balance out, or cancel, any learning effect that takes place. If counterbalancing worked, there should be no group effect—no significant difference between G1 and G2. Simple enough, but how does one know counterbalancing worked? A group effect

```
CMD                                    _□×
book>type dix-example-h10x2b.txt
DV: Completion Time (s)
F1: Icon Type, Natural, Abstract
F2: .
F3: Group
656,702,NA
259,339,NA
612,658,NA
609,645,NA
1049,1129,NA
1135,1179,AN
542,604,AN
495,551,AN
905,893,AN
715,803,AN

book>
```

FIGURE 6.20

Data in file `dix-example-h10x2b.txt`. The data are for the icon recognition experiment modified to illustrate counterbalancing. Headers lines are also included to improve the readability of the ANOVA table.

is investigated by treating group as a between-subjects factor. Of course, group is not a factor in the sense of a research topic. Nevertheless, the data can be organized with group as a between-subjects factor and the ANOVA can test for a *group effect*—a main effect of group on a dependent variable.

I'll illustrate this by modifying the icon design example in the previous section. Since the design was within-subjects, we'll assume counterbalancing was used to offset learning effects. With 10 participants, there are two groups with 5 participants per group. One group was tested with the natural icons followed by the abstract icons (NA). The other group had the conditions in the reverse order (AN). The modified data are shown in Figure 6.20. The between-subjects group identifier appears as a separate column of nominal data. Headers lines are also added. This is an optional feature of `Anova2` to improve the readability of the ANOVA table.

For the purpose of the ANOVA, the experiment is now a 2×2 design with one within-subjects factor (icon type with levels natural and abstract) and one between-subjects factor (group with levels NA and AN). Using `Anova2`, the ANOVA is performed on the data in Figure 6.20 using the same command, except specifying the new file, noting the presence of a between-subjects factor with two levels, and including the $-h$ option indicating the presence of header lines. (See Figure 6.21.) The group effect, seen along the top row, is not significant ($F_{1,8} = 0.466$, ns). This is good news. A non-significant group effect means counterbalancing worked. Any learning that may have taken place was balanced out. The primary result of the experiment remains the same, although the F and p values are slightly different because of the new partitioning of data in computing the variances. The result is still a significant effect of icon type on task completion time ($F_{1,8} = 30.68$, $p < .0005$).

There is a third effect in Figure 6.21. This is the two-way interaction effect between icon type and group. As seen in the ANOVA table, the effect was not significant

```
CMD                                                              _ □ ×

book>java Anova2 dix-example-h10x2b.txt 10 2 . 2 -h -a

ANOVA_table_for_Completion Time (s)
=================================================================
Effect                   df       SS            MS        F       p
-----------------------------------------------------------------
Group                     1     67744.800     67744.800   0.466   0.51424
Participant(Group)        8   1163747.200    145468.400
Icon Type                 1     13833.800     13833.800  30.680   3.6E-4
Icon Type_x_Group         1       125.000       125.000   0.277   0.61281
Icon Type_x_P(Group)      8      3607.200       450.900
=================================================================

book>
```

FIGURE 6.21

ANOVA for data in Figure 6.9.

($F_{1,8} = 0.277$, ns). If this effect is significant, it represents a phenomenon known as *asymmetric skill transfer* (Poulton, 1974), meaning there was a learning effect and that it was different transitioning from A to N than from N to A (see Chapter 5, section 5.12).

In many research experiments, counterbalancing is used for within-subjects factors without actually testing for a group effect. This is largely a matter of choice.

Consult the student exercises at the end of this chapter for some practice examples on the analysis of variance.

6.2 Chi-square test

A common statistical procedure for investigating relationships is the chi-square test, also known as the Pearson chi-square test, and sometimes using "squared" instead of "square." The pronunciation is *kī* (to rhyme with *sky*). The relationships are between categorical, or nominal-scale, variables representing attributes of people, interaction methods, systems, and so on. The data are commonly summarized in a *contingency table*—a cross tabulation organizing data in rows and columns with each cell containing counts or frequency data for the number of observations in the category. A chi-square test compares the observed values—the counts in the table—against expected values. The expected values are developed under the assumption that there is no difference among the categories in the table. The chi-square test is a non-parametric test since the categories are nominal-scale attributes and do not have a probability distribution associated with them. A hypothetical example will illustrate.

Consider a research project investigating whether males or females differ in their methods of scrolling when using a desktop computer system. To study this, a large number of users are observed. For each user it is noted whether they are male or female and whether they scroll using the mouse wheel (MW), the scrollbar by clicking and dragging (CD), or the keyboard (KB). The categories are Gender (male, female) and Scrolling Method (MW, CD, KB). Figure 6.22a provides the data in a 2 × 3 contingency table. One hundred and one users were observed, including 56 males and 45 females. Counts for usage of the scrolling methods were 49 (MW), 24 (CD), and 28 (KB). Figure 6.22b shows the data in a bar chart, as might appear in a research paper.

(a)

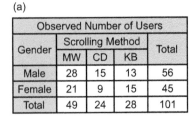

Observed Number of Users				
Gender	Scrolling Method			Total
	MW	CD	KB	
Male	28	15	13	56
Female	21	9	15	45
Total	49	24	28	101

(b)

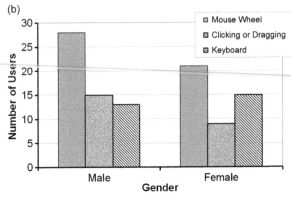

FIGURE 6.22

Contingency table example: (a) Data. (b) Chart.

A quick glance at the data and chart suggests that there may indeed be a difference between males and females in their methods of scrolling on desktop computer systems. Only 9 females used clicking and dragging, compared to 15 males. However, more males were observed overall, so the difference is not as dramatic as it seems. The issue, then, is whether the differences observed are real or simply due to random effects. To determine this, the chi-square test is used. The test statistic is written χ^2, using the lowercase Greek letter *chi*. As with the analysis of variance, the underlying assumption is "no difference" with the test, seeking to reject the assumption. Unlike the analysis of variance, however, a chi-square test is simple. The calculations are easily done using a spreadsheet application. Let's work through the details for this example.

The chi-square test is a comparison between the observed values and the expected values, with the expected values accounting for the different row and column totals. Figure 6.23a shows the expected values for the data in Figure 6.22a, under the no-difference assumption. Each expected value is the row total multiplied by the column total, divided by the grand total. For example, the Male-MW expected value is $(56 \times 49) / 101 = 27.2$. From the observed and expected values, a table of chi-squares is created, as shown in Figure 6.23b. Each chi-square is the square of (the observed value minus the expected value), divided by the expected value. For example, the Male-MW chi-square is $(28.0 - 27.2)^2 / 27.2 = 0.025$.

(a)

Expected Number of Users				
Gender	Scrolling Method			Total
	MW	CD	KB	
Male	27.2	13.3	15.5	56.0
Female	21.8	10.7	12.5	45.0
Total	49.0	24.0	28.0	101

(b)

Chi Squares				
Gender	Scrolling Method			Total
	MW	CD	KB	
Male	0.025	0.215	0.411	0.651
Female	0.032	0.268	0.511	0.811
Total	0.057	0.483	0.922	**1.462**

FIGURE 6.23

(a) Expected values and (b) chi-squares for the data in Figure 6.22.

Significance Threshold (α)	Degrees of Freedom							
	1	2	3	4	5	6	7	8
.1	2.71	4.61	6.25	7.78	9.24	10.65	12.02	13.36
.05	3.84	5.99	7.82	9.49	11.07	12.59	14.07	15.51
.01	6.64	9.21	11.35	13.28	15.09	16.81	18.48	20.09
.001	10.83	13.82	16.27	18.47	20.52	22.46	24.32	26.13

FIGURE 6.24

Chi-square critical values.

The final chi-square value is the sum of the individual chi-squares in the table. For the example data, the result is $\chi^2 = 1.462$, shown in the bottom-right cell in Figure 6.23b. Determining if there is a statistically significant difference among the cell entries involves comparing the final chi-square with values in a table of critical values. If the chi-square exceeds the critical value, the differences in the contingency table are statistically significant, implying there is a significant difference in the nominal-scale variables in the table. Two additional details are required: (a) the degrees of freedom, and (b) the required alpha level, or p-value, for significance. The degrees of freedom for the chi-square statistic is $(r - 1)(c - 1)$, where r is the number of rows and c is the number of columns. For the example, $df = (2 - 1)$ $(3 - 1) = 2$. The alpha level is chosen prior to testing. I'll use $\alpha = .05$ for the example. The critical value for significance is looked up in a table. Figure 6.24 gives the chi-square critical values for $df = 1$ to $df = 8$ using four common alpha levels. At $\alpha = .05$ and $df = 2$, the critical value is $\chi^2 = 5.99$. Since the computed value of $\chi^2 = 1.462$ is less than the critical value, the differences in the observed values (see Figure 6.22) are not statistically significant. Therefore, we conclude that there is no difference in the way males and females scroll using desktop computer systems.

As a convenience, this book's website includes a ChiSquare Java utility. It processes a text file containing a table of data, with the rows and columns containing the counts in the contingency table. Besides automating the calculation of the chi-square statistic, χ^2, the utility calculates and outputs the probability p, thus negating the need to use a look-up table. Figure 6.25 shows the utility processing a text file containing the data in Figure 6.22a.

```
CMD                                                    _|□|×|
text>type chisquare-ex1.txt
28   15   13
21    9   15

text>java ChiSquare chisquare-ex1.txt
Chi-square(2) = 1.462
p = 0.4814

text>_
```

FIGURE 6.25

Java utility to compute chi-square statistic and p.

Observed Number of People			
Opinion	Category		Total
	Student	Professor	Parent	
Agree	10	12	98	120
Disagree	30	48	102	180
Total	40	60	200	300

FIGURE 6.26

Contingency table showing the responses to a question about mobile phone usage during classroom lectures.

Let's work through another example, where the outcome is statistically signifi-cant and where a post hoc comparisons test is used to determine which conditions are significantly different from one another.

A researcher wishes to investigate whether students, professors, and parents agree in their responses to a question about mobile phone usage during classroom lec-tures. To study this, a large number of students, professors, and parents are randomly sampled and asked if they agree that students should be allowed to use mobile phones during classroom lectures. The categories are Opinion (agree, disagree) and Person (student, professor, parent). In all, 300 people were sampled, including 40 students, 60 professors, and 200 parents. The responses were: 120 agree and 180 disagree. The contingency table in Figure 6.26 shows the data organized by Opinion and Person. Evidently, respondents overall feel that the use of mobile phones during classroom lectures should not be allowed. Furthermore, the responses are in the same direction for all three categories of people. However, a closer look at the table reveals some variation among the categories. Although three times more students disagreed than agreed, only a few more parents disagreed than agreed. To determine if the differences in response are statistically significant, a chi-square test is used.

The calculations leading to the chi-square statistic are identical to those demon-strated for the last example. The result in this case is $\chi^2 = 20.5$ with $df = 2$. With reference to Figure 6.24, the chi-square statistic exceeds the critical value both for $\alpha = .05$ (5.99) and for $\alpha = .001$ (13.82). Clearly, there is a difference in opin-ions among students, professors, and parents on the question of interest. However,

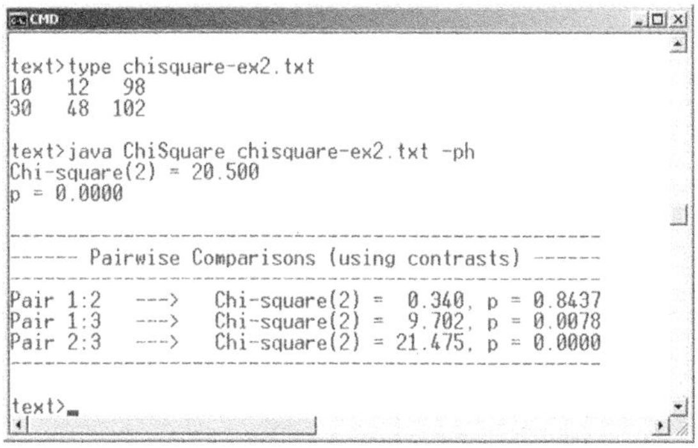

```
text>type chisquare-ex2.txt
10   12   98
30   48  102

text>java ChiSquare chisquare-ex2.txt -ph
Chi-square(2) = 20.500
p = 0.0000

------------------------------------------------------------
------ Pairwise Comparisons (using contrasts) ------
------------------------------------------------------------
Pair 1:2   --->   Chi-square(2) =  0.340, p = 0.8437
Pair 1:3   --->   Chi-square(2) =  9.702, p = 0.0078
Pair 2:3   --->   Chi-square(2) = 21.475, p = 0.0000
------------------------------------------------------------

text>_
```

FIGURE 6.27

Chi-square test including post hoc pairwise comparisons test.

since there were three categories of people, a post hoc pairwise comparisons test is required to determine which categories differ from one another. The `ChiSquare` utility on this book's website includes a `-ph` option to perform the post hoc comparisons. (See Figure 6.27.) The comparisons indicate statistical significance ($p < .05$) for the 1:3 and 2:3 comparisons. Thus, on the question at issue there is a difference in opinion between students and parents and between professors and parents. However, there is no difference in opinion between students and professors.[14]

Finally, let's consider an example using data from a paper published in the ACM SIGCHI conference proceedings. Ayyavu and Jensen researched tools to assist users in determining if websites are considered trustworthy (free of spam, predators, etc.) (Ayyavu and Jensen, 2011). In particular, they were interested in differences in the ratings provided by community-based tools versus heuristics-based tools. They examined Web Of Trust (WOT) as a community-based tool and McAfee's Site Advisor (MSA) as a heuristics-based tool. The tools were presented with 20,000 websites and for each site the tools provided an assessment of good (safe), bad (not safe), or unsure. After removing sites for which WOT or MSA gave an unsure rating, 18,650 remained. Ayyavu and Jensen presented the results for these sites in a contingency table, formatted as shown in Figure 6.28. Thankfully, most of the sites were deemed good, or safe. WOT rated 9.21 percent of the sites bad, or not safe. The figure was 3.36 percent for MSA. That seems like a substantial difference. To determine if the difference was statistically significant, a chi-square test was used. The result was $\chi^2 = 543.5$ with $df = 1$. That's well above the critical value of $\chi^2 = 3.84$ for $p < .05$ (see Figure 6.24). Ayyavu and Jensen concluded that there was a statistically significant difference between the assessments provided by the tools. In fact,

[14]The calculations for the pairwise comparisons are not included here. Interested readers are directed to the source code and comments in the ChiSquare java utility on this book's website or to Glass and Hopkins (1984, 392). The data in this example are from a chi-square test described by Glass and Hopkins pertaining to the attitude of school superintendents, teachers, and principals toward collective bargaining.

System	Set	Sample Size	% of Sample
WOT	Good	16,968	90.79%
WOT	Bad	1,722	9.21%
MSA	Good	18,062	96.21%
MSA	Bad	628	3.36%

FIGURE 6.28

Comparison of website assessments between Web Of Trust (WOT) and McAfee's Site Advisor (MSA).

(From Table 1 in Ayyavu and Jensen, 2011)

they reported that the difference was "highly significant," noting that the chi-square statistic exceeded the $p < .0001$ critical value (Ayyavu and Jensen, 2011, p. 2309).

A contingency table combined with a chi-square test is a simple and effective way to study relationships in HCI research. The relationships are frequently between attributes of people (males versus females, Mac users versus PC users, etc.) and their behaviors (e.g., preferred scrolling method, texting habits, etc.). But as the last example illustrates, the attributes may also involve systems and the behaviors of systems. A few additional examples of chi-square tests in the HCI literature are as follows: Bartneck, Verbunt, Mubin, and Mahmud, 2007; Kane, Wobbrock, and Ladner, 2011; Kindberg et al., 2008; Qvarfordt, Jönsson, and Dahlbäck, 2003). See also student exercises 6-6 to 6-8 at the end of this chapter.

6.3 Non-parametric tests for ordinal data

Non-parametric tests make no assumptions about the probability distribution of the population from which the underlying data are obtained. For this reason, non-parametric tests are applicable to a wider range of data than parametric tests. However, there is a downside to non-parametric tests: loss of information. While parametric tests such as the analysis of variance operate on interval or ratio data, most non-parametric tests deal with ordinal data (ranks). Non-parametric tests ignore any property of the scale of data except ordinality. If the data tested are in fact interval or ratio, non-parametric tests waste this knowledge by collapsing differences into ranks. For example, a trio of values such as 49, 81, 82 (perhaps student marks on an exam) is transformed to 1, 2, 3. Clearly information is sacrificed, since the middle value is now equidistant from the first and third. Non-parametric tests benefit by not being bound by parametric assumptions, but sacrifice the power to use all available information to reject a false null hypothesis.

In the examples ahead, non-parametric tests are described as they are typically used in HCI research—to analyze ordinal (and sometimes interval) data. The data are typically obtained through questionnaires (e.g., using a Likert scale), preference ratings, or assessments on a scale. Rather than using direct measurement of human responses, the data are obtained subjectively, from participants, or using heuristics or other non-empirical or semi-empirical methods.

Design	Conditions	
	2	3 or more
Between-subjects (independent samples)	Mann-Whitney U	Kruskal-Wallis
Within-subjects (correlated samples)	Wilcoxon Signed-Rank	Friedman

FIGURE 6.29

Choosing a non-parametric test based on experiment design and number of conditions.

The four most common non-parametric procedures are the Mann-Whitney U test, the Wilcoxon Signed-Rank test, the Kruskal-Wallis test, and the Friedman test. Each is used in a particular context, depending on the number of test conditions and the experiment design. (Figure 6.29 illustrates.) Between-subjects and within-subjects designs generate data that are from *independent samples* and *correlated samples*, respectively, as shown in the figure. Between-subjects designs generate independent samples because different participants are tested with each condition. Within-subjects designs generate correlated samples because the same participants are tested with each condition. Bear in mind that the conditions are levels of a single independent variable (factor) in the experiment.

The non-parametric tests in Figure 6.29 are demonstrated below through a series of hypothetical examples. As the problems are described and the data presented, it will be apparent which test is appropriate. Since the Kruskal-Wallis and Friedman tests operate on three or more conditions, a statistically significant outcome is usually followed with a post hoc pairwise comparisons test. This is also demonstrated. For each example, two versions of the data analysis are provided. One uses *StatView* (now *JMP*), a commercial statistics application. The other uses a Java utility provided on this book's website. The results are identical for both analyses. Let's begin.

6.3.1 **Example 1**

A researcher seeks to determine if there is a difference in the political leanings of Mac users versus PC users. Are Mac or PC users more likely to have political views leaning to the left or to the right? The experimenter randomly selects 10 Mac users and 10 PC users.[15] The participants are interviewed and asked a variety of questions about their political views. Each participant is assessed on a 10-point linear scale (1 = very left, 10 = very right) with the results stored in a file as a table with 10 rows and two columns. The first column contains the assessments for the Mac users, the second column for the PC users. The data are given in Figure 6.30.

---

[15] For simplicity, the number of participants in the examples is on the low side. Research where only questionnaire data are collected often includes substantially more participants or respondents than used in the examples.

Mac Users	PC Users
2	4
3	6
2	5
4	4
9	8
2	3
5	4
3	2
4	4
3	5

FIGURE 6.30

Assessments of the political leanings of Mac and PC users.

The mean score for the Mac users is 3.7 and for the PC users 4.5 (not shown). Evidently, the PC users are a little more "right-leaning." But is the difference real or is it just an artifact of the variability in responses? The data are potentially interval-scale, but the researcher senses that the intervals between successive codes are not equal, because they are based on a qualitative assessment. The data are at least ordinal, so a non-parametric test is chosen to answer this question. There are two conditions and the assignment is between-subjects, therefore the appropriate test is Mann-Whitney U (see Figure 6.29). The results are shown in Figure 6.31a using StatView (now JMP) and in Figure 6.31b using the `MannWhitneyU` Java utility from the book's website. There are numerous behind-the-scenes data manipulations and calculations leading to the test statistic, U.[16] The output also includes a normalized z-score (calculated from U) and p, the probability of obtaining the observed data under the null hypothesis of "no difference". Two z and p values are provided. The second set includes a "correction for ties." In most cases, the difference with the corrected values is minor.

For the example, $U = 31.0$ with $p = .1418$ (corrected for ties). Since p is greater than .05, the differences in the assessments have not met the customary threshold for statistical significance. The conclusion for the hypothetical experiment is that there is no difference in the political leanings of Mac users and PC users ($U = 31.0, p > .05$).

6.3.2 Example 2

A researcher is interested in comparing two new designs for media players. There is a particular interest in knowing if the designs differ in "cool appeal" for young users. Ten young tech-savvy participants are recruited and given demos of the two media players

---

[16] Readers interested in the details can examine the source code for the Java utility or search the Internet for "Mann-Whitney U". There are many sites detailing the step-by-step calculations leading to U. A good published source for all the tests described herein is Sheskin's *Handbook of Parametric and Non-parametric Statistical Procedures* (Sheskin, 2011).

(a)

Mann-Whitney U for Response
Grouping Variable: Category for Response

U	31.000
U Prime	69.000
Z-Value	-1.436
P-Value	.1509
Tied Z-Value	-1.469
Tied P-Value	.1418
# Ties	4

(b)

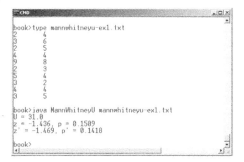

Mann-Whitney Rank Info for Response
Grouping Variable: Category for Response

	Count	Sum Ranks	Mean Rank
MAC	10	86.000	8.600
PC	10	124.000	12.400

FIGURE 6.31

Mann-Whitney U test for the political leanings of Mac and PC users: (a) StatView. (b) Java utility.

Participant	MPA	MPB
1	3	3
2	6	6
3	4	3
4	10	3
5	6	5
6	5	6
7	9	2
8	7	4
9	6	2
10	8	3

FIGURE 6.32

Ratings for "cool appeal" of two media players.

(MPA, MPB). The participants are asked to rate the designs for cool appeal on a 10-point linear scale (1 = not cool at all, 10 = really cool). The data are given in Figure 6.32.

The mean rating for media player A is 6.4 and for media player B 3.7 (not shown). It seems media player A fares quite well compared to media player B. However, there was some variability in the responses, so perhaps the difference was just a chance outcome. To test if the differences in the ratings are real, a statistical test is used. Since the data are interval-scale (see discussion for Example 1), a non-parametric test is chosen. There are two test conditions and the design is within-subjects, therefore the Wilcoxon Signed-Rank test is appropriate (see Figure 6.29).

(a)   (b)

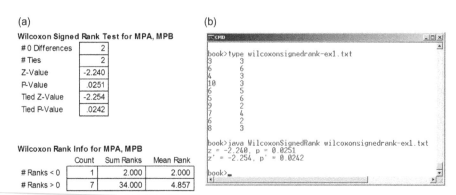

Wilcoxon Signed Rank Test for MPA, MPB

# 0 Differences	2
# Ties	2
Z-Value	-2.240
P-Value	.0251
Tied Z-Value	-2.254
Tied P-Value	.0242

Wilcoxon Rank Info for MPA, MPB

	Count	Sum Ranks	Mean Rank
# Ranks < 0	1	2.000	2.000
# Ranks > 0	7	34.000	4.857

FIGURE 6.33

Wilcoxon Signed-Rank test for the "cool appeal" ratings for two media players: (a) StatView. (b) Java utility.

The results are shown in Figure 6.33a using StatView and in Figure 6.33b using the `WilcoxonSignedRank` Java utility available on this book's website.

The test statistic for the Wilcoxon Signed-Rank test is a normalized z score. For the example, $z = -2.254$ with $p = .0242$ (corrected for ties). Since p is less than .05, the customary threshold for statistical significance is exceeded. The conclusion is that the two media players differ in "cool appeal" ($z = -2.254$, $p < .05$).

6.3.3 Example 3

The designers of a new GPS system for automobiles are wondering if age will be a factor in the acceptance of the product. They decide to conduct a small experiment to find out. Eight participants are recruited from each of three age groups: 20–29 years, 30–39 years, and 40–49 years. The participants are given a demo of the new GPS system and then asked if they liked it enough to consider purchasing it for personal use. They respond on a 10-point linear scale (1= definitely no, 10 = definitely yes). The data are given in Figure 6.34.

The mean scores by age group are 7.1 (20–29), 4.0 (30–39), and 2.9 (40–49) (not shown). It seems there is a difference, since the 20–29 year age group gave higher acceptability scores than the other two groups. However, there was also some variability in the scores. So the question remains: are the differences in the acceptability scores among the three age groups statistically significant, or are the differences simply a chance outcome? Since the data are interval-scale (see discussion for Example 1), a non-parametric test is chosen to help answer the question. There are three age groups and the design is between-subjects, therefore the Kruskal-Wallis test is appropriate (see Figure 6.29). The results are shown in Figure 6.35a using StatView and in Figure 6.35b using the `KruskalWallis` Java utility available on this book's website.

A20-29	A30-39	A40-49
9	7	4
9	3	5
4	5	5
9	3	2
6	2	2
3	1	1
8	4	2
9	7	2

FIGURE 6.34

Acceptability scores for three GPS systems by three age groups.

(a)

Kruskal-Wallis Test for Acceptability
Grouping Variable: Category for Preference

DF	2
# Groups	3
# Ties	7
H	9.421
P-Value	.0090
H corrected for ties	9.605
Tied P-Value	.0082

(b)

Kruskal-Wallis Rank Info for Acceptability
Grouping Variable: Category for Preference

	Count	Sum Ranks	Mean Rank
A	8	148.000	18.500
B	8	88.500	11.063
C	8	63.500	7.938

FIGURE 6.35

Kruskal-Wallis test for acceptability of a GPS system by three age groups: (a) StatView. (b) Java utility.

The test statistic is H, which follows a chi-square distribution with $df = k - 1$ (k is the number of groups). In the example, $H = 9.605$ with $p = .0082$ (corrected for ties). Since p is below the customary threshold for statistical significance (.05), the test shows a significant effect of age group on the acceptability of the GPS design ($\chi^2 = 9.605, p < .01, df = 2$).

There are three age groups, therefore a post hoc pairwise comparisons test is needed to determine which age groups are significantly different from one another. This is available in the Java utility using the –ph option.[17] (See Figure 6.36.) As is

[17] The Kruskal-Wallis pairwise comparisons test was implemented using the procedure described by Siegel and Castellan (Siegel and Castellan Jr., 1988, 213–214).

```
CMD                                                                    _|□|×|
book>java KruskalWallis kruskalwallis-ex1.txt -ph
H = 9.421, p = 0.0090
H' = 9.605, p' = 0.0082
--------------------------------------------------------------
----- Multiple Comparisons Test (alpha = .05) ------
--------------------------------------------------------------
Pair 1:2 -->  7.4375 >=  7.6103  ?   -
Pair 1:3 --> 10.5625 >=  7.6103  ?   * (significant)
Pair 2:3 -->  3.1250 >=  7.6103  ?   -
--------------------------------------------------------------
book>_
```

FIGURE 6.36

Post hoc pairwise comparisons for the Kruskal-Wallis test.

Participant	A	B	C	D
1	66	80	67	73
2	79	64	61	66
3	67	58	61	67
4	71	73	54	75
5	72	66	59	78
6	68	67	57	69
7	71	68	59	64
8	74	69	69	66

FIGURE 6.37

Quality of results for four variations of a search engine interface.

evident, the only statistically significant pairwise comparison was between pairs 1 and 3; that is, between the 20–29 year group and the 40–49 year group.

6.3.4 **Example 4**

A researcher has implemented four variations of a search engine interface (A, B, C, and D). Each interface uses a different dialogue for users to build their queries. The researcher wishes to know if the interfaces differ in the quality of results they produce. Eight participants are recruited and are given a demonstration of each interface and then asked to do a series of search tasks. The "quality of results" is assessed for each participant and for each search engine. The assessment uses a linear scale from 1 to 100 (1 = very poor, 100 = very good). A Latin square was used to balance the order of conditions, but this isn't important here. The data are given in Figure 6.37.

The mean scores for the search engines from A to D were 71.0, 68.1, 60.9, and 69.8 (not shown). The spread is only about 10 points between the highest and lowest assessments, so it unclear if there is any difference in the quality of results between the four interfaces. Nevertheless, it is worthwhile testing for significant

(a)

Friedman Test for 4 Variables

DF	3
# Groups	4
# Ties	2
Chi Square	8.475
P-Value	.0372
Chi Square corrected for ties	8.692
Tied P-Value	.0337

(b)

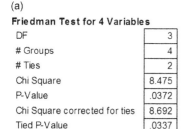

```
book>type friedman-ex1.txt
66      80      67      73
79      64      61      66
67      58      61      67
71      73      54      75
72      66      59      78
68      67      57      69
71      68      59      64
74      69      69      66

book>java Friedman friedman-ex1.txt
H(3) = 8.475, p = 0.0372
H'(3) = 8.692, p' = 0.0337

book>
```

Friedman Rank Info for 4 Variables

	Count	Sum Ranks	Mean Rank
A	8	24.500	3.063
B	8	19.500	2.438
C	8	11.500	1.438
D	8	24.500	3.063

FIGURE 6.38

Friedman test for quality of results for four search engine interfaces: (a) StatView. (b) Java Utility.

differences. Since the data are interval-scale (see discussion for Example 1), a non-parametric test is chosen to investigate further. There are four test conditions and the conditions were assigned within-subjects, therefore the Friedman test is appropriate (see Figure 6.29). The results are shown in Figure 6.38a using StatView and in Figure 6.38b using the Friedman Java utility available on this book's website.

The Friedman test statistic is H, which follows the chi-square distribution with $n - 1$ degrees of freedom ($n =$ number of conditions). As seen in the figure, there is indeed a difference in the quality of results between the four search engine interfaces ($\chi^2 = 8.692$, $p < .05$, $df = 3$). A post hoc pairwise comparisons test is needed to determine which search engine interfaces are significantly different from one another. This is available using the -ph option of the Friedman Java utility.[18] (See Figure 6.39.) With four conditions, there are six pairwise comparisons. Only two were significant: 1:3 and 3:4; that is, between interfaces C and A, and between interfaces C and D.

6.3.5 Discussion

In the examples above, the data were summarized using the means (averages) for each condition. This is common in HCI research for data of this sort. It is also valid. Since the assessment scales were described as "linear," the data are interval-scale.

---

[18] The test was implemented using Conover's F at $\alpha = .05$ for a two-tailed test.

```
CMD                                                            _ I□I x
book>java Friedman friedman-ex1.txt -ph
H(3) = 8.475, p = 0.0372
H'(3) = 8.692, p' = 0.0337

-------------------------------------------------------------
----------- Pairwise Comparisons (using Conover's F) -----------
-------------------------------------------------------------
Pair 1:2 --> abs( 3.063 -  2.438) >  1.132  ?    -
Pair 1:3 --> abs( 3.063 -  1.438) >  1.132  ?    * (significant)
Pair 1:4 --> abs( 3.063 -  3.063) >  1.132  ?    -
Pair 2:3 --> abs( 2.438 -  1.438) >  1.132  ?    -
Pair 2:4 --> abs( 2.438 -  3.063) >  1.132  ?    -
Pair 3:4 --> abs( 1.438 -  3.063) >  1.132  ?    * (significant)
-------------------------------------------------------------

book>
```

FIGURE 6.39

Post hoc pairwise comparisons for the Friedman test.

Therefore, the mean is the correct statistic for central tendency. However, many HCI experiments use questionnaires with response items presented on a Likert-scale or some other combination of numbers and verbal tags. Since the response items are subject to human interpretation, the data may not be interval-scale in the strictest sense (cf. temperature). If the scales are non-linear, then the quality of the data is compromised. In the worst case, the data degrade to ordinal and the appropriate statistic for central tendency is the median (middle value) or mode (most common value). In some research papers, questionnaire responses are summarized using the mean, while in other papers the median is used. On this subject we enter a grey area, with researchers holding different opinions on which measure is the correct measure. Some claim outright that Likert-scale responses are ordinal and that it is simply wrong to report means (e.g., Robertson, 2012). The truth is likely somewhere in the middle (i.e., between interval and ordinal).

The non-parametric tests demonstrated above are limited to single-factor analyses. The Friedman test, for example, can analyze many conditions, but the conditions are all levels of a single factor. The test cannot be used for multi-factor analyses, such as a 2×3 design or a $4 \times 2 \times 2$ design. (Of course, the parametric ANOVA is applicable to multi-factor experiments.) Although there are extensions of non-parametric tests to multi-factor experiments (Kaptein et al., 2010; Wobbrock, Findlater, Gergle, and Higgins, 2011), the value of these tools to HCI research is limited. Non-parametric tests are most commonly used to analyze questionnaire data or ratings, as in the examples above. Questionnaires are rarely administered for each condition in a multi-factor experiment (e.g., $4 \times 2 \times 2 = 16$ times). Typically, a single questionnaire is used when testing is finished, with the goal of gathering participants' comments and preference ratings on the conditions tested (perhaps in a multi-factor experiment). In this case, the non-parametric tests demonstrated above are fine. One possible exception is the use of non-parametric tests for ratio-scale data, which I discuss in the next section.

6.4 **Parametric versus non-parametric tests**

When alternative tests are available to study data in an experiment, a rationale is needed to choose among the possibilities. For statistical tests, the guiding principle is that of power. Statistical power is about improving the odds of getting it right with the null hypothesis: rejecting the null hypothesis when it should be rejected and not rejecting it when there is no (or insufficient) basis to do so. However, there are other issues to consider. Siegel (1957) suggests that an appropriate test is one where the measurement requirements of the test are consistent with the measurements used in the research. Of the four scales of measurement—nominal, ordinal, interval, ratio (see section 4.1.4 in chapter 4)—the pairings are simple. If the research data are ordinal, then a statistical test that operates on ordinal data is a good choice. Similarly, if the experimental data are ratio, then a statistical test that operates on ratio data is a good choice. In HCI, there is a common (and perhaps growing) practice that cuts across this simple principle. In this final section on hypothesis testing in HCI research, we venture into territory that was declared off-limits in this chapter's introduction: controversy. The incursion will be brief, however.

Parametric tests, such as the analysis of variance, assume the data are sampled from a probability distribution, such as the normal distribution. Provided this assumption is met (and a few others are), parametric tests have more statistical power and are more accurate and more precise than non-parametric tests. However, if the assumptions are not met, then the researcher must decide on the appropriate course of action. There are three possibilities: (1) proceed with the parametric test, (2) transform or clean the data in some manner to correct the violations and then proceed with the parametric test, or (3) use a non-parametric test. All three options have advantages and disadvantages. Proceeding with a parametric test on data that potentially violate underlying assumptions is a common approach. This may occur because researchers don't understand or don't have access to statistical tools that test the assumptions. Also, some researchers feel parametric tests are reasonably robust to violations and, in any event, the underlying assumptions are rarely met when analyzing real data (Erceg-Hurn and Mirosevich, 2008). Researchers with a particular concern for violations in assumptions are likely to choose one of the latter two options. However, both come at a cost. Transforming data using a log or power function is an effective way to correct the violations in assumptions. But as Siegel asks, "Will the process of 'normalizing' the distribution by altering the numerical values of the scores cause a distortion in the experimental effect under investigation?" (Siegel, 1957, p. 14). He notes that this is a question the investigator may not be able to answer. Sheskin adds, "One might view a data transformation as little more than a convenient mechanism for 'cooking' data until it allows a researcher to achieve a specific goal," while allowing "When used judiciously, data transformation can be a valuable tool" (Sheskin, 2011, p. 483). So the issues in transforming data are a matter for deeper consideration. The third option, which seems to be increasingly common in HCI research, is to proceed with a non-parametric test. Conveniently, this approach sidesteps questions about the probability distribution of the underlying data. However, the decision to use a non-parametric test on data that are potentially parametric but violate assumptions is not to be entered into lightly. Let's consider this point further.

For ordinal data, such as rankings or qualitative assessments on a scale, non-parametric tests are the logical choice. For ratio data, such as measurements of human performance, parametric tests are preferred, in part due to their increased power (the ability to reject a false null hypothesis) but also by the simple standard that the test-to-data pairing is correct. But do ratio-scale human performance measurements meet the requirements for parametric data? Put another way, are measurements such as the time or errors in completing tasks normally distributed? The answer to this question is never yes in a precise way. The data are samples and therefore inherit a multitude of haphazard, even capricious, tendencies. If the samples are expected to bring forth precise properties of a probability distribution, such as normality, then disappointment looms. There are numerous tests for normality, skewness, etc., and small sets of empirically sampled data will frequently fail. If the data are measures on a dependent variable collected in an experiment, a researcher may conclude that the data are not parametric and then proceed with a non-parametric test. But this may be unnecessary or unwise. Recall from our earlier discussions that non-parametric tests collapse data into ranks. As Sheskin notes, "When a researcher elects to transform a set of interval/ratio data into ranks, information is sacrificed" (Sheskin, 2011, p. 531). So choosing a non-parametric test for ratio-scale measurements that deviate from normality is to replace one deficiency with another. Restraint is advised. The procedures and instrumentation put in place to collect ratio-scale human performance data in experimental research should not be muted so casually, as occurs if the data are downgraded to ordinal (ranks). Let's examine a few related points.

In the 1950s and early 1960s, applied statistics in the social sciences experienced a broad migration to non-parametric tests. However, abandoning parametric tests—mainly the parametric ANOVA—in favor of non-parametric tests was largely unnecessary, as noted by Glass et al. (1972). The shift occurred because researchers asked the wrong question. They asked "Are the assumptions of the parametric ANOVA met?" instead of "What are the consequences of the inevitable violations in the parametric ANOVA?" The first of these two questions is easy to answer, as there are numerous "assumption tests" for parametric data.[19] However, the second question presents formidable challenges. For one, standards of rigor necessarily degrade when a researcher moves from studying a mathematical model under defined assumptions to studying that same model under violations to the

---

[19] Tests commonly used include the Kolmogorov-Smirnov test, the χ^2 goodness-of-fit test, Levene's test, Bartlett's test, the Shapiro-Wilk test, and Mauchly's test for sphericity. It is worth noting that these tests are themselves subject to assumptions. Some statisticians claim the implementation of assumptions tests in commercial software (e.g., SPSS) is fatally flawed and recommend these tests never be used (Erceg-Hurn and Mirosevich, 2008, p. 594).

Source Citation	Test	Source Citation	Test
Ali et al., 2009	Kruskal-Wallis	Kuzuoka et al., 2004	Wilcoxon
Banovic et al., 2011	Friedman	Liu et al., 2010	Kruskal-Wallis
Caniard & Fleming, 2007	Friedman	Munteanu et al., 2006	Friedman
Elmqvist et al., 2008	Friedman	Perugini et al., 2007	Mann-Whitney U
Farzam et al., 2008	Kruskal-Wallis	Rantanen et al., 2012	Mann-Whitney U
Findlater et al., 2008	Friedman	Seager & Fraser, 2007	Friedman
Gajos et al., 2008	Wilcoxon	Solovey et al., 2012	Friedman
Garcia et al., 2009	Mann-Whitney U	Stanton et al., 2008	Wilcoxon
Hayashi et al., 2012	Mann-Whitney U	Sylla et al., 2009	Mann-Whitney U
Hinckley et al., 2005	Kruskal-Wallis	Wilson et al., 2011	Friedman
Huhtala et al., 2011	Kruskal-Wallis	Wobbrock et al., 2009	Friedman
Jacko et al., 2004	Mann-Whitney U	Xiao et al., 2009	Mann-Whitney U
Kane et al., 2008	Wilcoxon		

FIGURE 6.40

Sample of 25 HCI research papers using a non-parametric test on ratio data.

assumptions. Examining the consequences of violations in assumptions requires empirical data, which are deviate, or simulated data, which are deviate by design. It's a difficult and highly complex assignment. But all is not lost. Considerable research into these issues exists (although not in HCI). In the end, there is evidence that the parametric ANOVA is reasonably robust to violations in the underlying assumptions.[20] Even with small sample sizes (e.g., $n = 3$), the consequences of violations in the assumptions underpinning the ANOVA are usually minor. Let's have a look at the use of non-parametric tests on ratio-scale data in HCI research.

Non-parametric tests, such as the Mann-Whitney U, Wilcoxon Signed-Rank, Kruskal-Wallis, and Friedman tests, are well-travelled in the HCI literature. In most cases the tests are used with questionnaire data and the like. That's appropriate since the data are ordinal (or perhaps interval). Yet there are examples where a non-parametric test was used on ratio data that were obtained experimentally. This use of non-parametric tests merits additional scrutiny. To investigate this, a small meta-analysis was undertaken using a sample of 25 publications from the HCI literature.[21] (See Figure 6.40.) What we find in studying these examples may provide insight into this application of non-parametric tests in HCI research.

[20] Readers interested in examining this point further are directed to the survey of related studies by Glass et al. (1972, 246–255). Of course, there are contrary opinions (see Erceg-Hurn and Mirosevich, 2008 for a summary).

[21] The papers were selected as follows. A search was undertaken using Google Scholar. The search was limited to HCI papers published by the ACM since 2004. The names of the four parametric tests described in this chapter were the search terms. Of hundreds of papers returned and examined, the first 25 were selected where an experiment was described and where a nonparametric test was used on ratio-scale data.

Each example publication in Figure 6.40 presents the methodology and results of an HCI experiment or user study. In each case, the effect of an independent variable on a dependent variable was tested using a non-parametric procedure. The dependent variables were ratio-scale performance measurements, so a parametric test could have been used. The dependent variables included the following: task completion time (Ali, Scholer, Thom, and Wu, 2009; Gajos et al., 2008; Hayashi, Pendleton, Ozenc, and Hong, 2012; Huhtala, Karukka, Salminaa, and Häkkilä, 2011; Jacko et al., 2004; Kuzuoka, Yamazaki, et al., 2004; J. Liu et al., 2010; Perugini, Anderson, and Moroney, 2007; Stanton, Kahn Jr., Severson, Ruckert, and Gill, 2008; Wilson, Brewster, Halvey, Crossan, and Stewart, 2011; Xiao et al., 2009), accuracy or errors (Banovic et al., 2011; Elmqvist, Henry, Riche, and Fekete, 2008; Findlater et al., 2010; Hinckley, Baudisch, Ramos, and Guimbretière, 2005; Kane, Bigham, and Wobbrock, 2008; Seager and Fraser, 2007; Wilson et al., 2011), distance (Caniard and Fleming, 2007; Rantanen, Verho, Lekkala, Tuisku, and Surakka, 2012), signal strength (Solovey et al., 2012), and counts such as number of clicks (Farzam et al., 2008), number of search sources (J. Liu et al., 2010), number of disorientations (Seager and Fraser, 2007), number of collisions (Solovey et al., 2012), number of objects dropped (García, Molina, Gonzalez, Martínez, and Martínez, 2009), and number of elements drawn (Sylla, Branco, Coutinho, and Coquet, 2009). Why were non-parametric tests used? In some cases, no rationale was given (Banovic et al., 2011; Elmqvist et al., 2008; Findlater et al., 2010; Hayashi et al., 2012; Hinckley et al., 2005; Kane et al., 2008; Kuzuoka, Yamazaki, et al., 2004; Rantanen et al., 2012; Stanton et al., 2008; Wobbrock et al., 2009). In other cases, the researchers expressed concern over violations in the assumptions of the parametric ANOVA. The following is a sample of the explanations leading to the choice of a non-parametric test: "The time data is not normally distributed" (Ali et al., 2009, p. 303), "The distributions are skewed" (Caniard and Fleming, 2007, p. 103), "[The] Shapiro-Wilk W test for non-normality suggests that the sample is unlikely to be from a normal distribution" (Farzam et al., 2008, p. 565), "[The data] did not meet the requirements for normality (Kolmogorov-Smirnov test)" (García et al., 2009, p. 260), "The distribution of task completion times was significantly different from a normal distribution" (Perugini et al., 2007, p. 968), and "The data did not fit a normal distribution" (Wilson et al., 2011, p. 150). In none of the papers cited did the researchers articulate concern for the loss of information in using a non-parametric test on ratio data. In eschewing the parametric test, these researchers were evidently concerned with the first of the two questions noted earlier: are the assumptions of the parametric ANOVA met? Of the 25 examples, only two went the extra distance to consider the second question: what are the consequences of the violations? Munteanu et al. reported:

> *Although we tested the data for normalcy, a non-parametric (distribution-free) test, Friedman's Rank Test for correlated samples, was also run and chi-square scores were computed, in order to confirm the validity of the F-scores obtained through ANOVA*

(Munteanu, Baecker, Penn, Toms, and James, 2006, p. 497).

The results of both the parametric and non-parametric tests were given. As it turns out, the tests lead to the same conclusion. Perugini et al. reported:

Since the distribution of task completion times was significantly different from a normal distribution, we also used the Mann-Whitney U test for non-parametric statistical significance. However, since the patterns of significant differences (p < .05) of the eight tasks were the same for the ANOVA and the Mann-Whitney U, we present the results for the ANOVA"

(Perugini et al., 2007, p. 968)

In both of these examples we see a hint of caution—that there is an issue around the use of a non-parametric test versus a parametric test. So which test is the correct test? At this juncture, it would be remiss to recommend strict testing of ratio data using a parametric test (despite violations in assumptions) or a non-parametric test (despite loss of information). Arguably, the balance tips in favor of parametric tests due to the added precision and statistical power. However, the practice of Munteanu et al. (2006) and Perugini et al. (2007) is laudable: examine both avenues, consider the outcome for each, and attune for possible contradictions.

STUDENT EXERCISES

6-1. The following data are from a hypothetical experiment comparing texting speeds on a mobile phone while sitting versus walking. Eight participants were tested.[22]

Participant	Texting Speed (wpm)	
	Sitting	Walking
P1	13	10
P2	14	11
P3	12	9
P4	9	13
P5	15	14
P6	11	8
P7	18	9
P8	9	11

Instead of counterbalancing, learning effects were offset by administering a practice session before testing. Perform an ANOVA on the data to determine if there is a difference in texting speed while sitting or walking. Write a brief report on your findings.

---

[22] To minimize the data transcription requirements, the number of participants in the student exercises is generally less than what is expected for real experiments.

6-2. A research project investigated the effect of distraction on driving. A driving simulator was used with the mean driving error (in pixels) measured under three distraction conditions: no distraction, call answering, and text messaging. Twelve participants were tested. The participants were divided into three groups with the distracter conditions administered according to a Latin square to offset learning effects. The results are shown in the table below:

Participant	Mean Driving Error (pixels)			Group
	No Distraction	Call Answering	Text Messaging	
P1	10	10	17	G1
P2	14	11	13	G1
P3	11	9	14	G1
P4	9	13	11	G1
P5	13	14	10	G2
P6	11	8	18	G2
P7	14	9	14	G2
P8	9	11	16	G2
P9	7	14	15	G3
P10	9	11	17	G3
P11	10	9	11	G3
P12	12	14	15	G3

Perform an ANOVA on the data to determine if there is an effect of distraction type on driving error. Write a brief report on your findings. Include a chart to illustrate the result and a post hoc multiple comparisons test, if appropriate.

6-3. Are gamers more adept than non-gamers in manipulating objects in 3D graphics environments? This question was investigated in an experiment with 10 participants, including five non-gamers and five gamers. Participants performed five object-manipulation tasks with task completion times logged for follow-on analyses. The five tasks were of equal difficulty. The data are shown below:

Participant	Task Completion Time (s)					Background
	T1	T2	T3	T4	T5	
P1	23	21	16	17	15	Non-gamer
P2	24	21	20	17	14	Non-gamer
P3	24	20	21	15	13	Non-gamer
P4	26	21	20	17	16	Non-gamer
P5	17	18	20	15	14	Non-gamer
P6	19	16	15	14	15	Gamer
P7	20	16	15	13	14	Gamer
P8	16	16	14	13	11	Gamer
P9	15	15	12	14	12	Gamer
P10	17	16	13	14	12	Gamer

Perform an ANOVA on the data to determine if there is an effect of participant background on task completion time. Also investigate whether learning occurred over the five tasks and whether the progress in learning, if any, was the same for both groups of participants. Write a brief report on your findings. Include a chart to illustrate the results.

6-4. An experiment with 12 participants sought to determine if interaction with touchscreen phones is improved using the flick gesture and whether the improvement, if any, is related to one-handed versus two-handed interaction. A variety of map-locating tasks were devised. All tasks were of equal difficulty. For each task, participants were presented with a starting location and were required to navigate to a final location using finger gestures on the map image. To avoid visual search in the task, the map and locations were familiar to participants. The system was configured to have a drag-only mode (flick disabled) and a drag + flick mode. The twelve participants were divided into two groups, counterbalancing the one-handed versus two-handed conditions. The results for task completion time are shown below:

| Participant | Task Completion Time (s) | | | | Group |
| | One-handed | | Two-handed | | |
	Drag-only	Drag+flick	Drag-only	Drag+flick	
P1	12	11	7	6	G1
P2	11	7	6	8	G1
P3	9	8	8	7	G1
P4	9	9	7	6	G1
P5	13	5	6	5	G1
P6	6	6	5	9	G1
P7	7	7	8	8	G2
P8	9	8	9	5	G2
P9	8	8	9	7	G2
P10	7	8	9	5	G2
P11	11	10	8	11	G2
P12	12	8	8	11	G2

Perform an ANOVA on the data to determine if there is an effect of hand use (one-handed, two-handed) or interaction method (drag-only, drag + flick) on task completion time for the map-locating task. Write a brief report on your findings.

6-5. Using Google Scholar, download and examine some HCI research papers. Find examples of factorial experiments where the F statistics were poorly reported or poorly formatted. Indicate what is wrong and suggest an improved way to report the result.

6-6. The data in Figure 4.5 show observations on male and female university students in their mobile phone usage habits. Use a chi-square test to determine if the data reveal a statistically significant difference between males and females in their tendency to use or not use a mobile phone while walking about campus. Perform the calculations using a spreadsheet application and the method shown for the data in Figure 6.22. Verify the results using the `ChiSquare` Java utility available on this book's website.

6-7. Verify the chi-square statistic of $\chi^2 = 543.5$ reported for the data in Figure 6.28 comparing the Web of Trust (WOT) and McAfee's Site Advisor (MSA) tools for assessing the safety of websites. Perform the calculations using a spreadsheet application and the method shown for the data in Figure 6.22. Verify the spreadsheet calculations using the `ChiSquare` Java utility available on this book's website. Ayyavu and Jensen (2011) reported that the chi-square statistic was highly significant at the $p < .0001$ threshold, with the WOT tool assessing significantly more sites bad (not safe) compared to the MSA tool. Of the 18,650 sites, WOT rated 1722 bad while MSA rated only 628 bad. What number of sites would the MSA tool need to assess bad in order for the chi-square test to *not* show statistical significance? In answering this question, consider the chi-square critical value for $p < .05$.

6-8. A researcher is interested in investigating whether Mac or PC users differ in their habits for using "wallpaper" on their desktop. (Wallpaper is a personalized background graphic.) A number of users on a university campus were approached and asked to provide two items of information. First, they were asked whether their main system was a Mac or PC. Second, they were asked about their wallpaper habits and, in particular, whether they (a) did not use wallpaper, (b) used personalized wallpaper but changed it less than once per month (<12 times in the last year), or (c) used personalized wallpaper and changed it more than once per month. The responses to the latter were coded as "none," "wallpaper static," and "wallpaper dynamic," respectively. The results are shown in the table below. Each cell contains the number of users in each category:

System	Wallpaper Habit		
	None	Wallpaper Static	Wallpaper Dynamic
Mac	13	8	25
PC	25	21	18

Perform a chi-square test on the data above to determine if Mac or PC users differ in their wallpaper habits. Write a brief report on your findings.

6-9. Users and computers (Part II). Extend the report for Part I of this exercise (see Chapter 5) to examine if user preference for a Mac or a PC differs by gender according to a chi-square test. Perform a similar test *by age*. For the age test, divide the respondents into equally sized nominal-scale groups: younger and older. (Use the median age to divide the groups.) This student exercise continues in Chapter 7 (Part III).

6-10. A telecommunications company has developed a new texting interface for their latest mobile phone. They are wondering if the phone will be equally acceptable to female and male users and decide to investigate by conducting a small experiment. Nine female and nine male participants (all experienced texters) are recruited and given a demo of the texting interface. The participants are then given the phone and allowed to test the texting feature for a period of one week. Afterward, they are asked to rate the texting interface on a 25-point linear scale: 1 = really bad, 25 = really good. The results are shown below:

Females	Males
25	18
25	14
19	13
21	15
22	17
19	19
15	18
18	20

Is there a difference in the ratings of the texting interface between females and males? Write a brief report on your findings.

6-11. A software company has developed a tool for personal project planning. The tool includes a variety of features that the company wishes to test with potential users. Eight participants are recruited and given a demonstration of the personal project planner and then asked to test the tool and to use four specified features: Drag and Link, Integration, In-context Create, and Outline. Afterward, the participants are asked to rate the features on a 5-point scale according to estimated frequency of use (1 = will never use, 5 = will use daily). The results are shown below:

Participant	Drag & Link	Integration	In-context Use	Outline
1	3	5	3	2
2	5	4	2	1
3	5	4	1	3
4	4	4	1	4
5	3	3	2	3
6	4	4	2	5
7	3	5	1	4
8	3	4	3	2

Is there a difference in the estimated frequency of use for the features in the personal project planner? Write a brief report on your findings. Note: This student exercise was inspired by the evaluation of a personal project planner by Jones et al. (2008). Their study used 21 participants who evaluated seven features of a personal project planner.

6-12. A toy company has designed and prototyped two computerized electro-mechanical pet dogs: Waggy and Scratchy. Through the wonder of software, the dogs have different "personalities." The company is interested in evaluating the toy dogs with children to assess the level of engagement. Eight children are recruited. The children are introduced separately to Waggy and Scratchy and then allowed to play with each dog for thirty minutes. (Counterbalancing is used, but this is not important here.) "Verbal engagement" is considered important so the sessions are videotaped. Afterward, the tapes are analyzed to tally the number of words spoken by each child while playing with each dog. The data are shown below:

Participant	Waggy	Scratchy
1	189	75
2	189	130
3	222	135
4	178	143
5	205	98
6	278	125
7	231	156
8	177	213

Is there a difference between Waggy and Scratchy based on the level of verbal engagement with the children? Since the data are ratio-scale, consider the merits of using a parametric versus non-parametric testing procedure. Write a brief report on your findings. Note: This student exercise was inspired by a similar evaluation described by Stanton et al. (2008). Their study used 11 autistic children. Five measures of behavioral interaction were analyzed (including verbal engagement).

Modeling Interaction

7

A model is a simplification of reality. Consider an architect's scale model of a building or a physicist's equation for the trajectory of a tossed ball. Both are reductions or simplifications of more complex phenomena. They are useful because they allow us to explore the phenomena, think about them, make changes, and so on, without actually constructing the building or throwing the ball. A great many problems in HCI are explored in this manner. This chapter is about modeling interaction—building models, testing models, using models, and thinking about interaction through models.

The term *model* is often used loosely, without a clear and simple definition. A mathematician's model is probably quite distant from a psychologist's or sociologist's model. To the mathematician, a model is a formal calculus tested through computer simulation. To the psychologist or sociologist it is often a verbal-analytic description of behavior. Pew and Baron (1983) elaborate on this: "There is a continuum along which models vary that has loose verbal analogy and metaphor at one end and closed-form mathematical equations at the other" (p. 664). This seems like a useful way to organize our discussion. Models using "loose verbal analogy and metaphor" describe phenomena. Let's called them *descriptive models*. Models using "closed-form mathematical equations" predict phenomena. Let's call them *predictive models*. This chapter opened with an example of each. An architect's model of a building is a descriptive model. A physicist's equation for the trajectory of a tossed ball is a predictive model.

There are many examples of descriptive and predictive models in HCI. The rest of this chapter is organized in two parts. In the next section I present descriptive models. Examples are presented, along with discussion on how each can provide insight into a design or interaction problem. Following this, I present a few examples of predictive models, with a similar organization.

7.1 Descriptive models

Descriptive models are everywhere. They emerge from a process so natural it barely seems like modeling. Look in any HCI paper with a title or section heading using words like *design space*, *framework*, *taxonomy*, or *classification* and there is a good chance you'll find a descriptive model, perhaps without knowing it. In many cases, the word *model* isn't even used. The general idea is developed in the next section.

7.1.1 Delineating a problem space

A descriptive model can be as simple as a dividing up a problem space. Taken as a whole, without divisions, the problem space is ... well, that's what it is, a space—vast and uncharted, a big fuzzy cloud. However, with a little thought and organization it becomes a partitioned domain. As a partitioned domain, we are empowered to think differently about the problem space, to get inside it and see the constituent parts or processes. We can focus on certain parts of the problem space, consider how one part differs from, or relates to, another, and weigh strengths, weaknesses, advantages, or disadvantages of certain parts over others.

Here is a non-HCI example, just to get started. Consider *politics*, a subject we all know a little about. Figure 7.1a gives the "big fuzzy cloud" model of politics. Of course, there is no model; it's just the thing itself, without delineation. If we really want to study politics, it would be useful to break it down, delineate it, categorize it, structure it, or whatever—so we can get inside the problem, define and understand its constituent parts, and begin the process of charting out a corner of the problem space as a research area. In Figure 7.1b, we see Johnson's (2007, 19)

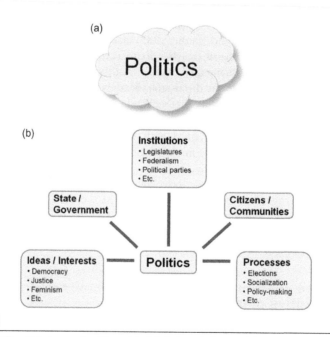

FIGURE 7.1

Politics: (a) The "big fuzzy cloud" model. (b) A descriptive model delineating the problem space.

delineation of the problem space for politics. This is a descriptive model for politics. Open any textbook on any subject and you are likely to find similar diagrams.

Johnson's chart in Figure 7.1b is beautifully crafted. It is organized as a semi-circular spoked wheel with politics at the center. Do you like the organization? Is there a different organization that might work better? Note the symmetry between "State/Government" (left) and "Citizens/Communities" (right). Nice. "Ideas/Interests" is mirrored with "Processes." Is that reasonable? What about "Federalism" under Institutions? That seems odd. Is federalism an institution? Perhaps Federalism, like Democracy, should be under Ideas/Interests. Enough said. The descriptive model in Figure 7.1b adds tremendous insight into politics. With it, we are empowered not only to think differently about the problem, but to think critically about it. With every tweak, refinement, and improvement we get a better model and, more importantly, we get a better understanding of the problem. That's the power of descriptive models.

In HCI, researchers often approach problems in a similar way. Let's have a look at a few descriptive models in HCI and examine how they are used to analyze a problem space and inform interaction design.

7.1.2 Quadrant model of groupware

An important area of research within HCI is computer supported collaborative work (CSCW). Computer applications to support collaboration are known as *groupware*. There are many facets to groupware, including teleconferencing, team writing, group voting, and so on. Is it possible to delineate the problem space of groupware into a descriptive model? Of course it is. And there are many ways to do this. The starting point, as always, is to just think about groupware, to consider aspects of it that differ in some way. These differences can assist in dividing the problem space into simpler components or processes.

One such possibility for groupware is to consider collaboration in terms of space and time. Spatially, users might collaborate in the same physical place or in different physical places. Temporally, users might collaborate at the same time or at different times. The spatial and temporal aspects of the collaboration are illustrated in a descriptive model known as the *quadrant model of groupware* (Johansen, 1991; Kaplan, 1997). (See Figure 7.2.) The model presents groupware as a 2×2 matrix with four cells, each representing a distinct quality of interaction. A group of colleagues co-authoring a report involves people working in different places and different times. This is labeled *group writing* and appears in the bottom-right cell. A team meeting where members use computer technology to present and discuss ideas involves people working in the same place and at the same time. This is labeled *PC projectors* and appears in the top-left cell.

The examples in Figure 7.2 are from a report published in 1991 (Johansen, 1991). There are numerous forms of collaboration common today that didn't exist in 1991. Think of camera phones, web cams, social networking, tweeting, and so on. All involve people collaborating or interacting with other people in some

	Same Time	Different Times
Same Place	Copy boards PC Projectors Facilitation Services Group Decision Room Polling Systems	Shared Files Shift Work Kiosks Team Rooms Group Displays
Different Places	Conference Calls Graphics and Audio Screen Sharing Video Teleconferencing Spontaneous Meetings	Group Writing Computer Conferencing Conversational Structuring Forms Management Group Voice Mail

FIGURE 7.2

Quadrant model of groupware.

(Adapted from Johansen, 1991, Figure 1)

manner. Can these interactions be positioned in the quadrant model of groupware? Probably. One use of a descriptive model is to identify common elements for inter-actions located in the same area of the problem space. Perhaps all such interactions should contain the same common elements, and if they don't, this might motivate a design change. The goal here is not to engage in this exercise for groupware, but only to suggest that descriptive models provide a context for this sort of analysis. The quadrant model of groupware seems to offer this possibility.

7.1.3 Key-action model (KAM)

Here is another descriptive model that might be useful in HCI. Computer keyboards today contain a vast array of buttons, or keys. Most desktop systems use a key-board with a row of function keys across the top and a numeric keypad on the right. Have you ever thought about the operation and organization of keys on a keyboard? Here's a descriptive model for this purpose. We'll call it the *key-action model* (KAM). With KAM, keyboard keys are categorized as either *symbol keys*, *executive keys*, or *modifier keys*. Symbol keys deliver graphic symbols to an application such as a text editor. These are typically letters, numbers, or punctuation symbols. Executive keys invoke actions in the application or at the system level. Examples include ENTER, F1, and ESC. Modifier keys do not generate symbols or invoke actions. Instead, they set up a condition that modifies the effect of a subsequently pressed key. Examples include SHIFT and ALT. That's about it for the KAM. It's a simple model. It has a name, it delineates a problem space, and it identifies three categories of keys; for each category it provides a name, a definition, and examples. I have not proposed a chart like in Figure 7.1b for politics. Perhaps you can do that. What do you think of KAM? Is it correct? Is it flawed? Do all keyboard keys fit the model? Can you think of additional categories or sub-categories to improve the model or to make it more accurate or more comprehensive? Do some keys have features of more than one category? Is the model useful?

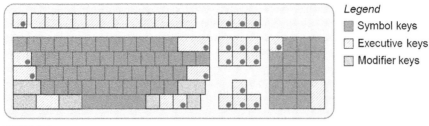

FIGURE 7.3

The key-action model (KAM) illustrated. Keys marked with (red) dots are executive keys that are not mirrored on both sides.

The questions above—by their very nature—are evidence of the power of descriptive models such as the KAM. The model piques our interest and suggests aspects of keyboard operation that merit consideration, particularly if a new design is contemplated. The most important question is the last. There is no greater measure of the merit of a model than its ability to tease out critical arguments on the potential, the capabilities, and the limitations in an interaction domain. Can the KAM do that? Let's see.

Figure 7.3 illustrates a keyboard with keys highlighted according to the KAM. It's a typical desktop keyboard with a wide space bar along the bottom, function keys along the top, a numeric keypad on the right, and non-alpha keys in various locations.

Let's think about the organization of keys in Figure 7.3 in terms of left- and right-hand usage. First, consider the executive keys (e.g., ENTER) and modifier keys (e.g., SHIFT).[1] On the keyboard's left we find seven such keys: SHIFT, ALT, CTRL, TAB, CAPS_LOCK, ESC, and WINDOWS. On the right we find no less than 22: SHIFT, ALT, CTRL, ENTER (x2), WINDOWS, RIGHT_CLICK, BACKSPACE, INSERT, DELETE, HOME, END, PAGE_UP, PAGE_DOWN, ←, ↑, →, ↓, PRNT_SCRN, SCROLL_LOCK, PAUSE, and NUM_LOCK. Because SHIFT, CTRL, ALT, and WINDOWS are mirrored, they do not pose a left- or right-hand bias and are eliminated from further discussion. Only three keys on the left (ESC, TAB, CAPS_LOCK) are without a right-side replica, thus, the numbers are three on the left, 18 on the right. These are identified by dots in Figure 7.3.

Before continuing, let's remember our goal. I am not here is to deliver a tutorial on keyboards, but to develop a descriptive model and demonstrate the ability of the model to delineate a problem space and potentially expose problems and suggest opportunities. The analysis in the preceding paragraph is a good example of this. Using the key-action model, we have identified a very peculiar bias in desktop keyboards. Let's continue.

With a 3:18 left-right ratio of executive keys, the desktop keyboard is clearly entrenched with a right-side bias. Simply put, the right hand is busy. Furthermore,

---

[1] For this discussion, we ignore the 12 function keys across the top.

with the emergence of the mouse in the 1980s, the right hand is even busier. Is it possible the right hand is, in fact, overloaded? Interactions that juxtapose executive-key activation and point-click operations are problematic for right-handed users. The right hand is just too busy. If the right hand is gripping the mouse and there is a need to press a right-side executive key, the options are to "reach over" with the left hand, or to release the mouse and acquire and activate the power key with the right hand. Not so good in either case. For users who manipulate the mouse with their left hand, the situation is quite different.[2] For "lefties," mouse operations efficiently mix with right-side power-key operations. In fact, a task analysis of common GUI tasks reveals an interesting phenomenon: the desktop interface is biased to favor left-hand mouse usage! But that's another story. Details are provided elsewhere (MacKenzie, 2003).

The key-action model only captures one aspect of keyboards, namely the actions associated with each key. Another way to think about keyboards is in the ambiguity of key presses. If pressing a symbol key always produces the same symbol, then the situation is simple. But if a key can produce two or more symbols, then this is worth thinking about. For this, a "key-ambiguity" descriptive model might be useful (MacKenzie and Soukoreff, 2002).

The key-action model delineates a design space for keyboards and allows for analyses to tease out design issues. Let's move on to another descriptive model.

7.1.4 Model of bimanual control

Humans are not only two-handed, they use each of their hands differently. This human behavior has undergone considerable study in a specialized area of human motor control known as *bimanual control* or *laterality* (Kelso, Southard, and Goodman, 1979; Peters, 1985; Porac and Coren, 1981; Wing, 1982). Studying the between-hand division of labor in everyday tasks reveals that most tasks are asymmetric: Our hands work together but have different roles and perform different tasks. Given this, and the knowledge that people are either right-handed or left-handed, examining the assignment of tasks to hands is a useful exercise. Guiard undertook such an exercise and proposed what he described as "a simple model, based on a non-quantitative physical approach, which aims at describing the logic of the division of labor that appears to govern the variety of human bimanual asymmetrical actions" (1987). This is the essence of a descriptive model. The result is Guiard's *model of bimanual control*—a simple three-part descriptive model identifying the roles and actions of the non-preferred and preferred hands. (See Figure 7.4.)

The points in Figure 7.4 are best explained through an exemplary illustration and narrative. In Figure 7.5, a right-handed graphic artist is sketching the design of

---

[2]Numerous straw votes by the author at presentations and lectures suggest that the vast majority of left-handed users manipulate the mouse with their right hand. The reason, it seems, is that most users learned to use a computer at an early age at school, where the mouse is positioned, and often anchored, on the right side of the keyboard.

Hand	Role and Action
Non-preferred	• Leads the preferred hand • Sets the spatial frame of reference for the preferred hand • Performs coarse movements
Preferred	• Follows the non-preferred hand • Works within established frame of reference set by the non-preferred hand • Performs fine movements

FIGURE 7.4

Guiard's model of bimanual control.

(From Guiard, 1987)

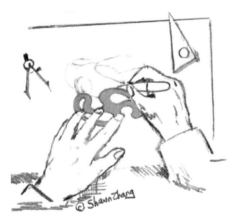

FIGURE 7.5

Two-handed interaction paradigm.

(Sketch courtesy of Shawn Zhang)

a new car. The artist acquires the template with the left hand (*non-preferred hand leads*). The template is manipulated over the workspace (*coarse movement, sets the frame of reference*). The stylus is acquired in the right hand (*preferred hand follows*) and brought into the vicinity of the template (*works within frame of reference set by the non-preferred hand*). Sketching takes place (*preferred hand makes precise movements*).

The roles and actions just described provide a provocative and fresh way of describing how humans approach common tasks. This is true both for every-day tasks and in the specialized context of human-computer interaction.

Guiard's research was published in a journal article in experimental psychology, not HCI. As originally published, no context for HCI was provided. Watershed

Task	Characteristics
Scrolling	• Precedes/overlaps other tasks • Sets the frame of reference • Minimal precision needed (coarse)
Selecting, editing, reading, drawing, etc.	• Follows/overlaps scrolling • Works within frame of reference set by scrolling • Demands precision (fine)

FIGURE 7.6

Relationship between scrolling and common GUI tasks.

moments in multi-disciplinary fields like HCI often occur when researchers, through due diligence, locate and adopt relevant research in other fields—research that can inform and guide their own discipline.[3] Guiard's work was located and studied by Paul Kabbash, a graduate student at the University of Toronto in the early 1990s. The paper by Kabbash, Buxton, and Sellen (1994) was the first in HCI to cite Guiard's 1987 work and adapt it to analyze and inform the problem space of two-handed computer input. Since then, Guiard's model has been widely adopted for HCI research in two-handed interaction (e.g., Cutler, Fröhlich, and Hanrahan, 1997; G. W. Fitzmaurice, Ishii, and Buxton, 1995; G. Kurtenbach, Fitzmaurice, Baudel, and Buxton, 1997; Malik and Laszlo, 2004; Morris, Huang, Paepcke, and Winograd, 2006; Yee, 2004). An example follows.

Scrolling is traditionally accomplished by dragging the *elevator* of the scrollbar positioned along the right-hand side of an application's window. Acquiring the elevator is a target acquisition task taking up to two seconds per trial. However, this action is in conflict with a basic goal of good user interfaces: unobtrusiveness and transparency. That is, users should not be required to divert their attention from the primary task (reading, editing, drawing, etc.) to acquire and manipulate user interface widgets.

Desktop affordances for scrolling changed dramatically in 1996 with the introduction of Microsoft's IntelliMouse, which included a scrolling wheel between the mouse buttons. Numerous copycat variations appeared afterward from other manufacturers. The so-called "wheel mouse" puts scrolling in the preferred hand. This is arguably bad for right-handed users because it increases the right-side bias noted in the preceding section. This insight—revealed in Guiard's descriptive model of bimanual control—presents an opportunity for design. An analysis of scrolling and the accompanying tasks reveals that scrolling is well suited to the non-preferred hand. Evidence of this is presented in Figure 7.6, which juxtaposes the properties of scrolling with tasks typically performed in concert with scrolling. (The reader is invited to compare the organization of bullets in Figure 7.6 with that in Figure 7.4, which presents the guiding principles in Guiard's model of bimanual control.)

---

[3] There are examples in HCI, for example, Card, English, and Burr's (Card et al., 1978) first use of Fitts' law (Fitts, 1954), or Norman's (1988) introduction of Gibson's affordances (1979).

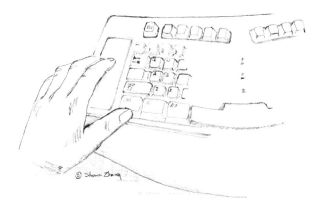

FIGURE 7.7

Scrolling interface example.

(Sketch courtesy of Shawn Zhang)

Figure 7.7 presents a scrolling concept for a right-handed user. On the keyboard's left a touch strip is shown, but a wheel is just as appropriate. There are many implementation issues, such as scrolling sensitivity and support for up/down paging, but these are not explored here. The point is simply that scrolling is an appropriate task for the non-dominant hand and that this is revealed through Guiard's model of bimanual control. See also Buxton and Myers (1986).

On a personal note, the idea of non-dominant hand scrolling was sufficiently appealing that I decided to re-engineer a Microsoft Intellimouse, separating the wheel assembly from the mouse. The new form factor allowed operation of the Intellimouse with the dominant hand while scrolling with the non-dominant hand. Figure 7.8a shows the setup for right-handed use. This setup was used for numerous demos and presentations. Two such presentations were given in February 1998 during a visit to Microsoft in Redmond, Washington. The first audience was the "mouse group" of Microsoft's Hardware Ergonomics Group. The idea seemed provocative enough. An impromptu meeting was arranged for the afternoon of the same day and the presentation was given again to the "keyboard group." The idea of non-dominant hand scrolling, as suggested by Guiard's model of bimanual control, was convincing. About two years later, Microsoft released the Office Keyboard, shown in Figure 7.8b. On the left side, the device includes some power keys and a scrolling wheel (see arrow)—perfect for right-handed users. Variations of keyboards with left-side scrolling were subsequently released by Microsoft and other keyboard manufacturers, including Logitech. In the end, however, the momentum and popularity of the wheel mouse were just too much. The benefit of non-dominant hand scrolling was insufficient to sway a satisfied user community toward a new interface paradigm. Today, most computer mice continue to include a wheel for scrolling.

FIGURE 7.8

(a) The author's re-engineered Microsoft Intellimouse with the wheel on left side of the keyboard. (b) Microsoft Office Keyboard with scrolling wheel on the left side.

7.1.5 Three-state model for graphical input

Another descriptive model is Buxton's *three-state model of graphical input* (Buxton, 1990). The model is a simple characterization of the operation of computer pointing devices in terms of state transitions. It is described as "a vocabulary to recognize and explore the relationship between pointing devices and the interaction techniques they afford" (Buxton, 1990, p. 449). In this sense, it is a paradigm of descriptive modeling. The three states are identified in Figure 7.9, annotated for mouse interaction.

From left to right in Figure 7.9, the states are Out of Range (State 0) for clutching or repositioning a mouse on a mouse pad, Tracking (State 1) for moving a tracking symbol (e.g., a cursor) on a display, and Dragging (State 2) for moving an icon on the display or for grouping a set of objects or a range of text. The model seems simple and obvious, and we might question its ability to add insight to the existing body of pointing device research. Yet the model can be extended to capture additional aspects of pointing device interaction such as multi-button interaction, stylus or finger input, and direct versus indirect input. See Buxton (1990) for further details.

As further evidence of the utility of Buxton's work, MacKenzie and Oniszczak (1998) used the three-state model to help characterize an interaction technique that didn't exist at the time Buxton's model was introduced. The insight led to a redesign

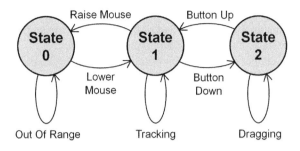

FIGURE 7.9

Buxton's three-state model for graphical input.

(Adapted from Buxton, 1990)

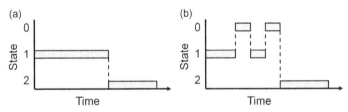

FIGURE 7.10

State transitions for dragging tasks: (a) Mouse. (b) Lift-and-tap touchpad. Dragging begins upon entering State 2.

(Adapted from MacKenzie and Oniszczak, 1998)

of an interaction technique that later appeared in the Blackberry Storm (Arthur, 2008a) and Apple MacBook (Arthur, 2008b). This work is briefly recounted here.

Never shy of innovation, Apple took a bold step in 1994 by commercializing a new pointing device in its PowerBook 500 notebook computer: the Trackpad touchpad (MacNeill and Blickenstorfer, 1996). Today, touchpads are the dominant pointing device for notebook computers, notepads, and other small mobile devices. One of the interaction techniques supported by touchpads is "lift-and-tap," where primitive operations like clicking, double-clicking, and dragging are implemented without a button. These new interaction primitives are easily represented by Buxton's three-state model. Figure 7.10 provides a simple comparison of the state transitions for dragging tasks (a) using a mouse and (b) using lift-and-tap on a touchpad.

Diagrams like this are evidence of the power of descriptive models such as Buxton's three-state model. Two observations follow: (1) lift-and-tap necessitates extra state transitions in comparison to a mouse, and (2) the use of state 1-0-1 transitions for lift-and-tap is confounded with clutching (not shown) which uses the same state transitions.[4] Among users' frustrations in using touchpads is that these

---

[4] *Clutching* refers to lifting the mouse to reposition it within its operating space.

primitives are difficult, awkward, or error prone. For example, if a touch following a lift is spatially displaced from the point of lifting, the system sometimes enters the Tracking state (State 1) instead of the Dragging state (State 2).

Armed with a deeper understanding of touchpad interaction, the state transitions on touchpads were redesigned. The additional pressure sensing capability of touchpads was used to implement state 1–2 transitions by "pressing harder."[5] A relay was added to provide both tactile and auditory feedback to inform the user of state transitions, much like the feedback in pressing a mouse button. Thus clicking, double clicking, and dragging were implemented on the touchpad, without a button, yet using the same state transitions as on a mouse. The complete details are presented in the 1998 proceedings of the ACM's SIGCHI (MacKenzie and Oniszczak, 1998).

Despite being introduced in 1990, Buxton's work continues to serve as a descriptive model for interactive systems. Contemporary applications include models for preview and undo (Appert, Chapuis, and Pietriga, 2012; Forlines, Shen, and Buxton, 2005), puck and stylus interactions for two-handed input (Hinckley, Czerwinski, and Sinclair, 1998), docking tasks for tabletop displays (Forlines, Wigdor, Shein, and Balakrishnan, 2007), camera control for spatial and temporal navigation of animated scenes (Burtnyk, Khan, Fitzmaurice, Balakrishnan, and Kurtenbach, 2002), modeling multi-touch on touchscreens (Wigdor et al., 2009), modeling panning and zooming on touchscreens (Malacria, Lecolinet, and Guiard, 2010), modeling the selection of moving targets (Al Hajri, Fels, Miller, and Ilich, 2011), and describing the rotation mode of a three DOF mouse (Almeida and Cubaud, 2007). In the latter case, an extra state was added ("State 3") to represent rotation.

Let's move across the continuum of the modeling space to models that work with closed-form mathematical equations—predictive models.

7.2 Predictive models

A predictive model is an equation. The equation predicts the outcome of a variable based on the value of one or more other variables (predictors). The outcome variable is a dependent variable, typically the time or speed in doing a task. It could also be accuracy, represented as spatial variability, error rate, or any other measure of human behavior. The only requirement is that the variable use continuous, or ratio-scale, data.

Most statistics sources call the predictor variable the *independent variable*. While correct, the terminology is problematic here. In experimental research, independent variable has a special meaning: it is a circumstance or characteristic that is manipulated. The vast majority of independent variables are nominal-scale attributes (e.g., device, feedback modality, display type, gender). This poses a problem, since a nominal-scale variable cannot serve as a predictor in a prediction equation

---

[5]The pressure sensing capability of a touchpad exists within the firmware as a separate mode of operation. In this mode, the device provides absolute x, absolute y, and z-axis data. The z-axis data corresponds to finger pressure on the touchpad surface.

(e.g., $3 \times device = ?$). Of course, independent variables in experimental research can also be ratio-scale attributes. Such variables can serve as predictors in prediction equations. Examples include distance to target, size of target, number of targets, angle of movement, system lag, joystick force, angle of tilt, decibel (dB) level of background noise, word size, number of choices, and so on. A predictor variable can also be a ratio-scale attribute of users such as age, years of computer experience, number of e-mails received per day, hours per day playing video games, geographic distance from a friend, and so on.[6]

Predictive models are useful in HCI. Like descriptive models, they allow a problem space to be explored. However, with a predictive model we are dealing with numbers, not concepts. In 1978 Card, English, and Burr (1978) presented what is likely the first predictive model in HCI. They conducted an experiment comparing the effect of four input devices (mouse, joystick, text keys, step keys) on users' speed and accuracy in selecting text on a CRT display. In many respects their work is straightforward; the methodology is as expected for an experiment with human participants. However, Card et al. went beyond a typical user study. Here are the first two sentences in the Discussion:

> While these empirical results are of direct use in selecting a pointing device, it would obviously be of greater benefit if a theoretical account of the results could be made. For one thing, the need for some experiments might be obviated; for another, ways of improving pointing performance might be suggested. (p. 608)

This is an inspired preamble to their discussion on building models—models of interaction that (a) embed a theoretical account of the underlying human processes and (b) serve as prediction tools for follow-up analyses of design alternatives. The remainder of their paper is about modeling using Fitts' law. They built and compared Fitts' law models for the mouse and joystick. Many dozens of HCI papers on Fitts' law have followed in the same vein. We will visit Fitts' law shortly, but first let's examine how a prediction equation is built.

7.2.1 Linear regression model

The basic prediction equation expresses a linear relationship between an independent variable (x, a predictor variable) and a dependent variable (y, a criterion variable or human response)

$$y = mx + b \tag{1}$$

where m is the slope of the relationship and b is the y intercept. (See Figure 7.11.)

---

[6]"Geographic distance from a friend" is an excellent example of the diverse and multi-disciplinary nature of HCI research. This ratio-scale circumstance was used both as an independent variable and as a predictor in a prediction equation for research on maintaining online friendships when people move apart (Shklovski, Kraut, and Cummings, 2006).

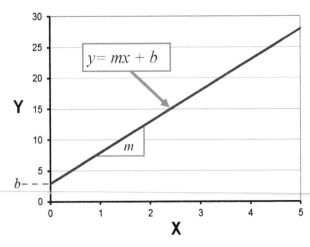

FIGURE 7.11

Linear relationship between an independent variable (*x*) and a dependent variable (*y*).

To build this equation, we first need a set of *x-y* sample points. Although any two ratio-scale variables will do, most commonly the *x-y* points combine the setting on an independent ratio-scale variable (*x*) with the measured value of a human response on a dependent variable (*y*). Since we are dealing with humans, variability is unavoidable, so the sample points are unlikely to lie on the line. They will scatter about. If the model is good, the points will be reasonably close to a straight line. How close is a key question.

Finding the best-fitting straight line involves a process known in statistics as *linear regression*. The objective is to find coefficients *m* and *b* in Equation 1 for the line than minimizes the squared distances (*least squares*) of the points from the line.[7] The result is the prediction equation—an equation that gives the best estimate of *y* in terms of *x*. Of course, the model is based on the sample points used in building the equation. If the data are good and the model is correct, a good prediction equation should emerge. There is also a built-in assumption that the relationship is linear, which is not necessarily the case. Let's visit an example in HCI.

As part of an experiment investigating text entry using a stylus on soft keyboards, MacKenzie and Zhang (2001) also wondered whether entry speed by stylus-tapping could be predicted from user's speed in touch-typing with a standard keyboard. The experiment involved 12 participants. The participants were given a pre-test to measure their touch-typing speeds. During the experiment, participants entered text using a stylus and a Qwerty soft keyboard displayed on an LCD tablet and digitizer. The pre-test touch-typing speed (independent variable) and

---

[7]Enter "linear regression" or "least squares" into Google or Wikipedia, and you will find all the details.

(a)

Participant	Stylus Tapping Speed (wpm)	Touch Typing Speed (wpm)
P1	18.2	42
P2	23.6	44
P3	26.0	32
P4	20.3	50
P5	20.3	36
P6	17.1	33
P7	24.0	74
P8	14.7	22
P9	20.3	31
P10	19.7	33
P11	22.4	25
P12	13.1	19

(b)

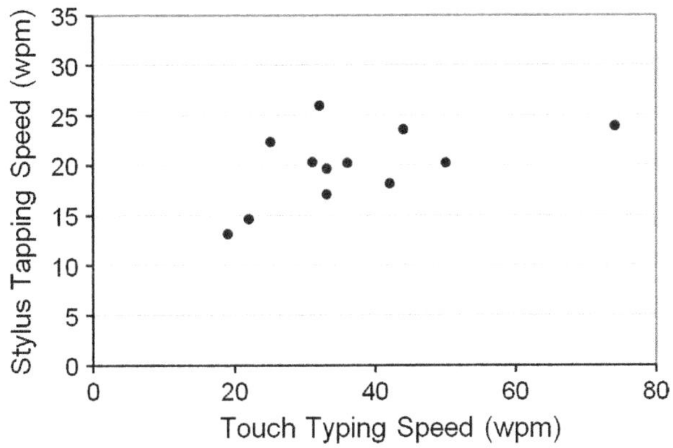

FIGURE 7.12

Relationship between stylus-tapping speed and touch-typing speed: (a) Data. (b) Scatter plot.

(Adapted from MacKenzie and Zhang, 2001, Fig. 4)

experimentally measured stylus-tapping speed (dependent variable) are given in Figure 7.12a for each participant.

Often as a precursor to building a prediction equation, a simpler question is posed: is there a relationship between the two variables? For this example, the question is this: do fast touch typists tend to be fast at stylus tapping?[8] Visualizing the data as a scatter plot helps (see Figure 7.12b). Yes, there seems to be a relationship. For example the slowest touch typist, P12 at 19 wpm, was also rather slow at stylus tapping (13.1 wpm). For the 12 points in the figure, the coefficient of correlation is $r = .5228$.[9] That's a modest positive correlation.

---

[8] The motivation is that proficient typists have a good visual image of letter positions on a Qwerty keyboard and, therefore, may require less visual scan time when using a stylus on a soft keyboard. Perhaps this phenomenon only applies to hunt-and-peck typists—typists who visually attend to the keyboard when typing. True touch typists tend to use muscle memory and do not visually attend to their keyboard. Perhaps they will exhibit a reverse phenomenon. More research is needed!

[9] The coefficient of correlation is computed in Microsoft Excel using the CORREL function.

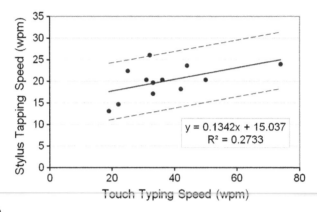

FIGURE 7.13

Scatter plot from Figure 7.12b embellished with linear regression line, prediction equation, squared coefficient of correlation (R^2) and dashed lines showing the 95% confidence interval.

The next step is to build the prediction equation—the best-fitting straight-line equation predicting stylus-tapping speed (y) from touch-typing speed (x). This is easily done using a spreadsheet application such as Microsoft Excel.[10] For the data in Figure 7.12a, the prediction equation is:

$$y = 0.1342\,x + 15.037 \tag{2}$$

Figure 7.13 is an embellished version of the chart in Figure 7.12b. As well as the scatter of points, it shows the line for the prediction equation along with the equation and the squared coefficient of correlation, $R^2 = .2733$. (By convention, R^2 is set in uppercase, r in lowercase.) R^2 is interpreted as the amount of variation in the data that is explained by the model. It is commonly articulated as a percent. So the model in Equation 2 explains about 27 percent of the variation of the data in Figure 7.12a. That's not very high, so in this case, the model is, at best, a modest predictor of stylus-tapping speed from touch-typing speed.[11]

One of the benefits of a predictive model is the potential to predict the outcome on a value of the predictor never actually visited. Note in Figure 7.12a that no participant had a touch-typing speed in the range of 60 wpm. Even so, we might

---

[10] First, the points are plotted as a "(XY) scatter" chart. With the points selected, the "Add Trendline" option from the Chart menu is used to add a linear regression line (trendline) to the chart. Options are available to include the equation and the squared correlation (R^2). If the goal is just to compute the slope (m) and intercept (b), then the SLOPE and INTERCEPT functions may be used.

[11] Low values of R^2 are common in the literature. Yin and Zhai (2006) report a linear regression model with $R^2 = .013$. As they noted, "the model accounted for very little of the variance in the actual selection (1.3%)."

conjecture that a user with a touch-typing speed of 60 wpm would have a stylus-tapping speed of:

$$y = 0.1342(60) + 15.037 = 23.1 \, wpm \qquad (3)$$

Given the scatter of points in Figure 7.12a, there is clearly some uncertainty surrounding this prediction. The standard error of estimate (*SE*) is a useful statistic for gauging this uncertainty. *SE* establishes confidence intervals around a prediction. For the data in Figure 7.12a, $SE = 3.39$ wpm.[12] Values within -1.96 *SE* and $+1.96$ *SE* of a prediction are within a 95% confidence interval. So for the model developed here, there is 95% confidence that a user whose touch-typing speed is 60 wpm will have a stylus-tapping speed between $23.1 - (1.96 \times 3.39) = 16.4$ wpm and $23.1 + (1.96 \times 3.39) = 29.7$ wpm. Dashed lines showing the 95% confidence window are included in Figure 7.13.

Usually linear regression models are reported giving the equation and R^2. Confidence intervals and *SE* are generally not given, although there are exceptions (Chung and Hossain, 2008; Johnsen, Raij, Stevens, Lind, and Lok, 2007; MacKenzie and Buxton, 1994). Sometimes the standard error is given separately for the slope and intercept coefficients in a linear regression model (Accot and Zhai, 2001; Cao et al., 2008; Pastel, 2006). Let's move on to a popular prediction model in HCI, Fitts' law.

7.2.2 Fitts' law

One of the most widely used models in HCI is Fitts' law. If an interaction involves a rapid-aimed movement, such as moving a finger or cursor to a target and selecting the target, there's a good chance someone has experimented with the interaction and used Fitts' law to model it. Fitts' law has three uses in HCI: (1) to learn if a device or interaction technique conforms to the model by building the prediction equation and examining the correlation for "goodness of fit," (2) to use the prediction equation in analyzing design alternatives, or (3) to use Fitts' *index of performance* (now *throughput*) as a dependent variable in a comparative evaluation. We'll examine each of these in the discussions that follow.

Since Fitts' law comes to HCI by way of basic research in experimental psychology, I'll begin with some background. Detailed reviews are provided elsewhere (MacKenzie, 1992; Meyer, Smith, Kornblum, Abrams, and Wright, 1990; Soukoreff and MacKenzie, 2004; Welford, 1968).

7.2.2.1 Background

Fitts was an experimental psychologist interested in applying information theory to human behavior. This was a common theme of research in the 1950s as it merged the idea of human performance with the contemporary and emerging mathematical concept of "information" in electronic communications. Fitts argued that the amplitude of an aimed movement was analogous to the information in an electronic

---

[12] The standard error of estimate (*SE*) is calculated in Microsoft Excel using the STEYX function. The formula assumes the data are from a sample, rather than the population.

signal and that the spatial accuracy of the move was analogous to electronic *noise*. Furthermore, he proposed that the human motor system is like a communications channel, where movements are like the transmission of signals. Fitts' analogy is based on Shannon's Theorem 17, expressing the information capacity C (in bits/s) of a communications channel of bandwidth B (in s^{-1} or Hz) as

$$C = B \log_2\left(\frac{S}{N} + 1\right) \tag{4}$$

where S is the signal power and N is the noise power (Shannon and Weaver, 1949, pp. 100–103).

Fitts presented his analogy—now his "law"—in two highly celebrated papers, one in 1954 (Fitts, 1954) and the second in 1964 (Fitts and Peterson, 1964). The 1954 paper described a serial, or reciprocal, target acquisition task where participants alternately tap on targets of width W separated by amplitude A (see Figure 7.14a). The 1964 paper described a similar experiment using a discrete task, where

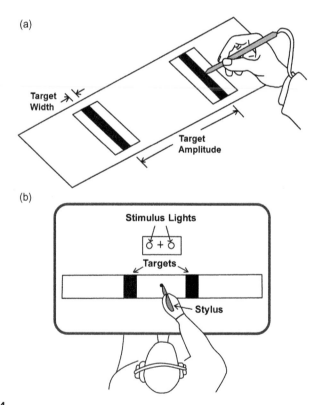

FIGURE 7.14

Experimental paradigm for Fitts' law: (a) Serial task. (b) Discrete task.

(Source: a, adapted from Fitts, 1954; b, adapted from Fitts and Peterson, 1964)

subjects selected one of two targets in response to a stimulus light (see Figure 7.14b). It is easy to imagine how to update Fitts' apparatus with computer input devices and targets rendered on a computer display.

The relationship Fitts examined is that between the amplitude of the movement task, the time taken, and the width, or tolerance, of the region within which the move terminates. In what may be the most understated conclusion in all of experimental psychology, Fitts summarized his findings as follows: "The results are sufficiently uniform to indicate that the hypothesized relation between speed, amplitude, and tolerance may be a general one." (Fitts, 1954, p. 389) Indeed, the robustness of Fitts' law is extraordinary. In the decades since Fitts' seminal work, the relationship has been verified countless times and in remarkably diverse settings, whether under a microscope or under water.

Fitts proposed to quantify a movement task's difficulty—*ID*, the *index of difficulty*—using information theory by the metric "bits." Specifically:

$$ID = \log_2\left(\frac{2A}{W}\right) \tag{5}$$

The amplitude (*A*) and width (*W*) in Equation 5 are analogous to Shannon's signal (*S*) and noise (*N*) in Equation 4. Note the offsetting influences of *A* and *W* in the equation. Doubling the distance to a target has the same effect as halving its size. An important thesis in Fitts' work was that the relationship between task difficulty and the movement time (*MT*) is linear. The following expression for *ID* was introduced later to improve the information-theoretic analogy (MacKenzie, 1992):

$$ID = \log_2\left(\frac{A}{W} + 1\right) \tag{6}$$

Because *A* and *W* are both measures of distance, the term in parentheses in Equation 6 is unitless. The unit "bits" emerges from the somewhat arbitrary choice of base 2 for the logarithm.

Fitts also proposed to quantify the human rate of information processing in aimed movements using *bits per second* as the units. This is a provocative idea, based purely on analogy, without a basis in human psychomotor behavior. Fitts' *index of performance*, now called *throughput* (*TP*, in bits/s), is calculated by dividing *ID* (bits) by the mean movement time, *MT* (seconds), computed over a block of trials:

$$TP = \frac{ID_e}{MT} \tag{7}$$

The subscript *e* in ID_e reflects a small but important adjustment, which Fitts endorsed in his 1964 paper. An adjustment for accuracy involves first computing the *effective target width* as

$$W_e = 4.133 \times SD_x \tag{8}$$

where SD_x is the standard deviation in a participant's selection coordinates.[13] Computed in this manner, W_e includes the spatial variability, or accuracy, in responses. In essence, it captures what a participant actually did, rather than what he or she was asked to do. This adjustment necessitates a similar adjustment to ID, yielding an "effective index of difficulty":

$$ID_e = \log_2\left(\frac{A}{W_e} + 1\right) \tag{9}$$

Calculated using the adjustment for accuracy, TP is a human performance measure that embeds both the speed and accuracy of responses. TP is most useful as a dependent variable in factorial experiments using pointing devices or pointing techniques as independent variables.

If using Fitts' law as a predictive model is the goal, then the movement time (MT) to complete a task is predicted using a simple linear equation:[14]

$$MT = a + b \times ID \tag{10}$$

The slope and intercept coefficients in the prediction equation are determined through empirical tests, typically using linear regression. The tests are undertaken in a controlled experiment using a group of participants and one or more input devices and task conditions.

7.2.2.2 Example

In this section I demonstrate how to build a Fitts' law predictive model, using a subset of the data from an experiment comparing pointing devices (MacKenzie and Jusoh, 2001). One device was an Interlink Electronics *RemotePoint*. The RemotePoint is a cordless pointing device operated in the air. Cursor position is controlled by a thumb-activated isometric joystick. Selection uses a trigger-like switch operated with the index finger. See Figure 7.15a. A Microsoft *Mouse 2.0* served as a baseline condition. Twelve participants performed a series of reciprocal point-select tasks across nine target conditions: $A = 40, 80, 160$ pixels crossed with $W = 10, 20, 40$ pixels. Using Equation 6, the target conditions span a range of difficulties from $ID = \log_2(40 / 40 + 1) = 1.00$ bits to $ID = \log_2(160 / 10 + 1) = 4.09$ bits. See Figure 7.15b.

The data for the mouse and RemotePoint conditions are given in Figure 7.16. There are nine rows, one for each A-W target condition. The three columns on the left are the target conditions (A, W, and the calculated index of task difficulty, ID). The remaining columns are based on the participants' responses. W_e is the *effective target width* (Equation 8). ID_e is the effective index of difficulty

---

[13] The effective target width (W_e) adjusts W to reflect a 4% error rate. For the full details and rationale, see Fitts (1964), Welford (1968, 145–149), MacKenzie (1992), or Soukoreff and MacKenzie (2004). For an argument against the adjustment for accuracy, see Zhai, Kong, and Ren (2004).

[14] It is important to distinguish between *building* a Fitts' law model and *using* a Fitts' law model. In building the model, ID_e should be used (so the model reflects both the speed and accuracy of participants' responses). In using the model, ID is used. The predictions will carry a 4% error probability.

(a)

(b)

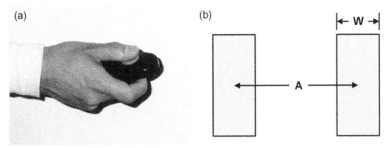

FIGURE 7.15

(a) Interlink Electronics RemotePoint. (b) Experiment task.

A (pixels)	W (pixels)	ID (bits)	Mouse				RemotePoint			
			W_e (pixels)	ID_e (bits)	MT (ms)	TP (bits/s)	W_e (pixels)	ID_e (bits)	MT (ms)	TP (bits/s)
40	10	2.32	11.23	2.19	665	3.29	13.59	1.98	1587	1.25
40	20	1.58	19.46	1.61	501	3.21	21.66	1.51	1293	1.17
40	40	1.00	40.20	1.00	361	2.76	37.92	1.04	1001	1.04
80	10	3.17	10.28	3.13	762	4.11	10.08	3.16	1874	1.69
80	20	2.32	18.72	2.40	604	3.97	25.21	2.06	1442	1.43
80	40	1.58	35.67	1.70	481	3.53	37.75	1.64	1175	1.40
160	10	4.09	10.71	3.99	979	4.08	10.33	4.04	2353	1.72
160	20	3.17	21.04	3.11	823	3.77	19.09	3.23	1788	1.81
160	40	2.32	41.96	2.27	615	3.69	35.97	2.45	1480	1.65
		Mean	23.25	2.38	644	3.60	23.51	2.35	1555	1.46

FIGURE 7.16

Experiment conditions (A, W, ID) and participants' responses (W_e, ID_e, MT, TP) for the standard mouse and the RemotePoint.

(Equation 9). MT is the mean movement time in milliseconds. TP is the throughput in bits/s (Equation 7).

A Fitts' law model can be built for both device conditions in Figure 7.16. The prediction equations use MT as the dependent variable and either ID or ID_e as the predictor variable. The main argument for using ID_e is that the model includes both the speed and accuracy of responses and therefore more fully encompasses participant behavior. The easiest way to build and demonstrate the models is to use a spreadsheet application. Figure 7.17 provides a visualization of the data as a scatter plot for each device. The chart also includes the regression lines, the prediction equations, and R^2. Both R^2 values are very high. The mouse model, for example, explains 97 percent of the variance in the observations.

The format of the prediction equations in Figure 7.17 can be improved. For the RemotePoint, the predicted time to move a cursor over a distance A to select a target of width W is:

$$MT = 597 + 408 \times \log_2 \left(\frac{A}{W} + 1 \right) \text{ms} \tag{11}$$

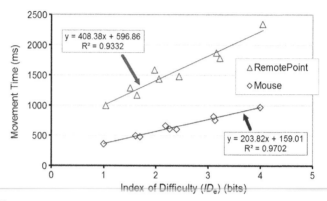

FIGURE 7.17

Scatter plot and regression lines for data in Figure 7.16b.

(Adapted from MacKenzie and Jusoh, 2001)

For the mouse, the prediction equation is:

$$MT = 159 + 204 \times \log_2\left(\frac{A}{W} + 1\right) \text{ ms} \tag{12}$$

What insight is found in the Fitts' law models in Figure 7.17? An initial observation is that point-select operations with both devices conform to Fitts' law (as is evident by the high values of R^2). This is the first use of Fitts' law, noted earlier. Also, it is apparent that the RemotePoint performed poorly compared to the mouse. The movement time was substantially longer for the RemotePoint, for all target conditions. The slopes of the regression lines demonstrate a substantially lower rate of information processing for the RemotePoint. The slope has units of ms/bit. The slope reciprocal, with a conversion to seconds, has units of bits/s. Thus a lower slope is a higher rate of information processing (throughput). The mouse is clearly a better device.[15] As an overall measure, the preferred calculation for throughput uses a division of means (Equation 7), as proposed by Fitts (1954). These values are along the bottom row in Figure 7.16. The throughput for the RemotePoint (1.46 bits/s) is less than half that for the mouse (3.60 bits/s).

There are many dozens of Fitts' law prediction models in the HCI literature. Some recent and representative examples are provided by Sällnas and Zhai (2003, Fig. 4), Wobbrock and Gajos (2007, Fig. 8), Po, Fisher, and Booth (2004, Fig. 2), Vertegaal (2008, Fig. 2), Rohs and Oulasvirta (2008, Fig. 11), Dixon, Guimbretière, and Chen (2008, Fig. 6), Perry and Hourcade (2008, Fig. 5), Baudisch, Cutrell, Hinckley, and Eversole (2005, Fig. 13), and Sproague, Po, and Booth (2006, Fig. 7).

---

[15]*Better*, here, refers to performance measured using task completion time, or Fitts' throughput. If the interaction involves standing in front of an audience, the *RemotePoint* is likely a better choice.

There is also some debate on the method of calculating throughput (see Soukoreff and MacKenzie, 2004; Zhai et al., 2004).

In the 1950s, when Fitts proposed his model of human movement, graphical user interfaces and computer pointing devices didn't exist. Yet throughout the history of HCI (since Card et al., 1978), research on computer pointing is inseparable from Fitts' law. The initial studies focused on device comparisons and model conformity. As the field evolved and matured, however, Fitts' law found its way into diverse topics—topics only peripherally related to pointing devices. Examples include expanding targets, hidden targets, fish-eye targets, crossing-based interfaces, path following, steering, pointing on the move, eye tracking, force feedback, gravity wells, multi-monitor displays, magic lenses, and so on. Research in these topics, and more, has thrived on the theory and predictive modeling techniques inspired and guided by Fitts' law. This is Fitts' legacy to research in human-computer interaction.

In looking back, the success of Fitts' law in HCI is due in no small measure to the endorsement the model received early on from Card, Moran, and Newell in *The Psychology of Human-Computer Interaction* (1983). Their model human processor (MHP) included two general psychological information theoretic models as guiding principles for the field (1983, 26–27). One was Fitts' law. The other was the Hick-Hyman law for choice reaction time.

7.2.3 Choice reaction time

The Hick-Hyman law for choice reaction time, like Fitts' law, arrived in HCI by way of basic research in experimental psychology—research seeking to model human behavior according to information processing principles (Hick, 1952; Hyman, 1953). The model also takes the form of a prediction equation. Given n stimuli, associated one-for-one with n responses, the time to react (RT) to the onset of a stimulus and choose the correct response is given by

$$RT = a + b\log_2(n + 1) \qquad (13)$$

where a and b are empirically determined constants. Reasonable values for the constants are $a \approx 200$ ms and $b \approx 150$ ms/bit (Card et al., 1983, p. 27, p. 76).[16] Figure 7.18 shows a typical setup for a choice reaction time experiment. At random intervals, a stimulus light is activated and the human responds by pressing the associated key as quickly as possible.

As with Fitts' law, the log term is analogous to the information content of the task and has units of "bits." There is an interesting twist to this for choice reaction time. If some of the choices are more probable than others, the information content of the task is reduced. This in turn reduces the choice reaction time. Let's explore this idea.

---

[16]The model is sometimes expressed as $RT = a + b\log_2(n)$ and sometimes without an intercept. See Card, Moran, and Newell (1983, 71–76) and Welford (1968, 61–70) for detailed discussions.

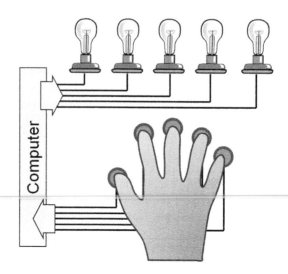

FIGURE 7.18

Paradigm for choice reaction time experiments.

For a set of alternatives with different probabilities, the information (H) is

$$H = \sum_i p_i \log_2 \left(\frac{1}{p_i} + 1 \right)$$ (14)

where p_i is the probability of occurrence of the ith item in the set. Consider a choice selection task where the choice is among 26 alternatives. If the alternatives appear with equal probability, the information content of the task is simply:

$$H = \log_2(27) = 4.75\,\text{bits}$$ (15)

If the alternatives appear with different probabilities, the information is reduced according to Equation 14. This occurs, for example, if the 26 stimuli are letters of the English alphabet and they appear with the same probability as in English writing. An example set of letter frequencies and probabilities for English is shown in Figure 7.19. The data were obtained from the British National Corpus[17] using the word-frequency list of Silfverberg et al. (2000).

Since e appears with greater frequency than, for example, z, the task is slightly easier because there is a small opportunity to anticipate the choices at the onset of a stimulus. In so doing, the reaction time is reduced. Overall, there is less uncertainty, or information, in the task. The information content of the task is reduced from 4.75 bits (Equation 15) to 4.25 bits (Equation 14, illustrated in Figure 7.19).

The Hick-Hyman law has surfaced in a few contexts in HCI research. Card et al. (1983, 74) describe an example of a telephone operator selecting among ten buttons

---

[17] ftp://ftp.itri.bton.ac.uk

Letter	Frequency	Probability (p)	$p \log_2(1/p + 1)$
a	24373121	0.0810	0.3028
b	4762938	0.0158	0.0950
c	8982417	0.0299	0.1525
d	10805580	0.0359	0.1742
e	37907119	0.1260	0.3981
f	7486889	0.0249	0.1335
g	5143059	0.0171	0.1008
h	18058207	0.0600	0.2486
i	21820970	0.0725	0.2819
j	474021	0.0016	0.0147
k	1720909	0.0057	0.0427
l	11730498	0.0390	0.1846
m	7391366	0.0246	0.1322
n	21402466	0.0711	0.2783
o	23215532	0.0772	0.2935
p	5719422	0.0190	0.1092
q	297237	0.0010	0.0099
r	17897352	0.0595	0.2471
s	19059775	0.0633	0.2578
t	28691274	0.0954	0.3358
u	8022379	0.0267	0.1404
v	2835696	0.0094	0.0636
w	6505294	0.0216	0.1203
x	562732	0.0019	0.0170
y	5910495	0.0196	0.1119
z	93172	0.0003	0.0036
		$H =$	4.25

FIGURE 7.19

Letters of the English alphabet, with frequencies and probabilities. Information (H) is calculated using Equation 14.

when the light behind a button comes on. Landauer and Nachbar (1985) applied the Hick-Hyman law in measuring and predicting the time to select items in hierarchical menus. Besides confirming the suitability of the law to this category of task, they also found empirical support that breadth should be favored over depth in hierarchical menus. Note that choice reaction is different from visual search, which is a linear function of the number of items. Landauer and Nachbar eliminated visual scanning in the task by ensuring that "the sets of choice alternatives were well practiced and well-ordered so that it was not necessary to search them sequentially to find the target location" (Landauer and Nachbar, 1985, p. 73).

Ruiz et al. (2008) used the Hick-Hyman law to model the perception, planning, and activation time for users to switch modes with their non-dominant hands in a tablet interface. Despite these efforts and a few others, the Hick-Hyman law has failed to gain the same momentum in HCI as Fitts' law (Seow, 2005). One reason is that the model alone is of limited use. In most situations there are additional behaviors coincident with choice reaction, such as movement or visual search and these complicate applying the model.

7.2.4 The keystroke-level model

One of the earliest and certainly one of the most comprehensive predictive models in the HCI literature is the keystroke-level model (KLM) by Card, Moran, and Newell (1980; 1983, ch. 8). Unlike Fitts' law and the Hick-Hyman law, the KLM was developed specifically for analyzing human performance in interactive computing systems. It was offered as a practical design tool, or as the authors called it, an *engineering model*. The model predicts expert error-free task completion times using the following elements:

- Task (or series of sub-tasks)
- Method used
- Command language of the system
- Motor skill parameters of the user
- Response time parameters of the system

The model is useful in situations where the sequence of interactions in performing a task is known. For example, if the task is "delete a file," the KLM can predict the time to do the task provided the interactions (operators) can be explicitly specified. If there are two or three different methods to do the task (e.g., mouse + menu selection versus keyboard + command entry), then the KLM can predict the time for each method. If used at the design stage, then design alternatives may be considered and compared.

The KLM is not useful if the details of the interactions are not known. A related model, GOMS (Goals, Operators, Methods, Selection rules), operates at a higher level and attempts, among other things, to predict the method the user will adopt (Card et al., 1983, ch. 5). This is complicated, as it builds upon the cognitive information processing activities of the user and also assumes that users act rationally in attaining their goals.

A KLM prediction requires a task to be broken down into a series of subtasks, or primitive operations. The total predicted time is the sum of the subtask times. The model works with four motor-control operators (K = keystroking, P = pointing, H = homing, D = drawing), one mental operator (M), and one system response operator (R):

$$t_{EXECUTE} = t_K + t_P + t_H + t_D + t_M + t_R \qquad (16)$$

Some operations are omitted or repeated, depending on the task. For example, if a keying subtask requires n keystrokes, t_K becomes $n \times t_K$. Each t_K operation is assigned a value according to the skill of the user, with values ranging from $t_K = 0.08$ s for highly skilled typists to $t_K = 1.20$ s for a novice working with an unfamiliar keyboard. The pointing operator, t_P, is a constant based on Fitts' law. The operators and their values from the original KLM are given in Figure 7.20.

7.2.4.1 Original KLM experiment

To validate the KLM, Card, Moran, and Newell conducted an experiment using 14 tasks performed using various methods. Task T1, for example, was "Replace one

Operator	Description	Time (s)

K	PRESS A KEY OR BUTTON
	Pressing a modifier key (e.g., shift) counts as a separate operation, Time varies with typing skill:
	    Best typist (135 wpm)
	    Good typist (90 wpm)
	    Average skilled typist (55 wpm)
	    Average non-secretary typist (40 wpm)
	    Typing random letters
	    Typing complex codes
	    Worst typist (unfamiliar with keyboard)
		
		0.08
		0.12
		0.20
		0.28
		0.50
		0.75
		1.20

P	POINT WITH A MOUSE Empirical value based on Fitts' law. Range from 0.8 to 1.5 seconds. Operator does *not* include the button click at the end of a pointing operation	1.10
H	HOME HAND(S) ON KEYBOARD OR OTHER DEVICE	0.40
$D(n_D, l_D)$	DRAW n_D STRAIGHT-LINE SEGMENTS OF TOTAL LENGTH l_D. Drawing with the mouse constrained to a grid.	$.9 n_D + .16 l_D$
M	MENTALLY PREPARE	1.35
R(*t*)	RESPONSE BY SYSTEM Different commands require different response times. Counted only if the user must wait.	*t*

FIGURE 7.20

Keystroke-level model (KLM) operators and values.

(From Card et al., 1983, 264)

5-letter word with another (one line from previous task)." It was performed on three different systems, each with a unique command set. On one system, POET, the required sequence of subtasks was as follows:

Jump to next line	**M K**[LINEFEED]
Issue Substitute command	**M K**[S]
Type new word	5**K**[word]
Terminate new word	**M K**[RETURN]
Type old word	5**K**[word]
Terminate old word	**M K**[RETURN]
Terminate command	**K**[RETURN]

The operators for each subtask are shown on the right. The task required four mental operations (M) and 15 keystroking operations (K):

$$t_{\text{EXECUTE}} = 4 \times t_M + 15 \times t_K \tag{17}$$

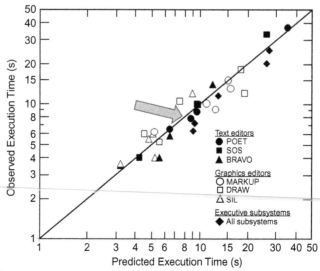

FIGURE 7.21

Observed versus predicted execution times for tasks in the KLM validation experiment. The arrow shows task T1 with POET.

(Adapted from Card et al., 1983, 277)

t_M was set to 1.35 s (Figure 7.20). t_K was set to 0.23 s, based on the mean keystroking time of the participants, determined in a five-minute pre-test. The predicted execution time for task T1 on POET was therefore

$$t_{EXECUTE} = 4 \times 1.35 + 15 \times 0.23 = 8.85 s \qquad (18)$$

In the experiment, twelve users performed the task an average of 27 times each. The mean execution time was 7.8 s ($SE = 0.9$ s). So the observation deviated from the prediction by $\approx 11\%$. The results were similar for the other tasks. Figure 7.21 shows the observed versus predicted task execution times for all 14 tasks (32 tasks, counting method variations). The coalescing of points about the diagonal is clear. This provides a general validation of the model. An arrow identifies the result for task T1 discussed above.

A model is a malleable tool that researchers can and should mold in any way that allows the model to tease out issues or opportunities in a problem space— opportunities to build a better interface or better interaction technique. Card, Moran, and Newell taught this in their *parametric analysis* or *sensitivity analysis* of the KLM. A predictive model is built on parameters. If parameters become variables and slide back and forth, what is the effect on the model's outcome? How sensitive are the predictions to changes in the parameters? This was explored in a series of arguments and demonstrations (1983, 287–293). Figure 7.22 is an example for an editing task. The figure charts $t_{execute}$ for three interaction methods as

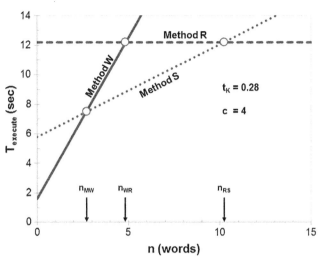

FIGURE 7.22

Parametric analysis showing the sensitivity of predictions for three methods based on changes in *n*—the location of an edit relative to the current location.

(Adapted from Card et al., 1983, 290)

a function of *n*—the distance in words from an initial location to the location of a misspelled word to correct. Viewing from left to right, optimal performance is achieved with Method W for $n < 2.7$, Method S for $2.7 < n < 10.2$, and Method R for $n > 10.2$. If the designer is choosing among candidate methods, and it is known that certain values of *n* are common, then the parametric analysis in Figure 7.22 provides precisely the information needed. A design choice is made supported by evidence obtained from a model of the interaction. Similar sensitivity analyses have appeared since Card et al.'s original KLM publication (e.g., Accot and Zhai, 2001; Clawson, Lyons, Rudnick, Iannucci, and Starner, 2008; W. D. Gray, John, and Atwood, 1993).

7.2.4.2 Modern applications of the KLM

Early experiments with the KLM related primarily to text editing and document management. The tasks were things like "delete a line of text," "add a label to a box," or "transfer a file to another computer, renaming it" (Card et al., 1983, p. 272). These tasks are just as common today as they were in the early 1980s; however, the available task methods are quite different. Transferring a file to another computer is good example. Today this task is likely to involve a mix of mouse and keyboard operations with a GUI-based FTP (file transfer protocol) application. In the original experiment, the task involved FTP as well, but the method only involved a keyboard. The subtask coding included 31 keystroking operations and 0 pointing operations.

Considering that the KLM is more than 25 years old, it is not surprising that some of the operators need updating. The pointing operator (P), for example, is a constant of 1.10 seconds. With the ubiquity of the mouse in today's GUIs, this operator could benefit from the additional fidelity afforded with a Fitts' law prediction. Using the mouse model from Figure 7.17, for example, a reasonable substitute for P is

$$t_P = 0.159 + 0.204 \times \log_2\left(\frac{A}{W} + 1\right) \tag{19}$$

If there are numerous mouse operations in a task undergoing KLM predictions, then the added precision in Equation 19 will improve the analysis. For example, if a subtask involves clicking a 1.2 cm wide toolbar button, having just clicked a neighboring button 3.2 cm away, then the pointing time is[18]

$$t_P = 0.159 + 0.204 \times \log_2\left(\frac{3.2}{1.2} + 1\right) = 0.45 \text{ s} \tag{20}$$

Alternatively, if the mouse pointer must move, say, 44.6 cm to reach the same toolbar button, the pointing time is

$$t_P = 0.159 + 0.204 \times \log_2\left(\frac{44.6}{1.2} + 1\right) = 1.22 \text{ s} \tag{21}$$

The predictions above include the terminating mouse-button click to select the target, unlike the original P operator.

As an example of applying the KLM to current GUI interaction, consider the editing operations to change the font style and font family for text while word processing. Figure 7.23 shows the operations to change "M K" to boldface in the Arial font.

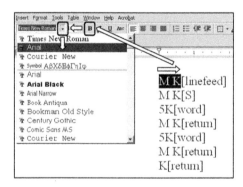

FIGURE 7.23

Mouse operations to change "M K" to boldface in the Arial font. The application is MS Word.

---

[18] For Fitts' law studies with the mouse, pointing times of 500 ms or less are common for easy tasks (ID < 3 bits). The minimum mouse pointing time in the original KLM was 800 ms (see Figure 7.20) which seems high.

The image is a screen snap for the editing performed above using Microsoft Word to characterize task T1. Four pointing operations are required: select the text, select Bold, select the drop-down arrow in the Font list, and select Arial.

A KLM coding of the subtasks is given in Figure 7.24.

Here, the pointing operator appears as P[A,W] to specify the movement amplitude and target width of the pointing task. The values shown were obtained using a ruler applied to Figure 7.23.[19] The execution time for each P operation is given in the right-hand column, computed using Equation 19. As there are four distinct subtasks, each is coded with a mental operator (M) as well as a pointing operator. The predicted task execution time is

$$t_{\text{EXECUTE}} = 4 \times t_{\text{M}} + \Sigma t_{\text{P}} = 4 \times 1.35 + 2.71 = 8.11\,\text{s} \tag{22}$$

As with the keystroking operator (K) in the original KLM, applications of the model using P[A, W] should use a pre-test to determine the coefficients in the Fitts' law model for the pointing device and method involved.

Of course, the same task can be done using the keyboard. A set of keyboard subtasks achieving the same effect is shown in Figure 7.25.

Here we see the same four mental operators; however, there is an assortment of keystroking actions, as per Microsoft Word. The KLM uses a separate keystroking

Mouse Subtasks	KLM Operators	t_P (s)
Drag across text to select "M K"	**M P**[2.5, 0.5]	0.686
Move pointer to Bold button and click	**M P**[13, 1]	0.936
Move pointer to Font drop-down button and click	**M P**[3.3, 1]	0.588
Move pointer down list to Arial and click	**M P**[2.2, 1]	0.501
	$\Sigma\, t_P =$	2.71

FIGURE 7.24

Mouse subtasks and KLM operators for editing operations in Figure 7.23.

Keyboard Subtasks	KLM Operators
Select text	**M P**[shift] 3**K**[→]
Convert to boldface	**M K**[ctrl] **K**[b]
Activate Format menu and enter Font sub-menu	**M K**[alt] **K**[o] **K**[f]
Type *a* ("Arial" appears at top of list)	**M K**[a]
Select "Arial"	**K**[↓] **K**(Enter)

FIGURE 7.25

Keyboard subtasks and KLM operators for the task in Figure 7.23.

---

[19] If the measurements are done on a display, they vary according to the display size and the zoom-factor of the document view. Since target amplitude and width appear as a ratio in Fitts' index of difficulty, scaling up or down does not affect the Fitts' law predictions.

value for pressing a modifier key, such as SHIFT. The predicted execution time using the keyboard is

$$t_{\text{EXECUTE}} = 4 \times t_M + 12 \times t_K = 4 \times 1.35 + 12 \times 0.75 = 14.40 \text{ s} \quad (23)$$

This prediction uses the "typing complex codes" setting for t_K (0.75 s; see Figure 7.20). Depending on the user, this value might be too high or too low. Figure 7.26 explores this by showing the sensitivity of the prediction to changes in the keystroking time, t_K. Markers on the keyboard line show the t_K settings from Figure 7.20. Of course, changes in t_K do not affect the mouse prediction. The keyboard is slower than the mouse over all but the fastest three settings for t_K. Given that these settings correspond to keystroking times while typing at 55+ wpm, it is unlikely the keyboard method would be faster than the mouse method for any user, including experts.[20]

Of course, the mouse model deserves the same scrutiny as the keystroking operations. The mouse predictions are sensitive to the slope and intercept coefficients in the Fitts' law model. The first subtask was a dragging operation. Strictly speaking, a separate Fitts' law dragging model is required, since it is known that dragging operations are less efficient than pointing operations (MacKenzie, 1992).

The example above is a common task on today's GUI systems. Other tasks offer a great range of possibilities for keystroke-level modeling. Examples include scrolling a document with a mouse wheel, finger or thumb input on a mobile phone (perhaps while walking), two-thumb input on a mini-Qwerty keyboard, or stylus input on a PDA. How are these tasks modeled with a keystroke-level model? Clearly, there are many issues to consider in contemporary applications of the KLM. Despite this—or should I say, *motivated by this*—researchers continue

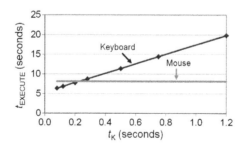

FIGURE 7.26

Sensitivity of prediction to keystroking time, t_K.

---

to use the KLM to model interactions in novel HCI contexts. Examples of recent KLM applications include models for attention shifts with mobile phones (Holleis, Otto, Hussmann, and Schmidt, 2007), stylus-based circling gestures (Hinckley et al., 2006), managing folders and messages in e-mail applications (Bälter, 2000), predictive text entry on mobile phones (Ahmed and Stuerzlinger, 2010; M. Dunlop and Crossan, 2000; Y. Liu and Räihä, 2010), task switching in multi-monitor systems (Hashizume, Kurosu, and Kaneko, 2007), mode switching on tablet PCs (Ruiz et al., 2008), and distractions with in-vehicle information systems (IVIS) (Pettitt, Burnett, and Stevens, 2007). In other cases, the KLM is an embedded component of a comprehensive yet general-purpose modeling tool. An example is *CogTool-Explorer* (Teo, John, and Blackmon, 2012).

Much of the work just cited extends the KLM by adding or refining operators to suit the application. For example, Ruiz et al. (2008) defined a new operator t_{INT}, the interval between a mode switch with the non-dominant hand and the beginning of the next action. Pettitt et al. (2007) define t_{RF} for "reach far," the time to reach from a car's steering wheel to an IVIS (in-vehicle information system). As mentioned above, a model is a malleable tool. Use it, modify it, to suit the problem.

In all cases, use of the KLM entails breaking a task into subtasks and building an overall prediction using Equation 16, perhaps updated with new or refined operators. If the particular KLM implementation is known to work, then the predictions may be used in a true design or engineering setting—the original intention. However, if the model is being extended or applied in a novel setting as part of a research initiative, then validation is required. This is typically done in a formal or semi-formal experiment, where the task is performed with users while task completion times are observed and measured. The predicted and observed times are compared. If they are the same or similar, the KLM is validated. Deviations between predictions and observations signal a problem, but not necessarily a problem in the KLM. The discrepancy may indicate a problem in the task coding. The insight can be valuable. As Hinckley et al. (2006, 187) note:

> [The discrepancy] shows where the techniques deviate from the model, indicating the presence of hidden costs. These costs might include increased reaction time resulting from planning what to do next, mental pauses, or delays while the user attends to visual feedback after performing an action. Our methodology cannot attribute these costs to a specific cause. It just lets us deduce that a hidden cost must exist in a specific portion of the task. This is sufficient to generate many insights as to where the bottlenecks to performance lie and what parts of a technique might be improved.

So, as with descriptive models, predictive models like the KLM are tools for thinking, for generating insight.

Hinckley et al. refer to reacting, planning, pausing, and attending as hidden costs contributing to deviations between predictions and observations. These intangibles are problematic: It is difficult to get inside a user's mind to know what he or she is contemplating, let alone attribute a time cost to mental processes in a model.

Arguably, the mental operator (M) in the KLM is its Achilles heel. It is a single operator, pegged at 1.35 s, and is used for all mental processes. The human mind is simply too rich to be distilled so uniformly.

For this reason, researchers often do not model or predict execution time, but instead, model or predict only the keystrokes or other primitive actions. This makes for a much simpler problem. Actions, such as keystrokes, stylus taps, finger gestures, button clicks, gaze shifts, menu accesses, and so on, often capture important aspects of an interaction method apart from the human performance element. And modeling such actions is relatively straightforward. The end result is a model that is accurate but limited. While optimizing an "action parameter" is a noble cause, the connection to user performance is tenuous at best. Hidden costs are real costs, and the earlier they are accounted for—that is, at the modeling or design stage—the better.

7.2.4.3 The KLM and (Predictive) text entry

A classic HCI example of keystroke-level modeling, minus the hidden costs, is text entry, particularly mobile text entry. The mobile phone keyboard, being ambiguous, bears a special challenge for text entry. The relevant statistic for this is *KSPC* (keystrokes per character), defined as the number of keystrokes required, on average, for each character of text entered using a given input method in a given language (MacKenzie, 2002). It is known, for example, that a mobile phone has $KSPC \approx 2.023$ for multi-tap and $KSPC \approx 1.007$ for predictive text entry (*T9*). If word completion or word prediction is added, $KSPC < 1$. However, these figures do not account for the performance costs of visually attending to the interface. Let's consider how these costs might be accommodated in a keystroke-level model.

The original KLM experiment did not include a task such as "enter a 43-character phrase of text." The task was likely considered too trivial to bother with, and that's a reasonable position. The KLM prediction would reduce to $43 \times t_K$, where t_K is the keystroking time of the participant, based on a pre-test for typing speed. In essence, the task would just confirm the pre-test.

However, if the target system is a mobile phone and the text-entry method is multi-tap, the task seems appropriate for a KLM prediction. Or is it? Consider the 43-character phrase "the quick brown fox jumps over the lazy dog." Entering it using multi-tap requires 88 keystrokes.[21] In this case, the KLM prediction reduces to $88 \times t_K$, where t_K is the keystroking time of the participant, based on a pre-test. Of course, the pre-test is on a mobile phone using multi-tap. Once again, the task simply confirms the pre-test. It is important to remember that the KLM is a model for expert users. The participants would be experts with multi-tap on mobile phones.

However, interaction with a mobile phone keypad is distinctly different from two-handed typing on a computer keyboard. A mobile phone is typically held in the

---

[21] The words (in keystrokes) are as follows: the (84433S) quick (778844422255S) brown (22777666966S) fox (33366699S) jumps (58867N7777S) over (66688833777S) the (84433S) lazy (55529999N999S) dog (36664S). S is the space key. N is a *next* key (e.g., ↓) to segment consecutive letters on the same key.

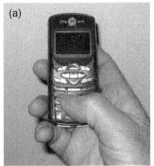
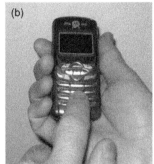
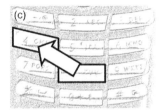

FIGURE 7.27

Interaction with a mobile phone keypad: (a) Thumb. (b) Index finger. (c) Fitts' law
movement for "h" preceded by "t."

hand with keys pressed either by the thumb of the supporting hand or by the index
finger of the opposite hand, as illustrated in Figure 7.27a and Figure 7.27b, respectively. Since only a single digit is used for input, the time for each key press can
be modeled by Fitts' law, as shown in Figure 7.27c for pressing *h* preceded by *t*.
Many multi-tap key presses are on the same key, but this too is a Fitts' law task
(with $A = 0$; $MT \approx 160\,\text{ms}$). So a more refined prediction for multi-tap text entry
can use the KLM pointing operator, with Fitts' law coefficients determined in a pre-
test. Silfverberg et al. (2000) developed this approach in detail, presenting separate
Fitts' law models for the thumb and index finger.

For touch typing on a Qwerty keyboard or multi-tapping on a mobile phone,
the KLM's mental operator (M) is not needed. The user knows what to do and
does it according to his or her keystroking expertise with the method. This is not
the case for predictive text entry. Systems that involve word completion, word
prediction, phrase prediction, or other language-based adaptive or predictive features are well known to tax the attention of users (e.g., Keele, 1973; Koester and
Levine, 1994a, 1994b; Silfverberg et al., 2000). Predictive text entry techniques
require the user to attend to and consider the system's behavior. Modeling this
requires the KLM's mental operator (M) or something similar. Let's consider the
possibilities.

Predictive text entry on a mobile phone (*T9*) requires only one keystroke per
character as a word is entered. The system uses an internal dictionary to map candidate words to the key sequence. When the user finishes the keystrokes for a word,

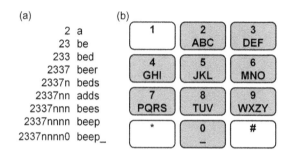

(a)

```
   2  a
  23  be
 233  bed
2337  beer
2337n  beds
2337nn  adds
2337nnn  bees
2337nnnn  beep
2337nnnn0  beep_
```

FIGURE 7.28

(a) Key sequence (*left*) and display progress (*right*) for input of *beep* using predictive text entry. Note: *n* is the *next* key (e.g., *). (b) Mobile phone keypad (for reference).

there is a good chance the desired word is displayed.[22] Unfortunately, "a good chance" isn't good enough; the uncertainty keeps the user on guard, monitoring the system's display. This creates an on-going attention demand ("Has my word appeared?"). Furthermore, input sometimes generates *collisions*—multiple words matching the key sequence. The words are presented in order of their probability in English and the user cycles through the possibilities to select the desired word. So there is an additional attention demand to navigate the list.

To further develop this idea, Figure 7.28a shows the key sequences (left) and display progress (right) for inputting "beep" on a mobile phone using predictive entry. For reference, a mobile phone keypad is shown in Figure 7.28b. The key sequence includes pressing *n* for *next* (e.g., *) to navigate the candidate list when collisions occur. After entering 2337, *beer* appears on the display. Four presses of next are required to navigate the list to reach the desired word. When the desired word appears, 0 is pressed to select it and append a space.

How are the interactions above modeled using the KLM? Clearly a raw break-down using only the keystroking operator (K) or the pointing operator (P) is inappropriate. The interactions require mental processing as well as keying or pointing. The KLM's mental operator (M) is for mentally preparing to take the next action (Card et al., 1983, p. 263). This doesn't seem appropriate here, since the user must *perceive*, *decide*, and *react*. Yet a variant of M is clearly needed. Figure 7.29 proposes a task coding with nine keying operations and five mental operations. M is coded as M_P, for performing a *physical match* between a stimulus (the presented word) and a code stored in the user's short-term memory (the desired word). After keying 2337, the user sees the wrong word. The user reacts by pressing next (*n*). A similar M_P occurs after each press of next until the desired word appears, whereupon the user presses 0 to select the word and append space. An assumption here is that the candidate words are presented to the user one at a time, as is typical of most mobile phones.

One question to ask in applying KLM principles to predictive interfaces is: what is an expert user? The question is not as odd as one might think. Remember, even the

---

[22] For English, one estimate is that 95 percent of the words can be entered unambiguously (Silfverberg et al., 2000).

$$\boxed{2}\boxed{3}\boxed{3}\boxed{7}\; M_P \boxed{n}\; M_P \boxed{n}\; M_P \boxed{n}\; M_P \boxed{n}\; M_P \boxed{0}$$

FIGURE 7.29

Key sequences and mental operators for the input of "beep" (see Figure 7.28).

Rank	Word	Keystrokes	Higher Ranking Colliding Word (rank)
47	if	43n0	he (15)
51	no	66n0	on (13)
63	then	8436n0	them (57)
72	me	63n0	of (2)
78	these	84373n0	there (35)
105	go	46n0	in (6)
118	us	87n0	up (56)
159	home	4663n0	good (115)
227	night	64448n0	might (141)
298	war	927n0	was (10)

FIGURE 7.30

Top ten ambiguous words requiring one press of next.

original KLM used a sliding scale for expertise. The keystroking operator (K) was tuned according to the typing skill of the user. Is there a similar sliding scale for the mental operator? Perhaps. Consider entering *the* (843), *of* (63), *and* (263), or other common words in English. Novices might monitor the display after entering 843 to confirm that *the* is displayed, but with a little practice, monitoring isn't necessary. 8430 produces *the*—no need to monitor the display! So the issue is not about tuning the value of M_P according to expertise, but in deciding when and where the mental operator is present.

The presence of, or need for, the M_P operator can be explored by examining a ranked list of English words and considering each word's position within ambiguous word sets. For this analysis, a ranked list of 64,000 unique words in English was drawn from the British National Corpus.[23] As it turns out, the top 46 words are either unambiguous or are at the front of the candidate list (if there are collisions). They are entered without pressing next. The 47th ranked word is *if*, which is ambiguous with *he* at rank 15. So, while *he* is entered with keys 430, *if* requires 43n0. The top ten such words are shown in Figure 7.30. The issue is whether users adopt behaviors that negate or reduce the presence of mental operations. No doubt, expert uses will expeditiously enter top-ranked words without hesitating to monitor the display. This behavior may also extend to top-ranked words that require presses of next. While empirical evidence is lacking, anecdotal evidence suggests that experienced users press *next* without hesitation while entering words such as *if* and *no*.[24]

---

[23] ftp://ftp.itri.bton.ac.uk. The list is an expanded version of that used by Silfverberg et al. (2000). It is available on this book's web site.

[24] The author knows this from personal experience as well as from conversations with other mobile phone users on this subject.

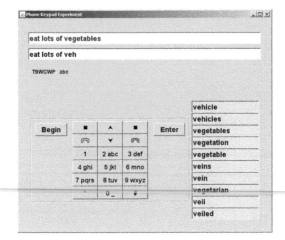

FIGURE 7.31

Input of *vegetables* using a GUI simulation of a phone keypad with word completion. After three key presses (834), *vegetables* appears as the third entry in the candidate list.

But how far down the list do such behaviors extend, and at what level of expertise do they begin? These are outstanding research questions. It is unlikely that any level of expertise would negate the need to monitor the display while entering *beep*, which is at rank 20,767 in the list. The word is simply too infrequent for sufficient skilled behavior to develop that would allow entry without mental operators.[25]

To move beyond keystroke-only modeling, heuristics are needed for the hidden costs—the mental operators. Two simple rules are *all-in* or *all-out*. An all-in model includes mental operators at every reasonable juncture (e.g., Figure 7.29). An all-out model recognizes an all-knowing absolute expert and excludes all mental operators. Assuming a reasonable value for the keystroking operator (K), the two approaches produce upper-bound (all-in) and lower-bound (all-out) execution time predictions. Neither is likely to occur in practice. More accurate predictions require a smarter heuristic, perhaps obtained through a creative pre-test.

Predictive text entry on a mobile phone is but one point in a rich and diverse problem space for text entry. Word completion adds to the mix by allowing entry of a full word after entering only part of it. A candidate list of complete words is generated with each key selection. If the desired word appears early, it is selected immediately, thus saving keystrokes. To explore mobile phone text entry involving word prediction and word completion, a Java GUI application was developed to test and demonstrate several setups.[26] The GUI simulation for word completion is shown in Figure 7.31.

---

[25] Of course, an obscure word that just happens to be entered frequently by a user would be expeditiously entered (i.e., no mental operators).

[26] The files, including an extensive API, and support files, are in `PhoneKeypadExperiment.zip`, available on this book's web site.

(a)   (b)

$\boxed{8}\boxed{3}\boxed{4}$ M$_V$ $\boxed{W}$ $\boxed{8}$ M$_V$ $\boxed{3}$ M$_V$ $\boxed{4}$ M$_V$ $\boxed{W}$

FIGURE 7.32

Key sequences and mental operators for input of *vegetables* (see Figure 7.31): (a) Visual check after third keystroke. (b) Visual check after each keystroke.

Keys are pressed by clicking on them with the mouse pointer or tapping on them with a stylus or finger. The entry of *vegetables* is shown. With each key press, a ten-word candidate list is generated.[27] After three key presses (834), *vegetables* appears in the third position in the candidate list. Clicking on it selects it, delivering it to the edit buffer. So four key actions produce 11 characters of text (*vegetables_*).

While there are fewer key actions, it is not certain that execution time or text entry speed will improve. What is a reasonable model for this interaction? Two possibilities are shown in Figure 7.32. If the candidate list is not generated until the third key action, or if the user chooses not to look until the third key action, the pattern in Figure 7.32a applies. The key action W is a selection on the candidate word. The mental operator M is coded as M$_V$, representing the time to visually scan the candidate words. It is clearly a different process than M$_P$—performing a physical match between a stimulus and a code in short-term memory. The visual search equation developed in Chapter 2 (section 2.7.2) is a logical substitute for M$_V$, but this is not explored here.

Figure 7.32b models a different scenario where the user is presented with and views the candidate list after each key action. Which behavior produces better performance? The behavior in Figure 7.32a is faster for the example (fewer operations), but what about English in general? This is a question for which an enhanced KLM can help. There are many design issues. A long candidate list bears a *cost* since it takes longer to visually scan but brings *benefit* since the desired word appears sooner. Viewing the list after each key action adds time to the interaction (*cost*) but allows entry of the intended word at the earliest opportunity (*benefit*).

The methods also differ between stylus or finger input and keyed input. For stylus or finger input, once the desired word appears and is located, it is selected directly. For keyed input, selecting the *n*th word in the candidate list takes an extra *n*−1 key actions, assuming arrows keys are required to navigate the list. And, as noted earlier, for mobile phone keyboards or stylus input, the pointing operator (P), in the form of a Fitts' law prediction, is more appropriate than the keystroking operator (K). Clearly there are many design choices and modeling issues that are ripe for a KLM analysis—one that includes a revised set of mental operators.

Models of predictive text entry in the HCI literature generally do not account for mental operations. The focus is usually on modeling or reducing keystrokes (M. Dunlop and Crossan, 2000; M. D. Dunlop, 2004; Gong and Tarasewich, 2005; Gong et al., 2008; MacKenzie, 2002; Pavlovych and Stuerzlinger, 2003; Ryu and Cruz, 2005).

---

[27]For convenience, discussions here speak of *key presses*. Since the interface uses soft keys, each key action involves a point-select operation using a mouse, finger, or stylus.

Models that predict text entry speed generally do so by incorporating only keystroking (K) or pointing (P) operators (MacKenzie and Soukoreff, 2002; Silfverberg et al., 2000).

7.2.4.4 Updating the KLM's mental operator (M)

Earlier I advocated updating the KLM's pointing operator (P) to include a Fitts' law prediction (P[A,W]). Perhaps the mental operator (M) also needs revisiting. Can the KLM's single mental operator (M) be replaced with a set of operators for the diverse interactions requiring user attention and cognition? M_P and M_V were suggested above as mental operations where the cognitive process involves physical matching or visual searching. But what are the execution times? What is the theory supporting these and other mental operators? Interestingly enough, the KLM's mental operator was not supported by any theory. The placement of KLM's mental operator involved heuristics to analyze the operations in a task and deduce where a mental operation was likely to occur (Card et al., 1983, p. 265). There was no theory offered on the cognitive processes or on the execution times expected for the operations, as is gleaned from experimental work in psychology or elsewhere. As noted, "The use of a single mental operator is a deliberate simplification" (Card et al., 1983, 263).

The value of M was estimated from the experimental data "by removing the predicted time for all physical operations from the observed execution time" (Card et al., 1983, 274). Then t_M was estimated by a least-squares fit of the time removed versus the estimated number of mental operations. The result was $t_M = 1.35\,\text{s}$ ($SD = 1.1\,\text{s}$).[28] The standard deviation was quite large (81% of the mean), suggesting that the method of estimating M was rough, at best.

M_P, physical matching, was motivated by Card et al.'s model human processor (1983, ch. 2), which includes a range of human behaviors called "simple decisions." Notably, these behaviors are not included in the KLM. Each behavior involves a stimulus that is connected to a response through one or more cycles of cognitive processing. The behaviors are given in Figure 7.33, along with a proposed

Proposed Mnemonic	Task	Execution Time (ms)	
		Card et al.	Figure 2-28 & Figure 2-30
M_S	Simple Reaction	240 [105 – 470]	277 [±44]
M_P	Physical Matching	310 [130 – 640]	510 [±59]
M_N	Name Matching	380 [155 – 810]	485 [±52]
M_L	Class Matching	450 [180 – 980]	566 [±96]
M_C	Choice Reaction	$200 + 150 \log_2(N + 1)$	
M_V	Visual Search		$498 + 41\,N$

FIGURE 7.33

Mental operators and proposed mnemonics for simple decision tasks, along with the nominal value and the range of execution times (ms).

---

[28] The value $t_M = 1.35\,\text{s}$ was used to calculate the predicted execution times in validating the KLM. Given that t_M was estimated from observed data in the same experiment, the observed versus predicted comparison in Figure 7.21 is of questionable value, because the predictions are derived from the observations.

mnemonic. There are two sets of nominal execution times, one provided by Card et al. and another from the experiment described earlier in Chapter 2 (see Figures 2.28 and 2.30). The range appears in brackets as the upper-bound and lower-bound from Card et al.'s values or as ±1 standard deviation for the values in Chapter 2. The execution times include the time for motor response (e.g., a button or key press).

Card et al.'s values were obtained by reviewing a large body of literature on human sensory-motor responses. The range of execution times in brackets is large because of the variety of experimental procedures and task conditions included in their review. Some conditions increase execution time while others decrease execution time. For example, reaction times are known to vary by the intensity of the stimulus: Increase the loudness (auditory) or brightness (visual) of a stimulus and the reaction time decreases. The values from Chapter 2 are offered as an example. They are considered accurate but limited to the task, apparatus, and procedure used in the experiment. For M_S, M_P, M_N, and M_L, the values fall within the range provided by Card et al., although in all cases the value is greater than Card et al.'s nominal value.

For a simple reaction (M_S), the user is attending to the system, waiting for the onset of a stimulus. When the stimulus appears, the user reacts by pressing a key or button. For physical matching (M_P), the user compares the stimulus to a code stored in short-term memory. When the stimulus appears and a match is deduced between the stimulus and the code in memory, the user presses a key or button. An example was given earlier (see Figure 7.29). Name matching (M_N) is similar to physical matching except the user abstracts the stimulus in some manner, deducing equivalence. For example, the user might press a key or button in response to the stimulus of a "key" regardless of its appearance (e.g., "key" versus "**KEY**" versus ⊶). For class matching (M_L), the user makes multiple references from long-term memory. An example is responding to the stimulus of a letter regardless of which letter appears.

The nominal execution times for the top four mental operators in Figure 7.33 are in the range of 240–566 ms. All values are well below 1.35 seconds, the value for the KLM's original mental operator (M) (see Figure 7.20). At the very least, the addition of new operators—more aligned with a user's perceptual and cognitive processes—should help with KLM modeling of interfaces that include adaptive or predictive features. There is also considerable overlap in the execution times, in view of the lower and upper bounds. These are illustrated in Figure 7.34. So predictions of tasks or subtasks enhanced with these operators, while behaviorally correct, will vary considerably.

The visual search operator (M_V) cannot be expressed as a nominal value, or even a range of values. The time depends on the number of choices the user must scan. For the example in Figure 7.31, where the user is searching for a word among ten choices:

$$t_{M_V} = 498 + 41 \times 10 = 908 \text{ ms} \tag{24}$$

If this delay is unacceptable, it can be lowered by reducing the size of the candidate list to five words:

$$t_{M_V} = 498 + 41 \times 5 = 703 \text{ ms} \tag{25}$$

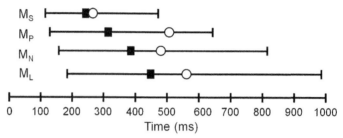

FIGURE 7.34

Nominal value and range of times (ms) for M_S, M_P, M_N, and M_L operators. Times are from Card et al. (1983, 65–76). Circles are means from experiment results in Figure 2.28 and summarized in Figure 7.33.

This time includes a match or no-match key press, which might be an over-simplification, depending on the interface. The difference of 205 ms is substantial and illustrates the kind of design trade-off that is possible if the range of interactions are analyzed and compared using a keystroke-level model. Let's consider another predictive model.

7.2.5 Skill acquisition

Not surprisingly, there is a relationship between skill and practice. Whether we are learning to play a musical instrument, fly an airplane, search a database, navigate a menu system, or touch type on a keyboard, we begin as *novices*. Initial performance is poor, but with practice we acquire skill. With continued practice, we become proficient, perhaps *experts*. If the skilled behavior is adequately represented by a ratio-scale variable, then the transition from novice to expert is well suited to predictive modeling.[29] In the model, the predicted or dependent variable is performance or skill, typically the time to do a specified task or the speed in doing the task. The independent variable is the amount of practice, typically in hours, days, years, trials, blocks, or sessions.

The relationship between skill and practice is non-linear. In the beginning, a small amount of practice yields substantial improvement. After a lot of practice, the same "small amount" produces only a slight improvement. It seems the best mathematical expression of the relationship is a power function of the form

$$y = b \times x^a \tag{26}$$

where x is the regressor or independent variable (amount of practice), y is the dependent variable (performance), and a and b are constants that determine the shape of the relationship. Represented in this form, the relationship between skill and practice is often called the *power law of learning* or the *power law of practice*

---

[29] This is generally not the case for playing a musical instrument or flying a plane. However, one can imagine unit tasks within these skills that are measurable with a ratio-scale variable and suitable for predictive modeling.

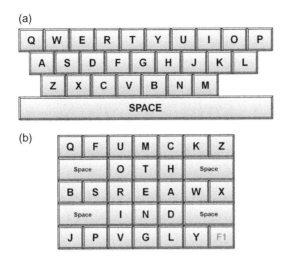

FIGURE 7.35

Soft keyboards layouts: (a) Qwerty. (b) Opti.

(Card et al., 1983, 27; Newell and Rosenbloom, 1981). The law dates at least as far back as the 1920s (Newell, 1990, p. 6).

If the dependent variable is the time to do a task, T, then Equation 26 can be recast as

$$T_n = T_1 \times n^a \tag{27}$$

where T_n is the time to do the task on the nth trial, T_1 is the time on the first trial. The trial number is n and a is a constant setting the shape of the curve. *Trial* is any practice indicator, such as task number, hours of practice, session number, etc. Note that a is negative, because the acquisition of skill means task completion time *decreases* with practice.

Alternatively, the dependent variable can be speed (S), the reciprocal of time. In this case, the model predicts "tasks per unit time," rather than "time per task." An example for speed might be text entry speed in "words per minute." Predicting speed, Equation 26 is recast as

$$S_n = S_1 \times n^a \tag{28}$$

where S_n is the speed on the nth trial, S_1 is the speed on the first trial, n is the trial number, and a is a constant setting the shape of the curve. In this form, a is positive since speed increases with practice. Furthermore, $0 < a < 1$ to reflect the diminishing return with practice. Let's develop an example.

An experiment compared two soft keyboard layouts for text entry using a stylus. (See Figure 7.35.) One layout had the familiar Qwerty letter arrangement. The other was Opti, a design intended to minimize stylus or finger movement for English text entry. The Opti layout was new to all participants. Because participants were familiar

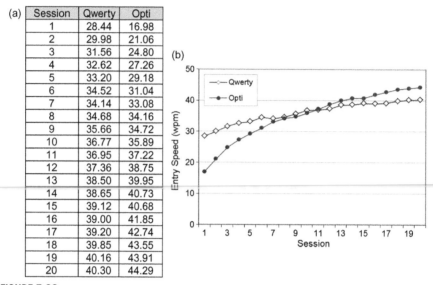

(a)

Session	Qwerty	Opti
1	28.44	16.98
2	29.98	21.06
3	31.56	24.80
4	32.62	27.26
5	33.20	29.18
6	34.52	31.04
7	34.14	33.08
8	34.68	34.16
9	35.66	34.72
10	36.77	35.89
11	36.95	37.22
12	37.36	38.75
13	38.50	39.95
14	38.65	40.73
15	39.12	40.68
16	39.00	41.85
17	39.20	42.74
18	39.85	43.55
19	40.16	43.91
20	40.30	44.29

FIGURE 7.36

Experiment demonstrating skill acquisition: (a) Data showing entry speed (wpm) by session. (b) Chart.

with the Qwerty layout, better performance was expected for the Qwerty condition, at least initially. To test the potential of the Opti layout, a longitudinal study was conducted. With the acquisition of skill, would Opti eventually outperform Qwerty? If so, how much practice is required to reach a crossover point? The experiment involved 20 sessions of text entry. (See MacKenzie and Zhang, 1999 for complete details.)

Figure 7.36a gives the summary data from the experiment. The independent variables are practice, labeled "Session" in the table, and layout (Qwerty and Opti). The dependent variable is text entry speed in words per minute (wpm). Since two layouts were compared, there are two patterns of learning to consider. These are shown in Figure 7.36b. The improvement with practice in both cases follows the conjectured non-linear pattern. The crossover point—where Opti becomes faster than Qwerty—occurred at session 11.

The curve for the Qwerty layout is more flat because participants were well along the learning curve at the beginning of the experiment, due to familiarity with the letter arrangement. Curve fitting each set of points to Equation 26 is easily done with a spreadsheet application such as Microsoft Excel. The result is shown in Figure 7.37. Both curves show a power function with the observed points clustered close to the line.

The prediction equation for each layout is shown in the chart. The equations appear in their default power form (see Equation 26), as produced by Microsoft Excel. The goodness-of-fit is given by the squared correlation coefficient (R^2), commonly articulated as the percentage of the variance explained by the model. For Opti, 99.7 percent of the variance is explained by the model, and for Qwerty, 98.0 percent. These are very high figures and attest that both models are excellent predictors.

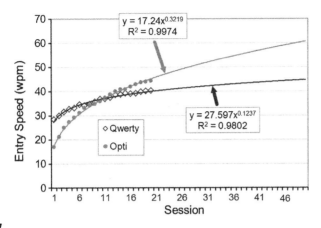

FIGURE 7.37

Power law of learning for Opti and Qwerty showing extrapolation to session 50.

Figure 7.37 also shows an extrapolation of the models to session 50. However, extrapolating beyond the testing range is risky. Although the correlations are high for both models, the ability to predict text entry speed diminishes the farther one ventures from the range of testing. For example, at session 50 the predicted text entry speed for Opti is:

$$S_{50} = 17.24 \times 50^{0.3219} = 60.7 \text{ wpm} \tag{29}$$

That's fast! Too fast, perhaps. Here's a simple exercise to demonstrate a model's ability (or inability!) to extrapolate. Using only the data for sessions 1–10 for Opti, the prediction equation is:

$$S_n = 17.03 \times n^{0.3319} \tag{30}$$

Using this equation to predict the text entry speed at session 20 yields:

$$S_{20} = 17.03 \times 20^{0.3319} = 46.03 \text{ wpm} \tag{31}$$

But the observed text entry speed at session 20 was 44.29 wpm (see Figure 7.36a). The prediction is generous by $(46.03 - 44.29) / 44.28 = 4.0\%$. So perhaps the prediction for session 50 is generous as well.[30]

---

[30] Perhaps the prediction for Opti at session 50 for 60.7 wpm is realistic. In the experiment, text phrases were drawn at random from a small set of just 70 phrases ($\approx$25 characters/phrase). The number of phrases per session was 50–60 early on, and 90–110 in later sessions. In view of this, participants were likely developing muscle memory with the phrases as the experiment progressed. This is similar to the highly over-learned motor skill one develops in other activities, such as buttoning a shirt, tying shoelaces, or entering a password (for people who never change their passwords). While this argument may have merit, it also means that the predicted text entry speed for session 50, while accurate, may apply only to the phrase set, not to English.

7.2.5.1 Skill acquisition research in HCI

Besides the experiment summarized above, there are other examples of the power law of learning in the HCI literature. The earliest is by Card, English, and Burr (1978), who compared a mouse, a joystick, and two keyboard techniques for selecting text on a CRT display. In building a learning model, they performed a log transformation on both the *x*-axis data (block) and the *y*-axis data (positioning time). With this change, the relationship is linear. The relationship for the mouse is shown in Figure 7.38. Similar log-log (linear) models are reported by Recker and Pitkow (1996) for mapping document access to document storage in a multimedia database, and by Seibel for a choice reaction task (reported in Newell 1990, 7).

Additionally, in *The Psychology of Human-Computer Interaction* (Card et al., 1983) there are skill acquisition models for reaction time (pp. 57–59) and execution time (pp. 284–285). There are numerous other sources in the HCI literature reporting predictive models of skill acquisition. Text entry is the predominant theme (Bellman and MacKenzie, 1998; Castellucci and MacKenzie, 2008; Clarkson, Clawson, Lyons, and Starner, 2005; Isokoski and Raisamo, 2004; Költringer, Van, and Grechenig, 2007; Lyons, Starner, and Gane, 2006; Lyons et al., 2004; MacKenzie et al., 2001; MacKenzie and Zhang, 1999; McQueen et al., 1995; Wigdor and Balakrishnan, 2003, 2004; Wobbrock, Myers, and Rothrock, 2006; Wobbrock, Rubinstein, Sawyer, and Duchowski, 2008; Zhai, Sue, and Accot, 2002). There are also examples in the literature where the progression of learning is presented in a plot but without including a model of the behavior (e.g., Itoh, Aoki, and Hansen, 2006).

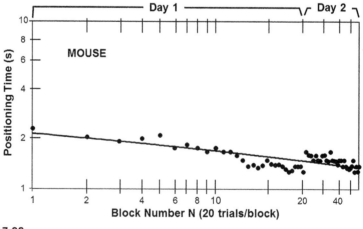

FIGURE 7.38

Skill acquisition for the mouse in a text selection task.

(Adapted from Card et al., 1978)

7.2.6 **More than one predictor**

The equations above predict the outcome on a dependent variable from a single predictor variable (independent variable). It is also possible to build a prediction model where the outcome is predicted from multiple predictors. In statistics the technique is called *multiple regression* and takes the form

$$y = a + b_1 x_1 + b_2 x_2 + b_3 x_3 + \dots \tag{32}$$

Let's begin with a hypothetical example. A researcher is interested in the relationship between the time taken to learn a computer game and the age and computing habits of players. Is age a factor in learning the game? Does the amount of daily computer use play a factor? Can the time to learn the game be predicted from a player's age and daily computer use? This last question suggests a prediction equation with multiple predictors. The dependent variable is y, the time to reach a performance criterion in playing the game. The two independent variables (predictors) are x_1, a player's age, and x_2, a player's daily computer use in hours. To explore the research questions above, an experiment was conducted. Fourteen participants were recruited. Their ages ranged from 16 to 40 years, and their use of computers ranged from two to eight hours per day. The participants were given basic instructions on the operation of the game. Then they were observed playing and learning the game in 15–20 minute segments over a period of one week. They continued to play until they reached a criterion score. The data are shown in Figure 7.39.

Participant	Time To Reach Criterion (hours)	Age (years)	Daily Computer Usage (hours)
P1	2.3	16	8
P2	2.1	17	7
P3	2.5	18	8
P4	3.6	23	6
P5	2.6	25	7
P6	5.3	26	5
P7	4.8	29	6
P8	6.1	31	4
P9	7.2	32	5
P10	7.3	35	3
P11	6.4	37	4
P12	8.1	38	2
P13	7.9	40	4
P14	2.3	16	8

FIGURE 7.39

Data for a hypothetical experiment testing the relationship between the time to learn a computer game and the age and daily computer use of players.

It is difficult to visually scan raw data and see patterns, so the first step is to import the data into a spreadsheet or statistics application and build scatter plots and other charts. Two scatter plots are shown in Figure 7.40. In both cases, a strong relationship is seen. Older participants generally took longer to reach the criterion in playing the game (Figure 7.40a). At $r = .9448$, the coefficient of correlation is high. The relationship is similarly strong between the time taken to reach the criterion score and players' daily use of computers. In this case, however, the relationship is negative. Players who self-report spending a lot of time each day using computers generally took less time learning the game (Figure 7.40b). The coefficient of correlation is $r = -.9292$, indicating a strong negative relationship.

Building a prediction equation using multiple regression is straightforward using any statistics application. Spreadsheet applications can also be used, depending on the features available. Microsoft Excel, for example, supports multiple regression using the Analysis ToolPak, which is available as an add-in. Regardless

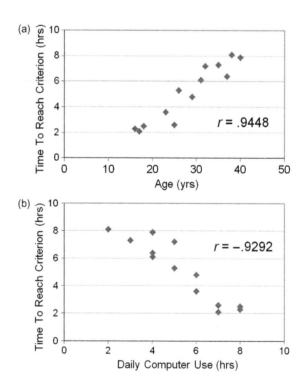

FIGURE 7.40

Relationships in the data between the time taken to reach a criterion score and (a) age and (b) daily computer use. The coefficient of correlation (r) is high in both cases.

of the tool used, a multiple prediction equation for the data in Figure 7.39 yields

$$y = 3.2739 + 0.1575x_1 - 0.4952x_2 \tag{33}$$

where y is the time taken to reach the criterion score, x_1 is a player's age, and x_2 is a player's daily computer usage in hours. The equation is accompanied with $R^2 = .9249$, meaning the model explains about 92.5 percent of the variance in the data. All in all, it's a very good model. Typically, other statistics are provided, such as the standard error of estimate for the prediction equation overall ($SE = .6769$, for the example above) and for each regression coefficient, and for the p-value for each coefficient.

As an example in the literature, MacKenzie and Ware (1993) studied the effect of lag (aka system delay or latency) on human performance while using a mouse in point-select tasks. The experiment followed a Fitts' law paradigm, manipulating target amplitude (A) and target width (W) in the usual manner. Lag was also manipulated by buffering mouse samples. Processing was delayed by multiples of the screen refresh period. The factors were target amplitude (A = 96, 192, and 384 pixels), target width (W = 6, 12, 24, and 48 pixels), and lag (8.3, 25, 75, and 225 ms). The A-W conditions yielded six levels of index of task difficulty (ID) ranging from 1.58 bits to 6.02 bits. The dependent variable was the movement time (MT in ms) to complete point-select tasks. The researchers presented four models for MT (see Figure 7.41). The first model in the figure is the traditional Fitts' law model. There is a single predictor, ID_e. The correlation is quite low, no doubt because of the additional variance introduced by the lag. The second model also uses a single predictor, lag. The fit is slightly better. The third model uses two predictors, ID_e and LAG. With $R = .948$, the fit is quite good.[31] The model explains 89.8 percent of the variance.

Model for MT (ms)[a]	Fit[b]	Variance Explained
$MT = 435 + 190\ ID_e$	$r = .560$	31.30%
$MT = 894 + 46\ LAG$	$r = .630$	39.80%
$MT = -42 + 246\ ID_e + 3.4\ LAG$	$R = .948$	89.80%
$MT = 230 + (169 + 1.03\ LAG)\ ID_e$	$R = .987$	93.50%
[a] LAG in ms, IDe in bits		
[b] $n = 48$, $p < .0001$ for all models		

FIGURE 7.41

Models for movement time (MT) based on index of difficulty (ID_e) and system lag (LAG).

(From MacKenzie and Ware, 1993)

[31] It is a convention for multiple regression to use uppercase R for the correlation coefficient.

The final model in Figure 7.41 reorganizes the independent variables to demonstrate an observed interaction effect between lag and task difficulty. Indeed, there is an improvement in the model: $R = .987$, explaining 93.5 percent of the variance. At lag $= 0$, the fourth model reduces to

$$MT = 230 + 169 \times ID_e \tag{34}$$

which is consistent with other Fitts' law models for the mouse. Each millisecond of lag in the fourth model adds 1 ms/bit to the slope of the prediction line. This is the sort of additional explanation that motivates adding extra predictors to regression models.

Similar uses of multiple regression in the HCI literature are reported by Accot and Zhai (2001), Cao et al. (2008), Rohs and Oulasvirta (2008), and Sears and Shneiderman (1991).

HCI researchers with a social science perspective tend to use multiple regression with a slightly different motivation. Social scientists are more interested in observing and explaining human behavior rather than in measuring and predicting human performance. Typically the research seeks to determine the relative impact of several behavioral factors (independent variables) on a dependent variable. A common method is *stepwise linear regression*. All variables are tested individually to determine which has the greatest explanatory power (highest R^2) on the variance in the dependent variable. A linear model is built using that variable. Then the remaining variables are tested one at a time against the model to determine which has the greatest explanatory power on the remaining variance. The process is repeated until all variables are added. For example, Dabbish et al. (2005) describe a model using "probability of replying to an e-mail message" as a dependent variable. The model was built using 12 predictor variables. Some contributed significantly and positively to the dependent variable (e.g., number of e-mails with only one recipient), some contributed significantly and negatively to the dependent variable (e.g., number of e-mails from close colleagues), while others had little or no effect (e.g., number of e-mails about scheduling). Even with 12 variables the model had a modest $R^2 = .37$. However, behavioral variables are, in general, less stable than performance variables, so overall Dabbish et al.'s model was good. Other researchers describe similar stepwise multiple regression models (Chung and Hossain, 2008; Iqbal and Bailey, 2006; Lampe, Ellison, and Steinfield, 2007; Seay and Kraut, 2007; Shklovski et al., 2006; Su and Mark, 2008).

One property of multiple regression deserves mention. When an additional predictor is added to the model, the correlation (R) always increases. It cannot decrease. Thus, caution is warranted in declaring the new model a "better model" simply because of a higher correlation.[32] The true test is whether the new predictor offers additional explanatory power relevant to the intended application of the model. MacKenzie and Ware's work was motivated to model interaction in virtual reality systems, where lag is common; thus, adding lag to the model makes sense.

---

[32] For example, if participants' shoe sizes were measured, then shoe size (SS) could be added as a predictor. The model's correlation would increase!

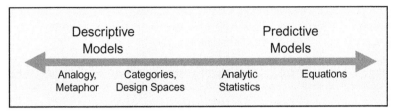

FIGURE 7.42

Model Continuum Model (MCM) with descriptive models at one end and predictive models at the other end.

7.3 **A model continuum model**

In this chapter, I have treated the problem space of modeling as a dichotomy—a space with two mutually exclusive zones: descriptive models and predictive models. While useful, this is in conflict with the model continuum suggested by Pew and Baron, which we examined at the beginning of the chapter. If the space is a continuum rather than a dichotomy, there will be identifiable points along the way. I will wrap up this chapter by proposing another model, a Model Continuum Model (MCM). (See Figure 7.42.)

Figure 7.42 is at best a suggestion, a work in progress. Certainly it lacks the organization and clarity of the descriptive model of politics in Figure 7.1. The model shows a continuum and places descriptive and predictive models at opposite ends. It suggests positions along the continuum where certain kinds of activities or processes might be placed according to their descriptive or predictive emphasis. Are there ways to improve the model? Perhaps the terms *qualitative* and *quantitative* should be added at each end.

This chapter presented the core ideas of descriptive and predictive models of human-computer interaction. The student exercises that follow take up and extend many of the ideas presented above.

STUDENT EXERCISES

7-1. Below is a "big fuzzy cloud" model of human-computer interaction.

Improve on this by proposing a descriptive model of human-computer interaction as per the discussions in Section 7.1.1: Delineating a Problem Space (see Figure 7.1).

7-2. Propose a descriptive model of text entry. (Hint: Do not try to encompass all aspects of text entry. Work with only two or three aspects of text entry that suggest a delineation of the problem space.)

7-3. Propose a descriptive model of _____. (Fill in with any HCI research topic.)

7-4. Review published papers in HCI to find a descriptive model. Summarize the model. Identify at least one weakness or limitation in the model and propose at least one improvement or extension to the model.

7-5. At a recent conference on human-computer interaction, a presenter used a Venn diagram to demonstrate the relationship between the disciplines of computer science (CS), human-computer interaction (HCI), and interaction design (ID):

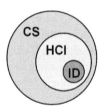

Critique this descriptive model. Suggest a revision to the model. Perhaps you can add one more circles to the Venn diagram to include an additional discipline or activity.

7-6. The following is a descriptive model for the design process (from Thornton, 2010). The model shows a continuum of activities that encompass design according to the philosophy of *design thinking* (Brown, 2009; R. L. Martin, 2009).

Design Thinking Continuum

Write a brief analysis of this model considering the following: What is *design thinking*? What is meant by *mystery, heuristic, algorithm,* and *binary code* as applied to design thinking? Why do the labels appear in two groups? Are there activities beyond each end of the continuum, as inferred by the arrows? (Hint: Search Google Scholar using the phrase "design thinking.")

7-7. The following is a descriptive model of multitasking (adapted from Salvucci, Taatgen, and Borst, 2009). The model shows a series of task pairings along a time continuum with concurrent multitasking at one end and sequential multitasking at the other end.

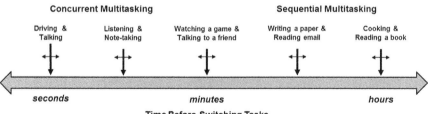

Write a brief analysis of this model considering the following: What is *multitasking*? What are *concurrent multitasking* and *sequential multitasking*? Identify at least three additional task pairings, where at least one of the tasks involves humans interacting with technology, and place each one in the model. Also, identify a task pairing that is positioned beyond the left extreme of the model and another beyond the right extreme of the model.

7-8. Besides the desktop keyboard, the key-action model (KAM) applies to keyboards on mobile devices:

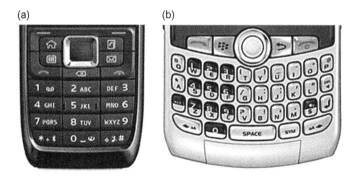

Create an illustration similar to Figure 7.3 for a mobile phone keyboard, such as above. Preferably use your own device. Propose some changes to the model to make it more representative of the keyboard.

7-9. Beaudouin-Lafon defines an *interaction model* (briefly) as "a set of principles, rules, and properties, that guide the design of an interface" (Beaudouin-Lafon, 2000, p. 446). Where are interaction models positioned in the "model continuum model" shown in Figure 7.42? Write a brief review of both models and propose a revised pictorial of the model continuum model that includes interaction models and other models reviewed by Beaudouin-Lafon.

7-10. Jacob et al. (2008) propose a framework for a category of interaction styles called Reality-Based Interaction (RBI). Their framework is a descriptive model. Summarize RBI and demonstrate how it meets the criteria described above for a descriptive model. Give examples.

7-11. The following data show the stylus tapping speed (S_{ST}) and touch typing speed (S_{TT}) for ten participants. Both variables are in words per minute (wpm).

Participant	Stylus Tapping Speed (wpm)	Touch Typing Speed (wpm)
P1	21.4	42
P2	23.6	44
P3	22.0	32
P4	24.0	50
P5	23.0	36
P6	17.1	33
P7	29.0	55
P8	14.7	22
P9	20.3	31
P10	19.7	33

What is the coefficient of correlation (r) between the two variables? What is the linear prediction equation for stylus tapping speed, given touch tapping speed? What percentage of the variation (R^2) is explained by the prediction model? Create a chart showing a scatter plot of the points, the prediction equation, and R^2.

7-12. The following chart was adapted from a Fitts' law study comparing target selection times for expanding and stationary targets (adapted from Zhai, Conversy, Beaudouin-Lafon, and Guiard, 2003). (Note: Expanding targets increase in virtual size when the cursor is close, thus potentially improving interaction.)

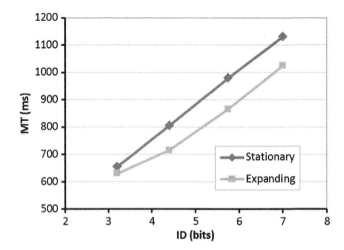

The authors did not build predictive models for the data sets, but they could have. Use a ruler or some other apparatus (e.g., Microsoft PowerPoint or Adobe PhotoShop) to reverse engineer the chart and create data sets for the Expanding and Stationary conditions. Enter the data into a spreadsheet application, such as Microsoft Excel. Create a new chart that, for each condition, includes the regression line, prediction equation, and R^2. Which condition is better in terms of *Throughput*? Explain.

7-13. The following chart was adapted from a study measuring the selection time for menu items based on the serial position of an item within the menu (adapted from Byrne, Anderson, Douglass, and Matessa, 1999, Figure 1).

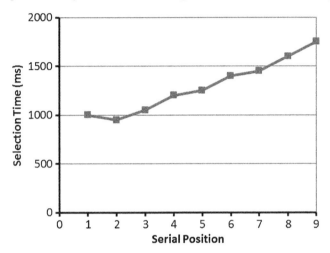

The scatter plot appeared without a regression line. Reverse engineer the chart and build a data set for the scatter plot. Recreate the chart, showing a regression line, regression equation, and R^2. What is the predicted time to select the fifth item in the menu? What is the 95 percent confidence interval for the prediction?

7-14. The data from a Fitts' law study with a mouse are given below:

A (pixels)	W (pixels)	ID (bits)	MT (ms)
192	16	3.70	654
192	32	2.81	518
192	64	2.00	399
320	16	4.39	765
320	32	3.46	613
320	64	2.58	481
512	16	5.04	872
512	32	4.09	711
512	64	3.17	567

Using a spreadsheet application, create a chart showing the scatter plot, regression line, prediction equation, and R^2. (Note: These data were used for Figure 4a in Wobbrock et al., 2008.)

7-15. Users and computers (Part III). Extend the report for Part II of this exercise (see Chapter 6) to determine if there is a relationship between the age of respondents and the number of hours per day of computer use. Since both variables are ratio-scale, the relationship may be explored using a scatter plot, regression line, and the coefficient of correlation (r). For the purpose of the report, consider the relationship strong, mild, or nil according to the following criteria:

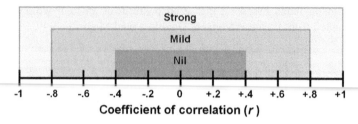

If the relationship is strong, propose a prediction equation that gives the number of hours per day of computer use as a function of a user's age.

7-16. The data from a choice reaction time experiment are given below:

Choices (n)	Reaction Time (ms)
1	155
2	265
3	310
4	365
5	400
6	425
8	505
10	530

Plot the data and build regression models using a few different relationships (e.g., linear, power). What model explains the most variation in the data? (Note: These data were reverse engineered from Figure 4 in Seow, 2005.)

7-17. The following chart was adapted from an experiment showing the relationship between error rate and target width in a target selection task using a camera phone (Rohs and Oulasvirta, 2008):

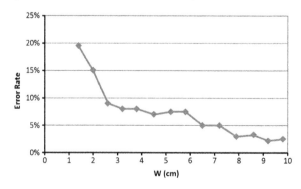

As expected, smaller targets tend to be incorrectly selected more often than larger targets. The relationship seems well suited to curve fitting using a power formula. Reverse engineer the chart and generate a set of *x-y* points where *x* = target width and *y* = error rate. Use a spreadsheet application to recreate the chart showing the scatter of points and the best-fitting curve. What percent of the variation in the observations is explained by the model?

7-18. A human operator attends to eight stimulus lights and presses one of eight keys when the corresponding light turns on. Two of the lights turn on more frequently than the others, accounting for 40 percent and 30 percent of all activations, respectively. The other lights activate with the same frequency. What is the information content of the task?

7-19. Below are the layouts for the Qwerty and Dvorak keyboards, as well as an alphabetic layout proposed by Card et al. (1983, 63). Assuming the layouts are implemented as standard physical keyboards, which design provides the most even split between left-hand and right-hand keying? (See Figure 7.19.) Propose a new design where the split is more even between hands.

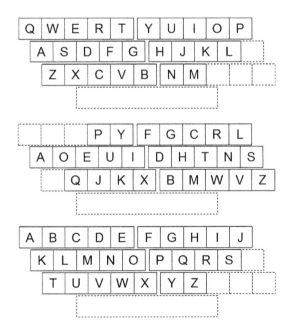

7-20. If the keyboards above are implemented as software keyboards on a desktop computer, the keys can be accessed (pressed) using a mouse. Use the Fitts' law mouse model given earlier (Equation 12) to compute the time to enter *the quick brown fox jumps over the lazy dog*. Convert the time to an entry speed in *words per minute* (wpm). Repeat for the Dvorak and Alphabetic layouts. Repeat using the RemotePoint Fitts' law model (Equation 11). In digitizing the keyboards, ignore the small gaps between keys in the images.

7-21. Repeat the exercise above for the Opti soft keyboard layout in Figure 7.35b. Of the four SPACE keys on Opti, assume the user chooses the one that minimizes the movement distances (e.g., for C_W, the user chooses the SPACE key at the top right).

7-22. Below is an illustration of a sequence of mouse operations to set "Small caps" as the formatting style for a word of text. The screen snap is from MS Word:

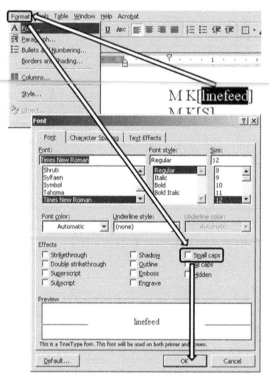

What is the predicted execution time for the task? What is the predicted execution time if the keyboard is used instead of the mouse? For this question, assume $t_K = 0.4$ seconds. For both questions, provide a KLM breakdown of all operations.

7-23. Use the KLM to predict the time to enter "I hate baking pies" on a mobile phone. Provide three predictions: one for multi-tap, one for predictive input using an "all-in" assumption for mental operators, and one using an "all-out" assumption for mental operations. In building the models, assume the keystroking operator (K) is nominally $t_K = 0.4$ seconds. For predictive input, the ordered collision sets at the ends of the words are as follows: I = {I}, hate = {have, gave, gate, hate}, baking = {baking, baling, caking}, and pies = {pier, pies, rids}.

7-24. Build a multiple regression model for the data in exercise 7-14 above. Treat *MT* as the dependent variable and *A* and *W* as predictors. What is the multiple regression equation? What is the percent of the variance explained by the model? Experiment with some transformations on *A* and *W* to obtain a better model (higher R^2). What transformation produces the highest R^2?

7-25. The following chart shows the relationship between text entry speed in characters per minute (cpm) over seven blocks of testing for three entry methods: GazeTalk (standard), GazeTalk (centered), and Dasher (adapted from Itoh et al., 2006, Fig. 4). The power law of practice is clearly evident in the chart; however, no model was provided in the publication.

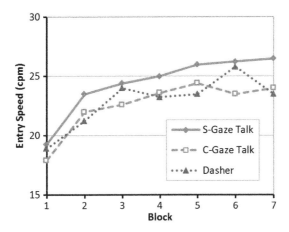

Reverse engineer the chart and generate a set of *x*−*y* points for each of the three entry methods. Use a spreadsheet application to recreate the chart showing the scatter of points and the best-fitting curve and prediction equation for each method. What percent of the variation in the observations does each model explain?

7-26. Conduct an experiment comparing two input methods for pointing and selecting. Use the `FittsTaskTwo` software from this book's website. Use any two methods of input. Consider using two input devices or a single input device operated in different ways. The setup dialog and a screen snap of the experiment procedure are shown below.

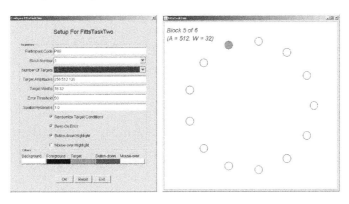

The software implements the multi-directional ISO 9241-9 protocol for evaluating non-keyboard input devices. Consult the API for complete details. Configure the software using three levels each of target amplitude and target width, with 13 targets per sequence (see above). Ask the participants to perform five blocks of trials for each condition. Consider other aspects of the experiment design as per discussions in Chapter 5 (Designing HCI Experiments). Write a brief report on your findings. Among the results to report, include ANOVAs for the effects of input method and block on movement time, throughput, and other dependent variables. Also include a chart with scatter data, regression lines, prediction equations, and squared correlations, as per Figure 7.17.

Writing and Publishing a Research Paper

8

In Chapter 4 I noted that publication is the final step in research (see section 4.1.1). It is fitting, then, to make our final step a chapter on writing and publishing a research paper.

Most HCI research papers present a novel interface idea, then describe an evaluation of the idea in a user study. User studies are designed (or should be designed!) according to accepted standards for experiments with human participants, as laid out in Chapter 5. Adhering to accepted standards is important in HCI and other fields since the practice brings consistency to the body of work that contributes to and defines the field. This practice extends to the final step in research—preparing and publishing the results.

8.1 Conference papers, journal papers

The main venues for publishing HCI research papers are conference proceedings or journals. Journals are considered the top tier for research publications. There are two primary reasons. First, journal submissions undergo a tightly controlled peer review to ensure the research is novel, correct, and carried out according to accepted standards in the field. The reviewers are experts in the subject matter and are enlisted by the journal's editor or by a member of the editorial board. Second, journals are archived in major libraries around the world; thus, research published in a journal is readily available to other researchers. For some disciplines such as physics, journal publications are virtually all that matter, with conference contributions viewed as little more than a summary of one's presentation at a meeting, the content of which appears (or will appear) in a journal publication. So the review of submissions to physics conferences is cursory, at best.

HCI is different. HCI conferences bring together researchers and practitioners, as noted in Chapter 1. The practitioners are the engineers and designers of products, and they are there to learn about the latest research in HCI. Life cycles and time-lines for such products are short. The big players, like Apple, Microsoft, and Nokia, announce new products regularly and with great fanfare. So reaching and influencing the designers and engineers of products requires HCI research to have a short timeline.[1] Unfortunately, the timeline from submission to publication in a journal is long—typically one to two years, sometimes more. For conferences the timeline is short—typically eight months, sometimes less. It is no surprise, then, that conferences and conference publications have emerged as an important vehicle for presenting and publishing research in HCI. Simply put, publishing in a conference proceedings is the quickest way to get one's work "out there." Furthermore, the archival advantage for journals no longer exists. Today, the term *archive* extends to online databases maintained by organizations such as the ACM or IEEE. The review process is also different. For some HCI conferences, the peer review process is as rigorous as it is with many journals. So the prestige of publishing in some HCI conferences, such as the ACM's annual SIGCHI conference, equals that of publishing in some journals.

Prior to publication, a research paper is a *manuscript*. In most cases, the venue for submitting is decided before writing begins. The decision will depend on many factors such as the subject matter, the timing and scope of the research, and the prestige of the conference or journal. Additional factors for considering a conference are location and travel costs, since acceptance of the manuscript implies attending the conference to present the research in a talk.

Journals generally have relaxed requirements for the format of submissions. This is reasonable since a journal submission, if accepted, undergoes a round or two of revision before publication. Revisions are introduced to improve the manuscript based on the referees' suggestions. Acceptance is often conditional on final approval by the journal editor or referees. Publication in a journal also includes professional copyediting by the journal staff. Hence, the formatting of the initial manuscript is not so important.

Conferences, on the other hand, have strict requirements on the format of submissions, including page length. There are a few reasons. For one, the timeline is short. The entire process is deadline-driven, with dates that are set for the initial submission, reviewer feedback, notification (accept or reject), and final submission. The initial submission must be formatted as per the conference requirements (see below), since there is very little time to rework a rough manuscript into the final camera-ready copy that is published.

Another reason for formatting the initial submission is that the responsibility lies with the author(s) to provide the final camera-ready copy that is published. Acceptance usually includes a request for "minor revisions," again, based on referees' suggestions. However, there is little or no vetting of the revisions or of the formatting within the manuscript, in part due to the short timelines. So formatting lies with the author and precedes the initial submission.

Before delving into formatting and presentation, let's examine the major parts of a research paper. The discussion that follows applies to conference or journal submissions that describe a user study.

---

[1] On timelines, see Research versus Engineering versus Design (section 4.1.4 in Chapter 4) for a contrary view.

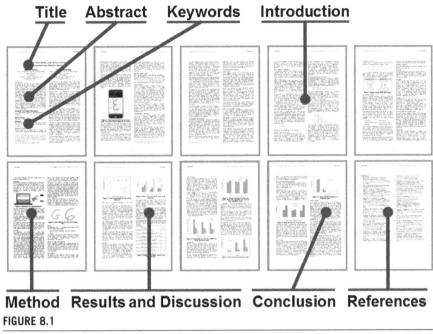

Title   Abstract   Keywords   Introduction

Method   Results and Discussion   Conclusion   References

FIGURE 8.1

Parts of a research paper. The backdrop paper is a 10-page conference contribution by Tinwala and MacKenzie (2010).

8.2 Parts of a research paper

In this section, I decompose a research paper into its constituent parts. For each part, we will examine the objectives and requirements. Figure 8.1 shows the major sections using a 10-page conference paper by Tinwala and MacKenzie (2010) as a backdrop. The text is seen in two columns, as is typical for conference papers. However, this is irrelevant from the perspective of the major sections and the content.

The sections in Figure 8.1 apply to the majority of, but not all, research papers in HCI. The backdrop paper describes a novel interface idea, which was evaluated in a user study. The user study is elaborated in the "Method" and "Results and Discussion" sections. Some HCI research papers do not describe a user study. The annual ACM SIGCHI conference, for example, welcomes other types of submissions, such as "Theory," "Argument," or "Systems, Tools, Architectures and Infrastructure."[2] Although in the minority, such contributions are important to HCI. And it is likely they do not include a user study (although they could). It is worth reiterating the important role of non-experimental research in HCI. However, our discussion here focuses on a traditional HCI research paper with a user study. Let's proceed.

---

[2] These contribution types were noted in the *CHI 2012* submissions web site (http://chi2012.acm.org/cfp-contribution-types.shtml).

8.2.1 Title

Every word tells! A title is short, so every word must contribute. The title must identify the subject area of the paper while at the same time narrowing the scope of the work. The backdrop paper in Figure 8.1 is titled "Eyes-free Text Entry With Error Correction on Touchscreen Mobile Devices." "Eyes-free Text Entry" identifies the subject area, but alone, this is too broad. Adding "With Error Correction" limits the scope of the work. Adding "on Touchscreen Mobiles Devices" further limits the scope. Some discretion is at work here. An overly broad title fails to indicate if the paper is relevant to a sub-topic within a subject area (e.g., error correction techniques as applied to text entry). Furthermore, an overly broad title is misleading. Using only "Eyes-free Text Entry" as the title implies that the work addresses a wider area of research than it actually does.

Titles are often in two parts with a separator (typically a colon) between the main title and a secondary title. There are no rules here. Either part can serve to broaden or narrow the scope of the work. Often the goal is to catch the attention of the reader, perhaps with a provocative claim or phrase; for example, "Silk From a Cow's Ear: Extracting Usable Structures From the Web" (Pirolli, Pitkow, and Rao, 1996). Another trick is to conjure up a name for a novel technique or method and then position the name in the title; for example, "Twitinfo: Aggregating and Visualizing Microblogs for Event Exploration" (Marcus et al., 2011). Combining Twit (for *Twitter*) and info (for information) into Twitinfo has the added benefit of creating a new keyword for future searches. If the aforementioned Twitinfo is adopted in subsequent research, the source is easily retrieved via a search engine using Twitinfo as a search keyword. In short, any title is fine provided it is concise, identifies the subject area, and narrows the scope of the work.

The title is followed by the names of, affiliations with, and contact information for the authors. This information is provided and positioned according to the submission requirements of the conference or journal.

8.2.2 Abstract

The abstract is written last. There is typically a size limit imposed, such as 150 words, so the abstract must be concise. No room to expound! The abstract is a single paragraph and should not include any citations. After the title, the abstract is likely the first part of the research paper that is read. The title has caught someone's interest; the abstract then delivers a succinct summary of the story within. After reading the abstract, the reader will decide if the rest of the paper is relevant and worth reading.

If the abstract is poorly written and fails to deliver on its essential objective (see next paragraph), then the paper has little chance of being read, or even worse, being accepted for publication. So edit, edit, edit. The abstract should be the best-written section of the paper. The English and grammar should be perfect, the content succinct and clear. A poorly written abstract foretells of a tough slog ahead for anyone with the patience to continue reading.

The objective of an abstract is two-fold. The abstract should tell the reader *what was done* and *what was found*. Both themes are highly condensed since the abstract is constrained in size. Nevertheless, this is the abstract's mission. An example of a well-crafted abstract is provided by Sandnes (2006, 245) in a paper titled "Can Spatial Mnemonics Accelerate the Learning of Text Input Chords?":

> *This study addresses to what extent spatial mnemonics can be used to assist users to memorise or infer a set of text input chords. Users mentally visualise the appearance of each character as a 3x3 pixel grid. This grid is input as a sequence of three chords using one, two or three fingers to construct each chord. Experiments show that users are able to use the strategy after a few minutes of instruction, and that some subjects enter text without help after three hours of practice. Further, the experiments show that text can be input at a mean rate of 5.9 words per minute (9.9 words per minute for the fastest subject) after 3 hours of practice. On the downside, the approach suffers from a relatively high error rate of about 10% as subjects often resort to trial and error when recalling character patterns.*

The first three sentences convey the topic of the research and what was done. The last three sentences convey what was found. The abstract is short (144 words). It fulfills its mandate, no more, no less. Note that there is no introductory material. Indeed, an abstract is not the place to introduce the subject matter of the paper. Unfortunately, treating the abstract as an introduction is a common flaw. This point deserves emphasis: *The abstract is not an introduction to the subject matter of the paper.* The reader has read the title and is now examining the abstract for further details. It is reasonable to assume, therefore, that the reader is familiar with the subject matter. Save the introductory material for the Introduction. Another common flaw in abstracts is the failure to give specific results. All too often, abstracts convey general conclusions and note that detailed results and discussions are found in the paper. Not good. Convey the most salient finding(s) in the abstract.

8.2.3 Keywords

Keywords are used for database indexing and searching. They allow others who are interested in the work to find it. Keywords are chosen by the author. They identify the subject matter and the scope of the work. For the backdrop paper in Figure 8.1, the keywords are "Eyes-free, text entry, touchscreen, finger input, gestural input, Graffiti, auditory display, error correction, mobile computing."

Since 1998, research papers published in ACM conference proceedings or journals are required to also include indexing and retrieval information according to the ACM's Computing Classification System (CCS). As the ACM notes, "This is beneficial to you because accurate categorization provides the reader with quick content reference, facilitating the search for related literature, as well as searches for your work in ACM's Digital Library and other online resources."[3] In applying the CCS,

---

[3] www.acm.org/about/class/how-to-use.

Categories and Subject Descriptors
H.5.2 [Information Interfaces and Presentation]: *User Interfaces*
– input devices and strategies (e.g., mouse, touchscreen)
General Terms
Performance, Design, Experimentation, Human Factors

FIGURE 8.2

Example of the ACM Computing Classification System.

research papers include "Categories and Subject Descriptors" and "General Terms."
(For conference submissions, the general terms are optional.) The descriptors and
terms are provided by the ACM, not the author. Since the CCS spans all of computer science, the choices are numerous. The descriptors and terms for the backdrop
paper in Figure 8.1 are shown in Figure 8.2. The terms are taken from the ACM's
CCS, which is available online (see URL in footnote). The formatting shown in
the figure (e.g., brackets, bold, italics) is required and must be strictly followed.
Although choosing descriptors and terms is a challenge, there is an easy way. Just
find a paper on the same or similar topic in the same proceedings or journal as the
paper in preparation and mimic that paper's descriptors and terms. In fact, the ACM
recommends this (see URL in footnote). Of course, care is warranted in the event of
an inappropriate descriptor in a published paper.

8.2.4 Introduction

The opening section of a research paper is typically called *Introduction*, although
other labels, such as *Background*, are fine as well. The introduction gives the context for the research. Usually opening comments characterize the state of the art and
indicate why the subject matter is interesting and relevant. A user interface problem
or challenge is identified and the reader is alerted, early on, to the solution that is
developed in the rest of the paper. It is common practice to give an overview of the
contents of the entire paper, usually at a convenient place within the first page or so
of the introduction. Figure 8.3 is an example from the backdrop paper (Figure 8.1).
The excerpt appears as the fifth paragraph in the introduction.

It is also desirable to state the contribution of the work. This is tricky, since it
entails laying down the bragging rights, so to speak, for a novel aspect of the work.
A statement like, "The approach presented here is the first example of . . ." is strong
but in most cases should be avoided. Usually it is sufficient to note that the idea
improves on existing practice, or something similar.

The introduction may span several sections. Any reasonable organization is fine.
Other sections may use the same level of heading as the introductory section, and
subsections may be added as appropriate. It's your story to tell! Take liberties to
prepare and organize the introduction as you see fit.

Usually a literature review is expected. This is typically organized in a separate
section, with an appropriate heading (e.g., *Related Work*). The literature review dis-
cusses earlier published work related to the subject matter of the research. Points

> In the following section, we briefly describe our original prototype. This is followed with a review of related work on automatic error correction. A redesign of the original prototype is then described followed by details of a user study to test the prototype.

FIGURE 8.3

Provide an overview of the entire paper early in the Introduction.

relevant to the current research are presented. A citation is included for each publication mentioned. Include figures, charts, or tables as appropriate.

The main ideas developed in the paper should be laid out in detail. Use formulas, screen snaps, sketches, or any appropriate visual aid to help the reader understand the solution to a problem that the research presents. The introduction usually finishes with a statement indicating the need to test the idea in an empirical evaluation. This sets the stage for the method section.

8.2.5 Method

The method section of a research paper tells the reader how the experiment was designed and carried out. Although the heading *Method* or *Methodology* is most common, this section is sometimes given other titles, such as *Evaluation, Experiment, User Study*, etc.

The method section should be written in an entirely straightforward fashion. Any creative flair conveyed in the introduction should come to a full stop here. The method section should read like a recipe. The reader wants to know what you did and how you did it. This information must be delivered in a style that is simple, clear, and predictable.

I noted earlier that a critical requirement of research is that it must be reproducible (see section 4.1.3). The method section delivers this crucial property. After reading the method section a reader might ask, "Could this research be reproduced?" If the reader is reviewing the manuscript for a conference or journal and answer is "no" or "I'm not sure," there is little chance of acceptance.

Predictability is important. It allows a reader to scour papers and quickly find key points and results. A reader will lose patience if it is a struggle to determine the independent and dependent variables, the number of participants, the tasks performed by participants, and other important details of the experiment. So keep it simple, make it predictable. On predictability, convention dictates that the method section is divided into the following subsections (and in the following order):

- Participants
- Apparatus
- Procedure
- Design

Let's examine each of these.

8.2.5.1 Participants

The participants section states the number of participants and how they were selected. Relevant demographic information is also given, such as age, gender, and related experience. Other details might be useful, such as level of education, first language, handedness, or whether the participants wore eye glasses or corrective lenses. The details to provide depend on the task and apparatus used in the experiment.

The information on participants identifies the *population* of people used and, therefore, the population to which the results apply. It is reasonable to limit the population pool to people with certain skills or attributes, if it makes sense for the research. An experiment on gaming devices, for example, might only enlist college-age users who play computer games more than 10 hours per week. That's fine, but the results may not generalize to other people.

The participants section is usually short—just a couple of sentences. However, if a property of the user (cf. the interface) is an independent variable, then the participants section is often more detailed. For example, Brajnik et al. (2011) describe an experiment where an independent variable was "expertise in judging websites for accessibility." The experiment included a group of experts and a group of non-experts. The participants section of the paper is quite detailed, as it is necessary to quantify the degree of expertise for both groups and to describe how such was determined and applied.

8.2.5.2 Apparatus

The *Apparatus* section describes the hardware and software. Other titles for this section include *Materials*, *Interface*, etc. Think of reproducibility when preparing this section. Give all the details necessary so that a skilled researcher could replicate the apparatus if he or she chooses. Of course, needless details can be excluded. Mention, perhaps, that the test computer was a Lenovo Thinkpad T60 running Microsoft Windows 7, but the amount of memory or the capacity of the hard drive is likely of no consequence. Some discretion is warranted. If the experimental task involved finger input on a touchscreen, then the make and model of the touchscreen should be given. Other details that might be relevant include the screen resolution, screen size, sampling rate, how the screen was held, or even the participants' finger sizes.

If the experiment used a custom interface, the development language (e.g., Java) and other relevant details should be given. It is particularly useful to provide screen snaps or photos of the interface. If comprehensive details of the interface were disclosed prior to the method section, then it is reasonable to simply refer the reader to the earlier material; for example, "the software included the algorithm described in the preceding section."

8.2.5.3 Procedure

The procedure section tells exactly what happened with each participant. State the instructions given, and indicate if demonstration or practice was used, etc. If

> The feedback mode conditions were counterbalanced using a
> Latin square. Aside from training, the amount of entry was 12
> participants × 3 feedback modes × 3 blocks × 4 phrases/block =
> 432 phrases.

FIGURE 8.4

A calculation reveals the total number of trials in the experiment.

participants completed a questionnaire before or after testing (or both), indicate this in the procedure section. It is also common to indicate if participants were paid, volunteered without pay, or were required to participate, for example, as part of a university course.

Typically, participants are tested over multiple conditions and perhaps multiple trials for each condition. Give the details. Usually there is a specific task that participants performed. Ensure the task is properly defined. What was the task? What was the goal of the task? When did timing begin and end? Were errors recorded? Give a precise definition of what constituted an error. Were participants allowed and instructed to correct errors? Did they correct all errors or only at their discretion? How were errors corrected? Were rest breaks allowed or encouraged? What was the total time for testing with each participant? And so on. Again, a screen snap of the interface may help. It is also useful to include a photograph of a participant performing the task.

8.2.5.4 Design

The design section summarizes the experiment in terms of the independent variables (factors and levels), the dependent variables (measures and units), or other relevant details. For short papers, these details are sometimes given in the procedure section. It is common to begin with a statement such as, "The experiment was a 3 × 2 within-subjects design." If counterbalancing was used, the way the conditions were administered to participants should be stated. Be thorough and clear! It's important that your research is reproducible.

A good way to conclude the design section is to indicate the total number of trials administered in the experiment. This can be revealed by a calculation that includes the number of participants and the variables and repetitions in the study. Figure 8.4 shows how this was done in the backdrop paper (Figure 8.1), which used a text entry task with feedback mode (three levels) as the main independent variable.

8.2.6 Results and discussion

Following the method section, the results of the experiment are given. It is common in HCI to combine the results with discussion. (Sometimes a discussion section follows the results section.) Note also that the heading *Results and Discussion* is at the same level as *Method*. (Results are not part of the method.)

> The mean task completion time for method A was 2.7 seconds. Method B was 9.1% slower with a mean task completion time of 3.0 seconds.

FIGURE 8.5

Reporting results in absolute and relative terms.

If there were outliers or problems in the data collection, state this up front and give details on any filtering of the data that took place before analysis. Before presenting the results it is common to describe the statistical approach and tests used in the data analysis.

Although there are no strict rules, it is common to use subsections that organize the results by dependent measures, beginning with the most important dependent variable. Often this is speed or task completion time. Then results are presented for accuracy or error rate, followed by results for other dependent variables.

For each dependent variable, begin with a broad observation, such as the overall mean, and then move to finer details such as the means for each test condition. The difference in the means between test conditions is the effect size. In HCI, effect size is typically given either as an absolute difference or as a relative difference, expressing the percent difference between one condition and another. Providing the means as absolute values and the difference as a percent is useful since the practical implications of results can be assessed. For example, if the mean task completion time was 3.0 seconds for Method A and 2.7 seconds for Method B, then the result can be presented as in Figure 8.5.

It is important to explain the results through discussion: What caused the differences in the measurements across experimental conditions? What detail in the interaction caused one method to be slower? Did one condition require more input actions? Were participants confused? Was the method hard to learn? Did participants experience fatigue or discomfort? Were corrective actions required as the task was carried out? Obviously the answers lie in the interactions used in the experiment and the observations made by the experimenter or obtained through a post-experiment questionnaire or interview.

There is very likely a difference in the observed dependent measures across experimental conditions. The difference may be real or it may be an artifact of the variability that occurs in experiments with human participants. Of course, finding a real difference is often the goal of the research: a novel interaction method improves on an existing interaction method. "Improves on" usually implies interaction that is faster, more accurate, more efficient, or better in some other quantifiable manner (e.g., fewer re-tries, less movement, higher quality results, etc.). Testing for a real difference typically involves doing an analysis of variance on the data, as described in Chapter 6. The results of this test are given in a succinct statement indicating the outcome. See Figure 6.5 for an example where the difference is real (i.e., statistically significant). See Figure 6.8 for an example where the difference is deemed a random effect (i.e., not statistically significant). In conveying the ANOVA results, bear in mind that the statistical tests are not the results per se. The results lie in the observations and measurements. So avoid characterizing the results in terms of statistics. Of course, finding a statistically significant effect of an independent variable on a dependent variable is important. But the statistical test is simply the supporting evidence. The result is the difference in outcome between the test conditions.

Experimental software is often designed to log a considerable amount of data. Sifting through the data is a daunting task; however, do not feel compelled to share all the data with the reader. Giving too many results or too much data is an indication that you can't distinguish what is important from what is unimportant. A key challenge, then, is deciding on which results to present and which not to present. Furthermore, there is generally no value added in giving results just "for the record." If there is no insight to be gleaned from a result, then don't include it.

Another way to make results interesting for the reader is through visuals. Bar charts, line graphs, 3D plots, or the like appear in most research papers in HCI, with examples appearing throughout this book.

The results and discussion section should compare the results with those in other research papers on a similar topic, citing prior work as appropriate. Is the new technique faster, slower, more accurate, less accurate?

The results and discussion section also summarizes information obtained through questionnaires or interviews given at the end of testing. Participant feedback is often enlightening. Include it. Discuss it. What does participant feedback suggest in terms of improvements to the interaction?

8.2.7 Conclusion

The conclusion summarizes what you did, restates the important findings, and restates the contribution. It is common to identify topics for future work, although developing new ideas is to be avoided in the concluding section.

The conclusion is often followed by an acknowledgment thanking funding sources as well as people who assisted in some way with the research.

8.2.8 References

The last section of a research paper is the reference list. The list contains the full bibliographic details on papers cited earlier in the paper. Only papers cited in the paper are included in the reference list. References should be formatted as stipulated by the conference or journal. Formatting details are discussed in the next section.

8.3 Preparing the manuscript

The experience in reading a research paper should be like the experience in listening to music. Hopefully the music is creative, interesting, and well executed.

Hopefully, as well, the listening experience is free of non-musical artifacts in the playback system or environment, such as static, noise, distractions, or other sounds. Music that is creative and well executed might fail to engage the listener due to these extraneous factors.

Similarly, a research paper seeks to present ideas that are creative and interesting. And the research must be well executed, in accordance with expected standards in the field and as described throughout this book. But there is more. Research that is creative and well executed might fail to engage the reader due to factors aside from the quality of the research. If the reader is distracted due to flaws in the delivery and presentation, he or she may have difficulty following and understanding the ideas. Soon enough, the reader's patience wears thin. So presenting ideas that are creative and well executed is not enough. The story must be properly assembled and presented.

In this section, I present ideas and suggestions on preparing a manuscript. The process is more about transparency than flair: writing in a straightforward style and constructing figures, tables, and other visuals that are simple, clear, and consistent. Easier said than done. But resist any temptation to jazz up the presentation. A research paper is a product of scholarship, not a marketing brochure.

8.3.1 Formatting

Formatting is about the minutia: the punctuation, spelling, capitalization, italics, quotations, abbreviations, numbers, variables, and so on. These properties of a manuscript are important for clarity and flow. The goal is to get the formatting right; actually, perfect. In fact, get it so perfect that the reader won't even notice. Remember, one of the first persons to read the paper will be a reviewer, who will make a recommendation for accepting or rejecting the paper. Will the reviewer critique the paper based on its value and novelty and put aside a confusing presentation or poor formatting that causes him or her to read, then re-read? Perhaps, but this is a chance you don't want to take. It is distinctly possible that a reviewer who struggles with formatting flaws and other distractions will eventually lose patience and render a negative opinion. The goal is to let the story of the research come through.

Formatting rules are too numerous to set out here. Fortunately, there are numerous references to assist. *The Publication Manual of the American Psychological Association* (APA) is recommended (APA, 2010). Chapter 4 in the latest edition (the 6th) is The Mechanics of Style. It contains a wealth of tips, actually *rules*, for formatting manuscripts. There are subsections on small details—proper use of the period, comma, semicolon, colon, double or single quotation marks, parentheses, brackets, slash—and subsections on broader details like capitalization, hyphenation, italics, abbreviations, statistics, and spelling. The APA also has a style website (www.apastyle.org) that is searchable on any topic of interest, including formatting rules.

Of course, a dictionary is also a valuable asset. Reputable dictionaries such as *Merriam-Webster's Collegiate Dictionary* or the *Oxford English Dictionary* are considered the final authority on spelling.[4] For some words there are differences in the American and British spellings (*labor* versus *labour*). Either form is generally accepted provided the choices are applied consistently throughout a manuscript. Dictionaries teach in other ways. A dictionary is a good source to determine if a word is capitalized (*Internet*), hyphenated (*e-mail*), not hyphenated (*online*), set as two words (*screen snap*), or set as a single word (*database*).

To facilitate formatting, conferences provide template files, typically in both Microsoft Word and LaTeX formats. The template embeds many of the formatting requirements such as the margin sizes, fonts for headings and text, line spacing, paragraph spacing, and so on. Generally, the manuscript is prepared directly in a renamed copy of the template file.

The template file also provides instructions and guidance on aspects of the paper under control of the author. These include writing style, the preparation of figures and other visual aids, formatting for citations and references, etc.

8.3.2 Citations and references

Citations and references are the connections that tie research together. Research submissions (e.g., for CHI) have formatting requirements for citations and reference lists. This is one area where HCI conferences generally deviate from the APA guidelines. The following is a quick view into the formatting of citations and references for conference submissions to CHI and many other HCI conferences.

8.3.2.1 Reference list

Figure 8.6 illustrates the formatting for five common types of publications in reference lists in HCI conference proceedings: a conference paper, a journal paper, a book, a chapter in an edited book, and an Internet document.

Citing web pages or documents downloaded from the Internet as the primary source for research is discouraged. However, if a relevant source is only available on the web or as a downloadable document, then it is reasonable to cite it. Unfortunately, there are not yet standardized rules for citing and referencing these sources. The example in Figure 8.6 includes four items: the source (e.g., author or organization), the title (set in italics), the URL, and the date the document was accessed.

The following is a checklist of common formatting rules for reference lists in conference publications:

- References are numbered.
- References are ordered alphabetically by first author's surname.
- For each author, the surname comes first, followed a comma, then the initials for the given names. Include a space between the initials if there is more than one (e.g., "Smith, B. A." not "Smith, B.A.").
- For the title of the publication, only capitalize the first word, the first word in a secondary title (e.g., after a colon), and proper nouns.

---

[4]Online versions are at www.merriam-webster.com/dictionary and http://oxforddictionaries.com.

1. Aula, A., Khan, R. M., and Guan, Z., How does search behavior change as search becomes more difficult? *Proceedings of the ACM SIGCHI Conference on Human Factors in Computing Systems - CHI 2010*, (New York: ACM, 2010), 35-44.

    Conference paper

2. Brajnik, G., Yesilada, Y., and Harper, S., The expertise effect of web accessibility *evaluation methods, Human-Computer Interaction*, 26, 2011, 246-283.

    Journal paper

3. Brown, T., *Change by design: How design thinking transforms organizations and inspires innovation*. New York: HarperCollins, 2009.

    Book

4. Buxton, W., There's more to interaction than meets the eye: Some issues in manual input, in *User centered system design: New perspectives on human-computer interaction*, (D. A. Norman and S. W. Draper, Eds.). Hillsdale, NJ: Erlbaum, 1986, 319-337.

    Chapter in book

5. ESA, *Electronic Software Association, Industry facts*, http://www.theesa.com/facts/, (accessed February 4, 2012).

    Internet document

FIGURE 8.6

Formatting examples for common types of publications in a reference list in a conference proceedings.

- Always include the year. Substitute "in press" for accepted but not-yet-published papers.
- Always include page numbers (except for complete books or web pages).
- The name of the publication is set in italics with all keywords capitalized (e.g., *Proceedings of the ACM SIGCHI Conference on Human Factors in Computing Systems—CHI 2011*).
- For journal publications, include the volume number in italics.
- If space permits, use the full name for conferences and journals. If space is tight, use abbreviated names for conferences and journals (e.g., *Proc CHI '99*). Do not mix full and abbreviated names; use one style or the other. If using abbreviated names, be consistent.
- Give the location and name of the publisher for conference papers and books (e.g., "New York: ACM"). Use the most economical yet understandable expression of the location (e.g., "New York," not "New York: NY"; but use "Cambridge: MA") and publisher (e.g., "Springer" not "Springer Publishing Company").
- Use *align left* (ragged right) for the reference list. (Note: The rest of the manuscript is justified.)
- Only include works that are cited in papers.
- Study and imitate!
- Be consistent.

8.3.2.2 Citations

Citations connect current research with prior research or other sources. Most commonly for conference submissions, citations appear as numbers in brackets. The following are examples and tips for correctly citing prior work.

A basic citation:

> A previous experiment [5] confirmed that...

Group multiple citations together. Separate the numbers with a comma followed by a space. Preface the list with "e.g.," but only if there are additional known sources supporting the same point:

> Our results are consistent with previous findings [e.g., 5, 7, 12].

Do not treat citations as nouns:

> It was proposed in [5] that...   *** Incorrect ***
> It was proposed by Smith and Jones [5] that...   *** Correct ***

There is an exception to this rule. When it is inside parentheses, a citation may serve as a noun:

> There are many user studies on this topic (see [6] for a review).

Quotations require a citation with a page number:

> Smith and Jones argue, "the primary purpose of research is publication" [14, p. 125].

If citing a specific point from a book, include the page number. If the point spans several pages, indicate the range, as shown here:

> Norman defines six categories of slips [15, pp. 105-110].

If a paper is referred to by author(s), cite the first author followed by "et al." (Latin for "and others") if there are three or more authors:

> Douglas et al. [5] describe an empirical evaluation using an isometric joystick.

Alternatively, include all the authors' names for the first appearance of the citation and use "et al." for subsequent appearances. Of course, all the authors' names appear in the reference list.

It is worth the effort to get the citations and references correct. Thompson Reuters' *EndNote* (www.endnote.com) is a tool that greatly simplifies that task. It works with a bibliographic database and a plug-in for word processors such as Microsoft Word. With EndNote, inserting a citation is as simple as copy (from the database) and paste (at the desired location in the manuscript). Formatting the bibliography is typically done by an option in the Tools menu or EndNote ribbon. The process formats both the citations within the manuscript and the references list at the end. Numerous styles are included with EndNote and they are easy to customize according to the submission requirements of a conference or journal.

8.3.3 Visual aids

Visual aids are powerful tools for conveying ideas and results. Few areas in experimental research have gained more from technological advances than the methods and tools for displaying results. Charts, tables, graphs, drawings, and photographs are now fully in the digital domain, with sophisticated tools for editing and stylizing the presentation.[5]

One of the most common results to present is the effect of an independent variable on a dependent variable. A bar chart is usually the most appropriate format, since most independent variables are nominal-scale attributes. An example is shown in Figure 8.7a. The chart shows the results of Zhu et al.'s experiment on teleoperation (Zhu, Gedeon, and Taylor, 2011). Participants used a scene camera while manipulating a robot arm to nudge rocks into a hole. The independent variable was camera control model (manual, natural, auto). The dependent variable was the number of rocks sunk in a specified time interval. As seen in the figure, the natural model performed best. (This was confirmed in an analysis of variance.) Note the presence of error bars. Error bars are an important reminder to the reader of variability in human responses. However, error bars add little insight unless they are appropriately labeled, for example, in the figure's caption (which was not the case in Zhu et al.'s paper).

If the variable shown along the *x*-axis is continuous, then a line chart is appropriate. In Zhu et al.'s experiment on teleoperation, participants proceeded under a time constraint. An additional result was provided on the number of rocks sunk in each of three 60-second intervals. (See Figure 8.7b.) The lines between intervals convey a sense of continuity as the experiment trials progressed.

Well before the Results and Discussion section, visuals are an important adjunct to text. Visuals can clarify concepts about the research or the technical details of an apparatus. In preparing a manuscript, try to find opportunities to assist the reader wherever possible. The methodology in particular can benefit from a judicious and targeted use of visuals. A powerful way to augment the procedure section of a research paper is through a photograph of a participant performing the experiment

---

[5]Of course, hand drawn sketches maintain a special appeal (see Figure 3.46 or Figure 7.5).

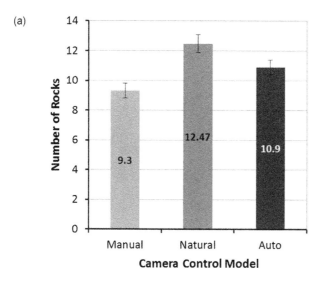

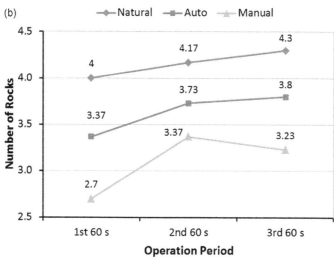

FIGURE 8.7

Charts presenting results: (a) Bar chart for categorical data. (b) Line chart for continuous data.

(Adapted from Zhu et al., 2011)

task. Two examples are shown in Figure 8.8. Part (a) shows a participant performing an eyes-free task with auditory feedback (Tinwala and MacKenzie, 2008). Part (b) is an experiment that involves Lego construction and identification (Ranjan, Birnholtz, and Balakrishnan, 2007). The photos help a reader understand the nuisances of the experiment task.

(a) (b)

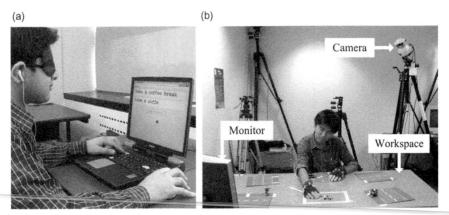

FIGURE 8.8

Photographs of experimental tasks: (a) Eyes-free input with auditory feedback (Tinwala and MacKenzie, 2008). (b) Lego construction and identification (Ranjan et al., 2007).

(Photo courtesy of Abhishek Ranjan)

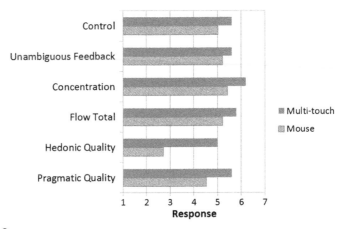

FIGURE 8.9

A chart summarizing participant responses from a questionnaire on target acquisition using multi-touch versus a mouse.

(Adapted from Leftheriotis and Chorianopoulos, 2011)

Summaries of Likert-scale questionnaire items may be presented as shown in Figure 8.9 (Leftheriotis and Chorianopoulos, 2011). The chart shows participants' impressions in a target acquisition task using multi-touch and a mouse. Seven is the most favorable response. Clearly participants preferred multi-touch, as this condition was rated higher on all items. The difference was particularly pronounced in the item about hedonic quality (pleasure) with scores of 5.1 for multi-touch compared to 2.8 for the mouse. A visual presentation, as here, helps the reader understand the results both in absolute and relative terms.

8.3.4 Writing for clarity

The goal in writing a research paper is communication. Effective communication demands clarity: "a clear mind attacking a clearly stated problem and producing clearly stated conclusions" (Day and Gastel, 2006, pp. 3–4). Clarity comes with economy—saying what needs to be said and little else. This theme appears in the ACM SIGCHI's template for research papers.[6] The template includes a section called "Language, Style, and Content," with recommendations organized in a bulleted list. The list begins:

- Write in a straightforward style.
- Avoid long or complex sentence structures.

So the goal in writing a research paper is to organize and deliver the story of the research in sentences that are simple and straightforward. This seems simple and straightforward. But it isn't. Writing with clarity and economy is a challenge that is never fully achieved. Even the most seasoned researcher continuously struggles to express ideas in the clearest and most succinct way possible. The guard must never be down, lest the prose enlarge and swell.

Writing with clarity is both a craft and an art. The craft is driven by rules, rigor, and precision. The art is creative, engaging human qualities such as imagination, inspiration, ingenuity, and originality. Succeeding at both, and with a balance that retains economy while delivering style, is a challenge. However, unlike fictional writing, the balance for scholarly writing leans toward craft. In scholarly writing, clarity trumps all.

It is outside the scope of this book to teach either the craft or art of scholarly writing. The topics include sentence structure, grammar, tense, flow, tone, continuity, economy of expression, and so on. It is a huge assignment. Besides, excellent sources on these and related themes already exist. Four sources are recommended below. The first three address scholarly writing as well as the methodology in experimental research. The fourth is the classic "Strunk and White," first published in 1919. At 105 pages, it packs more punch per page than any other source on writing style. It is not to be passed over.

1. The APA's *Publication Manual of the American Psychological Association* (APA, 2010)
2. Day and Gastel's *How to Write and Publish a Scientific Paper* (Day and Gastel, 2006)
3. Martin's *Doing Psychology Experiments* (D. W. Martin, 2004)
4. Strunk and White's *The Elements of Style* (Strunk and White, 2000)

---

[6] http://chi2012.acm.org/CHI2012USpaperformat.doc.

Original	Revised
In order to do this	To do this
Should be able to understand	Should understand
The software used was our	The software was our
Stacking objects one on top of the other	Stacking objects
Prior gaming experience	Gaming experience
With this goal in mind	With this in mind
Two paths that can be taken to reach the	Two paths to the
The selection was made based on	The selection was based on
The use of the homing keys helps	Homing keys help
The top five most frequent letters	The five most frequent letters
The rate at which the cursor moves	The rate the cursor moves
The ESC key on the keyboard	The ESC key
Each of the participants	Each participant
Can be used to show	Can show
The average value can be calculated as	The average is
When they were ready	When ready
It is worth mentioning that the number of	Notably, the number of
For the sake of consistency	For consistency
The number of keys the user has to press	The number of key presses
The time it takes to compose a message	The time to compose a message
Users who prefer to use the keyboard	Users who prefer the keyboard
This is not a recommended idea	This is not recommended
Three types of interaction techniques	Three interaction techniques
Should be able to quickly adapt	Should quickly adapt
At any given time	At any time
To the best of our knowledge	To our knowledge
The movement time required to	The movement time to
For the purpose of improving text entry	For improving text entry
Because the selection operation requires	Because selection requires
Sorted in the order of their similarity	Sorted by similarity
Is done using	Uses
The time taken to complete the task	The time to complete the task
Was developed in an attempt to	Was developed to
One point to note is that	Note that
Two different methods of input are	Two methods of input are
We ran an exploratory pilot study	We ran a pilot study
At their own discretion	At their discretion
Studies conducted in the past have found	Studies have found

FIGURE 8.10

Omit needless words.

There is one strategy leading to clarity of expression that I will dwell on in the closing paragraphs. It is, in this author's view, the single most powerful technique for transforming a loosely written manuscript into a succinct and clear research paper. The technique is simple: get rid of clutter.

If clarity is the prize, clutter is the curse. A profusion of words that fills space but adds nothing is certain to suffocate any research paper. Without doubt, the reader who faces a stream of added useless words will quickly tire. The superfluous words demand the reader's attention—so as not to miss a point—but in the end they encumber rather than enlighten. Every source on writing style has a take on this subject. Strunk and White's Rule #17 is to Omit Needless Words: "A sentence should contain no unnecessary words, a paragraph no unnecessary sentences, for the same reason that a drawing should have no unnecessary lines and a machine no unnecessary parts" (Strunk and White, 2000, p. 23). The APA's *Publication Manual* is more pedantic: "You can tighten long papers by eliminating redundancy, wordiness, jargon, evasiveness, overuse of the passive voice, circumlocution, and clumsy prose" (APA, 2010, p. 67).

A sampling of edits in view of Strunk and White's Rule #17 is found in Figure 8.10. The examples are real. They are from a much larger collection compiled by this book's author over many years while editing, co-authoring, or reviewing HCI manuscripts. In each case, redundant words are removed. The revised phrase is succinct. It delivers the same point with less energy demanded of the reader.

There is little to gain in analyzing each revision in Figure 8.10. Perhaps one observation is worthwhile, however: user studies that are written about in the past tense have already been *conducted*. Furthermore, they were conducted *in the past*. See the last example in the figure. Yes, every sentence should be parsed in this manner. Break it down. Get rid of every word that fails to contribute. The result is clarity and economy—a better manuscript.

When preparing the initial draft of a manuscript, relax. First and foremost, get the words and ideas down and into the manuscript. It would be nice if the editing that produced the revisions in Figure 8.10 surfaced in the first draft. But this is not likely and it needn't be attempted. Few writers are gifted enough to produce crisp prose in the first pass. So don't struggle to make the initial draft the final draft. But before submitting the manuscript, give it every ounce of editing that time permits. The reviewers will appreciate it, and the result may ultimately—and hopefully—achieve that final and essential step in research: a publication. Congratulations and good luck.

STUDENT EXERCISES

8-1. Use Google Scholar or the ACM Digital Library to locate several research papers from a recent conference proceedings. Study the abstracts to determine if they are succinctly and clearly written and if they convey what was done and what was found in the research. Choose two of the abstracts (perhaps the best and worst) and prepare a brief report or presentation on your analysis. Suggest improvements, as appropriate.

8-2. Design and administer a questionnaire to a group of people (participants). Collect data on characteristics of the participants and aspects of their interaction with technology. Analyze the data and write a report outlining the topic (Introduction), the methodology (Method) and the results (Results and Discussion).

Participants are drawn (ideally, at random) from a population. For this exercise, use a sample of university students or another population conveniently available, such as people at a local shopping mall or metro station or in the neighborhood where you live.

Narrow the population as appropriate. For example, if there is an interest in Apple Mac users, Twitter users, or people over the age of 50, then screen candidates and use only those from the desired population. Use at least 25 participants.

The participants may be given the questionnaire to complete. Alternatively, use an interview style and interact directly with participants. In the latter case, more reliable information is obtained since participants are more engaged and can ask for clarification.

So what data are of interest? A questionnaire usually begins by asking simple demographic information such as age and gender. Also solicit more specific information relevant to the topic, such as first language spoken, number of hours per day using a computer, hours per day playing video games, preferred browser (IE versus Firefox), preferred computer type (Mac versus PC), number of tweets sent per day, preferred texting method (multi-tap versus *T9*), estimated typing speed, and so on. There are numerous possibilities. Try to think of interesting relationships and ways to summarize, group, and graph the data.

Try to venture beyond the examples above. Remember, this is your research project! What other relationships are there? Do Faculty of Arts students differ from Faculty of Science students in . . . ? Does age or gender make a difference in . . . ? Do left-handed people prefer . . . ? Is the number of text messages sent per day related to . . . ? Are mobile phone users more likely to . . . ? Which pointing device do users of notebook computers prefer? Are people more likely to answer an incoming phone call if it is from a friend compared to a parent or co-worker? Is the latter behavior more prominent for males than females? Is there an age effect? Are Starbucks devotees more likely to use an iPod than customers at Timothy's? Are people with body piercings more likely to prefer a Mac to a PC?

Sounds like fun, right? Sure, but relationships need a plausible explanation. For example, it is unlikely people who wear glasses differ in their texting habits from people who don't wear glasses. But who knows? If a relationship such as this is investigated, that's fine, but develop a plausible reason for the difference (and include it in your report). If, in the end, the relationship sought doesn't surface, that's fine, too. But an explanation is necessary. Hint: use Google Scholar to determine if other researchers have investigated a similar topic. You may be surprised by what you find.

Think about the way information is gathered in the questionnaire. Do not ask participants their names. Instead, give each one a code (P1, P2, P3, . . .). Simple nominal-scale, or categorical, data are gathered as follows:

> What is your gender?   ☐ male ☐ female

If there is interest in knowing how many hours per day participants use a computer, the questionnaire could include

> Please indicate your computer usage:
> ☐ <2 hrs/day   ☐ 2-5 hrs/day
> ☐ 5-10 hrs/day   ☐ >10 hrs/day

Gathered in this manner, the responses are tabulated as counts, or number of respondents, per category. These data are useful to show categorical relationships such as computer usage (low, medium, high, very high) versus gender (male, female). Such data are organized in a contingency table and examined with a chi-square test (see section 6.2).

The same information is available as follows:

> How many hours per day do you use a computer? _____

Responses formed in this manner are examples of ratio-scale data. Provided there is a second ratio-scale characteristic, such as age, the degree of correlation (r) between the two variables can be shown. Also, a prediction equation can be built where one variable is predicted from the other (see section 7.2.1).

A 5-point Likert scale can be used with a preamble such as "Please indicate your level of agreement to the following statements." Here's an example:

> Mobile phone use should be banned during university lectures?
>
> | 1 | 2 | 3 | 4 | 5 |
> |---|---|---|---|---|
> | Strongly disagree | Mildly disagree | Neutral | Mildly agree | Strongly agree |

Are males or females more likely to agree with this statement? Who knows, but this student exercise—along with a chi-square test, provides a mechanism to find out.

For the report, use the standard two-column conference format, using the ACM SIGCHI conference submissions template. The final formatted report should be three or four pages and include citations and references to at least four papers.

8-3. Recruit 10 participants for a study on text entry. The study will use a paper mock-up of two soft keyboards. Prepare a handout sheet containing images of two keyboards. The top half of the sheet contains the heading "Method A," with a phrase of text below. Use "the quick brown fox jumps over the lazy dog." Below the phrase appears the keyboard. The bottom half of the sheet contains the heading "Method B," with same phrase below, and with a different keyboard below that. The general idea is shown below:

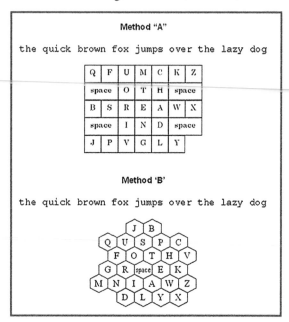

For the two keyboards, use the Qwerty and Opti layouts in Figure 7.35 or any other layouts of interest. (The Metropolis layout by Hunter et al. [2000] is shown in the figure above.) Another possibility is to use two sizes of the same keyboard layout. (Is entry speed faster on the larger keyboard or the smaller keyboard?) Ask participants to enter the phrase by tapping on the keyboard image using a non-marking stylus. They are to enter the phrase five times on one keyboard, then five times on the other keyboard. Use a watch or other timing device to record the entry time for each phrase. Enter the times on a log sheet. Divide the participants into two groups and counterbalance the order of testing (see section 5.11). After testing is complete, enter the data into a spreadsheet. Convert the entry time t (in seconds) to entry speed s (in words per minute) using:

$$s = \left(\frac{43}{5}\right) / \left(\frac{60}{t}\right)$$

where $43/5$ is the number of words and $60/t$ is the number of minutes. Analyse the data for significant effects using an analysis of variance, as outlined in Chapter 6. For the purpose of the ANOVA, the experiment has three independent variables: layout (A, B), phrase iteration (1, 2, 3, 4, 5), and group (AB, BA).

Write a research paper for the experiment, following the guidelines in this chapter. Use the standard two-column conference format, using the ACM SIGCHI conference submissions template. The final formatted report should be three or four pages. Include citations and references to at least four papers (e.g., research papers on soft keyboard layouts).

8-4. Recruit 10 participants for a study on text entry. Use a procedure similar to that described in the student exercise above. However, instead of using paper mock-ups, use the `SoftKeyboardExperiment` software provided on this book's website. The software supports five software keyboard layouts, as identified in the setup dialog (see below). Use any two. A screen snap of the experiment task is shown below. Note that data collection is automated in the software and includes additional dependent measures such as error rate and keystrokes per character (*KSPC*). Consult the API for further details.

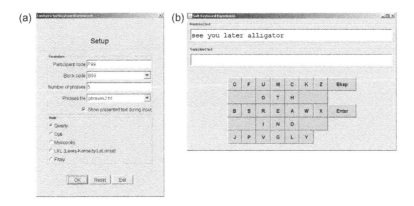

Write a research paper for the experiment following the guidelines in this chapter. Use the standard two-column conference format, using the ACM SIGCHI conference submissions template. The final formatted report should be three or four pages. Include citations and references to at least four papers (e.g., research papers on soft keyboard layouts).

8-5. How accurate are users in estimating their typing speed? Conduct a small experiment investigating this question. Recruit 10 participants and administer a brief questionnaire to each. Include a question asking them to estimate their typing speed on a desktop computer in words per minute. Then measure their typing speed using the `TypingTestExperiment` software provided on this book's website. The setup dialog and a screen snap of the experiment procedure are given below:

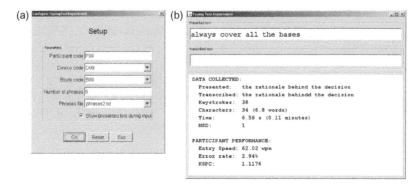

Configure the software for 10 phrases of entry. Compare the users' estimations with the observed typing speeds. Write a brief report on your findings.

References

Abrahams, P. (1987 November). President's letter: A farewell to NCC. *Communications of the ACM*, 899.

Accot, J., & Zhai, S. (2001). Refining Fitts' law models for bivariate pointing. *Proceedings of the ACM SIGCHI Conference on Human Factors in Computing Systems—CHI 2001*. New York: ACM. 193–200.

ACM. (2012). TOCHI author information. Retrieved 7 February 2012, from <http://tochi.acm.org/authors.shtml>.

Ahmed, S. A., & Stuerzlinger, W. (2010). Predicting the cost of error correction in character-based text entry technologies. *Proceedings of the ACM SIGCHI Conference on Human Factors in Computing Systems—CHI 2010*. New York: ACM. 5–14.

Akamatsu, M., MacKenzie, I. S., & Hasbrouq, T. (1995). A comparison of tactile, auditory, and visual feedback in a pointing task using a mouse-type device. *Ergonomics*, *38*, 816–827.

Al Hajri, A., Fels, S., Miller, G., & Ilich, M. (2011). Moving target selection in 2D graphical user interfaces. *Proceedings of INTERACT 2011*. Berlin: Springer. 141–161.

Ali, H., Scholer, F., Thom, J. A., & Wu, M. (2009). User interaction with novel web search interfaces. *Proceedings of OZCHI 2009*. New York: ACM. 301–304.

Almeida, R., & Cubaud, P. (2006). Supporting 3D window manipulation with a yawing mouse. *Proceedings of the Fourth Nordic Conference on Human-Computer Interaction—NordiCHI 2006*. New York: ACM. 477–480.

Almeida, R., & Cubaud, P. (2007). Nearly-integral manipulation of rotary widgets. *Proceedings of INTERACT 2007*. Berlin: Springer. 489–492.

APA, (2010). *Publication Manual of the American Psychological Association* (6th ed.). Washington, DC: APA.

Appert, C., Chapuis, O., & Pietriga, E. (2012). Dwell-and-spring: Undo for direct manipulation. *Proceedings of the ACM SIGCHI Conference on Human Factors in Computing Systems—CHI 2012*. New York: ACM. 1957–1966.

Argelaguet, R., & Andujar, C. (2008). Improving 3D selection in VEs through expanding targets and forced disocclusion. *Proceedings of the Nineth International Symposium on Smart Graphics—SG 2008*. Berlin: Springer. 45–57.

Arnault, L. Y., & Greenstein, J. S. (1990). Is display/control gain a useful metric for optimizing an interface? *Human Factors*, *32*, 651–663.

Arthur, K. (2008a). The Blackberry Storm's three-state screen. Retrieved 9 October 2008, from <http://www.touchusability.com/blog/2008/10/9/the-blackberry-storms-three-state-touchscreen.html>.

Arthur, K. (2008b). Three-state touch: Now Apple has it too! Retrieved 18 October 2008, from <http://www.touchusability.com/blog/2008/10/14/three-state-touch-now-apple-has-it-too.html>.

Asakawa, C., & Takagi, H. (2007). Text entry for people with visual impairments. In I. S. MacKenzie & K. Tanaka-Ishii (Eds.), *Text entry systems: Mobility, accessibility, universality* (pp. 304–318). San Francisco: Morgan Kaufmann.

Aula, A., Khan, R. M., & Guan, Z. (2010). How does search behavior change as search becomes more difficult?. *Proceedings of the ACM SIGCHI Conference on Human Factors in Computing Systems—CHI 2010*. New York: ACM. 35–44.

Ayyavu, P., & Jensen, C. (2011). Integrating user feedback with heuristic security and privacy management systems. *Proceedings of the ACM SIGCHI Conference in Human Factors in Computing Systems—CHI 2011*. New York: ACM. 2305–2314.

Baecker, R., Grudin, J. T., Buxton, W., & Greenberg, S. (1995). *Readings in Human-Computer Interaction: Toward the year 2000*. San Francisco: Morgan Kaufmann.

Bailey, R. W. (1996). *Human Performance Engineering: Designing High Quality, Professional User Interfaces for Computer Products, Applications, and Systems* (3rd ed.). Upper Saddle River, NJ: Prentice Hall.

Balakrishnan, R., Baudel, T., Kurtenbach, G., & Fitzmaurice, G. (1997). The Rockin'mouse: Integral 3D manipulation on a plane. *Proceedings of the ACM SIGCHI Conference on Human Factors in Computing Systems—CHI '97*. New York: ACM. 311–318.

Balakrishnan, R., & MacKenzie, I. S. (1997). Performance differences in the fingers, wrist, and forearm in computer input control. *Proceedings of the ACM SIGCHI Conference on Human Factors in Computing Systems—CHI '97*. New York: ACM. 303–310.

Balakrishnan, R., & Patel, P. (1998). The PadMouse: Facilitating selection and spatial positioning for the non-dominant hand. *Proceedings of the ACM SIGCHI Conference on Human Factors in Computing Systems—CHI '98*. New York: ACM. 9–16.

Bälter, O. (2000). Keystroke level analysis of email message organization. *Proceedings of the ACM SIGCHI Conference on Human Factors in Computing Systems—CHI 2000*. New York: ACM. 105–112.

Banovic, N., Li, F. C. Y., Dearman, D., Yatani, K., & Truong, K. N. (2011). Design of unimanual multi-finger pie menu interaction. *Proceedings of the ACM International Conference on Interactive Tabletops and Surfaces—ITS 2011*. New York: ACM. 120–129.

Barrett, R. C., Selker, E. J., Rutledge, J. D., & Olyha, R. S. (1995). Negative inertia: A dynamic pointing function. *Companion Proceedings of the ACM SICGHI Conference on Human Factors in Computing Systems—CHI '95*. New York: ACM. 316–317.

Bartlett, J. F. (2000 May/June). Rock 'n scroll is here to stay. *IEEE Computer Graphics and Applications*, 40–45.

Bartneck, C., Verbunt, M., Mubin, O., & Mahmud, A. A. (2007). To kill a mockingbird robot. *Proceedings of the ACM/IEEE International Conference on Human-Robot Interaction—HRI 2007*. New York: ACM. 81–87.

Baudisch, P., Cutrell, E., Hinckley, K., & Eversole, A. (2005). Snap-and-go: Helping users align objects without the modality of traditional snapping. *Proceedings of the ACM SIGCHI Conference on Human Factors in Computing Systems—CHI 2005*. New York: ACM. 301–310.

Beaudouin-Lafon, M. (2000). Instrumental interaction: An interaction model for designing post-WIMP user interfaces. *Proceedings of the ACM SIGCHI Conference in Human Factors in Computing Systems—CHI 2000*. New York: ACM. 446–453.

Belia, S., Fidler, F., Williams, J., & Cumming, G. (2005). Researchers misunderstand confidence intervals and standard error bars. *Psychological Methods*, *10*, 389–396.

Bellman, T., & MacKenzie, I. S. (1998). A probabilistic character layout strategy for mobile text entry. *Proceedings of Graphics Interface '98*. Toronto: Canadian Information Processing Society. 168–176.

Bickmore, T. W., & Picard, R. W. (2004). Towards caring machines. *Extended Abstracts of the ACM SIGCHI Conference on Human Factors in Computing Systems—CHI 2004*. New York: ACM. 1489–1492.

Blanch, R., Guiard, Y., & Beaudouin-Lafon, M. (2004). Semantic pointing: Improving target acquisition with control-display ratio adaptation. *Proceedings of the ACM SIGCHI*

Conference on Human Factors in Computing Systems—CHI 2004. New York: ACM. 519–526.

Bodnar, A., Corbett, R., & Nekrasovski, D. (2004). AROMA: Ambient awareness through olfaction in a messaging application. *Proceedings of the 6th International Conference on Multimodal Interfaces.* New York: ACM. 183–190.

Borman, L. (1996, January). SICGHI: The early years. *SIGCHI Bulletin,* 4–6.

Bouch, A., Kuchinsky, A., & Bhatti, N. (2000). Quality is in the eye of the beholder: Meeting users' requirements for internet quality of service. *Proceedings of the ACM SIGCHI Conference on Human Factors in Computing Systems—CHI 2000.* New York: ACM. 297–304.

Brajnik, G., Yesilada, Y., & Harper, S. (2011). The expertise effect of web accessibility evaluation methods. *Human-Computer Interaction, 26,* 246–283.

Brewster, S. A., McGookin, D., & Miller, C. (2006). Olfoto: Designing a smell-based interaction. *Proceedings of the ACM SIGCHI Conference on Human Factors in Computing Systems—CHI 2006.* New York: ACM. 653–662.

Brewster, S. A., Wright, P. C., & Edwards, A. D. N. (1994). The design and evaluation of an auditory-enhanced scrollbar. *Proceedings of the ACM SIGCHI Conference on Human Factors in Computing Systems—CHI '94.* New York: ACM. 173–179.

Brooks, F. P., Jr., Ouh-Young, M., Batter, J. J., & Kilpatrick, P. J. (1990). Project GROPE— Haptic displays for scientific visualization. *Computer Graphics, 24*(2), 177–185.

Brown, T. (2008, June). Design thinking. *Harvard Business Review,* 1–9.

Brown, T. (2009). *Change by Design: How Design Thinking Transforms Organizations and Inspires Innovation.* New York: Harper Collins.

Buck, L. (1980). Motor performance in relation to control-display gain and target width. *Ergonomics, 23,* 579–589.

Burtnyk, N., Khan, A., Fitzmaurice, G., Balakrishnan, R., & Kurtenbach, G. (2002). StyleCam: Interactive stylized 3D navigation using integrated spatial and temporal controls. *Proceedings of the ACM Symposium on User Interface Software and Technology— UIST 2002.* New York: ACM. 101–110.

Bush, V. (1945, July). As we may think. *The Atlantic Monthly,* 101–108 (reprinted in the ACM's *interactions,* March 1996).

Buxton, W. (1983, January). Lexical and pragmatic considerations of input structures. *Computer Graphics,* 31–37.

Buxton, W. (1986). There's more to interaction than meets the eye: Some issues in manual input. In D. A. Norman & S. W. Draper (Eds.), *User Centered System Design: New Perspectives on Human-Computer Interaction* (pp. 319–337). Hillsdale, NJ: Erlbaum.

Buxton, W. (1990). A three-state model of graphical input. *Proceedings of the IFIP TC13 Third International Conference on Human-Computer Interaction—INTERACT '90.* Amsterdam: Elsevier. 449–456.

Buxton, W., Hill, R., & Rowley, P. (1985). Issues and techniques in touch-sensitive tablet input. *Proceedings of SIGGRAPH '85.* New York: ACM. 215–224.

Buxton, W., & Myers, B. A. (1986). A study in two-handed input. *Proceedings of the ACM SIGCHI Conference on Human Factors in Computing Systems—CHI '87.* New York: ACM. 321–326.

Byrne, M. D., Anderson, J. R., Douglass, S., & Matessa, M. (1999). Eye tracking the visual search of click-down menus. *Proceedings of the ACM SIGCHI Conference on Human Factors in Computing Systems—CHI '99.* New York: ACM. 402–409.

Callahan, J., Hopkins, D., Weiser, M., & Shneiderman, B. (1988). An empirical comparison of pie vs. linear menus. *Proceedings of the ACM SIGCHI Conference on Human Factors in Computing Systems—CHI '88*. New York: ACM. 95–100.

Caniard, F., & Fleming, R. W. (2007). Distortion in 3D shape estimation with changes in illumination. *Proceedings of the Fourth Symposium on Applied Perception in Graphics and Visualization—APGV 2007*. New York: ACM. 99–105.

Cao, X., Li, J. J., & Balakrishnan, R. (2008). Peephole pointing: Modeling acquisition of dynamically revealed targets. *Proceedings of the ACM SIGCHI Conference on Human Factors in Computing System—CHI 2008*. New York: ACM. 1699–1708.

Card, S. K. (1982). User perceptual mechanisms in the search of computer command menus. *Proceedings of Human Factors in Computer Systems*. New York: ACM. 190–196.

Card, S. K., English, W. K., & Burr, B. J. (1978). Evaluation of mouse, rate-controlled isometric joystick, step keys, and text keys for text selection on a CRT. *Ergonomics, 21*, 601–613.

Card, S. K., Mackinlay, J. D., & Robertson, G. G. (1991). A morphological analysis of the design space of input devices. *ACM Transactions on Office Information Systems, 9*, 99–122.

Card, S. K., Moran, T. P., & Newell, A. (1980). Computer text-editing: An information-processing analysis of a routine cognitive skill. *Cognitive Psychology, 12*, 32–74.

Card, S. K., Moran, T. P., & Newell, A. (1980, July). The keystroke-level model for user performance time with interactive systems. *Communications of the ACM, 23*, 396–410.

Card, S. K., Moran, T. P., & Newell, A. (1983). *The Psychology of Human-Computer Interaction*. Hillsdale, NJ: Erlbaum.

Carroll, J. M., & Thomas, J. C. (1982). Metaphor and the cognitive representation of computing systems. *IEEE Transactions on Systems Man and Cybernetics, 12*, 107–116.

Casey, S. M. (1998). *Set Phasers on Stun: And Other True Tales of Design, Technology, and Human Error* (2nd ed.). Santa Barbara, CA: Aegean Publishing Company.

Casey, S. M. (2006). *The Atomic Chef: And Other True Tales of Design, Technology, and Human Error*. Santa Barbara, CA: Aegean Publishing Company.

Casiez, G., Vogel, D., Pan, Q., & Chaillou, C. (2007). RubberEdge: Reducing clutching by combining position and rate control with elastic feedback. *Proceedings of the ACM Symposium on user Interface Software and Technology—UIST 2007*. New York: ACM. 129–138.

Castellucci, S. J., & MacKenzie, I. S. (2008). Graffiti vs. Unistrokes: An empirical comparison. *Proceedings of the ACM SIGCHI Conference on Human Factors in Computing Systems—CHI 2008*. New York: ACM. 305–308.

Chapanis, A. (1965). *Man-machine engineering*. Belmont, CA: Wadsworth Publishing Company.

Chen, C. H., & Chien, Y. H. (2005). Reading Chinese text on a small screen with RSVP. *Displays, 26*, 103–108.

Chin, J., & Fu, W. T. (2010). Interactive effects of age and interface difference on search strategies and performance. *Proceedings of the ACM SIGCHI Conference on Human Factors in Computing Systems—CHI 2010*. New York: ACM. 403–412.

Chin, J., Fu, W. T., & Kannampallil, T. (2009). Adaptive information search: Age-dependent interactions between cognitive profiles and strategies. *Proceedings of the ACM SIGCHI Conference on Human Factors in Computing Systems—CHI 2009*. New York: ACM. 1683–1692.

Chung, K., & Hossain, L. (2008). Network structure, position, ties and ICT use in distributed knowledge-intensive work. *Proceedings of the ACM Conference on Computer Supported Cooperative Work—CSCW 2008*. New York: ACM. 545–554.

Clarkson, E., Clawson, J., Lyons, K., & Starner, T. (2005). An empirical study of typing rates on mini-Qwerty keyboards. *Proceedings of the ACM Conference on Human Factors in Computing Systems—CHI 2005*. New York: ACM. 1288–1291.

Clawson, J., Lyons, K., Rudnick, A., Iannucci, R. A., & Starner, T. (2008). Automatic Whiteout++: Correcting mini-QWERTY typing errors using keypress timing. *Proceedings of the ACM SIGCHI Conference on Human Factors in Computing Systems—CHI 2008*. New York: ACM. 573–582.

Cockburn, A., Gutwin, C., & Greenberg, S. (2007). A predictive model of menu performance. *Proceedings of the ACM SIGCHI Conference on Human Factors in Computing Systems—CHI 2007*. New York: ACM. 627–636.

Cooper, A. (1999). *The Inmates are Running the Asylum*. Indianapolis: Sams.

Cooper, A., & Riemann, R. (2003). *About face 2.0: The Essentials of Interaction Design*. Indianapolis: Wiley.

Cunningham, H. A. (1989). Aiming error under transformed spatial mappings suggest a structure for visual-motor maps. *Journal of Experimental Psychology: Human Perception and Performance*, *15*, 493–506.

Cutler, L. D., Fröhlich, B., & Hanrahan, P. (1997). Two-handed direct manipulation on the responsive workbench. *Proceedings of the 1997 Symposium on Interactive 3D Graphics*. New York: ACM. 107–114.

Czerwinski, M., Dumais, S., Robertson, G., Dziadosz, S., Tiernan, S., & van Dantzich, M. (1999). Visualizing implicit queries for information management and retrieval. *Proceedings of the ACM SIGCHI Conference on Human Factors in Computing Systems—CHI '99*. New York: ACM. 560–567.

Czerwinski, M., Horvitz, E., & Wilhite, S. (2004). A diary study of task switching and interruptions. *Proceedings of the ACM SIGCHI Conference on Human Factors in Computing Systems—CHI 2004*. New York: ACM. 175–182.

Dabbish, L. A., Kraut, R. E., Fussell, S., & Kiesler, S. (2005). Understanding email use: Predicting action on a message. *Proceedings of the ACM SIGCHI Conference on Human Factors in Computing Systems—CHI 2005*. New York: ACM. 691–700.

Daniels, P. T., & Bright, W. (Eds.). (1996). *The World's Writing Systems*. New York: Oxford University Press.

Dautenhahn, K., Walters, M., Woods, S., Koay, K. L., Nehaniv, C. L., & Sisbot, E. A., et al. (2006). How may I serve you? A robot companion approaching a seated person in a helping context. *Proceedings of the First ACM SIGCHI/SIGART Conference on Human-Robot Interaction*. New York: ACM. 172–179.

Day, R. A., & Gastel, B. (2006). *How to Write and Publish a Scientific Paper* (6th ed.) Westport, CT: Greenwood Publishing.

Dietz, P., & Leigh, D. (2001). DiamondTouch: A multi-user touch technology. *Proceedings of the ACM Symposium on User Interface Software and Technology—UIST 2001*. New York: ACM. 291–226.

Dillon, A., Richardson, J., & McKnight, C. (1990). The effects of display size and text splitting on reading lengthy text from screen. *Behaviour and Information Technology*, *9*, 215–227.

Dix, A., Finlay, J., Abowd, G., & Beale, R. (2004). *Human-Computer Interaction* (3rd ed.) London: Prentice Hall.

Dixon, N., Guimbretière, F., & Chen, N. (2008). Optimal parameters for efficient crossing-based dialog boxes. *Proceedings of the ACM SIGCHI Conference on Human Factors in Computing Systems—CHI 2008*. New York: ACM. 1623–1632.

Dragovic, M. (2004). Towards an improved measure of the Edinburgh handedness inventory. *Laterality: Asymmetries of Body, Brain and Cognition, 8*, 411–419.

Draper, M. H., Viire, E. S., Furness, T. A., & Gawron, V. J. (2001). Effects of image scale and system time delay on simulator sickness within head-coupled virtual environments. *Human Factors, 43*, 120–146.

Duggan, G. B., & Payne, S. (2008). Knowledge in the head and on the web: Using topic expertise to aid search. *Proceedings of the ACM SIGCHI Conference on Human Factors in Computing Systems—CHI 2008*. New York: ACM. 39–48.

Duh, H. B. L., Chen, V. H. H., & Tan, C. B. (2008). Playing different games on different phones: An empirical study on mobile gaming. *Proceedings of MobileHCI 2008*. New York: ACM. 391–394.

Dunlop, M., & Crossan, A. (2000). Predictive text entry methods for mobile phones. *Personal and Ubiquitous Computing, 4*, 134–143.

Dunlop, M. D. (2004). Watch-top text-entry: Can phone-style predictive text entry work with only 5 buttons?. *Proceedings of MobileHCI 2004*. Heidelberg: Springer-Verlag. 342–346.

Elmqvist, N., Henry, N., Riche, Y., & Fekete, J. D. (2008). Mélange: Space folding for multi-focus interaction. *Proceedings of the ACM SIGCHI Conference on Human Factors in Computing Systems—CHI 2008*. New York: ACM. 1333–1342.

Engelbart, D. (1970). U.S. Patent No. 3,541,541.

English, W. K., Engelbart, D. C., & Berman, M. S. (1967). Display selection techniques for text manipulation. *IEEE Transactions on Human Factors in Electronics, HFE-8*(1), 5–15.

Erceg-Hurn, D. M., & Mirosevich, V. M. (2008). Modern robust statistical methods: An easy way to maximize the accuracy and power of your research. *American Psychologist, 63*, 591–601.

Erickson, T., & McDonald, D. (Eds.). (2007). *HCI remixed: Reflections on Works that have Influenced the HCI Community*. Cambridge: MIT Press.

Evans, K. B., Tanner, P. P., & Wein, M. (1981). Tablet based valuators that provide one, two, or three degrees of freedom. *Computer Graphics, 15*(3), 91–97.

Fang, R., Chai, J. Y., & Ferreira, F. (2009). Between linguistic attention and gaze fixations in multimodal conversational interfaces. *Proceedings of the 2009 International Conference on Multimodal Interfaces*. New York: ACM. 143–150.

Farzam, R., DiMicco, J. M., Millen, D. R., Brownholtz, B., Geyer, W., & Dugan, C. (2008). Results from deploying a participation incentive mechanism within the enterprise. *Proceedings of the ACM SIGCHI Conference on Human Factors in Computing Systems—CHI 2008*. New York: ACM. 563–572.

Findlater, L., Jansen, A., Shinohara, K., Dixon, M., Kamb, P., & Rakita, J., et al. (2010). Enhanced area cursors: Reducing fine pointing demands for people with motor impairments. *Proceedings of the ACM Symposium on User Interface Software and Technology—UIST 2010*. New York: ACM. 153–162.

Fitts, P. M. (1954). The information capacity of the human motor system in controlling the amplitude of movement. *Journal of Experimental Psychology, 47*, 381–391.

Fitts, P. M., & Peterson, J. R. (1964). Information capacity of discrete motor responses. *Journal of Experimental Psychology, 67*, 103–112.

Fitts, P. M., & Posner, M. I. (1968). *Human Performance*. Belmont, CA: Brooks/Cole Publishing Company.

Fitts, P. M., & Seeger, C. M. (1953). S-R compatibility: Spatial characteristics of stimulus and response codes. *Journal of Experimental Psychology, 46*, 199–210.

Fitzmaurice, G. (1993). Situated information spaces and spatially aware palmtop computers. *Communications of the ACM, 36*(7), 39–49.

Fitzmaurice, G. W., Ishii, H., & Buxton, W. A. S. (1995). Bricks: Laying the foundation for graspable user interfaces. *Proceedings of the ACM SIGCHI Conference on Human Factors in Computing Systems—CHI '95*. New York: ACM. 442–449.

Foley, J. D., van Dam, A., Feiner, S. K., & Hughes, J. F. (1987). *Computer Graphics: Principles and Practice* (2nd ed.). Reading, MA: Addison-Wesley.

Forlines, C., & Balakrishnan, R. (2008). Evaluating tactile feedback and direct vs. indirect stylus input in pointing and crossing selection tasks. *Proceedings of the ACM SIGCHI Conference on Human Factors in Computing Systems—CHI 2009*. New York: ACM. 1563–1572.

Forlines, C., Shen, C., & Buxton, B. (2005). Glimpse: A novel input model for multi-level devices. *Proceedings of the ACM SIGCHI Conference on Human Factors in Computing Systems—CHI 2005*. New York: ACM. 1375–1378.

Forlines, C., Wigdor, D., Shein, F., & Balakrishnan, R. (2007). Direct-touch vs. mouse input for tabletop displays. *Proceedings of the ACM SIGCHI Conference on Human Factors in Computing Systems—CHI 2007*. New York: ACM. 847–856.

Freeman, M., Norris, A., & Hyland, R. (2006). Usability of online grocery systems: A focus on errors. *Proceedings of OzCHI 2006*. New York: ACM. 269–275.

Furnas, G. W. (1986). Generalized fisheye views. *Proceedings of the ACM SIGCHI Conference on Human Factors in Computing Systems—CHI '86*. New York: ACM. 16–23.

Gajos, K. Z., Wobbrock, J. O., & Weld, D. S. (2008). Improving the performance of motor-impaired users with automatically-generated, ability-based interfaces. *Proceedings of the ACM SIGCHI Conference on Human Factors in Computing Systems—CHI 2008*. New York: ACM. 1257–1266.

Gan, K. C., & Hoffmann, E. R. (1988). Geometrical conditions for ballistic and visually controlled movements. *Ergonomics, 31*, 829–839.

Garau, M., Slater, M., Vinayagamoorthy, V., Brogni, A., Steed, A., & Sasse, M. A. (2003). The impact of avatar realism and eye gaze control on perceived quality of communication in a shared immersive virtual environment. *Proceedings of the ACM SIGCHI Conference on Human Factors in Computing Systems—CHI 2003*. New York: ACM. 529–536.

García, A. S., Molina, J. P., Gonzalez, P., Martínez, D., & Martínez, J. (2009). A study of multimodal feedback to support collaborative manipulation tasks in virtual worlds. *Proceedings of the ACM Symposium on Virtual Reality Software and Technology—VRST 2009*. New York: ACM. 259–260.

Geven, A., Sefelin, R., & Tschelig, M. (2006). Depth and breadth away from the desktop: The optimal information hierarchy for mobile use. *Proceedings of MobileHCI 2006*. New York: ACM. 157–164.

Gibbs, C. B. (1962). Controller design: Interactions of controlling limbs, time-lags and gains in positional and velocity systems. *Ergonomics, 5*, 383–402.

Gibson, J. J. (1979). *The Ecological Approach to Visual Perception*. Hillsdale, NJ: Erlbaum.

Gillick, W. G., & Lam, C. C. (1996). U. S. Patent No. 5,530,455.

Glass, G. V., & Hopkins, K. D. (1984). *Statistical Methods in Education and Psychology* (2nd ed.). Englewood Cliffs, NJ: Prentice Hall.

Glass, G. V., Peckham, P. D., & Sanders, J. R. (1972). Consequences of failure to meet assumptions underlying the fixed effect analyses of variance and covariance. *Review of Educational Research, 42*, 237–288.

Goldberg, D., & Richardson, C. (1993). Touch-typing with a stylus. *Proceedings of the INTERACT '93 and CHI '93 Conference on Human Factors in Computing Systems—INTERCHI '93*. New York: ACM. 80–87.

Goldberg, J. H., & Helfman, J. I. (2010). Visual scanpath representation. *Proceedings of the ACM Symposium on Eye Tracking Research and Applications—ETRA 2010*. New York: ACM. 203–210.

Goldstein, M., Chincholle, D., & Backström, M. (2000). Assessing two new wearable input paradigms: The finger-joint-gesture palm-keypad glove and the invisible phone clock. *Personal and Ubiquitous Computing, 4*, 123–133.

Gong, J., & Tarasewich, P. (2005). Alphabetically constrained keypad designs for text entry on mobile phones. *Proceedings of the ACM SIGCHI Conference on Human Factors in Computing Systems—CHI 2005*. New York: ACM. 211–220.

Gong, J., Tarasewich, P., & MacKenzie, I. S. (2008). Improved word list ordering for text entry on ambiguous keyboards. *Proceedings of the Fifth Nordic Conference on Human-Computer Interaction—NordiCHI 2008*. New York: ACM. 152–161.

Gray, J. (1986, January). The role of menu title as a navigational aid in hierarchical menus. *SIGCHI Bulletin*, 33–40.

Gray, W. D., & Boehm-Davis, D. A. (2000). Milliseconds matter: An introduction to micro-strategies and to their use in describing and predicting interactive behaviour. *Journal of Experimental Psychology: Applied, 6*, 322–335.

Gray, W. D., John, B. E., & Atwood, M. E. (1993). Project Ernestine: Validating a GOMS analysis for predicting and explaining real-world task performance. *Human-Computer Interaction, 8*, 237–309.

Greene, J., & Haidt, J. (2002). How (and where) does moral judgment work? *Trends in Cognitive Science, 6*(1), 517–523.

Grinter, R., & Eldridge, M. (2003). Wan2tlk? Everyday text messaging. *Proceedings of the ACM SIGCHI Conference on Human Factors in Computing Systems—CHI 2003*. New York: ACM. 441–448.

Grudin, J. (2012). A moving target: The evolution of human-computer interaction. In J. A. Jacko (Ed.), *The Human-Computer Interaction Handbook: Fundamentals, Evolving Technologies, and Emerging Applications* (3rd ed.). Boca Raton: CRC Press. xxvii–lxi.

Guiard, Y. (1987). Asymmetric division of labor in human skilled bimanual action: The kinematic chain as a model. *Journal of Motor Behavior, 19*, 486–517.

Guy, I., Ur, S., Ronen, I., Perer, A., & Jacovi, M. (2011). Do you want to know? Recommending strangers in the enterprise. *Proceedings of the ACM Conference on Computer Supported Coorperative Work—CSCW 2011*. New York: ACM. 285–294.

Halligan, P. W., Zemen, A., & Berger, A. (1999). Phantoms in the brain: Question and assumption that the adult brain is "hard wired.". *British Medical Journal, 4*, 587–588.

Hancock, M. S., & Booth, K. S. (2004). Improving menu placement strategies for pen input. *Proceedings of Graphics Interface 2004*. Toronto: Canadian Information Processing Society. 221–230.

Hannagan, J., & Regenbrecht, H. (2008). *TwistMouse for Simultaneous Translation and Rotation. Technical Report*. University of Otago, Dunedin, New Zeland: HCI Group. Information Science Department.

Harada, S., Landay, J. A., Malkin, J., Li, X., & Bilmes, J. A. (2006). The vocal joystick: Evaluation of voice-based cursor control techniques. *Proceedings of the ACM Conference on Computers and Accessibility—ACCESS 2006*. New York: ACM. 187–204.

Harrison, B., Fishkin, K. P., Gujar, A., Mochon, C., & Want, R. (1998). Squeeze me, hold me, tilt me! An exploration of manipulative user interfaces. *Proceedings of the ACM SIGCHI Conference on Human Factors in Computing Systems—CHI '98*. New York: ACM. 17–24.

Harrison, D., & Hudson, S. E. (2009). Abracadabra: Wireless, high-precision, and unpowered finger input for very small mobile devices. *Proceedings of the ACM Symposium on User Interface Software and Technology—UIST 2009*. New York: ACM. 121–124.

Hart, S., & Staveland, L. (1988). Development of NASA-TLX (task load index): Results of empirical and theoretical research. In P. Hancock & N. Meshkati (Eds.), *Human Mental Workload* (pp. 139–183). Amsterdam: North-Holland.

Hashizume, A., Kurosu, H., & Kaneko, T. (2007). Multi-window system and the working memory. *Proceedings of HCI International 2007*. Heidelberg: Springer. 297–305.

Hauptmann, A. G. (1989). Speech and gestures for graphic image manipulation. *Proceedings of the ACM SIGCHI Conference on Human Factors in Computing Systems—CHI '89*. New York: ACM. 241–246.

Hayashi, E., Pendleton, B. A., Ozenc, F. K., & Hong, J. I. (2012). WebTicket: Account management using printable tokens. *Proceedings of the ACM SIGCHI Conference on Human Factors in Computing Systems—CHI 2012*. New York: ACM. 997–1006.

Hegel, R., Krach, S., Kircher, T., Wrede, B., & Sagerer, G. (2008). Theory of mind (TMD) on robots: A functional neuroimaging study. *Proceedings of the ACM/IEEE International Conference on Human-Robot Interaction—HRI 2008*. New York: ACM. 335–342.

Hemenway, K. (1982). Psychological issues in the use of icons in command menus. *Proceedings of the Conference on Human Factors in Computing Systems*. New York: ACM. 20–23.

Herot, C. F., & Weinzapfel, G. (1978). One-point touch input of vector information for computer displays. *Proceedings of SIGGRAPH 1978*. New York: ACM. 210–216.

Hick, W. E. (1952). On the rate of gain of information. *Quarterly Journal of Experimental Psychology, 4*, 11–36.

Hinckley, K., Baudisch, P., Ramos, G., & Guimbretière, F. (2005). Design and analysis of delimiters for selection-action pen gesture phrases in Scriboli. *Proceedings of the ACM SIGCHI Conference on Human Factors in Computing Systems—CHI 2005*. New York: ACM. 451–460.

Hinckley, K., Czerwinski, M., & Sinclair, M. (1998). Interaction and modeling techniques for desktop two-handed input. *Proceedings of the ACM Symposium on User Interface Software and Technology—UIST '98*. New York: ACM. 49–58.

Hinckley, K., Guimbretière, F., Baudisch, P., Sarin, R., Agrawala, M., & Cutrell, E. (2006). The springboard: Multiple modes in one spring-loaded control. *Proceedings of the ACM SIGCHI Conference on Human Factors in Computing Systems—CHI 2006*. New York: ACM. 181–190.

Hinckley, K., Pausch, R., Proffitt, D., Patten, J., & Kassell, N. (1997). Cooperative bimanual action. *Proceedings of the ACM SIGCHI Conference on Human Factors in Computing Systems—CHI '97*. New York: ACM. 27–34.

Hinckley, K., Pierce, J., Sinclair, M., & Horvitz, E. (2000). Sensing techniques for mobile interaction. *Proceedings of the ACM Symposium on User Interface Software and Technology—UIST 2000*. New York: ACM. 91–100.

Hinckley, K., Sinclair, M., Hanson, E., Szeliski, R., & Conway, M. (1999). The VideoMouse: A camera-based multi-degree-of-freedom input device. *Proceedings of the ACM Symposium on User Interface Software and Technology—UIST '99*. New York: ACM. 103–112.

Hirsch, J. E. (2005). An index to quantify an individual's scientific research output. *Proceedings of the National Academy of Sciences, 102,* 16568–16572.

Hodgson, G. M., & Ruth, S. R. (1985, July). The use of menus in the design of on-line systems: A retrospective view. *SIGCHI Bulletin,* 16–22.

Holleis, P., Otto, F., Hussmann, H., & Schmidt, A. (2007). Keystroke-level model for advanced mobile phone interaction. *Proceedings of the ACM SIGCHI Conference on Human Factors in Computing Systems—CHI 2007.* New York: ACM. 1505–1514.

Hornof, A. J., & Kieras, D. E. (1997). Cognitive modeling reveals menu search is both random and systematic. *Proceedings of the ACM SIGCHI Conference on Human Factors in Computing Systems—CHI '97.* New York: ACM. 107–114.

Howes, A., & Payne, S. J. (1990). Display-based competence: Towards user models for menu-driven interfaces. *International Journal of Man-Machine Studies, 33,* 637–655.

Huffman, D. A. (1952). A method for the construction of minimum redundancy codes. *Proceedings of the IRE, 40,* 1098–1101.

Huhtala, J., Karukka, M., Salminaa, M., & Häkkilä, J. (2011). Evaluating depth illusion as method of adding emphasis in autostereoscopic mobile displays. *Proceedings of MobileHCI 2011.* New York: ACM. 357–360.

Hunter, M., Zhai, S., & Smith, B. A. (2000). Physics-based graphical keyboard design. *Extended Abstracts of the ACM Conference on Human Factors in Computing Systems—CHI 2000.* New York: ACM. 157–158.

Hyman, R. (1953). Stimulus information as a determinant of reaction time. *Journal of Experimental Psychology, 45,* 188–196.

Igarashi, T., & Hughes, J. F. (2001). Voice as sound: Using non-verbal voice input for interactive control. *Proceedings of the ACM Symposium on User Interface Software and Technology—UIST 2001.* New York: ACM. 155–156.

Iqbal, S. T., & Bailey, B. P. (2006). Leveraging characteristics of task structure to predict the cost of interruption. *Proceedings of the ACM SIGCHI Conference on Human Factors in Computing Systems—CHI 2006.* New York: ACM. 741–750.

Ishii, H., & Ullmer, B. (1997). Tangible bits: Towards seamless interfaces between people, bits, and atoms. *Proceedings of the ACM SIGCHI Conference on Human Factors in Computing System—CHI '97.* New York: ACM. 234–241.

ISO. (2000). Ergonomic requirements for office work with visual display terminals (VDTs)—Part 9: Requirements for non-keyboard input devices (ISO 9241-9). International Organisation for Standardisation.

Isokoski, P., & Käki, M. (2002). Comparison of two touchpad-based methods for numeric entry. *Proceedings of the ACM SIGCHI Conference on Human Factors in Computing Systems—CHI 2002.* New York: ACM. 25–32.

Isokoski, P., & Raisamo, R. (2004). Quikwriting as a multi-device text entry method. *Proceedings of the Third Nordic Conference on Human-Computer Interaction—NordiCHI 2004.* New York: ACM. 105–108.

Itoh, K., Aoki, H., & Hansen, J. P. (2006). A comparative usability study of two Japanese gaze typing systems. *Proceedings of the ACM Symposium on Eye Tracking Research and Applications—ETRA 2006,* 59–66, New York.

Jacko, J. A., Barnard, L., Kongnakorn, T., Moloney, K. P., Edwards, P. J., & Emery, V. K., et al. (2004). Isolating the effects of visual impairment: Exploring the effect of ACM on the utility of multimodal feedback. *Proceedings of the ACM SIGCHI Conference on Human Factors in Computing Systems—CHI 2004.* New York: ACM. 311–318.

Jacob, R. J. K., Girouard, A., Hirshfield, L. M., Horn, M. S., Shaer, O., & Solovey, E. T., et al. (2008). Reality-based interaction: A framework for post-WIMP interfaces.

Proceedings of the ACM SIGCHI Conference on Human Factors in Computing—CHI 2000. New York: ACM. 201–210.

Jacob, R. J. K., Sibert, L. E., McFarlane, D. C., & Mullen, M. P., Jr. (1994). Integrality and separability of input devices. *ACM Transactions on Computer-Human Interaction, 1,* 3–26.

Javed, W., Ghani, S., & Elmqvist, N. (2012). PolyZoom: Multiscale and multifocus exploration in 2D visual spaces. *Proceedings of the ACM SIGCHI Conference on Human Factors in Computing Systems—CHI 2012.* New York: ACM. 287–296.

Jellinek, H. D., & Card, S. K. (1990). Powermice and user performance. *Proceedings of the ACM SIGCHI Conference on Human Factors in Computing Systems—CHI '90.* New York: ACM. 213–220.

Jenkins, W. L., & Connor, M. B. (1949). Some design factors in making settings on a linear scale. *Journal of Applied Psychology, 33,* 395–409.

Johansen, R. (1991). Groupware: Future directions and wild cards. *Journal of Organizational Computing and Electronic Commerce, 1*(2), 219–227.

Johnsen, K., Raij, A., Stevens, A., Lind, D. S., & Lok, B. (2007). The validity of a virtual human experience for interpersonal skills education. *Proceedings of the ACM SIGCHI Conference on Human Factors in Computing Systems—CHI 2007.* New York: ACM. 1049–1058.

Johnson, J. (2007). *GUI bloopers 2.0.* San Francisco: Morgan Kaufmann.

Johnson, J., Roberts, T. L., Verplank, W., Smith, D. C., Irby, C., & Beard, M., et al. (1989, Sept.). The xerox star: A retrospective. *IEEE Computer, 22,* 11–29.

Johnston, L. (2007). *Politics: An Introduction to the Modern Democratic State* (3rd ed.). Peterborough, Ontario: Broadview Press.

Jones, W., Klasnja, P., Civan, A., & Adcock, M. L. (2008). The personal project planner: Planning to organize personal information. *Proceedings of the ACM SIGCHI Conference on Human Factors in Computing Systems—CHI 2008.* New York: ACM. 681–684.

Kabbash, P., Buxton, W., & Sellen, A. (1994). Two-handed input in a compound task. *Proceedings of the ACM SIGCHI Conference on Human Factors in Computing Systems—CHI '94.* New York: ACM. 417–423.

Kabbash, P., MacKenzie, I. S., & Buxton, W. (1993). Human performance using computer input devices in the preferred and non-preferred hands. *Proceedings of the INTERACT '93 and CHI '93 Conference on Human Factors in Computing Systems—INTERCHI '93.* New York: ACM. 474–481.

Kammerer, Y., Nairn, R., Pirolli, P., & Chi, E. H. (2009). Signpost from the masses: Learning effects in an exploratory social tag search browser. *Proceedings of the ACM SIGCHI Conference on Human Factors in Computing Systems—CHI 2009.* New York: ACM. 625–634.

Kane, S. K., Bigham, J. P., & Wobbrock, J. O. (2008). Slide rule: Making mobile touch screens accessible to blind people using multi-touch interaction techniques. *Proceedings of the ACM Conference on Computers and Accessiblity—ASSETS 2008.* New York: ACM. 73–80.

Kane, S. K., Wobbrock, J. O., & Ladner, R. E. (2011). Usable gestures for blind people: Understanding preference and performance. *Proceedings of the ACM SIGCHI Conference on Human Factors in Computing Systems—CHI 2011.* New York: ACM. 413–422.

Kantowitz, B. H., & Elvers, G. C. (1988). Fitts' law with an isometric controller: Effects of order of control and control-display gain. *Journal of Motor Behavior, 20,* 53–66.

Kantowitz, B. H., & Sorkin, R. D. (1983). *Human factors: Understanding People-System Relationships.* New York: Wiley.

Kaplan, S. (1997, August). The CSCW column: The quadrant model of groupware. *SIGGROUP Bulletin, 18*, 11–14.

Kaptein, M., Nass, C., & Markopoulos, P. (2010). Powerful and consistent analysis of likert-type rating scales. *Proceedings of the ACM SIGCHI Conference on Human-Factors in Computing Systems—CHI 2010*. New York: ACM. 2391–2394.

Kaptein, M., & Robertson, J. (2012). Rethinking statistical analysis methods for CHI. *Proceedings of the ACM SIGCHI Conference on Human Factors in Computing Systems—CHI 2012*. New York: ACM. 1105–1114.

Kay, A., & Goldberg, A. (1977, March). Personal dynamic media. *IEEE Computer*, 31–41.

Keele, S. W. (1973). *Attention and Human Performance*. Pacific Palisades, CA: Goodyear Publishing Company, Inc.

Kelso, J. A. S., Southard, D. L., & Goodman, D. (1979). On the coordination of two-handed movements. *Journal of Experimental Psychology: Human Perception and Performance, 5*(2), 229–238.

Kiger, J. I. (1984). The depth/breadth trade-off in the design of menu-driven user interfaces. *International Journal of Human-Computer Studies, 20*, 201–213.

Kindberg, T., O'Neill, E., Beven, C., Kostakos, V., Fraser, D. S., & Jay, T. (2008). Measuring trust in Wi-Fi hotspots. *Proceedings of the ACM SIGCHI Conference on Human Factors in Computing Systems—CHI 2008*. New York: ACM. 173–182.

Kobayashi, M., & Igarashi, T. (2008). Ninja cursors: Using multiple cursors to assist target acquisition on large screens. *Proceedings of the ACM SIGCHI Conference on Human Factors in Computing Systems—CHI 2008*. New York: ACM. 949–958.

Koester, H. H., & Levine, S. P. (1994a). Learning and performance of able-bodied individuals using scanning systems with and without word prediction. *Assistive Technology, 6*, 42–53.

Koester, H. H., & Levine, S. P. (1994b). Modeling the speed of text entry with a word prediction interface. *IEEE Transactions on Rehabilitation Engineering, 2*, 177–187.

Költringer, T., Van, M. N., & Grechenig, T. (2007). Game controller text entry with alphabetic and multi-tap selection keyboards. *Extended Abstracts of the ACM SIGCHI Conference on Human Factors in Computing System—CHI 2007*. New York: ACM. 2513–2518.

Konig, W. A., Gerken, J., Dierdorf, S., & Reiterer, H. (2009). Adaptive pointing: Design and evaluation of a precision enhancing technique for absolute pointing devices. *Proceedings of INTERACT 2009*. Berlin: Springer. 659–671.

Kurihara, J., Vronay, D., & Igarashi, T. (2005). Flexible timeline user interface using constraints. *Extended Abstracts of the ACM SIGCHI Conference on Human Factors in Computing Systems—CHI 2005*. New York: ACM. 1581–1584.

Kurtenbach, G. (1993). *The Design and Evaluation of Marking Menus*. Toronto: University of Toronto.

Kurtenbach, G., Fitzmaurice, G., Baudel, T., & Buxton, B. (1997). The design of a GUI paradigm based on tablets, two-hands, and transparency. *Proceedings of the ACM SIGCHI Conference on Human Factors in Computing Systems—CHI '97*. New York: ACM. 35–42.

Kurtenbach, G. P., Sellen, A. J., & Buxton, W. A. S. (1993). An empirical evaluation of some articulatory and cognitive aspects of marking menus. *Human-Computer Interaction, 8*, 1–23.

Kuzuoka, H., Kosaka, J., Yamazaki, K., Suga, Y., Yamazaki, A., & Luff, P., et al. (2004). Mediating dual ecologies. *Proceedings of the ACM Conference on Computer Supported Cooperative Work—CSCW 2004*. New York: ACM. 478–486.

Kuzuoka, H., Yamazaki, K., Yamazaki, A., Kosaka, J., Suga, Y., & Heath, C. (2004). Dual ecologies of robot as communication media: Thoughts on coordinating orientations and projectability. *Proceedings of the ACM SIGCHI Conference on Human Factors in Computing Systems—CHI 2004*. New York: ACM. 183–190.

Lampe, C. A. C., Ellison, N., & Steinfield, C. (2007). A familiar face(book): Profile elements as signals in an online social network. *Proceedings of the ACM SIGCHI Conference on Human Factors in Computing Systems—CHI 2005*. New York: ACM. 435–444.

Landauer, T. K., & Nachbar, D. W. (1985). Selection from alphabetic and numeric menu trees using a touch screen: Breadth, depth, and width. *Proceedings of the ACM SIGCHI Conference on Human Factors in Computing Systems—CHI '85*. ACM. 73–77.

Laurel, B. (1991). *Computers as Theatre*. Reading, MA: Addison-Welsey.

Lee, S. K., Buxton, W., & Smith, K. C. (1985). A multi-touch three dimensional touch-sensitive tablet. *Proceedings of the ACM SIGCHI Conference on Human Factors in Computing Systems—CHI 85*. New York: ACM. 21–25.

Leftheriotis, I., & Chorianopoulos, K. (2011). User experience quality in multi-touch tasks. *Proceedings of the ACM Conference in Engineering Interactive Computing Systems—EICS 2011*. New York: ACM. 161–164.

Levy, S. (1995). *Insanely Great: The Life and Times of Macintosh, the Computer that Changed Everything*. New York: Penguin.

Lewis, J. R. (1994). Sample sizes for usability studies: Additional considerations. *Human Factors, 36*, 366–378.

Li, Y., Hinckley, K., Guan, Z., & Landay, J. A. (2005). Experimental analysis of mode switching techniques in pen-based user interfaces. *Proceedings of the ACM SIGCHI Conference on Human Factors in Computing Systems—CHI 2005*. New York: ACM. 461–470.

Liang, J., Shaw, C., & Green, M. (1991). On temporal-spatial realism in the virtual reality environment. *Proceedings of the ACM Symposium on User Interface Software and Technology—UIST '91*. New York: ACM. 19–25.

Lindeman, R. W., Sibert, J. L., Mendez-Mendez, E., Patil, S., & Phifer, D. (2005). Effectiveness of directional vibrotactile cuing on a building-clearing task. *Proceedings of the ACM SIGCHI Conference on Human Factors in Computing Systems—CHI 2005*. New York: ACM. 271–280.

Lindholm, C., Keinonen, T., & Kiljander, H. (2003). *Mobile Usability: How Nokia Changed the Face of the Mobile Phone*. New York: McGraw Hill.

Linzmayer, O. W. (2004). *Apple Confidential 2.0: The Definitive History of the World's most Colorful Company*. San Francisco: No Starch Press.

Liu, J., Cole, M. J., Liu, C., Bierig, R., Gwizdka, J., & Belkin, N. J., et al. (2010). Search behaviors in different tasks types. *Proceedings of the Joint Conference in Digital Libraries—JCDL 2010*. New York: ACM. 69–78.

Liu, Y., & Räihä, K. J. (2010). Predicting Chinese text entry speeds on mobile phones. *Proceedings of the ACM SIGCHI Conference on Human Factors in Computing Systems—CHI 2010*. New York: ACM. 2183–2192.

Lowry, O. H., Rosenbrough, N. J., Farr, A. L., & Randall, R. J. (1951). Protein measurement with the folin phenol reagent. *Journal of Biological Chemistry, 193*, 265–275.

Lyons, K., Starner, T., & Gane, B. (2006). Experimental evaluation of the Twiddler one-handed chording mobile keyboard. *Human-Computer Interaction, 21*, 343–392.

Lyons, K., Starner, T., Plaisted, D., Fusia, J., Lyons, A., & Drew, A., et al. (2004). Twiddler typing: One-handed chording text entry for mobile phones. *Proceedings of the ACM*

SIGCHI Conference on Human Factors in Computing Systems—CHI 2004. New York: ACM. 671–678.

MacDorman, K. F., Whalen, T. J., Ho, C. C., & Patel, H. (2011). An improved usability measure based on novice and expert performance. *International Journal of Human-Computer Studies, 27,* 280–302.

MacKenzie, I. S. (1992). Fitts' law as a research and design tool in human-computer interaction. *Human-Computer Interaction, 7,* 91–139.

MacKenzie, I. S. (2002). KSPC (keystrokes per character) as a characteristic of text entry techniques. *Proceedings of the Fourth International Symposium on Human-Computer Interaction with Mobile Devices—MobileHCI 2002*. Berlin: Springer. 195–210.

MacKenzie, I. S. (2003). Motor behaviour models for human computer interaction. In J. M. Carroll (Ed.), *HCI Models, Theories, and Frameworks: Toward a Multidisciplinary Science* (pp. 27–54). San Francisco: Morgan Kaufmann.

MacKenzie, I. S. (2009a). Citedness, uncitedness, and the murky world between. *Extended Abstracts of the ACM SIGCHI Conference on Human Factors in Computing Systems—CHI 2009*. New York: ACM. 2545–2554.

MacKenzie, I. S. (2009b). The one-key challenge: Searching for an efficient one-key text entry method. *Proceedings of the ACM Conference on Computers and Accessibility—ASSETS 2009*. New York: ACM. 91–98.

MacKenzie, I. S., & Buxton, W. (1994). Prediction of pointing and dragging times in graphical user interfaces. *Interacting with Computers, 6,* 213–227.

MacKenzie, I. S., & Isokoski, P. (2008). Fitts' throughput and the speed-accuracy trade-off. *Proceedings of the ACM SIGCHI Conference on Human Factors in Computing Systems—CHI 2008*. New York: ACM. 1633–1636.

MacKenzie, I. S., & Jusoh, S. (2001). An evaluation of two input devices for remote pointing. *Proceedings of the Eighth IFIP Working Conference on Engineering for Human-Computer Interaction—EHCI 2000*. Heidelberg: Springer-Verlag. 235–249.

MacKenzie, I. S., Kober, H., Smith, D., Jones, T., & Skepner, E. (2001). LetterWise: Prefix-based disambiguation for mobile text entry. *Proceedings of the ACM Symposium on User Interface Software and Technology—UIST 2001*. New York: ACM. 111–120.

MacKenzie, I. S., & Oniszczak, A. (1998). A comparison of three selection techniques for touchpads: *Proceedings of the ACM SIGCHI conference on human factors in computing systems—CHI '98*. New York: ACM. 336–343.

MacKenzie, I. S., & Riddersma, S. (1994). Effects of output display and control-display gain on human performance in interactive systems. *Behaviour and Information Technology, 13,* 328–337.

MacKenzie, I. S., Sellen, A., & Buxton, W. (1991). A comparison of input devices in elemental pointing and dragging tasks. *Proceedings of the ACM SIGCHI Conference on Human Factors in Computing Systems—CHI '91*. New York: ACM. 161–166.

MacKenzie, I. S., & Soukoreff, R. W. (2002). Text entry for mobile computing: Models and methods, theory and practice. *Human-Computer Interaction, 17,* 147–198.

MacKenzie, I. S., Soukoreff, R. W., & Pal, C. (1997). A two-ball mouse affords three degrees of freedom: *Extended Abstracts of the ACM SIGCHI Conference on Human Factors in Computing Systems—CHI '97*. New York: ACM. 303–304.

MacKenzie, I. S., & Teather, R. J. (2012). FittsTilt: The application of Fitts' law to tilt-based interaction. *Proceedings of the Seventh Nordic Conference on Human-Computer Interaction—NordiCHI 2012*. New York: ACM. to appear.

MacKenzie, I. S., & Ware, C. (1993). Lag as a determinant of human performance in interactive systems. *Proceedings of the INTERACT '93 and CHI '93 Conference on Human Factors in Computing Systems—INTERCHI '93*. New York: ACM. 488–493.

MacKenzie, I. S., & Zhang, S. X. (1999). The design and evaluation of a high-performance soft keyboard. *Proceedings of the ACM SIGCHI Conference on Human Factors in Computing Systems—CHI '99*. New York: ACM. 25–31.

MacKenzie, I. S., & Zhang, S. X. (2001). An empirical investigation of the novice experience with soft keyboards. *Behaviour and Information Technology*, *20*, 411–418.

MacNeill, D., & Blickenstorfer, C. H. (1996, May/June). Trackpads: Alternative input technologies. *Pen Computing*, *3*, 42–45.

Magerkurth, C., & Stenzel, R. (2003). A pervasive keyboard: Separating input from display. *Proceedings of the 1st IEEE Conference on Pervasive Computing and Communications—PerCom 2003*. New York: IEEE. 388–395.

Majaranta, P., Ahola, U. K., & Špakov, O. (2009). Fast gaze typing with an adjustable dwell time. *Proceedings of the ACM SIGCHI Conference on Human Factors in Computing Systems—CHI 2009*. New York: ACM. 357–360.

Majaranta, P., MacKenzie, I. S., Aula, A., & Räiha, K. J. (2006). Effects of feedback and dwell time on eye typing speed and accuracy. *Universal Access in the Information Society (UAIS)*, *5*, 199–208.

Malacria, S., Lecolinet, E., & Guiard, Y. (2010). Clutch-free panning and integrated pan-zoom control on touch-sensitive surfaces: The cyclostar approach. *Proceedings of the ACM SIGCHI Conference on Human Factors in Computing Systems—CHI 2010*. New York: ACM. 2615–2624.

Malik, S., & Laszlo, J. (2004). Visual touchpad: A two-handed gestural input device. *Proceedings of the Sixth International Conference on Multimodal Interfaces*. New York: ACM. 289–296.

Mappus, R. L., Venkatesh, G. R., Shastry, C., Israeli, A., & Jackson, M. M. (2009). An fNIR based BMI for letter construction using continuous control. *Extended Abstracts of the ACM SIGCHI Conference on Human Factors in Computing Systems—CHI 2009*. New York: ACM. 3571–3576.

Marcus, A., Berstein, M. S., Badar, O., Karger, D. R., Madden, S., & Miller, R. C. (2011). Twitinfo: Aggregating and visualizing microblogs for event exploration. *Proceedings of the ACM SIGCHI Conference on Human Factors in Computing Systems—CHI 2011*. New York: ACM. 227–236.

Martin, D. W. (2004). *Doing psychology experiments* (6th ed.). Belmont, CA: Wadsworth.

Martin, R. L. (2009). *The Design of Business: Why Design Thinking is the Next Competitive Advantage*. Boston: Harvard Business School.

Martinec, D. V., Gatta, P., Zheng, B., Denk, P. M., & Swanstrom, L. L. (2009). The trade-off between flexibility and maneuverability: Task performance with articulating laparoscopic instruments. *Surgical Endoscopy*, *23*, 2697–2701.

Masliah, M. R., & Milgram, P. (2000). Measuring the allocation of control in a 6 degree-of-freedom docking experiment. *Proceedings of the ACM SIGCHI Conference on Human Factors in Computing Systems—CHI 2000*. New York: ACM. 25–32.

Matias, E., MacKenzie, I. S., & Buxton, W. (1996). One-handed touch typing on a QWERTY keyboard. *Human-Computer Interaction*, *11*, 1–27.

McCallum, D. C., & Irani, P. (2009). ARC-Pad: Absolute + relative cursor positioning for large displays with a mobile touchscreen. *Proceedings of the ACM Symposium on User Interface Software and Technology—UIST 2009*. New York: ACM. 153–156.

McGrenere, J., & Moore, G. (2000). Are we all in the same "bloat"?. *Proceedings of Graphics Interface 2000.* Toronto: Canadian Information Processing Society. 187–196.

McQueen, C., MacKenzie, I. S., & Zhang, S. X. (1995). An extended study of numeric entry on pen-based computers. *Proceedings of Graphics Interface'95.* Toronto: Canadian Information Processing Society. 215–222.

Mehlenbacher, B., Duffy, T. M., & Palmer, J. (1989). Finding information on a menu: Linking menu organizaton onto the user's goals. *Human-Computer Interaction, 4,* 231–251.

Meyer, D. E., Smith, J. E. K., Kornblum, S., Abrams, R. A., & Wright, C. E. (1990). Speed-accuracy tradeoffs in aimed movements: Toward a theory of rapid voluntary action. In M. Jeannerod (Ed.), *Attention and Performance XIII.* Hillsdale, NJ: Erlbaum.

Miller, D. P. (1981). The depth/breadth tradeoff in hierarchical computer menus. *Proceedings of the Human Factors Society.* Santa Monica: Human Factors Society. 12–16.

Miller, G. A. (1956). The magical number seven plus or minus two: Some limits on our capacity for processing information. *Psychological Review, 63,* 81–97.

Moritz, M. (1984). *The little kingdom: The Private Story of Apple Computer.* New York: William Morrow.

Morris, M. R., Huang, A., Paepcke, A., & Winograd, T. (2006). Cooperative gestures: Multi-user gestural interactions for co-located groupware. *Proceedings of the ACM SIGCHI Conference on Human Factors in Computing Systems—CHI 2006.* New York: ACM. 1201–1210.

Munteanu, C., Baecker, R., Penn, G., Toms, E., & James, D. (2006). The effect of speech recognition accuracy rates on the usefulness and usability of webcast archives. *Proceedings of the ACM SIGCHI Conference on Human Factors in Computing Systems—CHI 2006.* New York: ACM. 493–502.

Myers, B. A. (1998, March/April). A brief history of human-computer interaction technology. *Interactions,* 44–54.

Nacenta, M. A., Regan, L., Mandry, K., & Gutwin, C. (2008). Targeting across displayless space. *Proceedings of the ACM SIGCHI Conference on Human Factors in Computing Systems—CHI 2008.* New York: ACM. 777–786.

New, B., Pallier, C., Brysbaert, M., & Ferrand, L. (2004). Lexique 2: A new French lexical database. *Behavior Research Methods, Instruments, and Computers, 36,* 516–524.

Newell, A. (1990). *Unified Theories of Cognition.* Cambridge, MA: Harvard University Press.

Newell, A., & Rosenbloom, P. S. (1981). Mechanisms of skill acquisition and the law of practice. In J. R. Anderson (Ed.), *Cognitive Skills and their Acquisition* (pp. 1–55). Hillsdale, NJ: Erlbaum.

Nielsen, J. (1994). Estimating the number of subjects needed for a thinking aloud test. *International Journal of Human-Computer Studies, 41,* 385–397.

Norman, D. A. (1983, April). Design rules based on analyses of human error. *Communications of the ACM, 26,* 254–258.

Norman, D. A. (1988). *The Design of Everyday Things.* New York: Basic Books.

Noyes, J. (1983). The QWERTY keyboard: A review. *International Journal of Man-Machine Studies, 18,* 265–281.

Oldfield, R. C. (1971). The assessment and analysis of handedness: The Edinburgh inventory. *Neuropsychololgia, 9,* 97–113.

Oulasvirta, A., Tamminen, S., Roto, V., & Kuorelahti, J. (2005). Interaction in 4-second bursts: The fragmented nature of attentional resources in mobile HCI. *Proceedings of the ACM SIGCHI Conference on Human Factors in Computing Systems—CHI 2005.* New York: ACM. 919–928.

Pan, B., Hembrooke, H. A., Gay, G. K., Granka, L. A., Feusner, M. K., & Newman, J. K. (2004). The determinants of web page viewing behavior: An eye-tracking study. *Proceedings of the ACM Symposium on Eye Tracking Research and Applications—ETRA 2004*. New York: ACM. 147–154.

Pastel, R. (2006). Measuring the difficulty of steering through corners. *Proceedings of the ACM SIIGCHI Conference on Human Factors in Computing Systems—CHI 2006*. New York: ACM. 1087–1096.

Pausch, R. (1991). Virtual reality of five dollars a day. *Proceedings of the ACM SIGCHI Conference on Human Factors in Computing Systems—CHI '91*. New York: ACM. 265–269.

Pavlovych, A., & Stuerzlinger, W. (2003). Less-Tap: A fast and easy-to-learn text input technique for phones. *Proceedings of Graphics Interface 2003*. Toronto: Canadian Information Processing Society. 97–104.

Pearson, G., & Weiser, M. (1986). Of moles and men: The design of foot controls for workstations. *Proceedings of the ACM SIGCHI Conference on Human Factors in Computing Systems—CHI '86*. New York: ACM. 333–339.

Penfield, W., & Rasmussen, T. (1990). *The Cerebral Cortex of Man: A Clinical Study of Localization of Function*. New York: Macmillan.

Permenter, K. E., Fleger, S. A., & Malone, T. B. (1987). Advanced human factors engineering tool technologies. *Proceedings of the Human Factors Society 31st Annual Meeting*. Santa Monica: Human Factors and Ergonomics Society. 345–349.

Perry, K. B., & Hourcade, J. P. (2008). Evaluating one-handed thumb tapping on mobile touchscreen devices. *Proceedings of Graphics Interface 2008*. Toronto: Canadian Information Processing Society. 57–64.

Perugini, S., Anderson, T. J., & Moroney, W. F. (2007). A study of out-of-turn interaction in menu-based, IVR, voicemail systems. *Proceedings of the ACM SIGCHI Conference on Human Factors in Computing Systems—CHI 2007*. New York: ACM. 961–970.

Peters, M. (1985). Constraints in the performance of bimanual tasks and their expression in unskilled and skilled subjects. *Quarterly Journal of Experimental Psychology*, *37A*, 171–196.

Peters, M., & Ivanoff, J. (1999). Performance asymmetries in computer mouse control of right-handers, and left-handers with left- and right-handed mouse experience. *Journal of Motor Behavior*, *31*(1), 86–94.

Pettitt, M., Burnett, G., & Stevens, A. (2007). An extended keystroke level model (KLM) for predicting the visual demand of in-vehicle information systems. *Proceedings of the ACM SIGCHI Conference on Human Factors in Computing Systems—CHI 2007*. New York: ACM. 1515–1524.

Pew, R. W., & Baron, S. (1983). Perspectives on human performance modelling. *Automatica*, *19*, 663–676.

Pirolli, P., Pitkow, J., & Rao, R. (1996). Silk from a cow's ear: Extracting usable structures from the Web. *Proceedings of the ACM SIGCHI Conference on Human Factors in Computing Systems—CHI '96*. New York: ACM. 118–125.

Po, B. A., Fisher, B. D., & Booth, K. S. (2004). Mouse and touchscreen selection in the upper and lower visual fields. *Proceedings of the ACM SIGCHI Conference on Human Factors in Computing Systems—CHI 2004*. New York: ACM. 350–366.

Poller, M. F., & Garter, S. K. (1984). The effects of modes on text editing by experienced editor users. *Human Factors*, *26*, 449–462.

Porac, C., & Coren, S. (1981). *Lateral Preference and Human Behaviour*. New York: Springer Verlag.

Potter, R., Berman, M., & Shneiderman, B. (1988). An experimental evaluation of three touch screen strategies within a hypertext database. *International Journal of Human-Computer Interaction, 1*(1), 41–52.

Poulton, E. C. (1974). *Tracking Skill and Manual Control*. New York: Academic Press.

Qvarfordt, P., Jönsson, A., & Dahlbäck, N. (2003). The role of spoken feedback in experience multimodal interfaces as human-like. *Proceedings of the Fifth International Conference on Multi-Modal Interfaces—ICMI 2003*. New York: ACM. 250–257.

Räihä, K. J., & Špakov, O. (2009). Disambiguating ninja cursors with eye gaze. *Proceedings of the ACM SIGCHI Conference on Human Factors in Computing Systems—CHI 2009*. New York: ACM. 1411–1414.

Ranjan, A., Birnholtz, J. P., & Balakrishnan, R. (2007). Dynamic shared visual spaces: Experimenting with automatic camera in a remote repair task. *Proceedings of the ACM SIGCHI Conference in Human Factors in Computing Systems—CHI 2007*. New York: ACM. 1177–1186.

Rantanen, V., Verho, J., Lekkala, J., Tuisku, O., & Surakka, V. (2012). The effect of clicking by smiling on the accuracy of head-mounted gaze tracking. *Proceedings of the ACM Symposium on Eye Tracking Research and Applications—ETRA 2012*. New York: ACM. 345–348.

Recker, M. M., & Pitkow, J. E. (1996). Predicting document access in large multimedia repositories. *ACM Transactions on Computer-Human Interaction (TOCHI), 3*, 352–375.

Rekimoto, J. (1996). Tilting operations for small screen interfaces. *Proceedings of the ACM Symposium on User Interface Software and Technology—UIST '96*. New York: ACM. 167–168.

Rekimoto, J. (1997). Pick-and-drop: A direct manipulation technique for multiple computer environments. *Proceedings of the ACM Symposium on User Interface Software and Technology—UIST '97*. New York: ACM. 31–39.

Richtel, M. (2009, July 28). In study, texting lifts crash risk by large margin, *The New York Times*, A1, Retrieved 21/23/11 from <http://www.nytimes.com/2009/2007/2028/technology/2028texting.html>.

Rider, R. E. (1974). U.S. Patent No. 3,835,464.

Roberts, D., Duckworth, T., Moore, C., Wolff, R., & O'Hare, J. (2009). Comparing the end to end latency of an immersive collaborative environment and a video conference. *Proceedings of the Thirteenth Symposium on Distributed Simulation and Real Time Applications*. New York: ACM. 89–94.

Robertson, J. (2012). Likert-type scales, statistical methods, and effect sizes. *Communications of the ACM, 55*(5), 6–7.

Rohs, M., & Oulasvirta, A. (2008). Target acquisition with camera phones when used as magic lenses. *Proceedings of the ACM SIGCHI Conference on Human Factors in Computing Systems—CHI 2008*. New York: ACM. 1409–1418.

Ruiz, J., Bunt, A., & Lank, E. (2008). A model of non-preferred hand mode switching. *Proceedings of Graphics Interface 2008*. Toronto: Canadian Information Processing Society. 49–56.

Rümelin, S., Rukzio, E., & Hardy, R. (2012). NaviRadar: A tactile information display for pedestrian navigation. *Proceedings of the ACM Symposium on User Interface Software and Technology—UIST 2012*. New York: ACM. 293–302.

Ryu, H., & Cruz, K. (2005). LetterEase: Improving text entry on a handheld device via letter reassignment. *Proceedings of the Nineteenth Conference of the Computer-Human Interaction Special Interaction Group (CHISIG) of Australia—OZCHI 2005*. New York: ACM. 1–10.

Sáenz, M., & Sánchez, J. (2009). Indoor position and orientation for the blind. *Proceedings of HCI International 2007*. Berlin: Springer. 236–245.

Sällnas, E. L., & Zhai, S. (2003). Collaboration meets Fitts' law: Passing virtual objects with and without haptic force feedback. *Proceedings of the IFIP Conference on Human-Computer Interaction—INTERACT 2003*. Amsterdam: IOS Press. 97–104.

Salvendy, G. E. (1987). *Handbook of Human Factors*. New York: Wiley.

Salvucci, D., Taatgen, N. A., & Borst, J. P. (2009). Toward a unified theory of the multi-tasking continuum: From concurrent performance to task switching, interruption, and resumption. *Proceedings of the ACM SIGCHI Conference on Human Factors in Computing Systems—CHI 2009*. New York: ACM. 1819–1828.

Sandnes, F. E. (2006). Can spatial mnemonics accelerate the learning of text input chords?. *Proceedings of the Working Conference on Advanced Visual Interfaces—AVI 2006*. New York: ACM. 245–249.

Seager, W., & Fraser, D. S. (2007). Comparing physical, automatic and manual map rotation for pedestrian navigation. *Proceedings of the ACM SIGCHI Conference on Human Factors in Computing Systems—CHI 2007*. New York: ACM. 767–776.

Sears, A., & Shneiderman, B. (1991). High precision touchscreens: Design strategies and comparisons with a mouse. *International Journal of Man-Machine Studies, 34*, 593–613.

Seay, A. F., & Kraut, R. E. (2007). Project massive: Self-regulation and problematic use of online gaming. *Proceedings of the ACM Conference on Human Factors in Computing Systems—CHI 2007*. New York: ACM. 829–838.

Selker, T. (2008, December). Touching the future. *Communications of the ACM, 51*, 14–16.

Sellen, A., Eardley, R., Iazdl, S., & Harper, R. (2006). The whereabouts clock: Early testing of a situated awareness device. *Extended Abstracts of the ACM SIGCHI Conference on Human Factors in Computing Systems—CHI 2006*. New York: ACM. 1307–1312.

Sellen, A. J., Kurtenbach, G. P., & Buxton, W. A. S. (1992). The prevention of mode errors through sensory feedback. *Human-Computer Interaction, 7*, 141–164.

Seow, S. C. (2005). Information theoretic models of HCI: A comparison of the Hick-Hyman law and Fitts' law. *Human-Computer Interaction, 20*, 315–352.

Shannon, C. E. (1951). Prediction and entropy of printed English. *Bell System Technical Journal, 30*, 50–64.

Shannon, C. E., & Weaver, W. (1949). *The Mathematical Theory of Communications*. Urbana, IL: University of Illinois Press.

Sheridan, T. B., & Ferrell, W. R. (1968). Remote manipulation control with transmission delay. *IEEE Transactions on Human Factors in Electronics, HFE-4*, 25–29.

Sheskin, D. (2011). *Handbook of Parametric and Nonparametric Statistical Procedures* (5th ed.). Boca Raton: CRC Press.

Shklovski, I., Kraut, R., & Cummings, J. (2006). Routine patterns of internet use and psychological well-being: Coping with a residential move. *Proceedings of the ACM SIGCHI Conference on Human Factors in Computing Systems—CHI 2006*. New York: ACM. 969–978.

Shneiderman, B. (1983, August). Direct manipulation: A step beyond programming languages. *IEEE Computer*, 57–69.

Shneiderman, B., & Plaisant, C. (2005). *Designing the User Interface: Strategies for Effective Human-Computer Interaction* (4th ed.). New York: Pearson.

Siegel, S. (1957). Nonparametric statistics. *The American Statistician, 11*(3), 13–19.

Siegel, S., & Castellan, N. J., Jr. (1988). *Nonparametric Statistics for the Behavioral Sciences* (2nd ed.). London: McGraw-Hill.

Silfverberg, M., Korhonen, P., & MacKenzie, I. S. (2003). International Patent No. WO 03/021568 A1.

Silfverberg, M., MacKenzie, I. S., & Korhonen, P. (2000). Predicting text entry speed on mobile phones. *Proceedings of the ACM SIGCHI Conference on Human Factors in Computing Systems—CHI 2000*. New York: ACM. 9–16.

Sjölie, D., Bodin, K., Elgh, E., Eriksson, J., Jaulert, L. E., & Nyberg, L. (2010). Effects of interactivity and 3D-motion on mental rotation brain activity in an immersive virtual environment. *Proceedings of the ACM SIGCHI Conference on Human Factors in Computing Systems—CHI 2010*. New York: ACM. 869–878.

Small, D., & Ishii, H. (1997). Design of spatially aware graspable displays. *Proceedings of the ACM SIGCHI Conference on Human Factors in Computing Systems—CHI '97*. New York: ACM. 367–368.

Smith, D. C., Irby, C., Kimball, R., & Harslem, E. (1982). The Star user interface: An overview. *Proceedings of the AFIPS Joint Computer Conference*. New York: ACM. 515–528.

Smith, D. C., & Irby, C. H. (1998). Xerox Star live demonstration. *Summary Proceedings of ACM SIGCHI Conference on Human Factors in Computing Systems—CHI '98*. New York: ACM. 17.

Smith, D. K., & Alexander, R. C. (1988). *Fumbling the Future: How Xerox Invented, then Ignored, the First Personal Computer*. New York: William Morrow.

Snowberry, K., Parkinson, S. R., & Sisson, N. (1983). Computer display menus. *Ergonomics, 26*, 699–712.

Solovey, E. T., Schermerhorn, P., Scheutz, M., Sassaroli, A., Fantini, S., & Jacob, R. J. K. (2012). Brainput: Enhancing interactive systems with streaming fNIRS brain input. *Proceedings of the ACM SIGCHI Conference on Human Factors in Computing Systems—CHI 2012*. New York: ACM. 2193–2202.

Song, H., Kim, B., Lee, B., & Seo, J. (2010). A comparative evaluation on tree visualization methods for hierarchical structures with large fan-outs. *Proceedings of the ACM SIGCHI Conference on Human Factors in Computing Systems—CHI 2010*. New York: ACM. 223–232.

Soukoreff, R. W., & MacKenzie, I. S. (2004). Towards a standard for pointing device evaluation: Perspectives on 27 years of Fitts' law research in HCI. *International Journal of Human-Computer Studies, 61*, 751–789.

Sporka, A. J., Felzer, T., Kurniawan, S. H., Ondrej, P., Haiduk, P., & MacKenzie, I. S. (2011). CHANTI: Predictive text entry using non-verbal vocal input. *Proceedings of the ACM SIGCHI Conference on Human Factors in Computing Systems—CHI 2011*. New York: ACM. 2463–2472.

Sprague, D. W., Po, B. A., & Booth, K. S. (2006). The importance of accurate VR head registration on skilled motor performance. *Proceedings of Graphics Interface 2006*. Toronto: Canadian Information Processing Society. 131–137.

Stanton, C. M., Kahn, P. H., Jr., Severson, R. L., Ruckert, J. H., & Gill, B. T. (2008). Robotic animals might aid in the social development of children with autism. *Proceedings of Human Robot Interaction—HRI 2008*. New York: ACM. 271–278.

Steed, A. (2008). A simple method for estimating the latency of interactive, real-time graphics simulations. *Proceedings of the ACM Symposium on Virtual Reality Software and Technology—VRST 2008*. New York: ACM. 123–129.

Strunk, W., Jr., & White, E. B. (2000). *The Elements of Style* (4th ed.). Needham Heights, MA: Pearson.

Su, N. M., & Mark, G. (2008). Communication chains and multitasking. *Proceedings of the ACM SIGCHI Conference on Human Factors in Computing Systems—CHI 2008*. New York: ACM. 83–92.

Sun, X., Zhang, Q., Wiedenbeck, S., & Chintakovid, T. (2006). Gender differences in trust perception when using IM and video. *Extended Abstracts of the ACM SIGCHI Conference on Human Factors in Computing Systems—CHI 2006*. New York: ACM. 1373–1378.

Sutherland, I. E. (1963). Sketchpad: A man-machine graphical communication system. *Proceedings of the AFIPS Spring Joint Computer Conference*. New York: ACM. 329–346.

Swensson, R. G. (1972). The elusive tradeoff: Speed vs accuracy in visual discrimination tasks. *Perception and Psychophysics*, *12*(1A), 16–32.

Sylla, C., Branco, P., Coutinho, C., & Coquet, M. E. (2009). Storytelling through drawings: Evaluating tangible interfaces for children. *Extended Abstracts of the ACM SIGCHI Conference on Human Factors in Computing Systems—CHI 2009*. New York: ACM. 3461–3466.

Talbot, M., & Cowan, W. (2009). On the audio representation of distance for blind users. *Proceedings of the ACM SIGCHI Conference on Human Factors in Computing Systems—CHI 2009*. New York: ACM. 1839–1848.

Tatler, B. W., Wade, N. J., Kwan, H., Findlay, J. M., & Velichkovsky, B. M. (2010). Yarbus, eye movements, and vision. *i-Perception*, *1*, 7–27.

Taylor and Francis. (2012). HCI style guidelines for final submissions. Retrieved 7 February 2012, from <http://www.tandf.co.uk/journals/authors/HHCIguidelines.pdf>.

Teather, R. J., Pavlovych, A., Stuerzlinger, W., & MacKenzie, I. S. (2009). Effects of tracking technology, latency, and spatial jitter on object movement. *Proceedings of the IEEE Symposium on 3D User Interfaces—3DUI 2009*. New York: IEEE. 43–50.

Teo, L. H., John, B., & Blackmon, M. (2012). CogTool-Explorer: A model of goal-directed user exploration that considers information layout. *Proceedings of the ACM SIGCHI Conference on Human Factors in Computing Systems—CHI 2012*. New York: ACM. 2479–2488.

Thornton, P. (2010, March/April). Design thinking in stereo: Brown and Martin. *interactions*, 12–15.

Tinwala, H., & MacKenzie, I. S. (2008). LetterScroll: Text entry using a wheel for visually impaired users. *Extended Abstracts of the ACM Conference on Human Factors in Computing Systems–CHI 2008*. New York: ACM. 3153–3158.

Tinwala, H., & MacKenzie, I. S. (2010). Eyes-free text entry with error correction on touchscreen mobile devices. *Proceedings of the Sixth Nordic Conference on Human-Computer Interaction—NordiCHI 2010*. New York: ACM. 511–520.

Tohidi, M., Buxton, W., Baecker, R., & Sellen, A. (2006). Getting the right design and the design right: Testing many is better than one. *Proceedings of the ACM SIGCHI Conference on Human Factors in Computing Systems—CHI 2006*. New York: ACM. 1243–1252.

Tullis, T. S. (1985). Designing a menu-based interface to an operating system. *Proceedings of the ACM SIGCHI Conference on Human Factors in Computing Systems—CHI '85*. New York: ACM. 70–84.

Van Cott, H. P., & Kinkade, R. G. (Eds.). (1972). *Human Engineering Guide to Equipment Design*. U.S. Government Printing Office.

Venolia, D. (1993). Facile 3D manipulation. *Proceedings of the INTERACT '93 and CHI '93 Conference on Human Factors in Computing Systems—INTERCHI '93*. New York: ACM. 31–36.

Venolia, D., & Neiberg, F. (1994). T-Cube: A fast, self-disclosing pen-based alphabet. *Proceedings of ACM SIGCHI Conference on Human Factors in Computing Systems—CHI '94*. New York: ACM. 265–270.

Venolia, D. S., & Ishikawa, S. (1994). U. S. Patent No. 5,313,230.

Vertanen, K., & Kristensson, P. O. (2009). Parakeet: A continuous speech recognition system for mobile touch-screen devices. *Proceedings of the ACM Conference on Intelligent User Interfaces—IUI 2009*. New York: ACM. 237–246.

Vertegaal, R. (2008). A Fitts' law comparison of eye tracking and manual input in the selection of visual targets. *Proceedings of the Tenth International Conference on Multimodal Interfaces*. New York: ACM. 241–248.

Villar, N., Izadi, S., Rosenfeld, D., Benko, H., Helmes, J., & Westhues, J., et al. (2009). Mouse 2.0: Multi-touch meets the mouse. *Proceedings of the ACM Symposium on User Interface Software and Technology—UIST 2009*. New York: ACM. 33–42.

Vogel, D., & Balakrishnan, R. (2010). Direct pen interaction with a conventional graphical user interface. *Human-Computer Interaction, 25*, 324–388.

Vogel, D., & Baudisch, P. (2007). Shift: A technique for operating pen-based interfaces using touch. *Proceedings of the ACM SIGCHI Conference on Human Factors in Computing Systems—CHI 2007*. New York: ACM. 657–666.

Weisband, S., & Kiesler, S. (1996). Self disclosure on computer forms: Meta-analysis and implications. *Proceedings of the ACM SIGCHI Conference on Human Factors in Computing Systems—CHI '99*. New York: ACM. 3–10.

Weiser, M. (1991, September). The computer for the 21st century. *Scientific American, 265*, 94–105.

Welford, A. T. (1968). *Fundamentals of Skill*. London: Methuen.

Wickens, C. D. (1987). *Engineering Psychology and Human Performance*. New York: HarperCollins.

Wigdor, D., & Balakrishnan, R. (2003). TiltText: Using tilt for text input to mobile phones. *Proceedings of the ACM Symposium on User Interface Software and Technology—UIST 2003*. New York: ACM. 81–90.

Wigdor, D., & Balakrishnan, R. (2004). A comparison of consecutive and concurrent input text entry techniques for mobile phones: *Proceedings of the ACM SIGCHI Conference on Human Factors in Computing Systems—CHI '04*. New York: ACM. 81–88.

Wigdor, D., Forlines, C., Baudisch, P., Barnwell, J., & Shen, C. (2007). Lucid touch: A see-through mobile device. *Proceedings of the ACM Symposium on User Interface Software and Technology—UIST 2007*. New York: ACM. 269–278.

Wigdor, D., Shen, C., Forlines, C., & Balakrishnan, R. (2006). Effects of display position and control space orientation on user preference and performance. *Proceedings of the ACM SIGCHI Conference on Human Factors in Computing Systems—CHI 2006*. New York: ACM. 309–318.

Wigdor, D., Williams, S., Cronin, M., Levy, R., White, K., & Mazeev, M., et al. (2009). Ripples: Utilizing per-contact visualizations to improve user interaction with touch displays. *Proceedings of the ACM Symposium on User Interface Software and Technology—UIST 2009*. New York: ACM. 3–12.

Williams, G. (1984, February). The Apple Macintosh computer. *Byte*, 30–54.

Wilson, G., Brewster, S. A., Halvey, M., Crossan, A., & Stewart, C. (2011). The effects of walking, feedback and control method on pressure-based interaction. *Proceedings of MobileHCI 2011*. New York: ACM. 147–156.

Wing, A. (1982). Timing and coordination of repetitive bimanual movements. *Quarterly Journal of Experimental Psychology, 34A*, 339–348.

Wobbrock, J. O., Chau, D. H., & Myers, B. A. (2007). An alternative to push, press, and tap-tap-tap: Gesturing on an isometric joystick for mobile phone text entry. *Proceedings of the ACM SIGCHI Conference on Human Factors in Computing System—CHI 2007*. New York: ACM. 667–676.

Wobbrock, J. O., Cutrell, E., Harada, S., & MacKenzie, I. S. (2008). An error model for pointing based on Fitts' law. *Proceedings of the ACM SIGCHI Conference on Human Factors in Computing Systems—CHI 2008*. New York: ACM. 1613–1622.

Wobbrock, J. O., Findlater, L., Gergle, D., & Higgins, J. J. (2011). The aligned rank transform for nonparametric factorial analyses using only ANOVA procedures. *Proceedings of the ACM SIGCHI Conference on Human Factors in Computing Systems—CHI 2011*. New York: ACM. 143–146.

Wobbrock, J. O., Fogarty, J., Shih-Yen, L., Kimuro, S., & Harada, S. (2009). The angle-mouse: Target-agnostic dynamic gain adjustment based on angular deviation. *Proceedings of the ACM SIGCHI Conference on Human Factors in Computing Systems—CHI 2009*. New York: ACM. 1401–1410.

Wobbrock, J. O., & Gajos, K. Z. (2007). A comparison of area pointing and goal crossing for people with and without motor impairments. *Proceedings of the ACM Conference on Computers and Assessibility—ACCESS 2007*. New York: ACM. 3–10.

Wobbrock, J. O., Myers, B. A., & Rothrock, B. (2006). Few-key text entry revisited: Mnemonic gestures on four keys. *Extended Abstracts of the ACM SIGCHI Conference on Human Factors in Computing Systems—CHI 2006*. New York: ACM. 489–492.

Wobbrock, J. O., Rubinstein, J., Sawyer, M. W., & Duchowski, A. T. (2008). Longitudinal evaluation of discrete consecutive gaze gestures for text entry. *Proceedings of the ACM Symposium on Eye Tracking Research and Applications—ETRA 2008*. New York: ACM. 11–18, 281.

Worden, A., Walker, N., Bharat, K., & Hudson, S. E. (1997). Making computers easier for older adults to use: Area cursors and sticky icons. *Proceedings of the ACM Conference on Human Factors in Computing Systems—CHI '97*. New York: ACM. 266–271.

Xiao, X., Luo, Q., Hong, D., Fu, H., Xie, X., & Ma, W. Y. (2009). Browsing on small displays by tranforming web pages into hierarchically structured subpages. *ACM Transactions on the Web, 3*, 1–36.

Yee, K. P. (2004). Two-handed interaction on a tablet display. *Extended Abstracts of the ACM SIGCHI Conference on Human Factors in Computing Systems—CHI 2004*. New York: ACM. 1493–1496.

Yin, M., & Zhai, S. (2006). The benefits of augmenting telephone voice menu navigation with visual browsing and search. *Proceedings of the ACM SIGCHI Conference on Human Factors in Computing Systems—CHI 2006*. New York: ACM. 319–328.

Zanbaka, C., Goolkasian, P., & Hodges, L. F. (2006). Can a virtual cat persuade you? The role of gender and realism in speaker persuasiveness. *Proceedings of the ACM SIGCHI Conference on Human Factors in Computing Systems—CHI 2006*. New York: ACM. 1153–1162.

Zaphiris, P., Kurniawan, S. H., & Ellis, R. D. (2003). Age related differences and the depth vs. breadth tradeoff in hierarchical online information systems. *Proceedings of the*

Seventh ERCIM International Workshop on User Interfaces for all. Berlin: Springer. 23–42.

Zhai, S. (1995). *Human Performance in Six Degree of Freedom Input Control. (Doctoral Dissertation).* University of Toronto.

Zhai, S., Conversy, S., Beaudouin-Lafon, M., & Guiard, Y. (2003). Human on-line response to target expansion. *Proceedings of the ACM SIGCHI Conference on Human Factors in Computing Systems—CHI 2003.* New York: ACM. 177–184.

Zhai, S., Kong, J., & Ren, X. (2004). Speed-accuracy tradeoff in Fitts' law tasks: On the equivalency of actual and nominal pointing precision. *International Journal of Human-Computer Studies, 61,* 823–856.

Zhai, S., Sue, A., & Accot, J. (2002). Movement mode, hits distribution and learning in virtual keyboarding. *Proceedings of the ACM SIGCHI Conference on Human Factors in Computing Systems—CHI 2002.* New York: ACM. 17–24.

Zhang, X., & MacKenzie, I. S. (2007). Evaluating eye tracking with ISO 9241—Part 9. *Proceedings of HCI International 2007.* Heidelberg: Springer. 779–788.

Zhao, S., Dragicevic, P., Chignell, M., Balakrishnan, R., & Baudisch, P. (2007). Earpod: Eyes-free menu selection using touch input and reactive audio feedback. *Proceedings of the ACM SIGCHI Conference on Human Factors in Computing Systems—CHI 2007.* New York: ACM. 1395–1404.

Zhu, D., Gedeon, T., & Taylor, K. (2011). Exploring camera viewpoint control models for a multi-tasking setting in teleoperation. *Proceedings of the ACM SIGCHI Conference in Human Factors in Computing Systems—CHI 2011.* New York: ACM. 53–62.

Zimmerman, T. G., Lanier, J., Blanchard, C., Bryson, S., & Harvill, Y. (1987). A hand gesture interface device. *Proceedings of the ACM SIGCHI Conference on Human Factors in Computing Systems—CHI + GI '87.* New York: ACM. 189–192.

Appendix

This appendix lists the software and Application Programming Interfaces (APIs) accompanying this book. The software is written in Java and, therefore, is platform independent (more or less). Each application is provided as a download on this book's website. The zip files contain the source and class files for the applications as well as related data files, images in the APIs, etc. An effective way to use this software is to unzip all the files into a single directory, then recompile all the files (`javac *.java`). Strictly speaking, recompiling is not necessary, but this is a good first step if changes to the source files are anticipated. It is also recommended to build a fresh collection of APIs (`javadoc *.java`) which are thereafter accessed from a browser by opening `index.html`.

Software on this book's website

- Anova2
- ChiSquare
- Nonparametric
- LetterGuessingExperiment
- ReactionTimeExperiment
- FittsTaskTwoExperiment
- FittsTaskTwoExperimentTrace
- TypingTestExperiment
- PhoneKeypadExperiment
- SoftKeyboardExperiment
- GraffitiExperiment
- GraffitiExperimentTrace

More software and downloads will be added as they become available. Please visit the website for further details: www.yorku.ca/mack/HCIbook.

Index

Note: Page numbers followed by *"f"* refer to figures respectively.

A

Abstract, 296–297
Access time, 9
Accidents, analyzing, 64–65
Acknowledgement, 303
ACM SIGCHI conference
  in 1983, 2, 15–17, 23
  in 1993, 103
Alpha, 196–197
American Psychological Association (APA), 158
Analysis of variance (ANOVA), 192–209, 224
  between-subjects designs, 202–203
  counterbalancing and testing for a group effect, 207–209
  post hoc comparisons, 201–202
  reasons for, 193–199
  test conditions, 199–201
  tool, 206–207
  two-way, 203–206
Apparatus section, 300
Apple Computer Inc., 14, 90, 128–129, 243, 293–294
Apple iPhone, 20, 107, 107*f*, 147
Apple II, 14
Apple MacBook, 242–243
Apple Macintosh, 15, 23*f*, 24*f*
  launch of, 22–23, 24*f*
Applied Information-Processing Psychology Project (AIP), 17
Archive, 293–294
Association for Computing Machinery (ACM), 158
Associative indexing, 4
Asymmetric skill transfer, 209
Attention, 63–65
  divided, 64
  selected, 64
Audition. *See* Hearing
Auditory illusion, 45–46, 46*f*
Axis labels, 76*f*

B

Big Brother, 22
"Big fuzzy cloud" model of politics, 234–235, 234*f*
Bimanual control, model of, 238–241
Birth of HCI, 15–23
  first ACM SIGCHI conference, 15–17
  launch of Apple Macintosh, 22–23
  psychology of human-computer interaction, 17–22

Books
  in reference list, 306*f*
Brain, 44–50
  cognition, 47–48
  memory, 48–50
  perception, 44–47
Breadth *versus* depth, in menu design, 24–25, 25*f*
British National Corpus (BNC), 50–51
Bush, Vannevar, 3–4, 149–150
Buxton's model, 242–243
CAPS_LOCK error, 112
Categorical data, 134–135
Cause-and-effect relationship, 145–147
CD gain and transfer function, 80–81
Chapter in books
  in reference list, 306*f*
Chi-square test, 209–214
  Java utility, 211, 211*f*
Choice reaction time, 18–19, 59, 255–257
Chunking, 50
Circumstantial relationship, 145–147
Citations and references, in manuscripts, 124–125, 305–308
  citations, 307–308
  reference list, 305–307
Clarity, writing for, 311–313
Class matching, 58, 58*f*
Close-ended questions, 173
Clutching, 243–244
Cognition, 47–48
Comparative evaluation, 143–145
Computer supported collaborative work (CSCW), 235
Conceptual models. *See* Mental models and metaphor
Conclusion, of research paper, 303
Conference paper, 293–294
  in reference list, 306*f*
Control-display relationships, 73–86
  CD gain and transfer function, 80–81
  latency, 81–84
  property sensed and order of control, 84–86
  spatial relationships, 75–79
Controlled experiments, 130–131
Correlational methods, 132
Counterbalancing, 177, 180*f*

D

Data collection, 165
Degrees of freedom (DOF), 77, 101–104

Dependent variables, 131, 160
Descriptive models, 93, 233–244
  bimanual control, model of, 238–241
  graphical input, three-state model for, 242–244
  key-action model (KAM), 235–236
  problem space, delineating, 234–235
  quadrant model of groupware, 235–236
Design section, of research paper, 301
Design-induced errors, 66–67, 115–116
Designing of HCI experiments, 157
Desktop metaphor, 12
Direct manipulation systems, 5–6
Discovery, 123
Divided attention, 64
Doing Psychology Experiments, 158
Dvorak simplified keyboard (DSK), 186

E

Ecological validity, 143
Edinburgh Handedness Inventory, 41
Effect size, in HCI research, 197
Effective target width, 252–253
Empirical research, 129
EndNote, 308
Engelbart, Douglas, 6–7, 7f
Engineering and design *versus* research, 126–129
Engineering model, 258
Entropy, in language, 53–54
Etch-A-Sketch, 103
Ethics Review Committee (ERC), 159
Euler, Leonhard, 177–178
Event-driven programming, 13–14
Executive keys, 236
Experiment design, signal-to-noise
      conceptualization of, 158f
Experimental methods, 130–132
Experimentation, 122
External validity, 140–143
Eye typing, 43–44
Eyes, 43–44, 43f

F

Factor. *See* Independent variables
Factorial experiments, 158, 161
Facts, research and, 122
Fat finger problem, 106–107
Fatigue effect, 177
Fitts' law, 123, 163, 167–168, 249–255
  background, 249–252
  example, 252–255
Fixations, 32
Focus advancement, 113–114

Focused attention. *See* Selected attention
Formatting, manuscript, 304–305
Friedman test, 214–215, 222

G

GOMS (Goals, Operators, Methods, Selection
      rules), 258
Grafacon, 8, 8f
Graphical user interfaces (GUIs)
  growth of, 23–24
Group effects, counterbalancing and testing for,
      206–207
Group writing, 235
Groupware, 235
Growth of HCI research, 24–25
Guiard's model, of bimanual control, 239f
Gulf of evaluation, 96–97
Gustation. *See* Taste

H

Handedness, 41–42
Haptic illusions, 46
Hard controls, 72–74
Hard keys, 94–95
HCI experiment, designing, 157, 160
  asymmetric skill transfer, 181–184
  confounding variables, 166–169
  control variables, 166
  counterbalancing, 177–180
  dependent variables, 163–165
  ethics approval, 159–160
  group effects, 181–184
  independent variables, 161–163
  Latin squares, 177–180
  longitudinal studies, 184–187
  methodology, 157–159
  order effects, 177–180
  participants, 171–173
  questionnaire design, 173–174
  random variables, 166
  task and procedure, 169–171
  within-subjects and between-subjects, 175–177
Hearing, 34–36
  envelope, 35
  loudness, 35
  pitch, 35
  timbre, 35
H-index, 125
Historical context, 2–3, 3f
  birth of HCI, 15–23
    First ACM SIGCHI conference, 15–17
    launch of Apple Macintosh, 22–23

psychology of human-computer interaction, 17–22
HCI and graphical user interfaces (GUIs), growth of, 23–24
HCI research, growth of, 24–25
invention of the mouse, 6–10
Ivan Sutherland's Sketchpad, 5–6
Vannevar Bush's "as we may think", 3–5
Xerox star, 11–15
Human error, 65–67
Human factors, 27, 29–30
  brain, 44–50
    cognition, 47–48
    memory, 48–50
    perception, 44–47
  human performance, 54–67
    attention, 63–65
    human error, 65–67
    reaction time, 56–59
    skilled behavior, 62–63
    visual search, 59–62
  language, 50–54
    entropy in, 53–54
    redundancy in, 52–53
  responders, 38–44
    eyes, 43–44
    limbs, 39–42
    voice, 42
  sensors, 30–38
    hearing, 34–36
    senses, 38
    smell and taste, 36–38
    touch, 36
    vision, 30–34
  time scale of human action, 28–29
Human Participant Review Committee (HRPC), 159
Human-computer interface with eye tracker, 42f
Hyperlinks, 124
Hypothesis testing, 191
  analysis of variance (ANOVA), 192–209
    between-subjects designs, 202–203
    counterbalancing and testing for a group effect, 206–207
    post hoc comparisons, 201–202
    reasons for, 193–199
    test conditions, 199–201
    tool, 206–207
    two-way analysis of variance, 203–206
  chi-square test, 209–214
  non-parametric tests for ordinal data, 214–222
  parametric *versus* non-parametric tests, 222–226

I

Ideas
  research topics, 148–150
  small aspects, 150–151
Implementation models, 89
Independent variables, 161–163, 244
Index of difficulty (ID), 167–168, 251
Index of performance, 251
Institutional Review Board (IRB), 159
Interaction elements, 71
  control-display relationships, 74–86
    CD gain and transfer function, 80–81
    latency, 81–84
    property sensed and order of control, 84–86
    spatial relationships, 75–79
  degrees of freedom, 101–104
  hard controls and soft controls, 72–74
  interaction errors, 110–116
  mental models and metaphor, 88–92
  mobile context, 105–110
  modes, 93–101
  natural *versus* learned relationships, 86–88
Interaction model, 285
Interaction stance, 161–162
Internal validity, 140–143
Internet document
  in reference list, 306f
Interval data, 136–137
Introduction, of research paper, 298–299
iPhone, 105–106, 128–129
  touchscreen selection, 107, 107f
Isometric joystick, 84–85
Isotonic joystick, 84–85

J

Journal papers, 293–294
  in reference list, 306f
Joysticks, 7, 8f, 84–85
Just noticeable difference (JND), 44–45

K

Key-action model (KAM), 236–238
Keys and modes, 93f, 94f
Keystroke-level model (KLM), 178, 258–274
  modern applications of, 261–266
  original experiment, 258–261
  and predictive text entry, 266–271
  and text entry, 266–271
Keywords, 297–298
Knee-controlled lever, 7–8, 8f
Kruskal-Wallis test, 214–215

L

Lag. *See* Latency
Language, 50–54
    entropy in, 53–54
    redundancy in, 52–53
Latency, 81–84
LaTeX, 305
Latin square, 177–178
Laws, 123
Learning effect. *See* Practice effect
Letter-guessing experiment, 53–54, 54*f*
LetterWise, 185
Light pen, 7, 8*f*
Likert-scale questionnaire, 136–137, 310*f*
Linear regression model, 245–249
Literature, awareness of, 151–152
Longitudinal study, 184–185
Long-term memory, 48

M

Mac, 15, 22–23
Manipulated variable, 131
Mann-Whitney U test, 214–215, 216*f*
Manuscript, 294
    citations and references, 305–308
    formatting, 304–305
    preparation, 303–313
    visual aids, 308–311
    writing for clarity, 311–313
The Many Loves of Dobie Gillis, 148, 149*f*
Mappings, 74–75
Martin, David, 158
McAfee's Site Advisor (MSA), 213
Measurement scales, 133–134, 134*f*
Memory, 48–50
Mental models and metaphor, 88–92
Menu design
    breadth *versus* depth in, 24–25, 25*f*
Merriam-Webster's Collegiate Dictionary, 304–305
Methodology, of research paper, 9, 63, 157–158, 299–301
    apparatus section, 300
    design section, 301
    participants section, 300
    procedure section, 300–301
Microsoft Excel, 100, 248
Microsoft *Intellimouse*, 242*f*
Microsoft PowerPoint, 95, 97–98
Microsoft Word, 73–74, 94, 305
Microsoft Windows, 23, 293–294
Mixed design, 177
Model, 252

Model Continuum Model (MCM), 283, 283*f*
Model human processor (MHP), 17–18, 19*f*
Modeling interaction, 233
    descriptive models, 233–244
        bimanual control, model of, 238–241
        graphical input, three-state model for, 242–244
        key-action model (KAM), 235–236
        problem space, delineating, 234–235
        quadrant model of groupware, 235–236
    model continuum model, 283
    predictive models, 244–283
        choice reaction time, 255–257
        Fitts' law, 249–255
        keystroke-level model (KLM), 258–274
        linear regression model, 245–249
        more than one predictor, 279–282
        skill acquisition, 274–279
Model-View-Controller, 14
Modes, 93–101
Modifier keys, 236
Motion time, 9
Motor homunculus, 38–39
Mouse, invention of, 6–10
Mouse configurations sensing rotation, 98, 99*f*
Mouse-to-cursor mapping, 75–76
Multiple regression, 279
Multi-touch demonstration, 107–108, 109*f*
Multi-touch sensing input devices, 105*f*

N

Name matching, 57–58, 58*f*
NASA-TLX, 174
National Computer Conference (NCC), 11
Naturally occurring attributes, 161
Navi key, 94
NaviRadar, 91
Needless words, omitting, 312*f*
Newell's time-scale model, 28–29
NLS (oNLine System), 6
Nokia, 293–294
Nominal scale, 134–135
Non-parametric tests, 191, 192*f*
    for ordinal data, 214–222
    versus parametric tests, 222–226
Non-verbal voice interaction (NVVI), 42
Null hypothesis, 193–194

O

Observation, 132–133
Observational methods, 130
Olfaction. *See* Smell
Open-ended questions, 173

Order effect, 177
Ordinal data, non-parametric tests for, 214–222
Ordinal scale measurements, 136
Organisation, of research paper, 295–303
Oxford English Dictionary, 304–305

P

PadMouse, 103, 105*f*
Paint Shop Pro, 89–90
Panning, 78
Parametric analysis, 260–261
Parametric tests, 191, 192*f*
    versus non-parametric tests, 222–226
Participants, 172
    section, of research paper, 300
Part-of-speech (POS) tagging, 52
Parts of research paper, 295–303, 295*f*
    abstract, 296–297
    conclusion, 303
    introduction, 298–299
    keywords, 297–298
    method, 299–301
    references, 303
    results and discussion, 301–303
    title, 296
Pearson chi-square test. *See* Chi-square test
Peer review, 293
Perception, 44–47
Personal digital assistants (PDAs), 187
Physical keys, 94–95, 94*f*
Physical matching, 21, 57, 57*f*
Pilot testing, 133
Pinyin, 51–52
Polhemus *G4*™, 82–83
Position-control, 84–86, 112–113
Positioning, 78
Post hoc comparisons test, 201–202
Power law of learning, 186, 274
Power law of practice, 274
Practice effect, 177
Predictive models, 244–283
    choice reaction time, 255–257
    Fitts' law, 249–255
    keystroke-level model (KLM), 258–274
    linear regression model, 245–249
    more than one predictor, 279–282
    skill acquisition, 274–279
Presentation style, of research paper, 295–303, 295*f*
Procedure section, of research paper, 300–301
The Psychology of Human-Computer Interaction, 17–22
Psychophysics, 44–45

Publication, 123–124
Publication Manual of the American Psychological Association (APA), 158, 304

Q

Quadrant model of groupware, 235–236
Questionnaire design
    for HCI experiments, 173–174
Qwerty keyboard, 186

R

Ratio-scale measurements, 137–138
Reaction time, 56–59
Reality-Based Interaction (RBI), 286
Redundancy, in language, 52–53
References, 124, 303
Refining ideas, 8
Relationships
    natural *versus* learned, 86–88
RemotePoint, 252
Repeated measures, 175
Reproducibility, standard of, 126
Research, 121–129
    circumstantial and causal relationships,
        145–147
    citations, references, impact, 124–125
    comparative evaluations, 143–145
    empirical, 129
    internal validity and external validity,
        140–143
    interval data, 136–137
    measurement scales, 133–134
    methods, 130–132
        correlational, 132
        experimental, 130–132
        observational, 130
    nominal scale, 134–135
    observation, 132–133
    ordinal scale measurements, 136
    publishing, 123–124
    questions, 139–140
    ratio-scale measurements, 137–138
    reproducible, 126
    research *versus* engineering *versus* design,
        126–129
    topics, 147–155
        finding, 150
        ideas, 148–150
        literature review, 151–152
        replicating the experiments, 151
        small aspects, 150–151
        "think inside the box!", 152–155

Research paper, writing and publishing, 293
  conference paper, 293–294
  impact of, 125
  journal papers, 293–294
  manuscript, preparing, 303–313
    citations and references, 305–308
    formatting, 304–305
    visual aids, 308–311
    writing for clarity, 311–313
  parts of, 295–303
    abstract, 296–297
    conclusion, 303
    introduction, 298–299
    keywords, 297–298
    method, 299–301
    references, 303
    results and discussion, 301–303
    title, 296
Responders, 38–44
  eyes, 43–44
  limbs, 39–42
  voice, 42
Response variable, 131
Results and discussion, of research paper, 301–303
Rockin'Mouse, 101–102, 102*f*
Roller Mouse, 103
Rotate mode, 97–98, 213*f*

S

Saccades, 32
Scientific foundations. *See* Research
Screen tips, 90
Scrollbar slider, 73
Scrolling interface, 241*f*
Selected attention, 64
Sensitivity analysis, 260–261
Sensors
  hearing, 34–36
  senses, 38
  smell and taste, 36–38
  touch, 36
  vision, 30–34
Sequence effect, 177
Sequential programming, 13–14
Shepard-Risset glissando, 45–46
Short-term memory, 48–49, 49*f*
Simple reaction time, 56, 56*f*
Sketchpad, 5–6
Skill acquisition, 274–279
  research in HCI, 278
Skilled behavior, 62–63
Smalltalk, 14

Smell, 36–38
SMS Pinyin, 51–52
SMS text messaging, 53
Soft controls, 43, 72–74
Spatial relationships, 75–79
Spatially aware display, 110, 110*f*
Special Interest Group on Computer-Human
    Interaction (SIGCHI), 15–17
Special Interest Group on Social and Behavioral
    Computing (SIGSOC), 15
Speech, 42
Speed-accuracy trade-off, 54–55
Spelling usage, in manuscript, 304–305
Standard error of estimate (*SE*), 249
Statistical significance, 196–197
Stepwise linear regression, 282
STEYX function, 249
Surface chart, 100
Sutherland, Ivan, 5–6
Symbol keys, 236

T

Tactile feedback, 36
Tactile illusions, 46
Tactition. *See* Touch
Take-off selection, 107
Task completion time, 131, 164, 180*f*
Taste, 36–38
Test conditions, 161–162, 181*f*
Text entry speed, 164
The Thinker, 148, 149*f*
Theory, defining, 122–123
Three-axis trackball, 102–103, 102*f*
Time scale of human action, 28–29
Title, 296
Tooltips, 90
Touch, 36
Transactions on Computer-Human Interaction
    (*TOCHI*), 158
Transformed spatial mapping, 76
TwistMouse, 98
Two-handed interaction paradigm, 239*f*
Two-way analysis of variance, 203–206

U

Usability evaluation, 131
Usability testing, 172
User errors, 115–116

V

Variables
  confounding, 166–169

control, 166
dependent, 131, 160, 163–165
independent, 161–163, 244
manipulated, 131
random, 166
response, 131
Variance, analyzing. *See* Analysis of variance
    (ANOVA)
Velocity-control, 84–86, 112–113
VisiCalc, 14
Vision, 30–34
fixations and saccades, 32
frequency, 31–32
intensity, 32
Visual aids, 308–311
Visual illusion, 45, 46*f*
Visual search, 59–62
Vocal joystick, 42
Voice, 42

W

Warrick's principle, 86–87
Web Of Trust (WOT), 213
Wheel mice, 103, 104*f*
Wilcoxon Signed-Rank test, 214–215
Windows, 23, 293–294
Windows, icons, menus, and a pointing device
    (WIMP), 14
Writing, 50
clarity, 311–313

X

Xerox Star, 11–15, 128
"(XY) scatter" chart, 248

Z

Zooming, 78–79

Printed and bound by CPI Group (UK) Ltd, Croydon, CR0 4YY

03/10/2024

01040324-0003